ENGLISH CATHEDRALS

English Cathedrals

A History

Stanford Lehmberg

Hambledon and London

London and New York

Hambledon and London

102 Gloucester Avenue
London, NW1 8HX

175 Fifth Avenue
New York, NY 10010
USA

First Published 2005

ISBN 1 85285 453 7

A description of this book is available from the
British Library and from the Library of Congress.

Typeset by Carnegie Publishing, Lancaster,
and printed in Great Britain by Cambridge University Press.

Distributed in the United States and Canada
exclusively by Palgrave Macmillan,
A division of St Martin's Press.

Contents

Illustrations

Text Illustrations

Plates

Between pages 114 and 115

Acknowledgements

During the years in which I have studied the cathedrals I have benefited from the assistance of many people. While I was a research student at Cambridge University in the 1950s I had the opportunity to study history with Christopher Morris, Geoffrey Elton, David Knowles, Herbert Butterfield and Norman Sykes, church music with Boris Ord, architecture with Nikolaus Pevsner and Jean Bony, and literature with C. S. Lewis. A greater constellation of scholars can hardly be imagined, and their kindnesses to me were remarkable. My friendship with the Very Reverend John Arnold, former dean of Durham, and the Venerable John Nurser, former chancellor of Lincoln, goes back to our student days; they and their wives often provided hospitality, just as their medieval predecessors might have done. Among the archivists I would acknowledge particularly the kindness of David Bowcock at Carlisle, Patrick Musset at Durham, Angela Doughty at Exeter, Penelope Morgan and Meryl Jancy at Hereford, Mark Curthoys at Christ Church, Oxford, Suzanne Eward at Salisbury, Linzee Colchester at Wells, and Barbara Carpenter Turner at Winchester. Some of these, sadly, are no longer alive. Others who have helped have been Nicholas Orme, Pamela Tudor-Craig Lady Wedgwood, Sir David Willcocks, Derek Beales, Michael Keall, John Harper and the Very Reverend Vivienne Faull. The authors and publishers are grateful to the following for permission to reproduce illustrations: Woodmansterne Ltd (plates 1–8); the Dean and Chapter of Hereford (pp. 85, 189); the Royal Commission on Historical Monuments of England (p. 45).

The author hopes that those who read this volume may share his love of these great churches and of their artistic and liturgical traditions.

Introduction

A cathedral by definition is a church, usually a large one, in which a bishop has his throne. The word derives from the Latin *cathedra*, chair or seat, in this case a reference to the bishop's throne or place of honour within the building. Early bishops came to speak *ex cathedra* – from their chair – when instructing their flocks. In later centuries statements on faith and morals made by a pope *ex cathedra* came to be regarded as being infallible.

The earliest cathedral was St John Lateran in Rome. Presented to the pope by Constantine, the site had formerly been part of the emperor's own residence. A few years later, in 324, Constantine began construction of a basilica on the Vatican hill, over what was believed to be the tomb of St Peter. When complete St Peter's was proclaimed by the pope to be 'the mother church and head of all churches of the city and of the world'.

Early cathedral churches were long rectangles, oriented east-west so that worshippers might face the Holy Land. Further symbolism was added when they assumed the shape of the cross and became cruciform. They then had twin transepts to the north and south of the central crossing, with the choir or clerical sanctuary and high altar to the east and a longer nave to accommodate lay people to the west. (The word nave came from the Latin *navis* or ship, suggesting that it was here that Christians would be borne to heaven.) It was common for the bishop's throne to be placed in an apse, a curving space at the extreme east end behind the high altar. A central tower came to crown the crossing or intersection of the nave, choir and transepts.

Great Italian edifices which followed the churches in Rome included the cathedrals in Florence, Orvieto, Pisa and Milan. In Spain elaborate cathedrals were erected in Cordova, Seville, Barcelona, Perpignan and Santiago de Compostella, a great site of pilgrimage. Germany saw the construction of cathedrals at Cologne, Frankfort, Freiburg, Mainz, Worms and Aachen.

Perhaps most famous and beautiful of all were the cathedrals of France. Chartres, Reims, Amiens, Beauvais, Bourges, Albi, Rouen and Notre-Dame in Paris surely rank among the greatest achievements of the middle ages and indeed the finest expressions of the human mind and spirit. The years just before and after 1200 witnessed an amazing flurry of construction. Notre-Dame and Chartres (where a fire consumed an older cathedral) date from the late twelfth century. Rouen was begun in 1202, Reims in 1211, Amiens in 1220, Beauvais in 1225.

Other forms of cathedral graced other countries. The classic Byzantine basilica is Hagia Sophia in Constantinople, built by the Emperor Justinian in 523–27 AD. Here the intention was to have a central altar which could be seen from all sides. Above it, and dominating the exterior view of the basilica, was a great central dome. Brilliantly coloured mosaics and gilding added to the church's splendour. In Italy, St Mark's in Venice is a monument to the Byzantine style.

Funding for these great edifices came from a variety of sources. In some cases royal patrons – emperors or kings – were involved. Many great noblemen wished to have a cathedral adorn their land and contributed to its building. The church itself was often rich; bishops and archbishops were common patrons. Some had inherited substantial estates; almost all received a large income from the church properties which they held and the rule of clerical celibacy meant that they could not pass on wealth to their children. In many places guilds of craftsmen or merchants made significant contributions, some of which are memorialized in stained glass. At Chartres, for instance, there are windows depicting the drapers, carpenters, coopers and cartwrights, as well as sculpture showing women working in wool. In some cities the mayor and municipal corporation sponsored building projects. Men and women who came to the cathedrals on pilgrimages, like those drawn to the shrine of St Thomas Becket at Canterbury, gave costly gifts, and a number of building campaigns can be linked to the popularity of shrines. Finally, ordinary men and women who came to worship left offerings. Individually they might not be large, but during the middle ages their total was significant.

Although bishops themselves were directly involved in the operation of their cathedrals during the early centuries, they came to be more and more removed. They had their own residences, often grand enough to be called palaces and frequently some distance from the cathedral, and they built private chapels in them. Many bishops, too, became important in politics, often serving as prominent ministers or chief advisers to medieval monarchs. In turn, the cathedrals came more and more to govern themselves. They were run by a dean, who was assisted by clergy who formed the cathedral chapter. Ordinary business affairs were left in the hands of the dean and chapter, with the bishop being involved only in important matters. Bishops came to visit their cathedrals rarely, perhaps preaching at Christmas and Easter, offering confirmation annually and conducting periodic episcopal visitations. In many cases bishops were not especially welcome at their cathedrals, for rivalry and bad feeling between bishops and deans was a common phenomenon.

It is the English cathedrals which interest us here. They should not be thought of in isolation, for they had many elements in common with cathedrals on the Continent of Europe. Nevertheless, they always had special characteristics which differentiated them from their counterparts in France, Germany or Italy. Following the Reformation they provided spiritual leadership for a national church, and later for the Anglican communion which spread throughout the world. Their buildings are great monuments of architecture. They provided homes for schools, choirs, organs and libraries. Many scholars, theologians, preachers and politicians held office in them.

The last quarter century has shown a remarkable growth of interest in the history of English cathedrals. This has been manifest primarily in the publication of histories of individual cathedrals. Beginning with an account of York Minster published in 1977, it has grown to include studies of Canterbury, Norwich, Rochester, Wells, Winchester, Lincoln, Durham, Gloucester and Hereford, with further volumes in preparation. In addition to these volumes dealing with a single cathedral there have been several books covering all the old cathedrals with many colour illustrations.

Both sorts of publications have their limitations. Books about individual cathedrals often reflect the special interests of the local communities involved and seldom attempt to relate the experiences of one cathedral to those of parallel institutions elsewhere. Most general accounts depend primarily upon beautiful pictures for their appeal and are content with superficial descriptions of cathedral history.

The present study hopes to bridge the gap between these sorts of books in a new way. It deals with all the cathedrals of England and attempts to draw together the strands of history affecting them. The earlier chapters, covering the years from St Augustine's mission to Canterbury in 597 to the coming of the Reformation about 1530, deal mainly with architecture and show how the cathedrals display the characteristics of the Norman, Early English, Decorated and Perpendicular styles which followed each other during these centuries. These chapters are followed by an account of the cathedrals under the Tudors and Stuarts. Concluding chapters carry the story of the cathedrals forward from 1700 until the end of the twentieth century.

The present volume is intended for serious general readers – those interested in the cathedrals of England and those who visit these great buildings – and tries to present an account which is both scholarly and accessible. The text is not burdened with elaborate footnotes, but a full bibliography has been provided and most quotations can be traced through it.

The Early Centuries, 597–1066

The history of England's cathedrals began at Canterbury in 597 AD. Christianity had come to the British Isles long before this, according to legend as a result of a missionary visit by Joseph of Arimathea, but more likely because of its acceptance by the Roman soldiers who conquered England in 43 and upheld Roman rule in Britain until 410. Canterbury, known to the Romans as Durovernum Cantiacorum, seems to have had a strong Christian element in its population by the fourth century and may have been home to an early bishop, but he does not appear to have established a cathedral. There are known to have been bishops at London and Lincoln; they must have had churches even if they were not yet called cathedrals.[1]

The Anglo-Saxon conquest, which began soon after the Roman withdrawal, brought new settlers from north Germany who held pagan beliefs. Early sources say that it was the Jutes who settled in Kent, while the Angles and Saxons overran the rest of what is now England, the Saxons living in Essex, Sussex and Wessex, the Angles in East Anglia, Mercia and Northumbria. Archaeological evidence suggests that the towns of Roman Britain experienced an economic decline in the fifth and early sixth centuries. Canterbury, for instance, became seriously depopulated and much of the land around it reverted to water meadows. But it continued to be the capital of Kent.

Because the Anglo-Saxon settlers remained pagan, Christianity survived primarily among the Celts in Wales and Cornwall. Despite biblical commands to convert others to their faith, the Celts had little interest in preaching to the Anglo-Saxons, but Celtic Christianity did spread to Ireland, as a result of St Patrick's missionary work, and to Scotland, where St Columba established a famous monastery at Iona in 563. Christianity did not return to northern England until 634, when Oswald, the ruler of Northumbria, asked the monks of Iona to send a missionary to his kingdom. They dispatched St Aidan, who like Columba chose to build his church on an island site, this time at Lindisfarne or the Holy Isle. Cathedrals were not part of the structure of the Celtic church, which relied on monasteries for spiritual leadership. Bishops lived in some of the monasteries, so they may have fulfilled some of the functions of cathedrals.

Although the king of Kent in the later sixth century, Æthelbert, was a pagan, he had married a Frankish princess from the Continent, Emma, a descendant of the famous ruler Clovis. Emma was a Christian, and although she did not convert her husband she brought with her a bishop and helped prepare the way for Christian missionaries. These were sent at the instance of Pope Gregory the Great, who supposedly became interested in England after seeing handsome Anglo-Saxon youths in a Roman slave market. Exclaiming that they were angels not Angles, he decided to dispatch a group of forty monks to Kent. Led by their prior, Augustine, they met Æthelbert on the Isle of Thanet and were given permission to preach and to establish a new church in Canterbury. According to the Venerable Bede, whose history of the English church was written shortly before his death in 735, the king was impressed by the holy life of the missionaries and by the miracles which followed their teaching. He allowed himself to be baptized, and many of his people followed his example. Æthelbert and his successors made substantial gifts to the church, which soon became a great landlord.[2]

After a visit to Arles, where he was consecrated bishop, Augustine returned to Canterbury and was recognized as archbishop and head of the church in England. It was here that he established the first English cathedral to have survived. Dedicated to the Saviour, it was known as Christ Church. Excavations undertaken in 1993, when the floor of the present nave was being replaced, revealed that it was oriented east-west and had apses at both ends. Augustine's building was enlarged in the tenth century, at which time the west end was reconstructed and a crypt fitted out to house the tomb of St Dunstan (d. 988), the restorer of the church following the Viking invasions. By the end of the Anglo-Saxon era Canterbury Cathedral had become one of the largest churches in northern Europe; it was probably almost 300 feet long and about 100 feet wide. The building was destroyed by fire in 1067.

Although Augustine and the men who established the cathedral were monks, it was not always organized as a monastery. During some periods the clergy who served the cathedral were allowed to marry and were given allowances for their personal expenses. Elaborate Benedictine liturgies were sung at the several altars in the cathedral, and beautiful manuscripts were already being produced in its writing room or scriptorium.

A second cathedral was begun at Rochester in 604. Bede tells us that Augustine consecrated two new bishops in that year, Mellitus and Justus.[3] They had not been among the archbishop's original companions but were part of a second mission sent by Pope Gregory in 601. Justus was made bishop of Rochester. In Bede's words, 'Augustine consecrated Justus in Kent itself, in the city of Dorubrevis which the English call Hrofaescaestrae, after one of their former chiefs whose name was Hrof. It is about twenty-four miles west of Canterbury, and in it King Æthelbert built the church of the apostle St Andrew'. The king also presented gifts of land, as he had done at Canterbury. For several centuries Rochester remained dependent on Canterbury; this was a unique relationship and is perhaps one of the reasons why Rochester remained the smallest diocese in medieval England. As at Canterbury, the clergy maintained some form of common life but were not organized as a monastery. Little is known about the Anglo-Saxon cathedral. Earlier writers thought that it had an apsidal east end separated from the nave by a triple arcade, but recent excavations have suggested that the building in question was not the cathedral and was indeed too small to have served such a purpose. The early cathedral may have been just to the east of the present building, which was perhaps erected alongside it so that the earlier structure could remain in use until the Romanesque church was completed.[4]

According to Bede, Mellitus 'was appointed to preach in the province of the East Saxons, which is separated from Kent by the River Thames. Its capital is the city of London, which is a trading centre for many nations'. Here Mellitus established a cathedral in honour of St Paul. Although the pope probably intended to transfer the seat of the archbishop from Canterbury to London, that did not happen. St Paul's Cathedral has always occupied its present site, at the summit of Ludgate Hill, which had earlier held a Romano-British temple dedicated to Diana. Again we know virtually nothing of the original cathedral. It was endowed with a landed estate, at Tillingham in Essex.

Pope Gregory instructed Augustine to send a bishop to York, which he intended to be the centre of Christianity in northern England. If the faith was accepted there, the bishop was to consecrate twelve other bishops, the same number that Augustine was to have in the south, and to become their archbishop or metropolitan, although remaining subordinate to the archbishop of Canterbury. This simple scheme, based more on continental practice than on knowledge of conditions in England, was never fully implemented but did become the basis for the future constitution of the English church. There had been Christians at York during the days of the Romans, and there was probably an early bishop of York in the fourth century. The first attempt at a cathedral, a small wooden building, may have been put up in 627 as a place of baptism for King Edwin of Deira, who had accepted Christianity in his middle years. It was soon replaced by a larger stone structure.[5] This seems to have fallen into decay in the next half century, while the Celtic form of Christianity preached by Aidan prevailed in the north. In 663 the Synod of Whitby decreed that St Augustine's Roman constitutions should prevail throughout England, and about 670 St Wilfrid restored the church, covering the roof with lead and filling the windows with glass. An archbishop was not permanently established at York until 735. The first man to hold the title was Ecgbert, who was a brother of the king of Northumbria and probably a pupil of Bede.

The 600s also saw the establishment of cathedrals at Winchester, Lichfield, Hereford and Worcester. A Roman church at Winchester had evidently been swept away by the Saxons but was followed in 635 by a new wooden building on the same foundations, just to the north of the present cathedral. The bishopric was established in 662. About 974 the community of secular priests was turned out and the cathedral became a Benedictine monastery. It was rebuilt, and the relics of Swithun, who was to become the cathedral's patron saint, were translated there. Ceadda, better known as St Chad, was responsible for building the first cathedral at Lichfield. A disciple of Aidan's, he had been consecrated bishop of Lindisfarne or York about 666 but soon resigned and was sent to be bishop to the Mercians. The first bishop of Hereford is often said to have been Putta, translated there from the see of Rochester in 669. According to Bede, he had a special interest in church music. A better documented figure is Cuthbert, briefly bishop of Hereford before being translated to Canterbury in 740. Bishop Æthelstan undertook the building of what was described as 'a glorious minster' at Hereford several decades before his death in 1056. The bishopric of Worcester dates to 680. Virtually nothing is known about the first bishop, named Bosel. A more important figure is St Oswald, who held the sees of Worcester and York concurrently for twenty years before his death in 992. His cathedral, a little north east of the present structure, has been described as a stately building with twenty-seven altars for use by members of its monastic community.

Wells, Durham and Exeter form a cluster of cathedrals established between 900 and 1066. The church at Wells was actually founded earlier, about 705, by Aldheld, bishop of the abortive see of Sherborne, but it was not given cathedral status until 909. Excavations have revealed its apse, east of the present cloister walk; the location may have been chosen because of the supply of fresh water from St Andrew's well nearby. At least seven Saxon bishops were buried in the cathedral, probably on either side of the high altar. The Saxon cathedral at Durham enjoyed the same magnificent site as the present building, a cliff overlooking a loop in the River Wear. The location had been chosen by Bishop Aldhune (or Eadlhun) when the seat of the bishopric was transferred to Durham from Chester-le-Street in 990. Excavations at Exeter, carried out in the 1970s, demolished the tradition that the Saxon minster had stood at the east end of the present cathedral and revealed the existence of several earlier buildings, as well as several early cemeteries, west of the existing façade. Asser was probably the first bishop of Exeter, from about 890. Later, Edward the Elder established a bishopric at Crediton, a few miles away. In 1050 Leofric returned to Exeter. Here he found only five books, seven bells and one mass vestment in the church, but after his generous donations there were crosses, chalices, censers, candlesticks, wall hangings, banners, reliquaries and service books, as well as five complete sets of mass vestments, altar frontals, choristers' robes, dalmatics, tunicles and staffs. Leofric also served as chancellor to King Edward the Confessor. Cornwall had an Anglo-Saxon cathedral at St Germans, but the bishopric was united with Exeter in 1080. The cathedral became a monastery and then a parish church; an ancient church survives on the spot.

During the years before 1066 there were also a number of embryo bishoprics, each of which would have had a Saxon cathedral. Many of these were founded as early as the seventh century. In addition to Sherborne, Chester-le-Street, Crediton and Cornwall, such bishoprics included Dorchester (Oxfordshire, not Dorset), Dunwich, Elmham, Hexham, Leicester, Lindisfarne, Lindsey, Ramsbury, Ripon and Selsey. A number of these, including Dunwich, Hexham, Leicester, Lindisfarne, Lindsey and Ripon, had been dissolved or transferred to other sites prior to the end of the Saxon era. Several others – Dorchester, Elmham, Ramsbury and Selsey – were still active in 1066.

Many of the English cathedrals suffered during the Viking invasions of England, which began about 800. Lindisfarne, Lindsey, Dunwich and Leicester were probably sacked in the first wave. A second wave of invasions began about 980. Led by Olaf Tryggvason, king of Norway, and Swein Forkbeard, king of Denmark, the Vikings sacked London in 982. In 1011 they turned to Canterbury, burning the cathedral and taking Archbishop Alphege and a number of townspeople captive. Alphege was kept a prisoner for several months and then clubbed or stoned to death in 1012, perhaps while his captors were drunk. The throne soon passed to one of the invaders, Cnut, who surprisingly proved to be a protector of the church. During his reign and that of his successor, Edward the Confessor (1042–66), the buildings were restored and the church entered what has been characterized as an age of vigour and progress. The life of the clergy was regularized as steps were taken to end the practice of clerical marriage. The laity were encouraged to attend services regularly and to receive communion in both kinds, often drinking the wine not directly from the chalice but through a small pipe or straw made of silver or ivory. Fasting before communion was enjoined. Lay people were taught the Creed and Lord's Prayer. In addition to sermons there were books for those who could read, including vernacular translations of the Bible and works like the Blickling Homilies, which were intended to prepare people for the end of the world expected in the year 1000. Attempts, not entirely successful, were made to persuade lay folk to abandon the worship of natural sites such as groves and fountains. Solemn liturgies included music and chant.

English cathedrals, then, were well established long before the Norman Conquest. None of the buildings survive and we know little about their architectural style. Most likely they resembled the Saxon parish churches which do remain in existence. Greenstead in Essex is a unique instance of a timber structure; during early phases of their existence some of the cathedrals were similar wooden buildings. There are early stone churches at Earls Barton and Brixworth (Northamptonshire), Deerhurst (Gloucestershire), Bradford-on-Avon (Wiltshire), Jarrow (County Durham) and Escombe (also Durham). Perhaps the finest of the pre-conquest churches is St Benet in Cambridge, used for a time as the chapel of Corpus Christi College. Constructed between 950 and 1050, it is an impressive building. Like it, some of the cathedrals may have displayed elements that foreshadowed the architecture of the Norman era.

2

Norman, 1066–1170

The Norman invasion marks one of the most important turning points in the history of the English church and its cathedrals. While still in Normandy William the Conqueror had displayed a great interest in the church, choosing strong bishops who would assist him in his rule. His coronation as king of England on Christmas Day 1066 was the first held in Westminster Abbey. Dedicated only months earlier, Edward the Confessor's building prefigured the coming of the Romanesque style, the great contribution of the Normans to English architecture.

One of William's chief interests was the establishment of effective new bishoprics throughout England. In them, and in most of the existing dioceses, he appointed Norman bishops. In a number of cases he followed a conscious policy, begun under the Anglo-Saxons, of transferring episcopal sees from small villages to larger cities. This was reaffirmed in ordinances adopted by an ecclesiastical council convened in 1075 by the new archbishop of Canterbury, Lanfranc of Bec. Thus Dorchester was abandoned in favour of Lincoln and Chichester took the place of Selsey. The see of Ramsbury was moved to Old Sarum, but when this continued to be a sparsely inhabited hilltop the site was moved once again in the thirteenth century to the nearby valley at Salisbury. Within a few years after William's death the bishopric of Norwich superseded establishments at Elmham and Thetford, and new cathedrals were built at Ely, Coventry, Bath and Carlisle. There were thus nineteen bishoprics and cathedrals in existence by the middle of the twelfth century.

Another of Lanfranc's goals was the establishment of monastic communities at many of the cathedrals, continuing an effort which had begun earlier. Within a few years there were ten monastic cathedrals. Canterbury, Bath, Coventry, Durham, Ely, Norwich, Rochester, Winchester and Worcester adhered to the Benedictine rule, while the small cathedral at Carlisle was a house of Augustinian canons. Since the bishop theoretically took the place of an abbot, these establishments were ruled by a deputy known as a prior and thus were known as cathedral priories. They came to house large communities – seventy was often regarded as the ideal number of monks. Their services included all the liturgies of the Benedictine rule, eight daily offices as well as several masses.

The remaining cathedrals – St Paul's in London, York Minster, Chichester, Exeter, Hereford, Lichfield, Lincoln, Salisbury and Wells – were run by clergy who did not take monastic vows. Hence these were known as secular cathedrals. Here the dean was the head of the cathedral establishment and was assisted by a chapter made up of canons or prebendaries. Again the numbers were large. Lincoln, which during the middle ages was a richly sprawling diocese, came to have fifty-eight prebendaries, followed by Salisbury with fifty-two. There were thirty at York and twenty or more at the remaining secular cathedrals.

In the monastic cathedrals revenues were held in common and all but the prior lived communal lives centred around the dormitory, refectory, scriptorium and cathedral choir. Administration was divided between a number of officers known as obedientiaries, including a receiver, sacrist, precentor, almoner, infirmarian and guest master. The prior's independent holding was often substantial, and his separate kitchen was able to provide lavish entertainment for prominent visitors and guests. The deanery at a secular cathedral also came to be a large establishment, often with its own chapel. The clergy of the secular cathedrals enjoyed individual incomes derived from specific landed estates or endowments known as prebends. Within a few years after the Norman Conquest they had abandoned common quarters in favour of individual houses in the cathedral close. Clerical celibacy was enforced in both monastic and secular cathedrals, and ecclesiastical courts were established to see that official policies were followed.

In order to maintain control of the country, William the Conqueror ordered the construction of a number of large stone castles. In some places cathedrals were located on adjacent sites. Durham, Lincoln and Rochester are the ideal places to view this arrangement today; at Durham and Lincoln castle and cathedral share easily defended hilltops, while the site at Rochester has the advantage of proximity to the River Medway. Fine stone for both castles and cathedrals was shipped to England from Caen in Normandy, and quarries were soon established in England, at such places as Barnack, near Ely, and Maidstone, close to Rochester.

Durham is the finest of the Norman cathedrals, and one of the world's greatest cathedrals of any period. It owes much to its site, ideal for a fortress but unusual for a cathedral, and to the fact that nearly all of it is in the same style. Virtually all of the existing building dates from the years between 1093 and 1133. It is thus of the same era as such French cathedrals as Vézelay, a masterpiece of the Romanesque style. But it exhibits specially English features, and it is right to regard it as the queen of Norman buildings.[1]

English and Welsh Cathedrals.

The foundation stone of Durham was laid by the bishop William of St Carileph on 11 August 1093. King William had called him to Durham in 1081. Both the nave and choir display the round arches which characterize Norman work; they are seen in the windows and in the arcades dividing the central space from the side aisles. Massive stone piers support these arches. Contrary to the notion that Norman buildings are simple in style, alternate pillars stopping short of the clerestory are elaborately decorated with zigzag and diamond-shaped patterns. These are interspersed with columns bearing groups of shafts which ascend all the way to the stone vaulted roof.

The vaults are historically the most significant part of the building, for they are generally acknowledged to date from about 1100 and to be the earliest rib vaults in existence. (The alternate view, that rib vaults were conceived at Saint-Denis in Paris and associated with Gothic architecture, is now discredited.) Rib vaults solved problems which had baffled earlier builders: they replaced wooden roofs which were unsatisfactory because they so often caught fire and rounded barrel or tunnel vaults made of stone which were so heavy that they threatened to collapse or spread. In rib vaults the essential structure is provided by thin stone ribs stretching diagonally across each bay of the structure, with straight ribs dividing each bay from the next. The areas between these ribs are then filled with very light-weight stonework resting on the ribs. As in earlier buildings, an exterior roof of lead is supported by a wooden framework installed above the stone vaults.

Both the east and west ends of Durham display work of a later date. On the west, poised dramatically atop the cliff, the entrance porch or Lady chapel known as the galilee was added about 1770 by Bishop Hugh de Puiset (often called Pudsey). Still Norman in style, it is less heavy and more elaborately detailed than the earlier work. It was originally intended as a place where women might worship, since St Cuthbert had dictated that they should not enter the cathedral proper; for centuries it has housed the tomb of the Venerable Bede, whose remains were translated to Durham at the time of Viking attacks on the monastery of Jarrow. At the opposite end of the cathedral the chapel of the nine altars, built in the thirteenth century, forms an eastern transept. The low central tower of the Normans was raised in the fifteenth century. The twin west towers are original but would have looked quite different during the Norman period, since we know that they were capped by lead spires until the seventeenth century.

A further remarkable piece of Norman work is the bronze knocker on the principal door to the cathedral from Palace Green. This is a reminder that Durham, like other cathedrals, was a place of sanctuary where those accused of crimes might seek refuge from the law: if the cathedral was locked for the night such persons might knock for admission. In addition there are remnants of the medieval monastic buildings around the cloister. Parts of the present deanery formed the medieval prior's lodging. The cathedral's furnishings include wall paintings of St Oswald and St Cuthbert dating from Bishop Pudsey's time. The choir stalls and baptismal font were installed in the 1600s, after Scottish prisoners of war housed in the cathedral following Oliver Cromwell's victory at Dunbar burned the original woodwork for warmth during a cold winter.[2]

Although the cathedral at Rochester lacks the grandeur of Durham and retains less of its Norman work, it is of considerable interest. The building of the early Norman cathedral can be credited to a remarkable bishop, Gundulph. A native of Normandy, he had been a monk at Bec with Lanfranc; he remained one of the archbishop's closest friends, accompanying him to Canterbury in 1070 and being appointed to the neighbouring see of Rochester soon thereafter. He was also a supporter of Lanfranc's successor Anselm. Indeed Anselm's collected letters include more addressed to Gundulph than to anyone but the king and the pope. Already fifty years old when he went to Rochester, Gundulph lived another thirty years and was responsible for transforming both the building of the cathedral and its staff, which he reorganized in 1083 as a monastic community of twenty-two monks, replacing a group of only five secular canons. It is interesting to note that the establishment of the monastery at Durham took place in the same year.[3]

A large square tower on the north side of the cathedral and slightly detached from it has been known as Gundulph's tower since the sixteenth century, but recent research shows that it was constructed before Gundulph's time and should not be associated with him. It was probably a defensive structure, not a bell tower, for it has no entrance on the ground level and lacks an internal staircase. In fact little of Gundulph's work survives. Two bays of a crypt, built with side aisles flanking a central nave, remain, and the solid side walls of the existing choir were probably also part of his cathedral. A devastating fire in 1137 necessitated major rebuilding. The present nave and west end date from this second building campaign in the twelfth century. It is often said that the low façade is dwarfed by the much taller castle adjacent to it, but in fact it is very satisfying architecturally, modest, well proportioned, and an honest expression of the nave and aisles beyond. The central doorway is flanked by two slender turrets and ornamented with a fine tympanum showing Christ in Majesty supported by two angels and surrounded by the beasts symbolizing the Evangelists. The twelve apostles appear on the lintel, and the door surrounds include statues of Solomon and the Queen of Sheba. Although the carving is badly weathered, it resembles French work, particularly the tympanum at Chartres, more than any other twelfth-century sculpture in England. The towers at each end of the façade are elaborately decorated with blind arcading of Norman arches. Although they are comparable in scale, they are not identical in design: the north tower rises four-square up to its top, but the highest stages of the south tower become circular. Both towers housed stairways which, together with a passage in the west wall, were probably used by choristers, especially on Palm Sunday, when it was common to begin the high mass in the churchyard with the singing of 'Gloria, laus et honor' (the origin of the modern hymn 'All Glory, Laud, and Honour'). Similar passageways exist in later buildings at both Wells and Salisbury. It takes some effort to imagine what the west end would have looked like with its original Norman windows – there were probably three small ones above the tympanum – for here, as in so many other cathedrals, a large Perpendicular-style window was inserted in the fifteenth century. The piers of the nave arcade are the most notable Norman feature of the cathedral interior. They are of interest because they display a variety of forms of design and shafting; they are not simply alternating patterns, as at Durham. They do not support a stone-vaulted roof, for Rochester has always had a wooden ceiling. There is a gallery of Norman arches and a clerestory of windows enlarged in later centuries.

The Norman cathedral at Winchester was far larger than either Rochester or Durham.[4] Its nave was 530 feet long: this was slightly less than Old St Paul's (586 feet) but longer than any other cathedral in England or, indeed, in Europe. (The longest nave on the Continent was that at Milan, at 475 feet). When viewed today, especially from the north, the nave of Winchester appears enormous, but as originally built it was 40 feet longer and had several more bays.

Winchester had been an important centre of royal government for centuries, sharing that honour with London until the twelfth century. William the Conqueror had actually gone to the trouble of being crowned at Winchester as well as at Westminster, perhaps in part because the royal treasury was still at Winchester. There had been three Anglo-Saxon churches here. The Old Minster (recently excavated) lay just to the north of the present cathedral, with part of its west end beneath the existing façade. A few feet north of that was the New Minster. There was also a Nuns' Minster. The Old Minster had been organized as a Benedictine monastery since 964 and monastic liturgies appear to have been recited without break from that date until the Dissolution of the Monasteries under Henry VIII, for the Old Minster remained in use until the new edifice was consecrated on 8 April 1093.

The bishop responsible for the new building was Walkelin. A kinsman of the king, Walkelin had been educated in Paris. He became bishop of Winchester in 1070, replacing Stigand, the Anglo-Saxon who had held both Winchester and Canterbury. Walkelin's brother Simeon came with him and was installed as prior of the cathedral monastery. Walkelin was probably responsible for determining the size of the new building, which went up with amazing speed. At the time of the consecration an apsidal choir, transepts, crossing tower and an eastern portion of the nave were probably complete. The remaining bays of the nave were finished by the end of the century. Stone came from Quarr on the Isle of Wight, timber from the king's wood at Hempage. The crossing tower fell in 1107 – it was said that this was a sign of God's displeasure that the anticlerical king William Rufus had been buried there, but more probably it reflected the fact that the building lay in a swampy area and had been raised on inadequate foundations.

Winchester was remodelled so thoroughly in the later middle ages that it is hard to imagine what it originally would have looked like. As we will see later, the east end was rebuilt in the thirteenth century, the choir reconstructed in the fourteenth, and the nave remodelled in the Perpendicular style during the first years of the fifteenth century. The existing west end also dates from this period. As at Rochester, the crypt is one of the best places to view the surviving Norman work, although it remains subject to flooding. The actual structure of the nave is Norman, but the round arches were cut down and turned into pointed Perpendicular arcades when the nave was given its elaborate stone vault by William of Wykeham, the great bishop who died in 1404.

Exterior views of Winchester are disappointing. The site is relatively small and unspectacular. The west end, lacking towers, is not impressive; also most of the wall space is taken up by the large west window. The central tower is squat and seems truncated, since it is not crowned by pinnacles. Only inside does one appreciate the size and richness of the structure, which has superb fittings and almost as many monuments as Westminster Abbey.

In eastern England, the cathedrals at Ely, Norwich and Lincoln display important work from the Norman period. It was Walkelin's brother Simeon who began the construction of the cathedral at Ely. After serving as prior at Winchester, he was made the abbot of Ely in 1081. Here there was already the great monastery begun in 673 by St Æsheldreda. It was always rich because of its connections with the royal family of East Anglia, to which Ætheldreda belonged. When the Domesday Book was compiled, shortly before the death of William the Conqueror, it was the second wealthiest monastery in the realm. Sacked by the Danes, it had been reconstructed in

970, but it was not grand enough for Simeon. Even though he was eighty-seven years old, he ordered construction of a new Romanesque structure to begin in 1083. Building, as usual, started with an apsidal east end, using stone from Barnack, and was sufficiently advanced for the church to be consecrated in 1106. Surprisingly, the diocese of Ely was not created until 1109, so the monastic church did not become a cathedral until that date.

Officially known as the Isle of Ely, the tiny cathedral city was indeed an island in the midst of swampy fenland throughout the middle ages. The site of the cathedral is sixty-eight feet above the surrounding water meadow. Thus the cathedral is not really on a hill, but it is sufficiently elevated to stand out as one approaches the city. The view is extraordinary. What one sees first is a single western tower rising above the principal entrance, together with the marvellous octagonal lantern that was placed over the crossing after the original crossing tower fell in the thirteenth century. Shortly after the lantern was erected the choir was rebuilt, but the nave still stands as one of the most imposing examples of Norman work. The west tower, later capped by an additional octagonal storey, is unusual in its placement and impressive in the strength of its ornamentation with round-headed blank arcades. Following the completion of the nave, a western transept was created to form the cathedral's façade. Its southern half still stands, terminated by a lower Norman tower, but the north tower collapsed or was demolished in the fifteenth century – the details of its fate remain cloudy – and was never rebuilt. Now there is only the crude buttress erected to provide needed support for what remained. The fact that this predates the dissolution of the monastery is attested by inscriptions or graffiti of the Tudor period. As at Durham, an entrance porch or Galilee was added following the completion of the original west end. It was not begun until the thirteenth century and it displays the pointed lancet windows and blind arches of the Early English style. In fact there is no better place to study the difference between Norman and Early English arches than here, where the galilee abuts the line of the original façade.

The most immediately striking aspect of the cathedral is its enormously long nave. This is now twelve bays but was originally thirteen, before the eastern bay was rebuilt as part of the octagon. This is not quite the longest nave in England: Winchester had fourteen bays and Norwich still does. But the nave of Ely does extend for more than 500 feet. Later rebuilding of the nave was limited to the insertion of larger windows in the clerestory. The carefully thought out ratio of heights was not changed; it remains 6:5:4 for the nave arcades, triforium and clerestory, a total of 105 feet. Although at first glance the great piers may look identical, in fact they alternate as at Durham, although none are elaborately carved and the difference in moulding is not great. The side aisles have groined vaulting but the nave itself has never had a stone vault. Like the transepts, it retains a wooden roof with recently restored paintings.

The Prior's Door leading from the cloister to the nave has a fine carved tympanum dating from about 1140. It bears a seated figure of Christ supported by two angels. It is reminiscent of the portal at Rochester; although it is smaller, it is much better preserved because of its protected location. The two sides of the doorway have carved scenes usually said to represent the labours of the months, a common medieval theme, but since there are fourteen rather than twelve figures it is evident that some modification has taken place. A similar if less elaborate doorway marks the monks' entrance into the cathedral.

Herbert de Losinga was responsible for the building of the cathedral at Norwich.[5] He had been prior of the monastery at Fécamp in Normandy before the death of William the Conqueror. After the accession of William Rufus in 1087 he was summoned to England and made head of Ramsey Abbey. But his ambitions were not satisfied, and in 1090 he paid the king £1000 for appointment as bishop of Thetford. At the same time his father was named prior of Winchester. Herbert was thus guilty of simony, and the new archbishop of Canterbury, Anselm, turned against both him and William Rufus. Hoping to gain forgiveness from Pope Urban II, Herbert set out for Rome. After receiving absolution he returned to England. In 1094 he transferred his see from Thetford to Norwich, and in 1096 he began construction of the cathedral there. Some chroniclers saw this as an act of penitence, but it seems likely that he would have begun building in any case. The cathedral was consecrated in 1101; by the time of Herbert's death in 1119 the choir, transepts and three eastern bays of the nave were complete. The remaining Norman work was finished by 1145. The speed of construction is notable and helps demolish the myth that cathedral building always dragged on for centuries. Both local Barnack and imported Caen stone were used.

Like Winchester, Norwich does not occupy a spectacular site, nor does it have a notable west end. Norwich castle is not far away, but it does not share its elevated location with the cathedral. The façade lacks towers and offers only a modest introduction to the fine interior; it is possible that the original plan included a west transept, as at Ely. The east end retains its original apsidal form and helps one visualize what several other Norman cathedrals looked like before Gothic alterations took place. Here the east end was never rebuilt, although it was relatively small, perhaps because there was no great shrine to be accommodated. The liturgical choir came to include three bays of the nave as well as the crossing area. The appearance of the interior during its early years must have been impressive: the walls were plastered and painted, and the crossing tower was lavishly decorated. Later centuries were to provide features that transformed both the exterior and interior. The Norman tower (so well built that, unusually, it has not caused later structural problems) must have been impressive even without a spire, but we know that it was capped by a spire of wood and lead as early as 1295. This was blown down in a great storm in 1362, and its replacement was destroyed by fire in 1463. The present stone spire was finally erected late in the fifteenth century. Rising to 315 feet, it is second only to Salisbury in height. Inside, the original wooden roof was replaced by an incombustible stone vault following the fire. The same pattern was followed in both the nave and choir; eight hundred carved and painted bosses ornament the intersections between the ribs of the lierne vaults. The Perpendicular period also saw the introduction of larger windows, especially at the west end of the choir clerestory. Their glass is not notable, but they produce an unusually well-lighted interior.

Little of the Norman cathedral remains at Lincoln, but what there is is extraordinary. As we have seen, the see was transferred from Dorchester to Lincoln about 1072 by Remigius, another former monk of Fécamp who was appointed bishop by William I. The site chosen, which may have housed an earlier church, was adjacent to the Conqueror's new castle and probably to an existing marketplace. It crowned the hill known as the Upper City, which had been occupied and walled by the Romans; since the surrounding land is flat, this eminence and the silhouette of the cathedral can be seen for miles around.

Lincoln Minster, as it came to be called, was also built very rapidly and was consecrated shortly before Remigius's death in 1091.[6] Not organized as a monastery, it had a chapter of twenty-two secular canons. Following a fire in 1123, the cathedral was given a stone vault by its third bishop, Alexander. None of it survives, so we do not know its exact form, but it may have been slightly earlier than the rib vaults at Durham. On 15 April 1185 the cathedral was seriously damaged by what contemporary chroniclers described as an earthquake. Since no other buildings seem to have been affected, it has been suggested that the calamity was actually caused by the collapse of the Norman vaults. In any case almost the entire cathedral was rebuilt in the new Early English style. Only the west end survived the disaster.

In its present form the façade of Lincoln, which is one of the most impressive in the country, includes work of two periods. The central portion is dominated by three large doorways, each surrounded by rows of elaborate carving. There are also two western towers, the lower stages of which display round-headed windows and blank arches. All of this represents what was originally a western transept, similar to the one partially preserved at Ely. But the Early English builders of the thirteenth century were not satisfied with it; they extended the sides beyond the towers and heightened the façade with several rows of blank lancet arches. Finally the architects of the late fourteenth century inserted large Perpendicular windows, cutting off part of the Norman design over the main doorway and jamming in a row of statues of kings. The remaining Norman sculpture ranks among the best in England. In addition to rows of elaborate shafts flanking the doorways, enlivened with human figures and animals, there are several sculpted scenes, the finest representing the Old Testament stories of Noah and the ark and Daniel in the lions' den and, from the New Testament, the Harrowing of Hell and the parable of Dives and Lazarus. Recently cleaned, they repay careful study.

The remaining cathedrals display less surviving Norman work. At Hereford Bishop Athelstan built what the Anglo-Saxon Chronicle called 'a glorious minster' thirty or forty years before the Norman Conquest, but it was destroyed in fighting with the neighbouring Welsh in 1055. According to the Chronicle the cathedral burned and the followers of Gruffud ap Llywelyn 'stripped and robbed it of vestments and everything'. Herbert de Losinga's elder brother Robert became bishop in 1079 and may have begun rebuilding, although Bishop Reynelm, who held the see from 1107 to 1115, is described as *fundator* (founder). The consecration took place under Robert de Béthune, who died in 1148. The nave and choir aisles display work of this period, including carved capitals; the variety of arches in the triforium of the south transept is particularly intriguing. But the choir was rebuilt in the thirteenth century and the west end had to be reconstructed following the collapse of the west tower in 1786. One bay was demolished and an undistinguished façade was put up.

When Leofric transferred the bishopric of Devon and Cornwall from Crediton to Exeter in 1050 he took over the Saxon building of an impoverished monastery. Rebuilding took place under the third bishop, William Warelwast; construction began in 1114 and the cathedral was consecrated in 1133. An apsidal east end, later demolished, was complete by that date. Most of the cathedral, however, was rebuilt in the Decorated style of the fourteenth century. The two towers are the remaining work of the Norman period. Their position is unique, for they form the transepts rather than being placed at the west end. The north tower has always been known as St Paul's, the south as St John's, so they presumably served as chapels dedicated to these saints. Although similar, the towers are not identical; that on the north has earlier arcading than the south. Both were originally topped by lead spires.

Bishop Ralph de Luffa is credited with building the cathedral at Chichester shortly after the see was moved from Selsey. It was consecrated in 1108 but damaged by fire in 1118 and again by a more serious conflagration that destroyed much of the city in 1187. Reconstruction retained the original plan, and much of the cathedral – the nave, crossing and western bays of the choir – is Norman. The nave is unusual because it has five aisles, not the three normally found in English cathedrals. The height of the interior was reduced when the cathedral was given a stone vault following the second fire, and shafts of dark Purbeck marble were attached to the piers of the nave to soften their appearance. Two panels from a twelfth-century choir screen have survived and are now displayed in a choir aisle. They depict the raising of Lazarus and Christ with Mary and Martha.

The cathedral at Worcester enjoys a fine site above the River Severn, reminiscent of that at Durham. Here the Anglo-Saxon bishop Wulfstan (actually Wulfstan II, since there had been an earlier bishop of that name) remained in office under William I and endorsed the king's ecclesiastical reforms. Supposedly saying, 'We pull down the work of our predecessors in order to add lustre to our own names', he undertook the erection of a new church in 1084. He was canonized in 1203, thus giving Worcester two saintly bishops (the other being Oswald, d. 992). The crypt is the main remaining example of Wulfstan's work. The two western bays of the nave provide a rare opportunity to study the transition from Norman to Early English architecture. The principal arches, dating from about 1170, are nearly round but are just beginning to have a pointed apex, while the triforium level displays groups of three round arches held together by a higher arch which clearly rises to a point. Zigzag carving and rosettes provide unusual ornamentation at this stage. Above, the clerestory windows – groups of three, the middle being taller – are round-headed. All of this is contrasted with the mature Gothic form of the fourteenth-century bays which make up the remainder of the nave. It has been suggested that here, especially in the triforium, we see England's first essay in the Gothic style.

There is also Norman work at Carlisle. This border town had been in the hands of the Scots until the end of the eleventh century. An Augustinian priory established in 1102 became the cathedral when the bishopric was formed in 1133. The choir was rebuilt in the thirteenth and fourteenth centuries and has a remarkable east window. Most of the nave was destroyed by the Scots during the Civil War of the seventeenth century. The truncated nave and most of the transepts are simple Norman work, with very sturdy circular piers, a blind triforium and a plain clerestory with triple opening. The church still lacks a proper west end.

Several of the great monasteries which were converted into cathedrals by Henry VIII display fine Norman architecture as well. Indeed it can be argued that Peterborough offers a more complete interior view of Norman work than any other cathedral, for little rebuilding has taken place in either the nave or the choir. The monastery had been founded by Peada, king of Mercia, about 650. It was sacked by the Danes in 870, rebuilt, and sacked again by Hereward the Wake in his campaign against William the Conqueror. Then there was a great fire in 1116. Rebuilding started in 1118 and the nave was probably begun about 1150. All in all there are more than twenty bays of the nave and choir. Although details such as mouldings were modified as building went forward, the church displays a rare unity provided by virtually identical main piers, a continuous large gallery with several forms of ornamentation above the round arches, and a clerestory which includes detached columns and another walkway high in the air. The nave is still crowned by its original wooden roof, flat in the centre with slightly canted sides. Its original painting, although restored, has not been fundamentally altered; it shows a glowing sky inhabited by monsters and saints, kings and musicians, and an architect recognizable because he holds an L-square and dividers. Transepts include an eastern aisle. The carving throughout is crisp and clean, partly because of the use of Barnack stone (the quarry was only nine miles away), which was much superior to the softer sandstone used at Hereford and Worcester.

The west end of Peterborough has a complex architectural history. In the original plan the nave would have been two bays shorter and would have included western towers. The northern one of these was built and remains in place. But it was then decided to lengthen the cathedral by two bays. The resulting façade is intriguing if not, perhaps, entirely satisfying. It is very wide, with small towers capped by spires at each end. Between these are three deep recesses housing entrances and windows. The central one, rather than being dominant, is smaller than those flanking it, and an entrance porch, reminiscent of galilees elsewhere, has been inserted into it, partly in an effort to stabilize the stonework. Construction of this west end was underway at the time when Norman Romanesque was giving way to Early English Gothic and the transition is evident, with hundreds of lancet arches adorning what remains fundamentally a Norman conception.[7]

The monastery at Gloucester dates back to about 680. The Benedictine rule was introduced in 1022 and the church was rebuilt in 1058. But, according to the chronicler William of Malmesbury, 'zeal and religion had grown cold' many years before the coming of the Normans; in 1072, when the Norman Serlo was appointed abbot, there were only two professed monks and eight novices. By the end of the century Serlo had been able to build up the number of monks to sixty. He began rebuilding the church in 1089 and it was consecrated in 1100. Pale Cotswold stone from a quarry at Painswick was used. Much of Serlo's building remains today, although it has been partly masked by alterations of the Perpendicular period.

The early Norman crypt at Gloucester reveals the Norman plan above, with an ambulatory and three radiating chapels. Above, the ambulatory also displays Norman features. But the dominant Norman work is the nave. The two western bays were later redesigned, but seven bays of the original structure remain. They are dominated by huge cylindrical columns, thirty-one feet high, placed so close together that they nearly hide the aisles. They completely dwarf the triforium, and the clerestory is nearly hidden in a rib vault installed after its wooden predecessor burned. But its appearance was totally altered in the fifteenth century, when Perpendicular-style tracery was placed over the original round arches. Outside, the west end is relatively unimpressive; it was rebuilt following the collapse of the Norman façade in 1420. The exterior of the building is dominated by its fine crossing tower, while the enormous east window makes the interior of the choir memorable.

St Werburgh's Benedictine abbey at Chester was elevated to cathedral status in 1540. The monastery had been founded in 1092 by Hugh Lupus, earl of Chester; the first monks, who came from Bec, were led by Anselm, who was at Chester briefly before becoming archbishop of Canterbury. The present building lacks tall towers to herald its presence from a distance or a striking setting – it is hemmed in by offices and commercial buildings. The finest architectural work dates from the thirteenth and fourteenth centuries and includes a remarkable set of choir stalls with misericords. Significant Norman work does remain in the façade, north transept, north-west tower and cloister. The unusually extensive nineteenth-century restorations, necessitated by the decay of the soft red sandstone of which the cathedral was built, make it difficult to be sure just what is Norman and what is Victorian.

At Oxford the cathedral, another of Henry VIII's new establishments, serves also as the chapel of the largest college, Christ Church. This was not the king's original intention, for he designated the abbey of Osney, across the river west of Oxford, as the cathedral of the new diocese. The view of it across the water meadows was one of the glories of Oxford, but the location proved inconvenient and in 1546 the cathedral was transferred to its present location, part of the monastery dedicated to St Frideswide which had been converted into Thomas Wolsey's college, known as Cardinal College prior to Wolsey's fall. Here the nave and south transept are Norman, as is the lower part of the choir, and there is a fine Norman doorway leading to the chapter house. Our appreciation of the Norman work is limited by the fact that Wolsey substantially reduced the length of the nave so that he could create Tom Quad and by the dominance of the exceptional pendant vault of the choir, added in the fifteenth century.

Little remains of the Augustinian abbey at Bristol that was turned into a cathedral in 1542. The gatehouse and chapter house are Norman, but the choir was rebuilt at the beginning of the fourteenth century. Rebuilding of the nave in the same unusual Gothic style was suspended at the time of the Dissolution, and the building was not completed until the nineteenth century.

The present buildings at Canterbury and York are not predominantly Norman, but some Norman work can be seen in both places. In fact three distinct phases of Norman construction have left traces at Canterbury. The first Norman archbishop, Lanfranc, was responsible for the earliest of these. When he came to Canterbury in 1070 Lanfranc found the fabric of the Anglo-Saxon cathedral in a damaged state following a fire of 1067. Assisted by his prior, Lanfranc began reconstruction in 1071. Gundulph, whose work at Rochester has already been noted, was also involved. We know that Lanfranc's nave had nine bays and was flanked by two towers. There was a large crossing tower; the small choir had only two bays and probably terminated in an apse. A portion of the crypt is the only work of this period to survive. It has three aisles, with vaults supported by two rows of columns decorated with patterns similar to those in the nave at Durham. There are also reliefs carved with foliage and grotesques reminiscent of details from the Bayeux Tapestry.

Soon after his arrival at Canterbury in 1093, Lanfranc's successor Anselm began a second round of building. His initial goal was to enlarge the choir – more space was needed to accommodate the monks, of whom there were then one hundred. By the 1120s this work was complete, and it must have been marvellous: the chronicler William of Malmesbury wrote that 'Nothing like it could be seen in England, either for the brilliancy of its glass windows, the beauty of its marble pavements, or the many coloured pictures which led the wandering eye to the very summit of the ceiling'. Here again what survives is the crypt, which contains some of the finest Romanesque sculpture in England. Most of this is in the form of capitals atop the columns which support the vault. The grotesques in St Gabriel's chapel are especially delightful. They are similar to, and perhaps based on, the ornamentation in illuminated manuscripts of the period.

Above ground, Anselm's choir was damaged by fire in 1174. In a way the fire was providential, since the martyrdom of Thomas Becket in 1170 and the growth of pilgrimage to his shrine meant that a larger east end was needed. The new architect, William of Sens, was instructed to retain as much of the earlier work as possible, and we know that a good deal of Anselm's building is buried within the walls of the present choir. But the style did begin to change; both pointed and round-headed arches may be seen, an early sign of transition to the Gothic. The south-east transept was not significantly altered, and its exterior merits examination. Low windows light the crypt. Above them there is a blind arcade of intersecting Norman arches, then large round-headed windows. Smaller windows light the clerestory, and the top of the transept boasts a round rose window. A smaller adjacent tower is richly embellished with Norman arches and capped by a lead spire. Another important Norman survival is the water tower, which forms part of the remarkable hydraulic system installed by Prior Wibert about 1150. Two early maps reveal its sophistication. A Norman staircase leading to the guest house (*aula nova*) and a Norman treasury or *vestiarium* also repay attention.

There is less Norman work visible at York. Here the Saxon cathedral was burned in September 1069 during a conflict between the Danes, Saxons and followers of William the Conqueror. Thomas of Bayeux, who was named archbishop in 1070, restored the church, but it was ruined when the Danes sacked the city in 1079. Thomas then decided to build a completely new church from the foundations up. It was probably complete by the time of his death in 1100. The cathedral was 362 feet long. Its eastern arm, as usual, terminated in an apse. The seven-bay nave was unusual in not having aisles; its central space was forty-five feet wide. Two western towers flanked the nave. Excavations have revealed amazingly strong footings including great timbers. The walls, generally seven feet thick, are partly of reused Roman masonry. The external faces were covered with hard white plaster lined in red to resemble ashlar. Some of the interior was also plastered. In 1137 the choir was damaged by fire. When rebuilt it was enlarged and the apse was squared, as in so many other buildings. But this did not satisfy Roger of Pont l'Evêque, who became archbishop in 1154. He built a magnificent new choir with an eastern transept, an idea perhaps borrowed from Cluny. None of this remains above ground, for the nave was rebuilt in the thirteenth century and the choir in the fourteenth. The visitor seeking Norman architecture will find it only in the crypt, where massive piers with zigzag and diaper decoration, charming capitals depicting dancers, and a rib vault remain.

The Normans also rebuilt St Paul's in London. Here again fire destroyed an earlier structure. John Stow's *Survey of London*, published in 1598, has a fine account of the cathedral's history.

In the year 1087, this church of St Paul's was burnt with fire, and therewith the most part of the city; which fire began at the entry of the west gate, and consumed the east gate. Mauricius the bishop began therefore the foundation of a new church of St Paul's, a work that men of that time judged would never have been finished, it was to them so wonderful for length and breadth; and also the same was built upon arches (or vaults) of stone, for defence of fire, which was a manner of work before that time unknown to the people of this nation, and then brought in by the French; and the stone was fetched from Caen in Normandy.[8]

An apsidal choir was raised over a crypt. The nave had twelve bays divided by clustered columns which were probably similar to those which survive at Peterborough. There were twin western towers, positioned outside the line of the nave aisles. The entire building was given rib vaults like those at Durham. Some Norman work is visible in Hollar's engravings of Old St Paul's, although the cathedral had been rebuilt and remodelled several times before it was destroyed in the Great Fire of London.

If some modern miracle could transport us back in time, we might be well advised to pick the date 1166, a century after the battle of Hastings. We would find great Norman cathedrals throughout England. The surviving buildings at Durham and Ely give us an idea of what Canterbury, York or St Paul's might have looked like, while Rochester helps us imagine the smaller Norman churches at such places as Worcester, Chichester or Carlisle.

Virtually all the cathedrals displayed fine sculpture and, in several cases, painted wooden ceilings, as well as imposing architecture. Their towers and spires often dominated the skyline. While the English cathedrals owed much to their French counterparts, it is right to call them Norman rather than Romanesque (as on the Continent), for they displayed their own characteristics. The most important development attributable to English builders is no doubt the introduction of rib vaults at Durham, but there are further English contributions to European architecture.

In the cathedral priories the full round of monastic offices was said or sung. Choirs of boys appear to have been established at such places at Canterbury. Solemn liturgies were also offered in the secular cathedrals. Cathedral libraries had come into existence in many places; we know that there were three hundred volumes in the library at Canterbury by the late twelfth century. In the writing rooms or *scriptoria* chronicles were kept and beautiful illuminated manuscripts written. At least informally, instruction in Latin and liturgy was provided for novices or other young men seeking to serve the church. Especially in the monastic cathedrals, guest houses provided hospitality for travellers and infirmaries helped care for the sick. Although services were conceived of as being offered to the greater glory of God rather than for the edification of humans, lay people were welcome to attend and must have been impressed by such events as Palm Sunday processions or great celebrations of Christmas and Easter; the liturgical year added warmth and colour to many lives which would otherwise have seemed barren.

3

Early English, 1170–1280

In the cathedrals of England, Gothic architecture superseded Romanesque during the last decades of the twelfth century; to put it in more specifically English terms, the Norman style gave way to Early English. The thirteenth century was the great age of E. E., as it is commonly abbreviated.

Nineteenth-century architects and ecclesiastical historians, among them A. W. N. Pugin and members of the Cambridge Ecclesiological Society, were especially fond of the new style, which they termed the 'first pointed architecture'. They referred, of course, to the fact that arches, including windows and doorways, now rose to a point rather than being round-headed. Certainly lancet arches were a characteristic of the new era; like a surgeon's lancet, they were tall, narrow, sharply pointed at the top. In the case of windows they were without stone tracery, thus being different from the larger, wider windows that were to come in later centuries. Pointed arches were not quite new in 1170; they had been used in the vaulting at Durham as early as 1130 and, as we have seen, they can be found alongside round arches at such places as the nave of Worcester. It may be that one inspiration for the pointed arches came from the areas of intersecting round arches often used by Norman builders to provide interesting designs for blank wall spaces: if two round arches are superimposed, the second beginning halfway through the area of the first, the result can be viewed as a narrow pointed arch. The chapter house at Bristol offers one of the best examples of this pattern, which can also be seen at Norwich and Durham.

Once introduced, pointed arches gained favour on account of their greater structural stability – because of their diagonal stress lines they were not as likely to cave in or spread as were round Norman arches. With them came new construction techniques that led to larger windows, brighter buildings, and a sense of lightness that contrasts with the massive heaviness associated with earlier cathedrals. Instead of a feeling that one is being weighed down in a Norman building, the spirit of a Gothic cathedral creates the sensation of soaring towards the heavens.

Architectural historians generally agree that the Gothic style was developed in France about 1140 and was first seen in England at some of the Cistercian abbeys, especially Malmesbury, where it is recognizable in work of the 1160s. It was employed at Canterbury beginning in 1174, at Wells in 1180, at Lincoln in 1192, at Salisbury in 1220, and at Westminster Abbey in 1245. During this period it is particularly interesting to note exact dates and see similar work appearing at several places almost simultaneously. Early English, obviously unique to England and Wales, came to have several characteristics in addition to the use of lancet arches. These included the replacement of simple rib vaults by increasingly complex vaulting with ornamental ribs, known as tiercerons; the use of different types of stone, especially Purbeck marble, to provide colour contrasts; the frequent employment of what is known as stiff-leaf ornament; and the greater use of sculpture, especially on the façades of Wells and Salisbury.

Rebuilding at Canterbury was necessitated by a fire which gutted the choir in 1174.[1] The monks had heard of the great cathedral which had just been completed at Sens in Normandy – some of them had likely seen it – and they resolved to bring one of its architects, William of Sens, to work for them. According to a chronicler it was William's 'lively genius and good reputation' that impressed them. William was instructed to retain as much of the existing structure as possible, so he kept the eastern transepts as they were and reused the lower part of the choir aisles. This meant that he was unable to alter the width of the building, though he could raise its height. His style is unique. No longer Romanesque but not yet fully Gothic, it reverts to classical Greek architecture in employing Corinthian or acanthus leaf capitals. The main arches point, but only barely; above them, the gallery is composed of pairs of pointed arches within a round-headed surround. The elevations are borrowed quite directly from Sens, but William has added a peculiarly English touch, the use of black polished Purbeck marble shafts on all four sides of the stone columns.

In 1178 William of Sens was preparing the centring for the choir vault when the scaffolding collapsed beneath him, dropping him to the floor fifty feet below. He was forced to return to France, where he died in 1180, and he was replaced by another William, known as William the Englishman, who completed a new area east of the choir. This addition had been made necessary by the growth of the cult of St Thomas Becket, the archbishop who had been murdered by Henry II's knights in 1170. The cathedral needed room to accommodate the throngs of pilgrims who streamed to pray to the holy blissful martyr. Becket's major shrine was established in the Trinity chapel, while the small corona to the east displayed a skull fragment for separate veneration. Here the large lancet windows provide a glorious bright space, but again the architecture is ambiguous, with both round and pointed arches visible. The general feeling, however, is clear: this is an Early English area, not a Norman one. William the Englishman was also responsible for building the crypts that lie under it, as well as the Trinity chapel and the corona.

Plans for the cathedral at Wells were laid by Bishop Reginald FitzJocelin de Bohun.[2] Reginald had been at Canterbury on 5 September 1174, the day of the fire, and it may be that the necessity of rebuilding there prompted him to undertake construction at Wells. Here the site was one of the finest in the country, for there were no surrounding buildings to block the view or restrict the building. Since the cathedral was not a priory, a full array of monastic buildings was not required, and work could proceed rapidly. It may have been undertaken as early as 1176 and was certainly in hand in 1179 or 1180. Although several breaks in construction have been identified, they were brief; the original plan was modified several times but never really altered. We do not know the name of the original master mason, but it has been speculated that he was a young man willing to break out of older moulds. Certainly he designed the first fully Gothic building in Britain – perhaps the first in the world.

There are now no round-headed arcades, but rather crisp pointed arches. Unusual features are the double-aisled transepts and the great north entrance porch, which displays particularly elegant blank arcading. The nave provides some of the finest Early English architecture anywhere. Ten bays long, it displays noble simplicity. Above the arcade of nearly identical pointed arches there is a triforium rather than a gallery (that is to say, it does not house a passageway) made up of a continuous range of identical lancets. This is uncommon – most other cathedrals have two smaller arches grouped together with a superior moulding – and it adds to a feeling of unity and, perhaps, enclosure. The capitals atop the shafts composing each archway repay study. Not only do they display the finest stiff-leaf carving in the country (and something completely unknown outside England); they also offer a number of amusing narrative subjects, the most famous being the toothache victim, his right hand clutching his mouth, and the hooded man attempting to remove a thorn from his foot, probably a reference to St Paul's complaint of a thorn in his flesh.

The nave and transepts of Wells were probably designed by Adam Lock, a master mason who came to Wells from Bristol about 1218 and whose portrait head, wearing a mason's cap, adorns the most western bay of the nave. The west front is probably the work of Thomas Norreys, who succeeded Lock in 1229. This broad façade, almost exactly twice as wide as it is high, is the cathedral's most famous feature, for it is an image screen displaying more than three hundred statues. It was completed by 1248. This is the grandest array of medieval sculpture in England; the similar façades at Salisbury and Exeter are derived from it but are smaller and less fine. The large number of statues is accommodated by including twin towers, set outside the line of the nave aisles, and by the clever device of having six buttresses which project from the main line of the wall, thus allowing statuary to be mounted on the sides of the buttresses as well as on the main north-south plane. Each statue is contained in its own canopied niche, separated from the next by shafts of Purbeck marble. We know that many of the statues were originally painted in bright colours, for traces of paint have been found on them. It is hard to imagine the impact that this brilliant display would have made. Probably most modern viewers would have found it gaudy and are happier with the present monochrome stonework; it may be that the medieval masons came to share that view, since recent examination shows that some of the statues remained unpainted. There were originally even more statues than can now be seen, since the Puritan iconoclasts of the seventeenth century pulled down those at the lowest level. (We can be grateful that they were not sufficiently energetic to tackle those they could not reach conveniently.) They did decapitate a few more figures, including Christ and Mary in the Coronation of the Virgin panel above the centre door.

Attempts have been made to identify each statue, but such work is largely speculative.[3] It may be that there was an attempt to depict the orders of angels, cherubim, seraphim, apostles, prophets and martyrs mentioned in the *Te Deum*. Certainly there are rows of saints and kings. It used to be thought that the figures above the central west doorway represented pairings of New and Old Testament figures, the Virgin Mary with the Queen of Sheba and Jesus with King Solomon. This is no longer accepted, but Sheba and Solomon are still there. Perhaps the finest sculpture can be found in the group of the four Marys, the Gospel procession, and the figures of a knight, priest, and deacon, all on the north tower. Some of the statues stand in front of holes in the wall. As was the case at Rochester, this arrangement made it possible for a choir, hidden in passageways behind the façade, to sing for processions in the churchyard, especially on Palm Sunday, one of the few days when the principal west door was opened.

The façade and its statuary were carefully cleaned with lime water between 1974 and 1986. The luminous honey-coloured stone which was then visible for a few years was surpassingly beautiful; now graying has set in and that transitory magic is gone. The façade remains one of the great glories of English architecture, but it must be said that it is not perfectly satisfying, for the upper parts of the towers were not completed as originally designed and what was finally built, several centuries after the completion of the main façade about 1295, is too simple and does not relate well to the work below. One wonders what the original design was. No trace of it remains; the designer may have dreamt of towers of an unheard of height, and short of that the façade could not have been made wholly successful. The eastern portion of the cathedral, together with the chapter house, dates from the fourteenth century and will concern us later.

Construction at Salisbury began about forty years after that at Wells.[4] Here again there was a virgin site, in a lush valley near the River Avon. The Norman cathedral had been on a nearby hilltop at Old Sarum; the decision to move was made during the reign of Henry III by Bishop Richard Poore and was finally approved by the pope in 1218. It is often said that the reasons were shortage of water and excessive winds at the earlier site, but it is likely that conflicts with the garrison of the neighbouring castle and a desire to build a grander edifice, comparable to that close by at Winchester, were of greater importance. Nothing but some foundations remains of the earlier building. Bishop Poore laid three stones at the new site in 1220, one for the pope, one for the archbishop of Canterbury and one for himself, and William Longespee, earl of Sarum, laid two more. The cathedral clergy migrated there on All Saints Day 1219; altars in the three eastern chapels were consecrated in 1225; consecration of the entire building took place in 1258. Stone came from a quarry at Chilmark, only twelve miles away. The building is 449 feet long. Besides Bishop Poore, those responsible for the building were the mason Nicholas of Ely and Elias of Dereham, a canon of Sarum. The plan, never altered, is elegantly simple. At the east end the Trinity chapel projects for two bays. There are then seven bays of the choir, an eastern transept of two bays, a wider main transept of three bays, and a ten-bay nave. The western façade is a wide screen, not growing out of the nave and its aisles. Entrance is normally through a fine north porch. Originally there was a separate bell tower, now demolished, though its site can still be seen north of the cathedral.

A number of writers have pronounced the interior perfect, or nearly so. If there is a weakness it lies in the lowness of the vault, which is only eighty-one feet high. No other English cathedral can match Salisbury's unity of style. The arcade is a continuous series of lancet arches, some left a rough gray colour and some a highly polished black. Capitals of the piers have dog-tooth, stiff-leaf and acanthus capitals. There is an elaborate gallery, each bay being subdivided into two groups of two arches each, all held together by a broad pointed arch with a foiled circle at the top. A succession of lancet windows, three to a bay, the central one taller, makes the clerestory. The fenestration of the aisles is handled similarly. The main transepts have an elaborate window pattern: three large lancets below, three groups of two lancets each above, and four lancets at the top, all recessed behind elegant mouldings with Purbeck shafts. The east end, behind the high altar, is handled similarly with five lancets at ground level, a five-arched triforium, and three high windows above. The ceiling has simple four-part rib vaults, very thin, with stiff-leaf bosses rather than carved figures. Some of the vaults are ornamented with painted roundels: originally thirteenth-century, they were renewed by Clayton and Bell in 1872. There is an elaborate fifteenth-century lierne vault at the crossing. On the outside one can see a number of flying buttresses bearing the weight of the vaults down to the ground but by-passing the main walls, which can then be used primarily for windows. This is one of the earliest uses of flying buttresses in England.

Beautiful though the west front is, especially when viewed across the broad expanse of the grassy close, it is the weakest feature of Salisbury Cathedral. Like the façade at Wells, on which it appears to have been based, it forms a screen wider than the nave itself; on the inside, the relationship between the west wall and the aisles leaves something to be desired. There seem to be too many different motifs, not integrated into a comprehensive system. The central porch, reminiscent of French work, is divided into three sections, of which only the centre one actually contains a door. There are smaller doors farther out on each side. These may seem insignificant, but in defence of the designer it should be said that the principal entrance to the cathedral was always intended to be the north porch; the west doors were used only for liturgical processions. A group of three large lancet windows, the central one taller than the others, dominates the façade. There are no towers, but rather only side turrets with low spires. As at Wells, these do not seem entirely satisfactory – they have the advantage of not competing with the great central spire, but since that was added later the original architect could not have had that goal in mind.

Sculpture is less important than at Wells, but the intention was to have a lot of it. In all there are five tiers of statues in the façade. Again echoing the Te Deum, these represent (starting at the top) angels; Old Testament prophets and patriarchs; apostles; doctors of the church, virgins, and martyrs; and, close to the ground level, eminent persons connected with the church and cathedral. These include Bishop Poore, Henry II, Henry VI and (from a more recent era) the Non-Juror Thomas Ken (d. 1711). The sculpture is not of the quality of Wells, for few of the original statues survive: some were destroyed by sixteenth- and seventeenth-century iconoclasts, while others simply appear to have decayed. What one sees today is largely the work of the Victorian architect Sir George Gilbert Scott, with the actual carving done by the sculptor J. F. Redfern and the local Osmond workshop.

Only six figures are old; these include the images of Peter and Paul on either side of the windows.

Salisbury's greatest glory is of course its spire, which has attracted countless artists, most notably the painter John Constable. Although it is of a slightly later date than the rest of the cathedral, it is convenient to consider it here. In fact no documentary evidence giving exact dates for the work survives, the best guess being that the upper stages of the tower and the spire were begun about 1300 and completed shortly after 1330. Even without the spire the central tower would have been impressive; to gain a sense of this, one can try using a hand or a piece of paper to blot out the view of the spire, either in real life or in a photograph, thus revealing the considerable size and elegance of the square tower itself. The spire rises to 404 feet. Its weight has been estimated at about 6300 tons. It was constructed around a complex scaffolding of timber posts and struts which at the higher levels rise from a central post, rather like the spokes of an umbrella. Although there had been earlier spires at Durham, Lincoln and Old St Paul's, they had been constructed of timber and lead; the stone spire at Salisbury is the first of its kind. It exterior is elegantly embellished with blank lancets at the lowest level, three tiers of diamond-shaped low relief carving on the ascending stonework, and a small lantern at the top.

Such a great structure has always caused trouble, in part because the original foundations and lower stages of the tower were not designed to carry such weight. Soon after its erection scissor-shaped arches were inserted in the eastern transepts to help prevent distortion of the stonework below. The strainer arches at the great crossing date from the early fifteenth century. Iron bars were added to the spire itself as early as the fourteenth century. There was considerable later work, supervised by such architects as Wren and Scott, and there were several twentieth-century campaigns of restoration, with Prince Charles once being photographed in a hard hat at the top of the spire to aid in fund raising. *

The original small cloister at Salisbury was enlarged in the later thirteenth century – there is no agreement about the exact date – and the chapter house was built at about the same time. Both are important architecturally, for they display a late form of Early English, often called the geometric style,

---

* The motivation for such demanding construction has been queried, most notably in the historical novel *The Spire* by William Golding (1964). Here the author attributes it to the ego of the bishop, who wishes to leave a lasting monument to his own authority. That may well be true; even if it is an exaggeration, the novel helps one feel the combination of excitement and fear that grew as the precarious spire rose ever higher.

which was to provide a transition to the Decorated style which followed it at the end of the century. The lancets of windows and arcades are grouped together: at the lowest level there are two groups of two lancet openings, each held together by a quatrefoiled circle above, while the entire area is surmounted by a large eight-foiled circle and elaborate moulding. There is still no stone tracery within the individual lancets. Such large windows make the octagonal chapter house very bright. Here the vault is supported by a slender central column of Purbeck marble. Seats for the clergy line the walls. Sixty carvings of Old Testament scenes form a frieze fitted into the arcading, while above the entrance a tympanum displays a seated figure of Christ surrounded by the four Evangelists.

The close at Salisbury is perhaps the finest in England. Laid out in the thirteenth century, it originally contained houses for the bishop, canons and vicars choral. The eighteenth century saw the construction of elegant homes within the close for members of the gentry; the grandest of these, Mompesson House, is now maintained by the National Trust.

As we have seen, the rebuilding of Lincoln Cathedral followed what was called an earthquake in 1185.[5] Whatever the disturbance may have been, it is clear that much of the eastern arm of the Norman cathedral collapsed. Originally there was no intention of reconstructing the entire cathedral, but rebuilding of the choir began in 1192. The structure that resulted is always known as St Hugh's Choir in honour of Bishop Hugh of Avalon, who died in 1200 and was canonized in 1220. The plan is unusual for its date in being apsidal. Nothing of the apse now exists, but excavations have revealed that it was of a unique hexagonal shape. It seems to have been based on the corona at Canterbury and, like the corona, was probably erected as a saint's chapel. Since Hugh had not yet been canonized when it was planned, the intention may have been to honour Remigius, the bishop who was responsible for building the Norman cathedral; efforts were being made to secure his canonization, but they were abandoned when Hugh's claims were put forward.

Several other unusual features of the choir can still be seen. The blind arcading which lines the other walls of the nave is double, one row of arches recessed behind another, and the spandrels display a row of carved figures. These contribute to the choir's visual opulence and probably represent local religious leaders; identification is difficult because the present heads are modern replacements of work that was destroyed by Puritan iconoclasts. The other unique design is the vaulting, often called crazy, mad or (more kindly) dionysiac. It is difficult to describe in such a way that one can visualize its form. Suffice it to say that each bay has two keystones, each keystone receiving two ribs from one side and one from the other. Not all the ribs are essential for functional purposes; some are decorative. Lincoln appears to be the place where these tiercerons were first used. The 'crazy' aspect refers to the fact that some of these do not run beyond the longitudinal ridge rib (itself a new feature), and that the two sides of each bay are not identical. The scheme was devised by the master mason Geoffrey de Noiers, who despite his name was very possibly English and who was inspired more by the work of William of Sens at Canterbury than by actual French buildings. The elevations of St Hugh's choir are not exceptional but are of great beauty. The large gallery has two arches for each bay, each subdivided into two more, and there is also a walkway at the clerestory level, with additional stone columns in front of the windows, foreshadowing the later use of double tracery.

Like Canterbury and Salisbury, Lincoln has two sets of transepts. Both were part of the same building campaign as St Hugh's Choir. The eastern transepts house four semicircular chapels, much ornamented with Purbeck shafts and stiff-leaf carving. The main transepts, slightly later in date, are most notable for the fenestration at their ends. The north transept has a door leading to the deanery, so the rose window near its apex is known as the Dean's Eye. Below this is a row of seven lancets, the central five pierced as windows and containing early grisaille glass. The south transept leads to an elaborate porch, sometimes referred to as a galilee, which was used as the bishop's entrance, so the rose window here was called the Bishop's Eye. It is later, dating from the fourteenth century, and was awkwardly fitted into the existing vaulting.

Next the nave was rebuilt to a somewhat different plan. It is more than ten feet higher than the choir, and its bays are wider. It is seven bays long, plus an odd bay between the west towers. There is still a gallery, now with triplet rather than twin openings per bay, and a clerestory passageway. The vault has been rationalized. There is still a ridge rib with tiercerons, but the pattern has become logical and symmetrical. Since some of the ribs are not functional, the whole conception of the vault has been altered; instead of a skeleton system of load-bearing ribs one now has a series of half-cone-shaped brackets. This change occurred first at Lincoln. The final stage in the rebuilding of Lincoln began in 1256, when permission was received to breach the city wall so that the cathedral might be extended to the east. The former apse was removed and replaced by the famous Angel Choir, so called because of the profusion of carved angels which adorns its arches. The work was complete by 1280, when St Hugh's remains were translated with great pomp and ceremony to a fine new shrine. This took up the eastern half of the Angel Choir; it was separated from the western portion, housing the high altar, by a double reredos. Here the style reached an extreme of elegance and ornamentation. The vaulting pattern is somewhat simplified from that in the nave but the roof bosses in the aisles are extraordinary, probably the finest in the country for their date (about 1260). They include foliage, identifiable as that of vine, oak, maple, ranunculus and water lily, and figures, some secular (a pair of wrestlers, a lady with a puppy) and some biblical (King David playing the harp, a Jesse tree, and the Coronation of the Virgin). There are also monsters and mermen. The east end is largely given over to four great windows, all in the form we have described as geometric, with groups of tall lancets held together by groups of foiled circles or *oculi* (eyes) above. The main east window is nearly sixty feet high.

The cloister probably dates from 1235–60, as does the chapter house. Similar to that at Salisbury, the chapter house is ten-sided with a vault supported by a central post. Its round west window rises above the cloister wall. While Lincoln does not have a proper close – motor traffic runs near the cathedral on several sides – there are a number of medieval buildings which housed its staff. These include homes of the vicars choral who sang the daily services and the fourteenth-century chancery, still the home of the chancellor.

Although Westminster Abbey was not a cathedral in the thirteenth century and is not one now, it must be included here. A technical reason is that the abbey did enjoy cathedral status during a brief period in the sixteenth century, following the Dissolution of the Monasteries. There are more important reasons also. Except for the absence of a bishop and the special association with the royal family, the abbey functioned very much like a cathedral priory, with daily sung services, monastic living quarters and a large library. In terms of architecture, too, the abbey buildings were comparable to those of a cathedral and are essential to understanding the architectural history of the age.[6]

We do not know the date of the foundation of the earliest church at Westminster. The Romans had occupied the site, the Isle of Thorney or Island of Thorns close to the marshy banks of the Thames. The first records of a monastery here date back to about 970, the time of St Dunstan. The earliest recorded association with the monarchy is the burial of Harold Harefoot in the abbey precincts in 1040. Far more important was the complete rebuilding of the abbey by Edward the Confessor beginning about 1050. His structure, which we may term Norman even though it antedated the Conquest, was dedicated on 28 December 1065. Soon thereafter Edward died and was interred in the abbey. Later in 1066 the coronation of William the Conqueror was held at Westminster, beginning an unbroken tradition that continues to the present.

We do not know a great deal about the Norman buildings. Judging from excavations and occasional recorded references there was an apsidal choir, transepts and a crossing tower, and two towers at the west end. The nave had six bays. It was no doubt inspired by the churches of Normandy, but it was longer than any of them which survive. Henry III added a Lady chapel at the east end about 1220. Initially it was incorporated in the subsequent rebuilding, which it may have helped inspire, but it was demolished in the early sixteenth century to make way for Henry VII's chapel. In 1222 the abbey was removed from the jurisdiction of the bishop of London and placed directly under the papacy.

The foundation stone of the present abbey was laid on 6 July 1245. Probably because of continuing royal support, building proceeded very rapidly; by 1255 the entire choir, transepts and first bay of the nave were complete. Four additional bays of the nave were built shortly thereafter and the translation of the body of Edward the Confessor, now a saint, took place in 1269.

As might be expected from the close connexion with a royal family which ruled both England and Normandy, the abbey was influenced by French buildings more than any of the cathedrals. It is especially dependent on Reims for its plan with a polygonal apse, ambulatory with radiating chapels and windows made up of clustered lancets. Some other windows have the shape of spherical triangles (triangles whose sides are arcs of a circle rather than being straight); these were borrowed from Amiens and the Sainte-Chapelle in Paris. Since the Sainte-Chapelle was finished only in 1248 the work at Westminster followed almost immediately; the architect, Henry of Reyns, must have been in close touch with his French counterparts, though it is generally believed that he was an Englishman who had some sort of professional relationship with Reims, probably during the years 1243–45, rather than a native of northern France. The proportions of the abbey also reveal French influences: it is taller than any other English church, the vault rising to a height of 103 feet, nearly thirty feet higher than Lincoln. The original building, excluding Henry VII's chapel, is 423 feet long and it built of stone from Reigate. Although voluminous building records survive – there are about a hundred fabric rolls in the Public Record Office – no scholar has yet been brave enough to utilize them for a detailed architectural history. It appears that work began at the east end, and that the cloister, chapter house and north porch were among the earliest parts to be completed, probably in 1250.

It is difficult to visualize the physical setting of the abbey in the thirteenth century. One must forget the paved streets and the swirling traffic of our own time and imagine a building set in the fields, with its close, the sanctuary, on the north side. It formed part of a complex that included the

Palace of Westminster, then a group of separate buildings rather than a single structure. As today, the abbey lacked a proper central tower, and the west end had no towers until Hawksmoor added them in the eighteenth century. During the middle ages the principal entrance was the elaborate north porch. Its tripartite form was based on French transept fronts like that at Chartres; there are three gables with large porches below them, and there was considerable statuary and stiff-leaf carving. Little of this remains, since the entire entrance has been rebuilt several times, most recently in the late nineteenth century. Above the gables there are lancet windows, with a rose window still higher up.

In appreciating the architecture of the interior one must again use one's imagination, in this case to visualize the building unencumbered by its scores of tombs and monuments. Some, of course, are medieval. These include royal tombs and lie mainly in chapels east of the high altar; the nave contains many monuments to statesmen and poets of the eighteenth and nineteenth centuries. In trying to conceive the east end as originally built one must blot out Henry VII's chapel. The original chancel, as at Reims, ends with five sides of an octagon and has radiating chapels. The area above the high altar is elegantly designed, with a lancet arcade topped by a gallery, then huge geometric windows (two lancets surmounted by a foiled circle). The sanctuary floor, which can be dated to 1268, is made up of mosaic fragments laid by Italian craftsmen who were members of the Cosmati family of Rome. The Italian workers also decorated the base of Henry III's tomb and installed a pavement of more than two hundred intertwined circles in the chapel of Edward the Confessor. The choir gallery is very elaborate, with double tracery, one set of shafts facing the choir itself and the other the passageway. This is an aspect of the abbey's Englishness; in France by this date galleries had been replaced by triforia without passageways.

Wall surfaces in both the nave and choir are adorned with beautiful diaper work, a feature that appears in no other English cathedral. These designs, which were carved in place, were borrowed from French churches, but in France they are usually found on exterior walls rather than internally. An unusual part of the south transept was a room above the east walk of the cloister. Originally probably a royal pew from which dignitaries could watch the ceremonies without being seen themselves, this has been converted into a modern muniment room. The architects of the nave who followed Henry of Reyns were John of Gloucester and Robert of Beverley; the nave was not completed until the fifteenth century, but the later masons, including Henry Yeveley, kept to the original plan and the building retains a sense of unity. Its earlier part was vaulted by 1269, copying the system of ridge ribs with one additional tierceron developed a few years earlier at Lincoln. The choir had been roofed with a simpler pattern of quadripartite vaulting. Throughout the building the fenestration at both the ground and clerestory levels consists of twin lancets capped by a single foiled circle – the typical geometrical pattern. The gallery is also lit by its own set of windows, in the choir and transepts single foiled circles inside spherical triangles but in the nave sets of three circles inside a flat-bottomed triangle.

The sculptural embellishment of the interior of Westminster Abbey is the richest ever undertaken in a medieval building of comparable dimensions. The transept ends are especially interesting; here the soffits of the lancet windows are ornamented with carvings of musical angels. There are also sculptures of kings, including the Confessor. The vault of the royal pew has fascinating bosses depicting centaurs and dragons as well as men.

The chapter house, completed by 1250, is similar to those at Salisbury and Lincoln. It is octagonal (that at Lincoln had ten sides), and its windows are larger than had been seen earlier. They take up almost the entire wall space; their pattern, more elaborate than Lincoln's, has four lancets (two groups of two) held together by two sets of foiled circles, pushing the geometric style to its limit. The vault resembles that at Lincoln. The pavement is made up of mid thirteenth-century tiles. It is amazing that these survive, especially in a building where so much reconstruction has taken place. They depict an archer, a horseman, a king, a queen and a pilgrim, as well as foliage and rose window designs. During the later fourteenth century the House of Commons met in the chapter house. It was then that paintings depicting the Apocalypse and Last Judgment were added to the wall arcades. Following the Dissolution of the Monasteries the chapter house was used for a variety of purposes; records of the Exchequer and other courts were stored there from the reign of Edward VI until 1866. The windows were bricked up in the seventeenth century and the dangerous vault taken down in the eighteenth, but both were carefully restored by Sir George Gilbert Scott. The chapter house is unusual in having a crypt, also octagonal, underneath its main storey. Further undercrofts remain, now housing the chapel of the pyx and a museum displaying the funeral effigies of monarchs. These underground chambers were part of the Confessor's original building.

Lesser examples of Early English architecture can be seen in several other cathedrals. At Chichester the Norman building was damaged by fire in 1187. This necessitated demolition of the apsidal east end and its reconstruction as a straight-ended retrochoir with corner chapels. Here the work, which is contemporary with building at Canterbury and Lincoln, represents the transition between Norman and Gothic; the main arches of the arcade and triforium remain round-headed, but pointed arches are also used in the triforium and dominate the clerestory. Later in the thirteenth century the retrochoir was adapted to house the shrine of St Richard of Chichester, bishop from 1245 to 1253. The cathedral was also given a stone vault to reduce the likelihood of another conflagration.

If Chichester embodies the transition from Norman to Early English, Lichfield enables us to see the change from the geometric style to the full-fledged Decorated which followed it. The early history of the diocese is complicated. The first bishop was Chad (or Ceadda), a disciple of Aidan at Lindisfarne. After serving briefly as bishop of Lindisfarne or York, Chad was named bishop to the Mercians and fixed his see at Lichfield, where he built some sort of church prior to his death in 672. The Normans first transferred the see to Chester, then to Coventry, and finally to Coventry and Lichfield jointly. This arrangement continued until the Reformation, at which time the church in Coventry lost its cathedral status and was destroyed. (The cathedral at Coventry gutted by bombing in the Second World War was not the medieval cathedral but rather a nearby parish church which had been raised to cathedral status in 1918.)

By the thirteenth century Chad had become a popular saint, and the cathedral at Lichfield needed to be rebuilt to accommodate his shrine. A new choir was begun about 1220, with transepts following about 1230, the chapter house about 1240, nave about 1260, and west front about 1280. The building is famous for its spires – it is the only English cathedral to have three of them. The crossing tower and central spire were built about 1300 and the twin west spires a few years later. The east end was reconstructed beginning about 1310 and the Lady chapel added about 1325.

In terms of architectural style we may call the nave Geometric, that is, late Early English. The ground-level windows have three lancet panels with three trefoiled circles over them. The triforium has a typical geometric design. The clerestory windows are particularly interesting, since they are in the form of spherical triangles, each holding three trefoiled circles. These must have been borrowed from Westminster Abbey, a fact that helps date work on the nave. The Lady chapel also adopts motifs from Westminster. The chapter house is unusual in shape, an elongated octagon approaching an oval. By the time the west front was begun the Decorated style was coming into vogue. That elaborate structure, which will be considered in greater detail later, has something like a hundred statues and three small doors as well as its two towers and spires. The chancel as finally rebuilt in the fourteenth century displays window tracery of typically Decorated style in its elaborateness, with some patterns arguably Perpendicular.[7]

The choir of Worcester Cathedral gives us another fine example of Early English architecture. It was rebuilt beginning in 1224; together with the retrochoir, Lady chapel and eastern transepts it forms almost a miniature cathedral in itself. The east window wall has two groups of five lancets, still separate and not grouped as they would have been later in the century. The triforium has a double arcade and the clerestory, as at Lincoln, offers a walkway fronted by a second set of stone arches. There is much Purbeck marble, columns with finely carved capitals, and (high up) statuary springing from the spandrels of the arches. King John was interred in the choir in 1232, while later, in the early Tudor period, a chantry chapel was erected for Henry VIII's elder brother Prince Arthur. The nave, although not reconstructed until the fourteenth century, continues the basic design of the choir rather than adopting the full-fledged Decorated style.

As few other bits and pieces deserve to be mentioned. At Hereford the north transept was rebuilt by Bishop Acquablanca or Aigueblanche (1240–68) in an unusual Geometric form, the triforium arches ending in a triangular pattern with nearly straight sides rather than the normal curved arcs. The small clerestory windows are circles with six cusps. The large seven-bay choir at Carlisle was begun about 1220 but little of it survives; following a fire in 1291 the east end was rebuilt and rather surprisingly boasts one of the finest Decorated windows in the country. At St David's, if we may journey on to Wales, the tower collapsed in 1220 and was rebuilt. It now displays lancet openings, while the new choir has fourteen lancets, separated by multiple mouldings, at its east end. The eastern extension of the cathedral at Rochester is Early English, 1220–27; it is notable for its massiveness and solidity. There is neither a triforium nor aisles but rather a series of tombs. The transepts are also thirteenth century. As we have seen, the west end at Peterborough was not completed until the early thirteenth century. The transepts at York date from about 1250 and are Early English, though the rest of the building is a little later and will be considered as Decorated. The north transept contains the famous Five Sisters window – five separate lancets – with important grisaille glass. Chester has the only early thirteenth-century chapter house to survive in its original state. There are fine lancet windows and an elegantly vaulted vestibule. The refectory, also thirteenth century, has an exceptional stone staircase set into the thickness of the wall leading up to an unusual stone pulpit. At Ely the Norman apse was pulled down in 1234 and the new east end completed by 1252. The ground floor has a beautiful group of three tall lacets surrounded by dog-tooth shafts; above them there are two tiers of five stepped lancets, the upper ones lighting the roof area above the vaults. All of this enhanced the shrine of St Ætheldreda. The retrochoir and Lady chapel at Winchester date from 1202, though the chapel was elaborately redone about 1500.

4

Decorated, 1280–1350

Late in the thirteenth century Early English gave way to the Decorated style. This remained dominant until the middle of the fourteenth century, when it in turn was superseded by Perpendicular architecture. Decorated buildings are most easily recognized by their window patterns. The windows themselves have become larger; they are often very wide in relationship to their height. They display elaborate tracery, no longer the simple circles which were characteristic of geometric Early English. The architects and master masons obviously took delight in devising these imaginative designs; in many cases they provided several different forms of tracery for adjoining windows rather than repeating a single pattern, as was common both earlier and later. There are other characteristics of the Decorated style as well. Doorways, arches and blank arcading are influenced by the new window patterns. Occasionally one finds ogee arches with compound curves of two parts, one convex and one concave, something like an S-shape. Tombs and monuments display stylistic similarities. Vaults are various, sometimes elaborate rib vaults but more often lierne vaults in which additional non-structural ribs add elegant ornamentation. Examples of Decorated tracery can be found in many cathedrals, most notably Wells, Exeter and York. There are lierne vaults at Exeter, Bristol, Ely, Wells and Gloucester, with ogee arches as well at Bristol and Exeter. The finest Decorated doorway is probably that leading to the cloister at Norwich; it is ornamented with elaborate carving and sculpture.[1]

Not all architectural historians agree about the definition and dating of Decorated architecture.[2] It seems most logical to regard window patterns which are basically groups of two or three lancets held together with a circle at the top as belonging to the last phase of Early English, commonly known as Geometric and dating approximately 1250–80. Here the individual lights are still lancets; the chief difference from earlier work is that instead of being side-by-side though separate they now have been conjoined to provide a single wider window. The circles are used to fill the space at the top so that a single pointed arch can be erected over the grouping; even if there are several circles and they are foiled, they are still simple, relatively unimaginative patterns which are repeated throughout an entire nave, choir or Lady chapel. Only in the last two decades of the thirteenth century is this geometric work replaced by the more elaborate and ingenious designs described above. It is these that should properly be identified as Decorated. Aesthetic judgments of Decorated work vary as well. Because of its variety, imagination and unique Englishness it is the favourite of some critics, while others reject it as being too elaborate and fussy, with decorative patterns sometimes obscuring the structure or use of a part of the building. Both views are legitimate.

The best place to study the difference between Early English and Decorated is Wells.[3] As we have seen, the present nave and image screen at the west end date from 1180–1240 and are among the purest examples of Early English. The east end was rebuilt beginning about 1285 or 1290, by which time Decorated had been accepted. By about 1340 the new choir, retrochoir, transepts and chapter house were complete.

The east end – the area over the high altar – offers a fine place to assimilate the chief characteristics of the Decorated style. The great east window is composed of seven lights with a pattern of quatrefoils and diamond-shaped tracery above it. It is as wide as it is high; the dimensions are in part dictated by its placement above an arcade leading to the Lady chapel, but they also reflect the taste of the Decorated builders. The area behind the altar, the retrochoir, is one of the most unusual and delightful spaces in the country, for it is vaulted with a series of fans supported by central pillars such as we have seen earlier in some chapter houses. They look almost like palm trees. There is a similar pillar in the octagonal chapter house; springing from it are thirty-six ribs, more than twice as many as at Westminster Abbey.

Window tracery in both the chapter house and Lady chapel is clearly Decorated, though the windows are taller than that over the altar. The interior of the Lady chapel has some early ogee arches at the doorway and sedilla. Examination of the exterior shows flying buttresses and a group of small openings above the great east window, lighting the area between the vaulted ceiling and the exterior lead roof. The choir vaults are simple liernes, with only a few additional ribs creating a diamond-shaped pattern in the centre of each bay. The crossing tower was heightened about 1313, and it was soon found necessary to strengthen its base by inserting huge strainer arches into the transepts. In shape they can be described as an inverted arch placed on top of a normal one or as two intersecting ogee curves. The tower was originally capped by a low spire, but it burned in 1438 and was not replaced. The stairway leading to the chapter house, built a few years earlier than the chapter house itself and still displaying geometric arches, passes over the chain gate and gives access to the vicars' close, a long narrow street of small houses for the men who sang in the cathedral choir, together with the dining hall of the vicars choral. These medieval survivals, the best of their kind in England, date from about the 1340s and are still partly used for their original purpose.

If Wells is the best place to compare the Early English and Decorated styles, the ideal cathedral for studying fully developed Decorated is Exeter.[4] Because of its proximity, Wells must have influenced Exeter, especially in the provision of an image screen at the west end. Salisbury may have been an even more important model; it is likely that Walter Bronescombe, who was enthroned as bishop of Exeter in April 1258, was present at the consecration of Salisbury Cathedral that September. Rebuilding of the Norman cathedral at Exeter began in 1275, the year in which Salisbury was completed. Although the styles are different, the cathedrals are alike (and unusual) in being of a piece throughout. They were built rapidly, Salisbury in two generations and Exeter in three, the original plans never being altered significantly, even though younger master masons succeeded their seniors. Virtually everything at Exeter, except for the Norman towers which remained as transepts, is Decorated. The other exception is the chapter house, a rectangular structure dating from the second quarter of the thirteenth century and thus Early English, though the higher parts were redone in the Perpendicular architecture of the fifteenth century.

During the rebuilding the cathedral was divided into two parts so that services could continue in the nave while the east end was reconstructed. A wooden partition was probably erected; it is interesting to note that following the Civil War of the seventeenth century, when Anglican worship was outlawed, the building was again divided so that Presbyterians could use the choir and Congregationalists the nave. Irregularities in the ground level appear to have made work on the east end difficult, for the area east of the Norman apse was lower than the floor of the earlier choir. The problem was partly solved by placing a crypt under one of the chapels, that dedicated to St James. The new choir and high altar were consecrated in 1328, but the Lady chapel was completed earlier and Bronescombe's successor Peter Quinil was buried there in 1291.

The Norman towers were modified by the insertion of Decorated windows during the last years of the thirteenth century and opened up on the inner side so that they became transepts. The presbytery or retrochoir (the area east of the high altar, between it and the Lady chapel) was completed at about the same time. Here again the palm-tree effect is unforgettable. The roof vaults are also exceptional; there are three pairs of tiercerons in each cell, yet all the ribs are truly supporting, not merely ornamental. Building dates can be determined more precisely than is usually the case because of the survival of a large number of the original fabric rolls. They tell us, among other things, that forty-nine carved bosses and eight corbels were painted in 1301–2 and that fifteen windows were glazed two years later. The four bays of the presbytery were originally built without any triforium arcades or clerestory galleries, but these were introduced into the plan of the choir itself when it was built a few years later and the size of the columns was increased slightly to accommodate them. The presbytery was then modified to follow the choir pattern, though the arcades are shallower and the passageways of no practical use. The original choir stalls were replaced by Gilbert Scott in the 1870s but their misericords remain. (Misericords are the seats of the stalls. Taking their name from *misericordia*, the Latin word for mercy, they could be tipped up so that a cleric or singer obliged by the liturgy to kneel for long periods might rest his body against them, a merciful accommodation of human weakness.) The Exeter misericords are the earliest surviving set in England; they range in date from 1230 to 1270. Subjects include an elephant, a lion, a mermaid, a siren, a centaur, Aristotle saddled and a knight fighting a bear. Other seats simply have stiff-leaf or naturalistic foliage.

The elaborate stone pulpitum which forms a screen at the entrance to the choir was completed about 1325. It includes Corfe marble columns and images. Rebuilding of the nave began at this time. Here some of the existing Norman walling was reused; this is the reason the nave appears so massive. The fabric rolls document a payment of £15 for sixty sets of columns for the triforium arcade. One of the notable features of the nave is the minstrels' gallery, set into the north triforium. It probably dates from the 1350s and depicts fourteen angels playing musical instruments, among them a recorder, viol, trumpet, zither, bagpipe, timbrel and cymbals. This is a visual reminder that such instruments were often used in medieval liturgies and that organs, though already extant, had not yet acquired their present role.

The west front of Exeter is the legacy of Bishop John Grandisson, who died in 1369. There are in fact two elements here: the original façade, which includes a very wide Decorated window of nine lights topped by an enormous circle holding spherical triangle tracery, and in front of it an image screen reminiscent of Wells, with figures of kings and saints carved in the fourteenth and fifteenth centuries. The statue of St Peter high in the apex is said to be a portrait of Grandisson, whose funerary chapel is incorporated in the wall to the right of the central doorway.

It is best to study the Decorated window patterns from the exterior, where

Wells, the Vicars' Close, seen from the Cathedral tower. (*Royal Commission on Historical Monuments of England*)

one can concentrate on the stone tracery without being distracted by the stained glass, some of which is fourteenth century. Here at Exeter, more than in any other cathedral, one appreciates the desire of the builders to provide a variety of tracery designs rather than simply repeating an accepted pattern. The late thirteenth-century Lady chapel demonstrates this well, but it is even more instructive to examine the nave tracery. This can be done most easily on the north side. Here the shapes used in the upper parts of the windows include trefoils, quatrefoils, spherical triangles and quadrangles, and dagger shapes (called mouchettes). All of these were favourites of the designers working in Paris, for instance on the south transept of Nôtre-Dame, about 1250. It is likely that the Master of Exeter (unfortunately we do not know his name) had seen them. Yet he did not simply borrow them; he was a genius who made them his own, and a part of the English building vocabulary.

Much of York Minster dates from the Decorated period, but it is not as good a place to study the style as Exeter or Wells. At York the rebuilding of the Norman cathedral took place over several centuries; the dates are about 1225 to about 1475.[5] This means that there are Early English, Decorated, and Perpendicular elements present. But the succession of architects was obviously eager to maintain a continuity of appearance, and some elements of the different styles are therefore played down. The Decorated work is a particularly strong example of this.

The transepts were the first part of the minster to be rebuilt. The south transept came first. Plans may have been made as early as 1220 and work was probably complete by 1244, when King Henry III came to York to visit the shrine of St William. The north transept followed about 1253. In both the style is clearly enough Early English; the windows, both at the ground level and in the clerestory, are separate lancets, although the triforium does display the Geometric motif of grouped arches topped by foiled circles. The south transept holds three large lancet windows, the central one double, while the north transept has the celebrated 'Five Sisters', a row of five lancets each fifty-five feet high, filled with grisaille glass. Both transepts have fine rose windows.

The chapter house, the largest in England, was built between 1260 and 1285. Like many similar structures it is octagonal, but it is almost unique in not having a central column to support the vault. (The only other example is at Southwell, which during the middle ages was a collegiate church rather than a cathedral.) Although this was probably originally designed as a stone tierceron vault, it was actually built in wood – lighter weight, but looking much the same, with bosses and painted designs (now Victorian).

The chapter house may be regarded as the earliest English building to aim at the total substitution of window for wall. The patterns of the large five-light windows are typical late geometric, but in the adjacent vestibule (finished in 1290) they assume imaginative if perhaps awkward Decorated shapes.

Then, beginning about 1291, the nave was tackled. Masons' marks indicate that some of the workmen who had been employed at the chapter house now moved to the nave, but there appears to have been a new master mason, identified only as Simon of York. Stylistic evidence suggests that he was familiar with contemporary work at Troyes Cathedral. He was succeeded about 1310 by Hugh de Boudon, probably a former under-master and possibly from the York suburb of Bootham. The large scale of the nave – each bay spans twenty-seven feet – was probably dictated by the earlier Norman structure. Like the chapter house the nave was originally intended to have a stone vault, but in the end it too was vaulted in wood with ribs made to look like stone. This work was not completed until 1346. The fact that most of York was vaulted in wood was dramatized in 1984, when the roof of the south transept was consumed by fire. The vault in question was actually a nineteenth-century replacement; the original nave vault had burned earlier, in 1840.

The nave windows date from about 1300 and hence ought to be Decorated, but they do not resemble the Decorated windows we have described earlier. At York the tracery patterns are unimaginative and are repeated throughout the nave. In the aisles there are simple groups of three conjoined lancets below and three quatrefoiled circles above. The larger clerestory windows are of five lights topped by a large circle filled with trefoil and quatrefoil tracery. It is as if the Decorated style had never existed; the tracery seems half geometric and half Perpendicular. The interior elevation of the nave is unusual and interesting. The triforium has disappeared as a separate storey. Its arches remain, but the mullions of the clerestory windows above them have been extended down so that the upper half of each wall presents a unified appearance.

If the windows of the nave seem routine in appearance, that is made up for by the extraordinary west window. Often called 'the Heart of Yorkshire' because of the heart shape which is part of its wonderfully fanciful curvilinear tracery, it dates from 1338 and has been attributed to the architect Ivo de Raghton. Fifty feet wide and nearly twice as high, it is flanked by two smaller windows that also display tracery which is clearly Decorated. The upper parts of the western towers date from the mid fifteenth century and are equally clearly Perpendicular, but because they are of comparable complexity they blend well with the fourteenth-century work and also with the early fifteenth-century crossing tower. There is none of the clash of styles that we noted at Wells. The east arm of the Minster (choir and presbytery) was rebuilt between 1361 and 1400, by which time it ought to be classified as Perpendicular, but here again the masons generally conformed to an earlier style and there is little noticeable break between the nave and the choir. The stone screen or pulpitum which separates the choir from the nave and transepts dates from the end of the fifteenth century and is the work of the mason William Hyndeley. Its niches hold fifteen statues of English kings from William the Conqueror to Henry VI, all but one original. The great east window, completed in 1405, is divided into a number of rectangular panels by Perpendicular stone tracery. It is the second largest east window in England, its size being exceeded only by the so-called 'Crécy' window at Gloucester. The small eastern transepts also have enormous Perpendicular windows. The windows at York hold much of the nation's treasury of medieval glass.

The cathedral at Bristol is not as well known as it should be, perhaps because it was not a cathedral in the middle ages and perhaps because the nave and façade are nineteenth century. As we will see, the Augustinian abbey at Bristol was one of the former monasteries given cathedral status by Henry VIII in 1542. The Norman church had been rebuilt between 1298 and 1330, the plan being attributed to Abbot Knowle, who died in 1332.[6] The chancel and aisles are extraordinary. The form is that of a hall-church in which the aisles are of the same height as the central space. This concept is relatively common among parish churches of the later middle ages, but its use in a cathedral is unique. It means that there is no triforium or clerestory. The large east window has elaborate Decorated tracery, as do the windows of the aisles, where there are two alternating patterns. They are ingenious, but it is the aisle vaults which are unforgettable. Here a pointed arch at the level where the aisles might be expected to be vaulted helps support a horizontal stone bar, somewhat similar to a tie-beam on the arched braces of a timber roof. Above that each bay has two cells of vaulting supported by the horizontal bar. There are also large dagger-shaped openings at the lower level and carved figures on the bars. The vault of the central choir is less surprising; it has diamond-shaped lierne patterns at the centre of each bay, rather like Wells. The tombs of abbots in the Lady chapel are surrounded by remarkable ogee arches forming a star pattern. The transepts and crossing remain basically Norman, with some Perpendicular windows added. Construction of the nave was abandoned at the time of the Dissolution of the Monasteries; it was finished in the 1880s by the architect G. E. Street, who retained the basic design of the choir so that the cathedral today has a unified fourteenth-century appearance.

Ely also has extraordinary work of the Decorated period: the Lady chapel and the octagon. Those responsible were the leading clergy, Bishop John Hotham, Prior John of Crauden, and the sacrist, Alan of Walsingham. They felt that a proper Lady chapel was needed and in 1321 laid the foundation stone for a rectangular building north of the choir, approached through the north transept. But in February 1322 the Norman crossing tower fell down and attention was diverted from the Lady chapel to replacing the former square tower by the marvellous octagon designed by Alan of Walsingham. We know that Alan was a goldsmith as well as a monk but have no inkling what inspired his remarkable invention; there was a Norman octagonal tower at Swaffham Prior, not far from Ely, but it is so small that it is hardly comparable. The name of the ingenious carpenter who constructed the wooden lantern at Ely is also known. He was William Hurle, who later worked at Westminster and Windsor.

The Ely octagon takes up a very large space; one bay of the nave, the choir and each transept was taken over to form a space much grander than that of the former crossing. The lower stages of the octagon are stonework. This supports a great wooden lantern which admits a flood of light into the centre of the cathedral. Since there are two sides of the octagon for each of the main directions of the cathedral, the octagon appears to be twisted so that no side is parallel to an exterior wall. Although the wooden structure was renewed by Sir George Gilbert Scott in the nineteenth century, the Decorated window pattern has been preserved. Outside, flying buttresses help support the octagon and the stonework includes big Decorated windows, again at an angle to the main axis of the building. A fine view can be obtained from the top of the south tower at the west end. Inside, the shafts which carry the lantern make way for eight corbelled niches with carvings telling the story of Ely's patron saint Ætheldreda. This remarkable narrative sculpture dates from about 1325. The octagon has inspired a number of later structures. Perhaps the most famous of these is the tower of St Botolph's church in Boston, Lincolnshire (the Boston 'Stump').[7]

Once the octagon was completed work on the Lady chapel could be resumed. The room is dominated by its large windows. These now hold clear glass; the chapel would have appeared richer and warmer with the original coloured glazing. Tracery is Decorated but repetitive, and the east window has horizontal sone bars dividing its eight lights into upper and lower sections, each nearly rectangular. This is essentially Perpendicular, and since the date of completion is about 1353 that is not surprising. Below the windows there is a row of seats, as if in a chapter house, and much elaborate carving, including elegant ogee-arched niches holding statues relating to the life and miracles of the Virgin, now sadly defaced by Tudor iconoclasts. Throughout much of its life the Lady chapel was used as a parish church. This function ceased only in 1938.

The choir stalls at Ely are also worth noting. Originally they stood under the octagon, though they have now been moved further east. They were completed about 1342 and, like the wooden octagon, were probably the work of William Hurle. The back stalls have canopies based on ogee arches as well as a complete set of forty-six misericords. The front stalls have thirteen more. The scenes, many of them humourous, include monkeys, men playing dice, hunters, wrestlers, the Virgin and a unicorn, and a pelican in her piety. Prior Crauden's chapel, a part of the east end, offers another fine example of the Decorated style at Ely.

Before the Reformation Chester was also a Benedictine abbey, in this case dedicated to St Werburgh. Here our interest centres on the choir, which was rebuilt beginning about 1300. It has passageways at both the triforium and clerestory levels, as at Exeter, though the work at Chester appears to be earlier. It has been claimed that it looks Burgundian, like the nave of the cathedral at Nevers, perhaps because during the Welsh wars of the fourteenth century the area around Chester was full of Burgundians – knights, engineers, masons – called in by Edward I. Once again there are fine misericords, with scenes including angels with the instruments of the passion, a woman beating her husband, and the tale of Tristan and Iseult. The south transept, also Decorated, was built about 1340; the larger north transept remained Norman. The nave followed, beginning about 1360. Since Chester Cathedral was built of unusually soft sandstone it was worked over more by Victorian restorers than most of its peers, and in many cases it is hard to be sure what features are original or whether work by Scott is a faithful copy of what went before.

The cathedral at Carlisle has one of the finest Decorated windows to be found anywhere. Here, as we have seen, a Norman building was given an Early English choir, but by the time the masons reached the east end the Decorated style had come in. Thus the easternmost bay of the chancel is Decorated, as is the east window. It is very large, being fifty-one feet high. Below there are nine glass panels or lights, divided 4–1–4. Above the central light is tracery based on a pointed oval, while heart-shaped patterns are placed at the sides. All of these basic forms are filled with exuberant quatrefoils and mouchettes. Most of the stained glass is now nineteenth century, but near the top a small scene showing a seated Christ is original fourteenth-century work. The stalls are also fourteenth century. Among the subjects depicted on the misericords are such miscellaneous things as the Coronation of the Virgin and a boar killing a man. The piers of the chancel are also worth examining. The capitals are carved in stiff-leaf patterns and also have small figures exemplifying the labours of the months, January as Janus with two heads, February sitting by the fire, March digging the ground, and so on.

Some fourteenth-century work at Lincoln demands our attention as well. The pulpitum or stone screen separating the choir from the nave and crossing is a beautiful example of Decorated design. The background is diaper work, divided halfway up by a band of leaves. The central doorway and the niches flanking it are crowned by ogee arches and rich carving. Inside, the structure includes a vaulted chamber and a staircase leading to the organ loft. Also of this period are the Bishop's Eye, the huge rose window inserted in the south transept, and the upper stages of the crossing tower. The tower was heightened between 1307 and 1313. It includes a stage for bells and originally had a lead spire which was blown down in 1548 and never replaced. The interior of the tower was vaulted with a lierne pattern in the later fourteenth century.

As we have seen, the finest fourteenth-century doorway is probably that leading from the nave to the cloister at Norwich. It is early Decorated, about 1310, topped by a semi-circular arch rather than an ogee shape, and it includes fine statuary: a seated Christ in the centre surrounded by angels, and then two more figures on each side. These have been repainted in something approaching their original colours. The whole east range of the cloister is of more or less the same period, beginning about 1297. Each bay has a large opening topped by typical Decorated tracery, basically spherical triangles enclosing trefoils. The east walk of the cloister at Westminster Abbey was also rebuilt in the mid fourteenth century.

About 1350 the architectural style dominant in medieval England changed one last time, as Decorated gave way to Perpendicular. The next chapter will analyze its characteristics and describe its place in the building of the medieval cathedrals.

5

Perpendicular, 1350–1530

The last of the great medieval styles of architecture in England is known as Perpendicular Gothic. It gradually supplanted the Decorated style about the middle of the fourteenth century and lasted until about 1530, near the mid point in the reign of Henry VIII. Few religious buildings were put up after that date, partly because the changes and controversies of the Reformation unsettled the church and partly because so much building had taken place in the last century or two that further construction did not seem necessary. There are, however, some survivals of late Perpendicular work into the seventeenth century. Most of these, rather than being churches, are secular buildings, a number of them at the universities. Good examples are the hall of Trinity College (1604) and the library of St John's College (1625), both at Cambridge. The introduction of classical architecture, which can be viewed as one aspect of the English Renaissance, finally brought an end to Gothic building: Ralph Symons, who designed the Trinity College hall, can be regarded as the last of the Perpendicular architects, while Inigo Jones, who built James I's Banqueting House in Whitehall, was the first to introduce the fully developed Classicism of ancient Greece and Rome.[1]

In examining the characteristics which identify architecture as Perpendicular we should, as usual, look first at the windows and their tracery. Perpendicular windows are very large, often taking over most of the exterior wall space. Unlike most Decorated windows, their height is always much greater than their width; some Perpendicular windows, especially those at the east end of cathedrals or in transepts, are amazingly high. Sometimes these windows, although they still culminate in a pointed arch, are contained within a rectangular space with a square head at the top. Tracery is relatively simple and repetitive; once a suitable pattern was found it was repeated through an entire building, or whatever part of one was being constructed. During the earlier years of the period much tracery was based on elongated hexagons, creating patterns resembling a rectangle, its larger sides vertical rather than horizontal, but with areas at the top and bottom resembling two sides of a triangle, thus producing an overall design with six sides. Later work has other patterns but they remain simple. Such tracery fills only the upper part of the window, generally only the area where the sides begin to curve toward each other. Below, large windows are generally divided into a number of rectangular panels held in place by stone bars. In fact it was such glazing bars that originally gave Perpendicular its name: the windows hold both horizontal and vertical bars, which run perpendicular to each other.

The patterns of arches are characteristic as well. Part of the basic vocabulary of Perpendicular was the four-centred arch. Such arches were laid out by holding a compass at four different points, one pair higher than the other, so that each side of an arch was based on arcs that sprang from two centres. Piers, arcades, doorways and window surrounds have typical moulding patterns. Vaults, as before, come in several forms. Tiercerons and lierne vaults continue, generally with relatively simple logical patterns, but the greatest of the mature Perpendicular buildings have fan vaults, a uniquely English development. Pendants appear toward the end of the period. In general individual ribs no longer bear the weight of the vaults but are superseded by cones. On the exterior, flying buttresses disappear and are replaced by solid buttresses turned at a ninety-degree angle to the main building so that they take up only a minimal amount of wall space. We will see all of these things in the individual buildings to which we now turn.

Although Old St Paul's in London was destroyed by the Great Fire of 1666, surviving engravings made by Wenceslaus Hollar show its architectural design and reveal the basic elements of the Perpendicular style. Dates are uncertain. The chronicler John Stow wrote of new work – the rebuilding of the Norman cathedral – beginning in 1256, but it was probably not completed until the fourteenth century and both the eastern crypt and the twelve-bay choir above it display Perpendicular piers and fenestration. The Lady chapel, behind the high altar, had enormous windows, clearly Perpendicular in style, one of them a very wide seven-light window which dominated the east end of the cathedral. Above it there was a great rose window, similar to that at Nôtre-Dame in Paris. Perpendicular windows also terminated the side aisles. Hollar also left a view of the chapter house designed by William de Ramsey and built in the fourteenth century. Again it has enormously tall Perpendicular windows and a typically Perpendicular arch over its principal entrance. Ramsey was also responsible for the design of the cloisters.[2]

At Gloucester and Winchester parts of a Norman cathedral were elaborately remodelled to suit the new fashion. Although the Benedictine abbey at Gloucester did not become a cathedral until the 1540s, the medieval structure certainly ranked with the cathedrals. Rebuilding of the Norman church began after 1327, when Edward II was murdered at Berkeley Castle nearby and buried at Gloucester. Revenues flowed in from pilgrims visiting his tomb and enabled Abbot John Thoky to begin a great remodelling scheme. Here the staunch Norman building was not torn down, but the style was altered by the insertion of Perpendicular windows and stone panelling which masked the round Norman arches.

Work began with the south transept about 1330.[3] This is earlier than the date we have suggested for the beginning of the Perpendicular period and shows that late Decorated and early Perpendicular coexisted for a decade or two. The south transept is dominated by what can be regarded as the earliest existing Perpendicular window. Possibly it was the work of court architects, probably attracted to Gloucester because of the royal tomb there, but the unusual vaulting – cones supported from below – is similar to that at Bristol. The window itself displays horizontal tracery dividing its lower level into rectangular lights; this simple tracery, which may be though to be tentative and awkward, is based on elongated hexagons. It can be dated to 1331–37. The north transept was similarly reworked in the 1370s.

The remodelling of the choir is more spectacular. The round Norman arches of the main arcade and triforium remain, but they are masked by Perpendicular panelling added about 1337. Some ribs run all the way from the floor to the vault, a height of ninety-two feet, while others are broken up to allow the insertion of a large number of small arches with pointed foiled heads. These form blank ornamentation over the Norman stonework and are left open as they front the gallery. The clerestory windows were enlarged and given Perpendicular forms. The great east window was the largest in the world when it was built, in about 1350. It is seventy-two feet high and thirty-eight feet wide and contains more than 1500 square feet of glass. Its sides are canted; this unusual pattern provided greater structural stability and allowed more room for glass. In all there are fourteen lights, four in each of the wings and six in the centre. Most of the stained glass one sees today is original; there are Decorated elements in the glass work even though the stone frame is clearly Perpendicular. The window was designed soon after the famous English victory at Crécy in the Hundred Years War, and it contains a number of heraldic and nationalistic elements. The choir stalls also date from the fourteenth century and have the fanciful misericords typical of that era.

The east range of the cloisters (1351–77) is at least as important as the east window, for it has the earliest fan vault. The same forms can be found in the south walk, built about thirty years later. Stone cones, springing from a central column and assuming a semi-circular shape at the top, are ornamented with Perpendicular tracery; they touch each other overhead but leave a central space which is ornamented with foiled circles. Since the cloister was built for monks, there are a number of carrels where they might

study, and the cloister is glazed to keep out at least some of the cold winter
winds – in many places this was not done, and the cloister arcades remained
open to the elements.

Rebuilding of the nave at Gloucester was undertaken about 1420. This
work included the west front (unexciting, with a large window but no towers) and the two adjoining bays of the nave itself. The south porch, which
is the main entrance, also dates from this time. The Early English tower was
replaced with the present Perpendicular structure in 1450, and rebuilding of
the Early English Lady chapel was begun about the same time. It was kept
low so as not to interfere with the east window of the choir. The library is
earlier, fourteenth century; it has a fine wooden roof and, at each end, large
Perpendicular windows.

At Winchester, as at Gloucester, the great Norman building was modernized
during the fourteenth century.[4] Here the nave was not demolished and
rebuilt but rather reworked in the new style. Work began under Bishop
William of Edington, a leader in both church and state who was consecrated
in 1346, but the chief activity came under his successor, William of Wykeham, bishop from 1366 to 1404, who is remembered as the patron of
Winchester College and New College, Oxford. His master mason, William
Wynford, transformed the nave from Norman to Perpendicular by reducing
the size of the piers and recutting the arches so that they have pointed heads.
The triforium was replaced by a small gallery; this enabled the clerestory to
be enlarged and Perpendicular windows to be inserted. No totally Perpendicular building is so heavy, yet the style seems appropriate and the nave
conveys a feeling of unity. The nave remains low – it is only seventy-eight
feet high – but Wynford's ingenious vault, which includes liernes and
tiercerons, creates an illusion of height. The fine mouldings, some rising all
the way from the floor to the vault, counteract the stoutness of the columns
and seem almost like fountains of stone spraying upwards.

The Norman façade had two towers and extended forty feet beyond the
present west end. It was demolished, probably because it had partially collapsed or become insecure. The new Perpendicular west end is
disappointing. It is essentially no more than a section through the nave and
aisles, dominated by a large window of forty-four panels arranged in nine
lights (3 + 3 + 3). It was damaged in the Civil War and is now filled with a
jumble of old glass. The western porches have details which are probably
derived from Gloucester. There are small turrets but one feels the lack of
towers, and the Norman crossing tower does little to enhance the exterior
view, since it is low and has no pinnacles or other ornaments. The Lady
chapel was extended at about the same time as the façade. Its new east bay

has large Perpendicular windows on three sides. The cathedral's furnishings are unusually elaborate; they include many tombs and monuments, considerable sculpture, and, in the Lady chapel, early Tudor wall paintings. Whatever its failings, Winchester is impressive, partly because of its great length. It remains the longest cathedral in Europe.

Rebuilding the nave at Canterbury was undertaken by Archbishop Simon of Sudbury in 1377.[5] Complete reconstruction was necessary, according to a contemporary document, 'on account of the notorious and evident state of ruin' of the nave. Demolition of the façade was carried out at Sudbury's own expense. The supervisors of the new work were the subprior, John Goodnestone, and John Roper, a leading local citizen, but the chief credit must go to Henry Yeveley, the architect. In 1360 Yeveley had been appointed master of the king's masonry, a title that remained his for life. He worked at Windsor Castle, the Tower of London, and Westminster Abbey for Edward III, the Black Prince, and Richard II. He was a contemporary of William Wynford and their styles, though personal, are similar. After his death in 1400 his work at Canterbury was continued and completed by his friend and partner John Lote. The great pulpitum or screen separating the choir from the crossing is Lote's work. Lote also rebuilt the great cloister, for here again the Norman work was demolished by Yeveley.

Although the design of the Canterbury nave is of a piece, construction fell into several distinct phases. Work had to be abandoned in 1381, when the archbishop was murdered in the Peasants' Revolt, but it was resumed ten years later under Prior Thomas Chillenden and Archbishop Thomas Arundel. By 1405 the nave was complete. The west end – a western transept – was built by Thomas Mapilton, whose design echoed Yeveley's. Its windows are the tallest in the country. This façade included the south-west tower; the north-west Norman tower, dating back to Lanfranc's days, remained in place until the 1820s, by which time it was ruinous and was replaced by a replica of Mapilton's work. It is hard to imagine Canterbury with the unmatched towers, but a number of surviving prints testify to its appearance.

As at Winchester the dimensions of the nave were determined by its Norman predecessor, but the new work could of course be taller. In fact it appears higher than its eighty feet, primarily because of the effect of the splendid lierne vault which is one of Yeveley's masterworks. Shafts rise from the floor level to the springing of the ribs without being interrupted by a gallery (it has been replaced by Perpendicular panelling) or the clerestory. Each bay has a series of four hexagons with bosses which form a row of stone flowers along the ridge rib. The fact that the subordinate ribs are unusually slender adds to the illusion of distance.[6] The nave windows, too, are remarkable, both for their size and for the medieval glass which they contain. The exterior elevation is noble and dignified, without excessive ornament; the windows take up almost all the space between the buttresses. Mapilton's south-west tower has more decorative detailing, and the south-west porch (1400), which forms the principal entrance to the cathedral, is still more elaborate. Its two tiers of niches are now filled with nineteenth-century statues, the originals probably having fallen prey to Reformation iconoclasts. The actual west doorway, used for ecclesiastical processions, is inconspicuous; it is dwarfed by the huge west window. The pavement of the nave was replaced in 1993, providing an opportunity for archaeologists to undertake excavations which confirmed the dimensions of the earlier structure.

Canterbury also has one of the earliest fan vaults. Similar to that in the cloister at Gloucester, it was erected in the chapel of Our Lady Martyrdom (also known as the dean's chapel) in 1460. The central tower, which houses the famous Bell Harry, was rebuilt at the expense of Archbishop John Morton beginning in 1496 and completed under Archbishop William Warham. The architect was John Wastell. The tower rises to a height of 235 feet; inside, it has another remarkable fan vault, more florid than that in the chapel. Christ Church Gate, the great gatehouse giving access to the cathedral close, was built in 1507, partly as a memorial to Henry VII's elder son Prince Arthur, who had died five years earlier.

Perhaps the greatest of the Perpendicular buildings, and one which is unusual in that it is entirely in that style, is the chapel of King's College, Cambridge. Although never a cathedral, its great windows, delicate fan vault and unity of plan are unforgettable. Although it is no longer a cathedral, Bath Abbey was intended to be one, and it is stylistically very similar to King's although it was built by different masons, Robert and William Vertue rather than John Wastell. Construction began in 1499, after Bishop Oliver King, who had been French secretary to both Edward IV and Henry VII, had a dream of angels ascending and descending a ladder to heaven. He also heard voices saying (ambiguously), 'Let a King restore the church'.

The ecclesiastical history of Bath is complicated. There was a college of secular canons as early as 781. Monastic rule was established under St Dunstan, and King Edgar was crowned at Bath in 973. Shortly after 1066 John de Villula of Tours, who had been named bishop of Wells, established himself also at Bath, following the Norman decree that bishops' sees should be in larger towns. Although the bishops continued to reside at Wells, the see was known as Bath and Wells and the bishop had thrones in both cathedrals until the reign of Henry VIII, when Bath was demoted and became a parish church.

We know nothing about the Saxon building and very little about its Norman successor. This had probably decayed severely by Bishop King's time. The new Perpendicular cathedral was much smaller than its predecessor, and (because of the coming of the Reformation) it took a very long time to complete. Only the choir and the north transept were complete when the monastic establishment was dissolved in 1539. The south transept was finished in the early seventeenth century by Bishop James Montague, but the nave was not completed until the nineteenth century.

Perhaps the finest feature of Bath Abbey is its fan vault, which is almost identical to that at King's College and is in fact a few years earlier. The Vertue brothers had promised Bishop King that there would be 'none so goodly neither in England nor France'. Their design was carried throughout the building, which retains a stylistic unity despite its chequered building history. Since this was a cathedral rather than a chapel, it did have transepts and a crossing tower. There are no west towers, only turrets much like those at King's; the façade is dominated by the carved ladders and ascending angels which flank the large window. The east window is even bigger, and, like a number of late Perpendicular windows, it is contained within a rectangle and thus has a square head. There are low side aisles but the interior elevations do not include a gallery or triforium. The flying buttresses which form a striking feature of the exterior are larger than necessary structurally and were probably included by the Vertues for their visual delight.

The vault is also the most arresting feature of Christ Church Cathedral at Oxford. This was one of Henry VIII's new cathedrals; his chief minister Thomas Cromwell believed that the medieval diocese of Lincoln was too large to be administered effectively and carved out the new see of Oxford in 1539. The former religious house at Osney, outside Oxford, originally served as the cathedral, but in 1546 the see was transferred to St Frideswide's, a former nunnery possibly founded by the saint herself in the eighth century. The existing Norman building was soon to be reduced in size when it was fitted into Tom Quad of Thomas Wolsey's new college, originally called Cardinal College but renamed Christ Church after his fall. The cathedral is unique in several ways: it serves as a college chapel as well as a cathedral, and it is the smallest of the English cathedrals.

The interior is dominated by a Decorated east window and by the extraordinary vault of the choir. This was almost certainly constructed about 1500 by a west-country architect, William Orchard, who had just finished erecting a similar vault in the university's Divinity School. These are not fan vaults; instead they are liernes, notable for the pendants which hang down like lanterns at the edges of each bay, seemingly springing from the lierne ribs. In fact they are independent of the liernes and are held in place by strong invisible ribs which ride above the main vault. Only in the space between the vault and the exterior roof is the ingenious engineering clear.

A pendant vault is one of the chief features of Henry VII's chapel at Westminster Abbey as well. This perhaps represents the climax of the whole development of English medieval vault design. The vaults themselves are fully circular fans of amazingly shallow masonry (the areas between the ribs are only four inches thick). Pendants descend from the centre of each fan. The apsidal ambulatory which forms the east end has even more remarkable vaulting: six closely spaced circular fans with central pendants. Once again the pendants are separately suspended by invisible ribs riding on top of the fans. The side aisles are also vaulted with fans and pendants.

The rest of the chapel is remarkable too. Originally it was intended as a resting place for the bones of Henry VI, but when the campaign to have him canonized faltered the chapel was redesignated as the burial place for Henry VII. Construction began in 1503 and was virtually complete when the first of the Tudor monarchs died in 1509. It is possible that the architect was Robert Vertue but a more likely guess is another royal mason, Robert Janyns, who had worked on Henry VII's tower at Windsor. The splendid effigies of Henry Tudor and his wife Elizabeth of York were made by the Italian sculptor Pietro Torrigiano. There are also twelve saints in Renaissance roundels, while St Sebastian and his tormentors are depicted in an apsidal chapel. The exterior again represents the last and most elaborate phase of Perpendicular design. Its buttresses are ornamented with carved panelling and capped by large circular turrets, while the spaces between them have been turned into bays with projecting panels of window, thus allowing more glass than would be possible on a single flat plane. The unique flying buttresses are pierced with circular designs, making it clear that they serve aesthetic more than structural purposes. The heraldic glass in the east window was lost to bombing in the Second World War (as was Henry VII's nose, now replaced by a wood copy from his original funeral effigy in the abbey museum) and in its place one now sees, perhaps incongruously, a tribute to the airmen who served during the war. The bronze gates to the chapel are filled with Tudor heraldry.[7]

There are Perpendicular bits in many of the cathedrals which were built earlier. These include the crossing towers at Worcester (1357) and Durham (built in two stages, about 1465 and 1483) as well as that at Gloucester (1450). All of these are similar and elegant, though one might wish for pinnacles at Worcester and Durham, as at Gloucester. The west towers at Wells were not finished until 1436 and fail to live up to the glorious façade below; the central tower, given its present form about 1440, is more pleasing. The fine lierne vaults at Norwich date from the 1460s (nave) and 1470s (choir); they house more than a thousand magnificent bosses carved between 1300 and 1515. Chapter houses were erected at Hereford and Worcester in the late fourteenth century and at Exeter in the early fifteenth. The Lady chapel at York is also late fourteenth century.

Henry Yeveley has been credited with work in many places. He probably designed the elaborate reredos, known as the Neville Screen, which stands behind the high altar at Durham. As we will see later, it held dozens of statues prior to the Reformation. At Westminster Abbey he built the west porch and the south and west walks of the great cloister. One of his last works was the east walk of the cloister at Gloucester; it was finished by Lote after his death. Portions of the cloisters at Norwich and Wells are also of this period.

6

Stained Glass

Although parish churches contain much fine stained glass, most of England's medieval glass is to be found in the cathedrals. As befits their status, Canterbury and York hold the largest collections, but remarkable work is to be found in a number of other cathedrals as well.[1] The earliest reference to glass comes from Benedict Biscop, the abbot of Monkwearmouth, who sent to France in 675 for craftsmen to glaze the windows at his monastery. Nothing more is known of his enterprise; indeed virtually no glass earlier than 1100 survives. From then until 1530, however, many religious establishments were enriched by glorious stained glass, most of it made by foreign glaziers and paid for by kings, bishops, abbots, noblemen and occasionally craft guilds.

Medieval glass was made from sand, lime and potash melted together in a furnace. It was then formed into sheets, generally rectangles about 24 inches by 15 inches but sometimes circles 24 inches in diameter. Most glass was white. The only colour that could be introduced into molten glass was ruby, obtained by adding copper oxide. This had to be coated onto the side of a sheet of white glass, since an entire sheet containing copper became opaque. In the fourteenth century it was discovered that white glass painted with a liquid containing silver salt would turn yellow when fired; the exact shade could be made to vary from lemon yellow to orange, depending on the quantity of silver salt used and the length of the firing. Other colours, and all designs, were painted onto the white glass, which was then refired – it would thus be more accurate to refer to painted glass rather than stained glass. In the fifteenth century it was discovered that small holes could be drilled into sheets of glass; these might then be filled with circular coloured inserts or 'jewels', which were fused in by a subsequent firing.

Designs, sometimes based on illuminated manuscripts or cartoons which could be reused, were transferred to whitewashed boards or, later, to parchment. Panes of glass were then placed on these and cut to the required shapes by touching them with a hot iron and then dropping water or spitting on the heated areas so as to create a crack. A small notched implement called a glazing iron was used to cut the smaller pieces into the exact size needed. When the painting and staining were complete, the glass was placed on an iron tray and given a final firing over hot coals. After cooling the pieces were laid out atop the design and joined together by bars of lead grooved in an 'H' shape to hold the glass. Joints in the lead were soldered together, a cement-like preparation was used to make the panels watertight, and iron bars were added to provide strength so that the window would not be damaged by wind. Until the late thirteenth century iron armatures were often used to divide the window into geometrical areas – circles and qua-trefoils were common. These were later abandoned because they interfered with the composition of larger subjects. As we have seen, bar tracery using stone ribs was introduced at the beginning of the Decorated period; earlier windows were in the form of lancets without stone bars.

During the thirteenth century groups of glaziers are known to have existed at Bath, Canterbury, Chester, Durham, Lincoln, London, Norwich, Salisbury and Oxford. Glaziers' guilds were established at London and York in the fourteenth century. By the sixteenth century the craft was dying out, partly because of the Reformation and partly because Henry VII and Henry VIII preferred to patronize foreign artists.

Periodization is perhaps less important for stained glass than it is for architecture; despite some breaks, glasswork can be thought of as following a more or less continuous development. Nevertheless we can speak of work from the Early English period, including the narrative panels at Canterbury and grisaille windows at Lincoln, Salisbury, Westminster Abbey and York; Decorated style windows at such places as Exeter, Wells, Bristol, Gloucester and Ely; and Perpendicular or International Style glazing at Canterbury, York, Exeter and Durham.

Stained-glass windows are often thought of as a poor man's Bible, since their depictions of biblical scenes were accessible to those who could not read. This was of course particularly important prior to the translation of the Bible into English. The famous Abbot Suger of St-Denis in France is sup-posed to have said that 'the pictures in the windows are there for the purpose of showing simple people who cannot read the Holy Scriptures what they must believe'. The point should not be exaggerated, however, for many of the biblical scenes were too small or were mounted too high up for observers to benefit from their details. While one can appreciate the overall effect of the coloured glass by walking through cathedrals, those who would examine the windows carefully are well advised to use binoculars and to sit where they can study subjects and styles at leisure.

The earliest surviving stained glass at Canterbury dates from the beginning of the twelfth century.[2] It was part of the choir completed by Prior Conrad in 1130. Four of the windows were saved after the great fire of 1174 and subsequently installed in other parts of the cathedral. These include the figures of David, Nathan, Roboham and Abia, which are now divided between the south-west transept window and the nave west window.

Of greater importance are the windows commissioned for the new choir designed by William of Sens and installed between 1178 and 1220. These are unusual because they are part of a very clear programme of iconography, probably devised by Prior Benedict, who left Canterbury to become abbot of Peterborough in 1177. Some eighty-eight figures originally illustrated the genealogy of Christ as related in St Luke's Gospel. These were placed in the clerestory of the choir, including the eastern transepts and the apsidal east end of the Trinity chapel. Thirty-five of these windows can still be seen, although none are in their original positions. Among those reinstalled in the south-west transept are figures of Abraham, David, Josiah and Methuselah. A second series of twelve 'Bible windows' depicted New Testament scenes flanked by parallel 'types' drawn from the Old Testament. Placed in the choir aisles and corona, these included the Ascension, Pentecost and the Tree of Jesse. Only two full windows remain; they are now in the ambulatory on the north side of the choir. Each window contains a number of separate panels. Several of these depict the Magi: in one panel they are shown fast asleep in one bed while an angel hovers overhead; another shows them conversing with King Herod. A complete group of three scenes has the adoration by the Magi and shepherds in the centre, flanked by oval panels showing Solomon and the Queen of Sheba accompanied by attendants on camels and, on the other side, Joseph in state with his brothers. One may also see Noah in the ark and the parable of the sower. Other figures include Isaiah, Moses, Lot and Simon of Cyrene. Another notable medallion depicts the miraculous draught of fishes.

A third set of twelve windows in the ambulatory of the Trinity chapel was devoted to the life of St Thomas Becket and miracles attributed to him. The miracle windows, though heavily restored, are among the best examples of early Gothic glass. It is remarkable that a figure of Thomas himself survived the iconoclastic campaigns of the sixteenth and seventeenth centuries. There is also a view of Becket and Henry II during a moment of reconciliation and a depiction of the armed knights who murdered the archbishop. Tales of miracles include those experienced by such obscure medieval figures as Henry of Fordwich (a maniac), Petronella (an epileptic nun), Hugh the cellarer of Melrose Abbey (a sick monk), and Sir Jordan Fitzeisulf (a friend of St Thomas whose son died because the father failed to undertake a pilgrimage to Becket's shrine).

The great west window at Canterbury is one of the finest works of a later period, the beginning of the fifteenth century. At the top are six prophets who wear hats to distinguish them from the apostles depicted with halos in the row below. The main lights hold figures of kings. There were once twenty-one of these showing the rulers from Canute to Henry VI; the eight which remain are probably Canute, Edward the Confessor, Harold Godwinson, William I, William II, Henry I, Stephen and Henry III. Fifteenth-century figures of archbishops and apostles, originally in other parts of the cathedral, may be seen here as well. The most famous of the twelfth-century panels reinstalled in the west window shows Adam delving.

There is even more medieval glass at York than at Canterbury, and much of it is of the highest quality.[3] All periods of Gothic building are represented. There is late twelfth-century glass in the nave, thirteenth-century grisaille in the transept windows known as the Five Sisters, the great west window of 1339, and a large east window completed in 1408. Remarkably, this heritage remained undisturbed by either the Reformation or the Civil War, although two nineteenth-century fires did inflict some damage. Much of the medieval glass benefited from sensitive restoration by the York Glaziers Trust following the Second World War.

We are told that St Wilfrid ordered the installation of windows in York Minster as early as 670 in order to prevent the entry of birds and rain. The earliest surviving glass was made in the twelfth century; it was apparently removed from the Norman choir and placed in other locations about 1335. Twenty-seven figurative panels remain. These include a depiction of Daniel in the lions' den, now reset in the central lancet of the Five Sisters windows, and a king from the Jesse tree which has been placed in one of the nave aisles. Other remarkable windows show the supper at Emmaus, the miraculous draught of fishes, and Saints Peter and Paul at the gates of heaven. A view of St Benedict in a cave has been shown to be based on an illuminated manuscript now in the Vatican Library. This glass is characterised by dark, intense colours; green, purple and blue hues suggest a mood of luminous mystery.

Much of the thirteenth-century glass is grisaille. Since most of the glass used is white, these windows admit far more light than earlier work and make it possible to appreciate the architecture more fully. Here geometric designs are based on cross-hatching or stiff-leaf foliage. The Five Sisters windows in the north transept are perhaps the finest example of grisaille work in England, although they have suffered from repairs involving leading which tends to obscure the original patterns. Some windows, as noted, have also been altered by the insertion of figurative panels. The five lancets are of the same height, fifty-five feet; above them in the gable are seven stepped lancets, the first and last left as blank arches.

The glass in the chapter house dates from the later thirteenth century. Here a compromise has been made between the brightness of the grisaille and the dark colours of the original choir windows. The chapter house windows have grisaille backgrounds but figure panels are set into them, running in a series of bands. Unlike the earlier work, these are based on a unified scheme. Twenty of the 140 panels illustrate Christ's passion, death and resurrection. A number of other windows are dedicated to single saints – Katherine, Margaret, Nicholas, John the Baptist and St Denys. Incidents associated with the life of St William of York are also depicted.

Most of the glass in the nave is fourteenth century; the glazing dates from the period between 1291 and 1339. Here again horizontal bands of coloured figures are set on backgrounds of white glass. The windows of the clerestory are simpler and probably earlier than those below; ornament includes heraldic shields as well as figures. The nave aisle windows have two rows of figures shown under canopies. Backgrounds are grisaille, with naturalistic foliage recognisable as oak and maple leaves. In many cases individual donors, mainly clergymen, presented the windows and were allowed to determine the subject matter. A particularly interesting window is that given by Richard Tunnoc, a rich goldsmith and bellfounder; he is shown presenting a model of the window to St William of York. The top canopy is filled with bells, while the side borders depict apes playing musical instruments. A related panel shows two men casting a bell. A window in the north nave aisle shows St Peter, the minster's patron, holding a model of the church as well as an enormous key to the gates of heaven.

The minster's west window includes the famous heart-shaped tracery often called the 'Heart of Yorkshire'. In 1339 Archbishop William Melton gave 100 marks for the glazing, which was entrusted to a master named Robert. Melton wished the window to commemorate eight of his predecessors, who are shown standing under canopies with their hands raised in blessing. Another row of figures shows apostles. Higher up are panels of the joys of the Virgin Mary – the Annunciation, Nativity, Resurrection, Ascension and Coronation of the Virgin. There is a wealth of carefully executed ornament; Master Robert's technique included the use of yellow stain to produce brilliant effects on blue glass as well as on white.

The great east window was commissioned from the glazier John Thornton of Coventry in 1405. The contract specified that the work was to be completed within three years and that the iconography was to include historical figures. The window is immense, 76 feet high and 32 feet wide, with about 1680 square feet of glass. The iconographic programme reads from the top down. At the apex God is shown holding a book inscribed with the letters alpha and omega. The tracery lights contain angels, patriarchs, prophets and saints. The highest three rows of main lights have scenes from the Old Testament; the next nine rows are based on the Revelation of St John the Divine.

The bottom row (most easily seen) depicts the leaders of the church in York and northern England. The central figure is that of Walter Skirlaw, consecrated bishop of Durham in 1388. In 1398 Skirlaw was named archbishop of York but his election was set aside. The resulting controversy was ended only by Skirlaw's death in 1406. Nevertheless he had agreed to pay for the east window, which remains a monument to him. The window is one of Europe's great masterpieces of stained glass, although it is divided up into many small details. Thornton used a great deal of white glass and yellow stain; the figures contrast strikingly with rich backgrounds of blue or ruby glass. He was more interested in three-dimensional design than were his predecessors. Some panels, especially those showing the Elders before the Throne of God, are crowded with figures, yet each head retains its own individuality. Thornton was made a freeman of York in 1410 and is known to have been alive as late as 1433.[4]

Because of the importance of their Early English architecture, we should expect to find important glass at Lincoln, Salisbury and Westminster Abbey. In fact all three have some early thirteenth-century grisaille, but what survives is disappointing. Lincoln once had a series of grisaille windows incorporating figures; it appears that these may have been typologies showing the relationship between Old and New Testament events, as at Canterbury. Only the Last Judgment in the north rose window remains in its original place. Other scenes have been reinstalled in the east windows of the choir aisles and in the lancets of the transepts. These include a cycle of the life and miracles of the Virgin as well as depictions of the regional saints Ætheldreda and Hugh of Lincoln.

The choir of Salisbury had a series of biblical windows which were admired by the traveller Celia Fiennes in the seventeenth century. Sadly, little escaped James Wyatt's restoration of 1788; his craftsmen hauled off most of the medieval glass and dumped it in the city ditch. Surviving fragments show grisaille painted with at least ten different designs – trefoils, cinquefoils and stiff-leaf foliage set on cross-hatched lines. Part of a Jesse tree and a figure of St Stephen can still be seen. The slightly later windows in the chapter house are better preserved; they have figures of angels, prelates and kings as well as armorial shields. The earliest grisaille glass with naturalistic leaf forms was made for Westminster Abbey about 1250. Some of this was lost in the Second World War but bits survive. There are also seven figured panels dating from the thirteenth century, but most of these have been removed to the abbey museum or the muniment room. The three east clerestory windows of the apse, pieced together by Sir Christopher Wren at the beginning of the eighteenth century, contain a figure of Edward the

Confessor, and some coats of arms can be seen in St Edmund's chapel. The Jerusalem Chamber also has a few medieval scenes, including the Massacre of the Innocents.

Some of the finest fourteenth-century glass is at Gloucester.[5] As noted, the great east window was the largest in the world when it was built, about 1350. Most of the original glass remains in place. It has often been thought that the shields at the base of the window form a memorial to those who took part in Edward III's French campaign of 1346–49, which included the victory at Crécy, but it is possible that they may relate instead to the king's Scottish expedition or are simply a roll of the leading noblemen of the time. The main part of the window is a triptych of tiers of figures in Gothic niches: there are mitred bishops (probably bishops of Worcester, since Gloucester was part of that diocese in the middle ages), tonsured abbots (no doubt local), saints, apostles and at the top Christ and the Virgin Mary, surrounded by angels carrying palms. The figures and canopies are made of painted grisaille and yellow stain, with coloured glass reserved for the background.

The east window at Exeter is somewhat earlier and has a more complicated history. The original window of nine lights was put in when the east end was rebuilt about 1300. The stone tracery, which had probably decayed, was replaced with Perpendicular work in 1390. The fine figures of Isaiah, Moses and Abraham were retained, and new glass, some of it depicting St Sidwell, St Helena, St Edward the Confessor and St Edmund, was added by a glazier named Robert Lyen. The window suffered damage during the Reformation and was restored in the eighteenth and nineteenth centuries. In 1942 an air raid destroyed more of the glass, so following the war the window had to be reglazed again, when medieval glass from other parts of the cathedral was set into it. This includes fifteenth-century figures of the Virgin and Child and Saints Catherine, Barbara and Martin.

Among the bits and pieces at Wells are a Crucifixion (about 1315), a Resurrection showing several crowned kings and queens and a mitred bishop bursting from their tombs (about 1340), and a figure of St Gregory standing under a remarkably three-dimensional canopy (also about 1340). The Lady chapel at Ely has a charming panel showing an angel musician holding hammers to strike bells as well as some other figures in niches. The east window of the Lady chapel at Bristol includes a Jesse Tree from the same period.

Work from a later period includes new windows for Durham Cathedral made about 1440 by the resident glass painter Richard Glayzier and glass for the new east end of Winchester, commissioned at the beginning of the sixteenth century by Bishop Richard Fox. Here the east window has figures of the Virgin and St John the Baptist as well as trumpeting angels and a scroll bearing Fox's motto ('Est Deo Gratia').

7

Medieval Tombs and Monuments

The English cathedrals hold most of the country's great heritage of medieval tombs and monuments. Mirroring the social history of the time, most of them are memorials to members of the royal family and great noblemen or to bishops and other prominent churchmen. As might be expected, the largest number of royal burials were at Westminster Abbey, while most of the archbishops of Canterbury were interred in Canterbury Cathedral. There are artistically important monuments, both to clergy and lay aristocrats, in many other cathedrals as well.[1]

The earliest burials were beneath the floor, with only coffin lids visible. The oldest surviving monumental effigy in England is from the coffin lid of Abbot Gilbert Crispin of Westminster Abbey, who died in 1117 or 1118. This has now been removed to the abbey cloister; its primitive carving has a low-relief figure of the abbot, bare headed and holding his staff of office. Tomb chests placed on the floor of churches became common at the beginning of the thirteenth century. Although early examples, like the tomb of Hubert Walter at Canterbury, did not include effigies, figures soon became popular. Local stone, Purbeck marble and alabaster were among the materials used. Sometimes the carvings were elaborately painted with vivid colours. Gilt bronze effigies were introduced in the later fourteenth century, a particularly fine one being that of the Black Prince at Canterbury Cathedral. The sides of tomb chests were often ornamented with blank arches, trefoils and quatrefoils, and other decorative patterns; they also sometimes held figures of mourners or angels. The Decorated period saw the introduction of monumental canopies overarching the tombs. During the age of Perpendicular architecture tombs were frequently enclosed within screens of stonework and were often part of chantry chapels.

The collection of medieval monuments in Westminster Abbey is one of the richest in the world.[2] These are located east of the high altar, in an area which remains quieter and more solemn than the nave, dominated as it now is by tourists and by monuments to politicians and poets, mainly of the nineteenth century. Presiding over the royal tombs is the shrine of St Edward the Confessor, which despite iconoclastic assaults remains the most complete of its kind surviving in a Protestant country.[3] Erection of the shrine was undertaken by Henry III in 1241; he regarded it is one of the most important achievements of his reign. It was intended to house the Confessor's relics, which had been gathered in a reliquary chest. According to surviving descriptions, this was made of gold ornamented with gems; it had a gabled roof and included statutes of Christ surrounded by censing angels and St Edward flanked by bishops. This was placed on a stone base raised on four steps, where pilgrims might kneel when they came to pray. The shrine, constructed of Purbeck marble, was elaborately decorated with inlaid glass and gems. A protective cover could be raised by ropes attached to pulleys in the vault in order to reveal the treasures. In the later middle ages the royal coronation ring was kept in this shrine whenever the king was abroad, presumably because of the security offered by the holy place. The reliquary was dismantled on the orders of Thomas Cromwell in July 1536, but the base remains and the Confessor's body was probably reburied under it. What survives is impressive but a mere shadow of the splendour of the original shrine.

St Edward's shrine was located behind the high altar in an area which came to be known as the Confessor's chapel. Henry III decided that he wished to be buried there and this began the tradition of the abbey serving as the chief mausoleum of English monarchs. Henry's remains, originally interred before the high altar, were moved to a position north of the Confessor's tomb and placed within an elaborate tomb whose base contains a large piece of prophyry, standing on a floor of Cosmati mosaic work. The bronze image of Henry III, cast by an artisan named William Torel in 1291, is one of the glories of medieval sculpture.

Torel also made an effigy of Eleanor of Castile. Her tomb chest includes coats of arms similar to those found on the Eleanor Crosses which mark the route taken by her funeral cortège. Her husband Edward I is buried on the north side of the Confessor's shrine, but without an effigy. Edward III (d. 1377) was memorialized by a fine effigy probably made by John Orchard; his fourteen children are depicted as weepers. The base of the tomb, almost certainly designed by Henry Yeveley, includes figures of five angels. The monument to Edward III's queen, Philippa of Hainault, included coloured jewels and beads ornamenting the black and white marble, now mutilated, and more than seventy statuettes. Yeveley was also commissioned to make the base for the monument to Richard II and his wife Anne of Bohemia, begun after her death in 1394. The copper effigy of Richard II was probably made by Nicholas Broker and Godfrey Prest.

Henry VI, at one time a candidate for sainthood, lies in a Purbeck tomb chest designed by Yeveley. His silvered and gilt effigy, once among the most splendid in the abbey, has lost its head, hands and regalia; what one now sees are replacements made of fibreglass in the 1970s. Above the tomb, according to instructions in the king's will, was constructed a chantry chapel with two turrets containing spiral staircases. The only non-royal burials in the Confessor's chapel are those of John of Waltham, bishop of Salisbury, a friend of Richard II, and Richard Courtenay, bishop of Norwich, who died while attending Henry V at Harfleur.

Nearby, radiating chapels arranged around the ambulatory contain a number of further non-royal tombs. Henry V's standard-bearer Sir Louis Robessart has a splendid monument with heraldry showing a sultan's head and a Catherine wheel. The tomb of John of Eltham, a masterpiece of alabaster, was made by craftsmen from Nottingham. Records tell us that thirty-five medieval tombs were made by the Limoges workshop. These include the monument to William de Valence (d. 1296), which was constructed of eighty pieces of Limoges enamel screwed onto a wooden base. Cardinal Simon Langham (d. 1376) has another tomb chest made by Henry Yeveley and Stephen Lote.

Three fine monuments remain within the sanctuary, on the north side of the high altar. These were made about 1300 by Michael of Canterbury, who was the chief architect to the court and designed one of the Eleanor Crosses. Edmund Crouchback (d. 1296) is shown facing the altar, wearing a striped coat ornamented by glass jewels. His wife Eveline, countess of Lancaster, is given a graceful effigy, although she died when she was only fourteen. A third tomb depicts the prominent nobleman Aymer de Valence, earl of Pembroke (d. 1324).

Archbishops Lanfranc (d. 1089) and Theobald (d. 1161) had been buried at Canterbury cathedral, but their remains were removed from the Trinity chapel when it was converted into the shrine for Thomas Becket. Lanfranc was reinterred in the north-east transept and Theobald in the Lady chapel in the east bays of the north nave aisle. Becket's shrine was the chief glory of the medieval cathedral. Despite an effort to prevent nearby burials which might detract from the uniqueness of the saint's shrine, several archbishops did find adjacent resting places. The first of these was Hubert Walter (d. 1205), who was respected by the monks for his efforts to block the establishment of an archiepiscopal foundation at Lambeth. His tomb, unique in style and one of the earliest in which the sarcophagus is not buried below ground level, does not include an effigy, although its lid does hold six large sculptured heads. These are not identified and their meaning is open to doubt, but it has been suggested that they represent the several communities of religious and secular persons Walter had served in his dual capacities of archbishop and justiciar. Walter was followed by Stephen Langton (d. 1228), who more than anyone else had been responsible for the establishment of Becket's shrine; he was interred in the chapel of St Michael in the south-west transept.

Archbishop John Pecham (d. 1292) did not originally intend to be buried at Canterbury but was persuaded that his position made it appropriate. He has the most elaborate early monument; the wooden effigy, now stripped of its silver mitre, lies on a tomb chest surmounted by an elaborate Gothic arch and gable. The artisan was once again the London-based Michael of Canterbury. This was to form a model for many of the fourteenth- and fifteenth-century tombs. These include the monuments to Simon Meopham (d. 1333), John Stratford (d. 1348), Simon Sudbury (d. 1381 – beheaded in the Peasants' Revolt), William Courtenay (d. 1396), Henry Chichele (d. 1443), Thomas Bourchier (d. 1486), John Morton (d. 1500) and William Warham, the last of the pre-Reformation archbishops (d. 1532). Meopham's tomb, despite its exceptionally fine materials and craftsmanship, is simpler than most and may be meant to convey a sense of humility. Among the finest effigies are those of Pecham, Stratford, Courtenay and Chichele. The designer of Stratford's tomb was probably William Ramsey, the earliest practitioner of the Perpendicular style in south-east England. Chichele's monument, probably made by William Mapilton, is one of the earliest examples of the 'double-decker' tomb: its upper level shows the archbishop richly clothed in his cope and mitre, while below lies an effigy of equal size depicting a naked, decaying cadaver. An inscription reads, 'I was born a poor man: and afterwards raised to be primate here. Now I am cast down and turned into food for worms'. Morton lies in the crypt; Warham was interred in the Martyrdom, in one of the cathedral's largest monuments. Several priors were also given tombs, the most notable being Henry of Eastry (d. 1331), William Sellyng (d. 1494) and Thomas Goldstone II (d. 1517).

The finest tombs of laymen are those of Edward the Black Prince (d. 1376), designed by Henry Yeveley with a gilt bronze effigy, and Henry IV and his queen, Joan of Navarre, whose fifteenth-century alabaster likenesses have been attributed to the sculptor Robert Brown. These are in the Trinity chapel. Effigies of women are uncommon. The finest, beside that of Joan, is that of Lady Margaret Holland (d. 1439), who lies between her two husbands, John Beaufort, earl of Somerset (d. 1410), and Thomas, duke of Clarence (d. 1421). The large alabaster tomb was designed by the master mason Richard Beke; its detailed carving depicts even the pins which hold the duchess's wimple in place. The heraldic symbols of Lady Margaret and her husbands were originally incorporated in stained-glass windows adjoining the monument, but these do not survive. The crypt contains tombs of two more non-royal ladies, the rich benefactress Joan, Lady Mohun (d. 1404) and Elizabeth, Lady Trivet (d. 1433).

Although the other cathedrals were less important as burial sites, they contain many monuments of great interest. At York the finest of these is the tomb of Archbishop Walter de Gray (d. 1255) in the south transept. His Purbeck effigy lies under a marble canopy; the freestone top and finials, reminding one of the shape of a reliquary, fit perfectly but are in fact eighteenth century additions. The tomb of Archbishop William de Greenfield (d. 1315), probably made by the master mason Simon, is surmounted by a cusped ogee arch and pinnacle typical of the Decorated period, while the tomb of Archbishop Henry Bowet (d. 1423) is a good example of Perpendicular work. An unusual memorial is the tomb of Thomas Haxey, the cathedral treasurer who died in 1425; it was probably originally a double-decker, like Archbishop Chichele's, but only the cadaver survives.

Finer than any of these is the effigy of King John (d. 1216) at Worcester. Made of Purbeck marble about 1230, it is of superb craftsmanship and is almost perfectly preserved. The king's figure is realistically carved in high relief; there are two bishops censing his head and a lion at his feet. Originally painted and ornamented with inset semi-precious stones, it established a new standard for monument-making in England. Worcester also has one of the best of the early sixteenth-century chantry chapels, built for Henry VII's elder son Prince Arthur. Although the figures were mutilated by iconoclasts, the delicate Perpendicular tracery which surrounds the chapel remains intact.

The tomb of Edward II at Gloucester, like that of John at Worcester, is of national importance. Erected at the order of Edward III, following his father's murder at Berkeley Castle in 1327, it has one of the earliest alabaster effigies, beautifully carved, lying beneath an elaborate limestone canopy. The form of the monument is reminiscent of a saint's shrine; this is appropriate since it attracted many pilgrims. The other great tomb at Gloucester holds the remarkable wooden effigy of Robert, duke of Normandy, William the Conqueror's eldest son. Robert is shown wearing chain mail, his legs crossed and a crown on his head. The elaborately painted figure is recumbent on a tomb chest dating from the fifteenth century. We know that the effigy was broken into pieces by Puritan soldiers during the Civil War; it has been well restored, although an arm and hand are probably not in the original position. The cathedral also has an unusual effigy of Abbot Serlo (d. 1104) and an alabaster figure of Abbot Thomas Seabroke (d. 1457), lying in a chantry chapel in the south aisle.

Most of the great tombs memorialized bishops. Hereford had the famous shrine of St Thomas Cantilupe, the thirteenth-century bishop credited with performing many miraculous cures. Valuable treasures were removed in 1538 and the shrine itself demolished about 1550. An earlier tomb in the north transept survived, however. It does not have an effigy of the saint, but there are carved figures of sixteen warriors as weepers, the earliest known figures of weepers in the country. Although these are sometimes thought to have been relatives of Cantilupe's, it has recently been suggested that they are meant to be soldiers of Christ, their feet resting on allegorical beasts, defending Cantilupe as he enters Paradise. No other tombs appear to have been defaced. They include those of Bishops Peter de Aigueblanche (d. 1268), similar to Gray's tomb at York, John Stanbury (d. 1474) and Richard Mayeu (d. 1516). Unusually, the precentor John Swinfield (d. 1311) was accorded a tomb in the retrochoir, its surround carved with a rebus showing pigs feeding on acorns. Hereford is also unusual in having a monument to a woman, Joanna de Bohun (d. 1327), whose finely painted effigy lies in the Lady chapel, and two fine tombs of soldiers, Peter de Grandisson (d. 1358) and Sir Richard Pembridge (d. 1375). Both are depicted wearing armour; Grandisson's effigy is elaborately painted, while Pembridge's is made of alabaster.

The most famous of the bishops of Winchester, William of Wykeham (d. 1404), has that cathedral's finest monument, a mitred effigy reposing on a tomb chest. This was part of a chantry chapel, as were the tombs of bishops William of Edington (d. 1365), Henry Beaufort (d. 1446), William Waynflete (d. 1486) and Thomas Langton (d. 1500). Perhaps the last great chantry to be erected in England is that of Stephen Gardiner (d. 1555), the conservative bishop who was deprived under Edward VI but reinstated by Queen Mary. There are also tombs of Prior William of Basing (d. 1295) and Sir Arnold de Gaveston (d. 1302), the father of Edward II's favourite Piers Gaveston. Sir Arnold, a veteran of the Seventh Crusade, holds his sword and shield; he was the first layman to be buried in the cathedral.

One of the earliest tomb chests incorporating an effigy is that of Bishop Henry Marshall of Exeter (d. 1206), located on the north side of the presbytery. The figure is of high sculptural quality, made of polished Purbeck marble. The bishop wears mass vestments and a mitre. His right hand is raised in blessing and has a large episcopal ring; his left hand holds a crozier. His body rests on a crouching lion, perhaps symbolising Satan whom he has beaten down under his feet. The finest monument at Exeter is that to Bishop Walter Bronescombe (d. 1280) in the Lady chapel. His unusual effigy made of black basalt, still displaying vivid colours, lies on a fifteenth-century tomb chest beneath a large arched canopy. Like Marshall, Bronescombe is shown with vestments, mitre and staff. Two more thirteenth-century monuments are the tombs of Bishops Simon of Apulia (d. 1223) and Peter Quinil (d. 1291). The most important monument from the fourteenth century is that of Bishop Walter Stapledon (d. 1326), which lies in the choir north of the high altar. An effigy of his brother Sir Richard Stapledon (d. 1320) shows the knight's armour as well as his squire, groom and horse. From about the same date is the tomb of Humphrey de Bohun, earl of Hereford (d. 1322), also depicted in armour; the effigies of the second earl of Devon and his wife Margaret de Bohun, their feet resting on the swans which formed part of their crest, are from the end of the century. The chantry chapel of Sir John Speke (d. 1518) also has an effigy clad in contemporary armour. As a *memento mori* the tomb of Precentor William Sylke (d. 1508) is surmounted by a cadaver.

A few tombs from Old Sarum were transferred to Salisbury in 1226. The first person to be buried in the new cathedral was William Longespée, earl of Salisbury and half-brother to King John (d. 1226). His stone effigy rests on a wooden base with lancet arcading. William Longespée the Younger died in 1250 while on a crusade and was buried at Acre, but he was given a Purbeck effigy at Salisbury. Another warrior, John de Montacute (d. 1389), fought at Crécy and Poitiers; he has a tomb chest of Bath stone but again it is empty. The chantry chapel of Robert Lord Hungerford (d. 1459) includes a fine effigy, including what must be one of the finest sculptured dogs of the middle ages. Sir John Cheyney (d. 1509) has an alabaster effigy. Among the bishops suitably entombed are Giles Bridport (d. 1262), Simon of Ghent (d. 1315), Richard Mitford (d. 1407), John Blyth (d. 1499) and Edmund Audley (d. 1524).

At Norwich, as elsewhere, few civic leaders were buried in the cathedral. In this case the priory's long-standing dispute with the city about jurisdictions may be partly responsible. Exceptions are the tombs of John Berney (d. 1374), a merchant and MP for Norwich, and John Heydon (d. 1480), a gentleman of Baconsthorpe. Several early monuments are now lost. These included memorials to the boy-saint William of Norwich (d. 1144), to whom many miracles were attributed, and Bishops Walter Suffield (d. 1256) and John Salmon (d. 1325). The earliest surviving monument is to Bishop John Wakering (d. 1425); his tomb chest has seven original figures holding symbols of the Passion. Perhaps the finest monument is the elaborate tomb chest with a painted effigy and a large canopy which is part of the chantry chapel of Bishop John Goldwell (d. 1499). Before the Reformation it was served by three chantry priests.

Wells has the tomb chest of Bishop Ralph Shrewsbury (d. 1363), topped by crenellations, and the elaborate tomb of Bishop William of March (d. 1302), an unsuccessful candidate for sainthood. The early fourteenth-century tomb of Prior Sutton survives at Christ Church Cathedral in Oxford. The prominent magnate John Lord Neville (d. 1388) was interred in the cathedral at Durham. The Angel Choir at Lincoln contains the tomb of Bishop Henry Burghersh (d. 1340), who was also Edward III's lord chancellor, with canons of the cathedral as weepers; the tomb of Bishop Grosseteste has been lost. At Rochester one may see the thirteenth-century monuments to Bishops Gilbert Glanville (d. 1214), Lawrence of St Martin (d. 1274) and John Bradfield (d. 1283). Ely has the tombs of a number of bishops, their dates ranging from 1254 (Hugh of Northwold) and 1256 (William of Kilkenny) to 1505 (Richard Redman). There is also a monument to John Tiptoft, earl of Worcester (d. 1490), who among other things was an influential Speaker of the Commons. The greatest survivals at Ely, however, are the sixteenth-century chantry chapels of Bishop John Alcock (d. 1500) and Bishop Nicholas West (d. 1533). Alcock's chapel is one of the most sumptuously decorated in the country; as one writer has observed, it demonstrates the middle ages going out in a blaze of glory.

Monumental brasses inserted into the 'ledger stones' in the floor above burial sites became common in the late thirteenth century and were enormously popular in the fifteenth and early sixteenth centuries. They were concentrated in East Anglia and Yorkshire and were more common in parish churches than in cathedrals, probably because they were not regarded as being grand enough for bishops and aristocrats. Most of the original brasses do not survive; they fell prey to iconoclasts or to those eager to melt them down for their metal. One of the cathedrals once noted for its brasses was Hereford, where as many as 170 empty indents were recorded in the eighteenth century. A brass in Cantilupe's shrine was made in 1287 by a London workshop; the only portion to survive is a figure of St Ethelbert. Bishop John Trilleck (d. 1360) is depicted with his staff and miter beneath a gothic canopy with coats of arms. The brass monuments to the archdeacon Richard Rudhale (d. 1476), the mayor John Stockton (d. 1480), the sheriff Richard Delamare (d. 1435) with his wife and two dogs, and Sir Richard Delabere (d. 1514) with his wife and twenty-one children also remain. One of the earliest brasses honouring an ecclesiastic is that of Archbishop William Greenfield (d. 1315) in York Minster. Exeter has fifteenth-century brasses depicting Canon William Langton (d. 1414) and Bishop John Booth (d. 1478), both shown kneeling in prayer. The only other cathedrals with two or more medieval brasses are Salisbury, Wells and Oxford. One of the late brasses is that of Ralph Pulvertoft, master of the charnel house at Norwich, who died about 1505. A handful of incised stone slabs also survive, the finest perhaps being that of Bishop William of Bitton II (d. 1274) at Wells. Another unusual form is the heart monument: Winchester has a half-effigy of Bishop Aymer de Valence (d. 1260) holding his heart in his hands. Finally we may mention the unique monument and chantry chapel of Thomas Hatfield (d. 1381) at Durham, in which provision was made for a new episcopal throne raised high on a platform above the bishop's tomb chest.

8

Life in a Medieval Cathedral

During the later middle ages there were nineteen cathedral churches in England. Nine of these – Chichester, Exeter, Hereford, Lichfield, Lincoln, St Paul's in London, Salisbury, Wells, and York – were secular cathedrals, served by a dean, chapter and inferior clergy who were in holy orders but not monks. The remaining ten cathedrals were monastic in organization. Bath, Canterbury, Coventry, Durham, Ely, Norwich, Rochester, Winchester, and Worcester were Benedictine priories, while the cathedral at Carlisle was staffed by Augustinian canons. In organization and finance the two types of cathedrals differed significantly.[1]

The clergy who served in the secular cathedrals were called canons or prebendaries. The word *canon* originally meant 'rule', and cathedral canons had at first lived under a rule, in a sort of communal life, even though they had not taken monastic vows. Their lives may have been regulated by rules drawn up by bishops; the most famous and influential of these was the set of orders promulgated by Bishop Chrodegang of Metz about 755.

By the time of the Norman Conquest, canons had begun to acquire individual property. As this happened, they abandoned their communal life and established homes in separate houses near the cathedral. For a time it was common for them to be married, but this arrangement ended by the thirteenth century. They gained their financial support from individual endowments – lands and the right to collect rents, fees and tithes from parish churches – which were called prebends. The canons thus became prebendaries, who could be referred to by naming their principal estate, such as the prebend of Masham at York. For our purposes the terms *canon* and *prebendary* are virtually synonymous, and they were used more or less interchangeably during the middle ages. But they do have different origins and different technical meanings. For legal purposes they were often conjoined: the full title of a canon at Lincoln, for instance, was canon of Lincoln and prebendary of Buckden (or whatever other prebend he might hold).

The number of canons in the secular cathedrals before the Reformation varied considerably, but it was always surprisingly large, at least in comparison to modern cathedral establishments. Lincoln – a vast and rich diocese before the 1540s – had fifty-eight prebendaries. Salisbury followed with fifty-two. York, though the seat of an archbishop, had only thirty-six. Lichfield, one of the poorest cathedrals, had more canons than St Paul's in London; the numbers were thirty-two and thirty respectively. There were twenty-seven canons at Hereford and Chichester, twenty-four at Exeter, and twenty-two at Wells.

The chief officer in every secular cathedral was the dean. The bishop was rarely present. He might celebrate mass or preach at Christmas and Easter, and he would normally be consecrated, enthroned, and eventually buried in the cathedral, but it was the dean who presided over meetings of the cathedral chapter, joined with the canons in holding title to cathedral property, and was generally responsible for all activities of the cathedral. He had the cure of souls for all the cathedral clergy. His income was much larger than that of other canons, and he was expected to live grandly and entertain on a large scale. Many deans held other positions in the church concurrently, and a number were named bishops later in their careers. Although deans were supposed to be elected by members of the cathedral chapter, royal nomination became common in the later middle ages, with the actual election being no more than a formal confirmation of the monarch's choice.

Three other great officers were found in the secular cathedrals; they, together with the dean, formed the *quatuor personae* spoken of in medieval texts as forming the four cornerstones of the cathedral's spiritual and material fabric. Ranking next to the dean, though much inferior to him in wealth and prestige, was the precentor. He was in charge of the cathedral services, the music and liturgy, the choir and song school. The chancellor kept the seal of the chapter and acted as its secretary, but his chief functions related to education and scholarship. Most cathedrals had schools which operated under the general supervision of the chancellor. He was usually the cathedral librarian and archivist, and he was responsible for arranging the reading of lessons at services and for scheduling sermons. The treasurer was not, as might have been expected, given control of cathedral finances. Instead he guarded the cathedral's treasures – plate, vestments, relics – and provided the lights, candles, incense, bread and wine, and other things needed at the altars. He was responsible for the regulation of the clock and bells as well.

Each of these great officers commonly had a deputy who assisted him and performed his duties in his absence. The subdean might be especially important in cases where the dean himself was non-resident or frequently absent from his cathedral church. At Lincoln the subdean was specifically charged with the duty of hearing confessions from members of the cathedral staff and assigning penances. As deputy to the precentor, the succentor was usually the real director of music in the choir and at the high altar. At Exeter, for instance, we know that he lived with the choristers and taught in the song school. The vice-chancellor's chief deputy seems to have arranged the lessons for the choir offices and assigned lectors. The sacrist – deputy to the treasurer – often assumed the routine duty of providing the material articles required by the liturgy (bread, wine and lights). In some places archdeacons were also counted as officials of the cathedral. They were really assistants to the bishop and helped him oversee the parishes of the diocese, but they sometimes held prebends and were treated as guests of the cathedral, being allotted stalls in the choir next to those of the other great officers. In all, therefore, there could be nine principal officials in each secular cathedral, but they were rarely all present and primary responsibility remained in the hands of the dean and his three chief colleagues.

One would hardly expect that such large numbers of canons would be resident at the cathedral continuously, especially when many of them held posts in parish churches, at court or in the universities. In fact the problem of non-residency presented great difficulties in the middle ages, and there were complaints of cathedrals being poorly served because few members of the senior staff were actually present. Eventually a satisfactory accommodation was reached, under which a small number of prebendaries were designated residentiary canons. To them were given the real responsibilities of running the cathedral, and they came to receive additional compensation: as well as the revenue that came to individual canons from their prebends, the cathedral had common funds that were divided only among the resident- iaries. Besides these, the resident clergy were given quite substantial sums for participation in obits (endowed masses and memorial observances).

At York, where there were sometimes only two or three residentiaries in the fifteenth century, a clear distinction grew up between two types of canons. Those who did not actually reside were principally royal clerks and university scholars, while the four great officers and a few other active administrators formed the much smaller group of residentiaries. York appears to have been unique in that even the non-residentiary canons had small houses in the immediate vicinity of the minster. At St Paul's the resi- dentiary canons were called stagiaries. There were ordinarily eight of them. Five canons generally resided at Lincoln, although there were occasionally only three and sometimes as many as seven. Six or seven are common elsewhere; numbers fluctuate, and it is not unusual to find as few as four.

By the end of the middle ages the rewards of residence had grown so great that there were more canons wishing to reside than could easily be accom- modated or paid without prejudice to those already residing. It was probably for this reason that the cost of assuming residence was set very high. A non- residentiary who wished to come into full residence was required to declare his intention of doing so well in advance. If this was agreed to, the new residentiary would be required to attend every cathedral service for three-quarters of the first year. In addition, staggering responsibilities for hospitality were laid upon him. At St Paul's new stagiaries had to keep open house daily at breakfast time; entertain the other stagiaries, one by one, at dinner each quarter; feast the choir twice a year; and provide semi-annual banquets to which were invited the bishop and all the canons (including non-residents) as well as the mayor and aldermen, judges and other leading royal officials.

All of this could easily cost 1000 marks (£667). Indeed, new statutes enacted for York in 1541 complained that major residence (the term given to the first year, with its strict requirements) did cost 1000 marks, so that only the richest clergy could contemplate it. (To put this in perspective it may be useful to recall that the subsistence level for poor persons was thought to be only £6 a year.) Even at a relatively remote and poor cathedral like Lichfield, no canon was allowed to take up residence unless he was able to spend at least £40 a year of his own money in the city, and he was required to pay the dean 100 marks, the money to be used partly for maintenance of the cathedral building and partly for church ornaments. After the first year, or in some places a somewhat longer period of time, canons could enter into what was called the lesser residence, which required their presence for only half of the year.

By the beginning of the Tudor period, the residentiary canons were generally well established, well off, and prepared to live out their lives in the relative comfort of the cathedral close. Indeed all but one of the fifty residentiaries of York during the century and a half before 1500 died in office. (The single exception went on to become bishop of London.) They were educated men, almost all graduates of Oxford or Cambridge; occasionally, as at Hereford, they were given leaves of absence for a year or two so that they could undertake advanced study at the university. A number of surviving wills of fifteenth-century canons testify to their wealth and the luxury of their homes. Their private libraries were often among the largest in the country.

The principal responsibility of the cathedral clergy was the maintenance of the daily round of services, the *Opus Dei* of prayer and praise. The mass was, of course, the central act of worship before the Reformation, and it was celebrated several times a day: there was the morrow mass at dawn and the mass of the Virgin Mary in the Lady chapel as well as the solemn high mass celebrated at the principal altar. But the mass was not the only service sung in the cathedrals, for the Use of Salisbury or Sarum and its local variants, especially the Uses of Hereford, York, Lincoln and Bangor, prescribed eight

Hereford breviary, 1262–68, antiphon for St Æthelbert (Hereford Cathedral Library, MS P.IX.7, fol. 262r). (*Dean and Chapter of Hereford*)

other daily observances. These were matins (sung during the night, before daylight), lauds (offered at daybreak), prime, terce, sext, none, vespers and compline (celebrated just before retiring). By the fifteenth century some liberties had been taken with timing. At Lincoln matins continued to be sung at midnight between Michaelmas and Easter until 1548, but between Easter and Michaelmas it was postponed until about 5 a.m.; elsewhere night matins was transferred to the early morning, just before the morrow mass, and was followed immediately by lauds. The Lady mass was usually celebrated at about 9 a.m. Terce was said while the celebrant was preparing for high mass, at 10 a.m. Sext and nones were sung after the mass, often together. Such a schedule occupied most of the morning but left the early afternoon free for other activities.

All of these services included psalms and prayers, and all were generally sung. Simple plainsong chant usually sufficed for the lesser offices of prime, terce, sext and none. Although awkwardly timed, matins and lauds often contained some more elaborate polyphony, as did compline. Vespers, at which the liturgy included the *Magnificat*, had come by the late fifteenth century to be the most important of the offices musically. Antiphons and hymns were sung at matins, lauds, vespers and compline; on Sundays and festivals the *Te Deum* concluded matins.

The principal mass of the day might be sung with relative simplicity on ordinary weekdays, but on Sundays and high holy days it was celebrated with great magnificence. Polyphonic music would then alternate with chant or replace it altogether in the Ordinary of the mass (the *Gloria, Credo, Sanctus* and *Benedictus*, and *Agnus Dei*), and antiphons and motets appropriate to the season could be included. The Marian masses sung in the Lady chapels provided the greatest opportunity for the performance of elaborate polyphonic music sung by trained choirs of men and boys. Cathedrals that had shrines honouring the memory of saints and martyrs would provide regular services there as well.

In addition to these daily observances, there were masses for the dead, celebrated at designated altars or in chantry chapels. Distinctive liturgies were prescribed for Holy Week. Some other occasions demanded special observance: the installation of new bishops, deans or mayors, for instance, or ceremonial visits by civic dignitaries or members of the royal family, or funerals of prominent persons. In addition, processions through the cathedral close and out into the streets of the city were common; these might culminate in high masses performed in the choir. Palm Sunday processions were especially elaborate and could include special liturgical practices, such as that in which musicians sang through the holes in the façade of the cathedrals at Wells and Salisbury.

It is impossible to say how frequently lay men and women attended cathedral services in the years preceding the Reformation. Certainly some came to the masses on festival days, and many would have seen the processions of priests and singers. Civic ceremonies were probably well attended. Lady masses were also popular with lay people, perhaps because of the elegance of the music as well as on account of the growth of Marian devotion. The appeal of shrines may have been declining, but they remained a focus for worship and veneration of relics until they were dismantled under Henry VIII. The laity were not likely to attend matins, lauds and compline because of the inconvenience of the hours, and it is unlikely that many were attracted to the lesser offices. Evidence is lacking, but we may suppose that vespers appealed to lay persons, just as its successor, evensong, does today. Certainly John Wheathampstead, the abbot of St Albans in the mid fifteenth century, believed that 'wherever the Divine Service is more honourable celebrated the glory of the church is increased and the people are aroused to much greater devotion'. But cathedral services were offered mainly for the glory of God, not the edification of man, and there was no provision for participation by a congregation of worshippers.

These elaborate services obviously could not be maintained by the small number of residentiary canons, who were not in any case chosen because of their skill in music. It was the vicars choral who actually sang the several daily masses and other canonical hours. These men are usually thought of as being deputies for the non-resident prebendaries – this is the origin of the term *vicar* and the accompanying notion that these men vicariously performed the duties of others who were absent. As early as the twelfth century, canons were required to appoint vicars, who initially lived in the homes of the vicars and ate at their tables. However, residentiaries were often expected to have vicars, just as were their non-resident colleagues, and it soon became clear that the vicars had duties that were quite different from those of the canons whom they represented.

Skill in singing was a requisite for the vicars choral at least as early as the twelfth century. In a number of the cathedrals, medieval statutes provide that vicars serve a probationary year before achieving permanent tenure in their offices. During this time they were supposed to learn the psalms, antiphons and hymns by heart; if they had not mastered all this material they might (as at Wells in 1488) be granted permanent status on condition that they memorize the remaining psalms and hymns by a certain date.

The number of vicars choral varied from place to place. At the beginning there were theoretically as many vicars as there were canons in the cathedral chapter. Thus Lincoln, Wells and Salisbury were supposed to have more than fifty vicars, York thirty-six. But these numbers were not in practice always maintained. A visitation of 1437 revealed that there were only thirty-four vicars at Wells, and only twenty-three were actually paid in 1500. Salisbury had only thirty-one in 1468, fourteen in 1547. At Lincoln there were twenty-five in 1501. York could afford only twenty in 1509. When John Colet became dean of St Paul's in 1505 he was shocked to find that the thirty vicars had dwindled to six. But St Paul's was unusual in having twelve minor canons who joined the vicars in singing its services. Exeter had twenty-four vicars choral, Hereford twenty-seven. At Chichester there were seventeen in the 1480s and fourteen in 1521 but only twelve in 1524. The four laymen added to the choir in 1529 as the result of a grant from Bishop Sherburne were required to have special skill in singing, and we know that some were married, since an unusual provision allowed Dorothy Somer to continue receiving the stipend allocated to her husband Henry following his death, so long as she remained single, or even if she married another singing man. There were supposed to be twenty-seven vicars choral at Lichfield, although the full number was not always maintained. Lichfield was unusual in not permitting vicars to hold other offices (for instance as chantry priests) and this probably reduced the value of vicars' positions to the point where it was hard to recruit new singers.

At most of the cathedrals vicars choral were required to be in holy orders. At Exeter all twenty-four had to be priests. It was more normal for a handful of vicars to be priests while the others remained in minor orders, as deacons, subdeacons or even acolytes. Two laymen were admitted at Wells in 1489 on condition that they take holy orders as soon as possible. In some cathedrals there were clear distinctions between vicars who were priests and those who were not. The priests at Lincoln, for instance (in 1501 there were fifteen, out of a total of twenty-five vicars choral), were called the vicars of the first form and sat above the vicars of the second form, who had so far taken only minor orders.

As the attachment of the vicars to individual canons gradually weakened during the later middle ages, the vicars acquired residences and incomes of their own. The earliest residential accommodation was the Bedern at York. Here thirty-six small houses or sets of chambers were erected near the east end of the minster as a result of the bequest provided by one of the canons as early as the 1240s. In the fourteenth century the vicars were able to add their own chapel and a common dining hall, and at the end of the century a pedestrian bridge was built to link the Bedern and the cathedral gatehouse, so that the vicars would not face danger or inconvenience in having to cross a busy road. The Bedern no longer exists, although foundations of its buildings were exposed in the 1970s when the area was redeveloped.

At Lincoln a hall, kitchen and some chambers for vicars choral were erected in 1309, on the bishop's order. Some of these early buildings survive in what is now called vicars' court. They are of interest architecturally became a number of chambers (originally six in the best of the surviving houses) opened off a central staircase. Such a plan was to become common in the colleges at Oxford and Cambridge, but the work at Lincoln probably antedates that at the universities. This arrangement was not adopted elsewhere, however; in other places vicars choral had individual small houses with separate entrances.

Vicars' closes survive intact at Hereford, Lichfield, and Wells. The vicars' college at Wells was founded and endowed by Bishop Ralph of Shrewsbury in 1348 so that the vicars 'might be freer to serve God, live more respectably and nearer the church, attend divine service constantly, and meet together for meals in a companionable way, but without idle and scurrilous gossip'. Forty-two small houses, facing one another along two sides of an enclosed street, provided ample accommodation. A chapel and library terminate the close at its north end; an attractive refectory, with a large fireplace, was built at the south, and in 1457 Bishop Beckington ordered the construction of a covered way over the chain gate, linking the refectory directly to the cathedral, as at York. The quadrangle now known as the cloisters at Hereford was constructed just after 1472. Here there were twenty-seven small two-roomed houses, a hall with a kitchen, and a chapel; the cloister was connected to the south-east transept of the cathedral so that vicars would not be troubled by inclement weather. At Lichfield the vicars' close, similar in appearance, consisted of sixteen houses built in the fifteenth century adjoining an older hall that was reconstructed in 1458.

Similar arrangements existed at the other secular cathedrals. The minor canons of St Paul's had a hall by 1272 and houses in the 1350s. At Exeter the vicars choral had acquired buildings comparable to those at Wells by the end of the fourteenth century. These were on the west side of the close, in Kalendarhay, an area that had belonged to a religious guild called the Kalendar brethren before being transferred to the vicars. Twenty houses were still standing in 1850; the vicars' hall remained until the Second World War but was destroyed by the bombing of 1942. The vicars' close at Chichester was under construction by 1400, and the hall was already in use then. One side of this close remains; a local antiquarian has attacked the conversion of the other half to shops, fronting on South Street, as an early twentieth-century act of urban vandalism. Salisbury was the last of the secular cathedrals to acquire a vicars' dining hall. Evidence of this comes only in 1409, and it seems that the vicars choral of Salisbury never had their own individual houses.

By the beginning of the sixteenth century the vicars choral of the secular cathedrals had acquired a remarkably large degree of independence from the dean and chapter. They had their own officers, their own statutes and their own revenues (the income came from lands and rents just as that of the dean and chapter did, and from obits and other payments for services). In some places they also maintained their own bakehouse and brewery. These arrangements changed little during the Reformation, at least until the later years of Elizabeth's reign, when the marriage of most vicars dictated an end to their communal life.

The polyphonic music sung at vespers, the Lady mass and the high mass on festive occasions also required boys with unchanged treble voices. The number of choristers did not vary greatly from place to place. Everywhere there were fewer boys than one would find in a modern cathedral choir. Salisbury and Exeter had fourteen choristers apiece; York, Lincoln and Lichfield, twelve. There were ten at St Paul's, eight at Chichester, six at Wells and only five at Hereford.

As early as the twelfth century, St Paul's arranged to have its choristers live in the almonry, under the care of the official called the almoner, but this arrangement was borrowed from monastic houses and was not repeated in any of the other secular cathedrals. A different pattern was established at Lincoln, where in 1264 the bishop provided endowments, a choristers' house and regulations for the boys' life and instruction. This plan was followed at Salisbury and Wells, where a master of the choristers was appointed, serving under the supervision of one of the residentiary canons. Hereford and Exeter placed the boys in the care of the succentor. By the later fifteenth century the role of organists had become important; sometimes the organists also served as masters of the choristers, but sometimes the two positions remained separate. Schoolmasters were appointed as well, to teach in the song schools associated with the cathedrals.

Two further groups of men were included in the staff of the secular cathedrals. Both were involved in serving chantries, the endowments that provided masses and prayers for the repose of the souls of the dead. In cases where prominent persons had given large revenues to the cathedral there might be separate chantry chapels with a priest whose principal duty was the celebration of a daily mass at the chantry altar. Smaller bequests provided for obits, in which persons would be remembered on the anniversary of their death.

Many of the chantries traced their origins to the thirteenth and fourteenth centuries. For some reason fewer seem to have been founded during the fifteenth century, but the early Tudor period witnessed a rebirth of interest in these establishments, particularly notable since it occurred only a few years before they were dissolved and made illegal by Acts of Parliament. Most of the secular cathedrals have remains of early Tudor chantry chapels. Chantries were important to faithful lay people because they ensured that masses would be celebrated throughout all the early morning hours, when the laity would be able to attend. At Lincoln, for instance, there were continuous celebrations from 5 until 11 a.m. every day but Good Friday, 'so that the faithful will not lack services'.

The priests who served chantries were known by several names. Most often they were called cantarists or altarists. At Exeter chantry priests were termed annuellars (in Latin *annuellarii*), the word obviously being derived from the original practice of celebrating a mass for a person's soul on the 'annual' or anniversary of his or her death. It was possible for those vicars choral who were priests to hold chantry appointments; indeed, this provided an essential income for many of them. But other clergy were needed as well. At York in the 1540s, twenty-one vicars choral were serving nineteen chantries, but a further twenty-four chantries were staffed by a separate group of cantarists. At Lincoln fifteen vicars held chantry appointments, but there were thirty-five other cantarists. One of the vicars choral of Hereford resigned in 1517 to become a full-time chantry priest. Fourteen out of the twenty-one chantries at Hereford and nine of the fourteen at Chichester were served by vicars choral. The situation in the other cathedrals was similar. Cantarists had assistants, younger men who were not priests, to help them in the celebration of their offices, particularly by ensuring that supplies of bread, wine and wax were available as needed. These men were sometimes called clerks of the second form, or secondaries, since they sat in the second row of choir stalls, below the vicars choral and cantarists but above the choristers. Rather confusingly, they are referred to as altarists at Salisbury and Wells – the term more commonly designated the chantry priests themselves, not their helpers – and at Lincoln they are called the poor clerks. Many of the secondaries had been choristers; when their voices broke they remained at the cathedral with modified duties. Generally they were expected to attend the grammar school, and they received modest stipends for doing so. At Lincoln and Hereford they were specifically admonished to be faithful in attending school and not to wander about as they had done. They were supposed to come regularly to at least some of the cathedral services, and very likely they joined in singing them: at Lincoln they are sometimes called the poor clerks choral. Those who could not sing, perhaps while their voices were unstable, could be assigned the duty of blowing the organ, for this was one of the responsibilities of the poor clerks. Secondaries often had preference for appointment as vicars choral, and when they were old enough to be ordained priests they might be named cantarists.

Halls of residence were established for the cantarists at a number of cathedrals, generally later than the houses for the vicars choral. St Paul's, which not surprisingly had more chantries than any other cathedral, was the first to reserve chambers in the churchyard for its cantarists; these became known as Presteshouses or St Peter's College. A common hall of residence, called the Monterey College, was provided at Wells in 1399. St William's College at York was established in 1461 to provide a home for twenty-four chantry priests who were not vicars choral and could not live in the Bedern. Substantial parts of this building still survive. The fifteenth century also saw the building of a house for the cantarists in the close at Lichfield. Although there had been talk of providing a home for the annuellars of Exeter as early as the 1380s, a residence was not actually built until the late 1520s. It was called Peter's House or New Kalendarhay. Lincoln was the only cathedral to have a common hall and common endowments for its clerks of the second form. There were thus four separate houses or colleges at Lincoln, accommodating the choristers, poor clerks, junior vicars choral and senior (or priest) vicars.

All four of the Welsh cathedrals – Bangor, Llandaff, St Asaph and St David's – were secular in organization. They were much smaller and poorer than their English counterparts. The eight vicars choral of St David's were organized as a corporation with their own seal for making leases. There were also four choristers. About 1717 an antiquarian described the ruins of the vicars' houses and common hall, which he likened to those at Hereford. It must have been difficult for the other Welsh cathedrals to maintain the full round of services properly, for there were only four vicars choral at St Asaph and two at Bangor. All the Welsh cathedrals served also as parish churches.

The monastic cathedrals were quite different from their secular counterparts. For one thing, they housed much larger numbers of people. Seventy was often regarded a the ideal number of monks for a large Benedictine house, and the greater cathedral priories approximated that size. Like other Benedictine houses, they seem to have reached their peak shortly before the disaster of the Black Death in the fourteenth century but to have recovered substantially by 1500.

The monastic population of Durham is unusually well documented. Here the number of monks varied between eighty and a hundred during the years between 1274 and 1348. There were fifty-two deaths from the plague in 1349, leaving only thirty-nine monks in 1350, but the population soon returned to about seventy and remained there until 1539.

It is difficult to collect comparable figures for the other cathedral priories; records are usually incomplete and what survives has generally not been analyzed. One can set out figures for the early sixteenth century, but many of them represent the situation just before the Dissolution of the Monasteries, when trouble clearly lurked just around the corner and monastic populations declined rapidly. In 1540 Durham still had seventy monks and Canterbury fifty-eight. There were forty-five at Winchester and forty-one at Worcester. All the other houses were smaller; the numbers were in the twenties at Ely, Bath, Rochester and Carlisle, only in the teens at Norwich and Coventry.

Not all of these men actually lived in their mother house, for several of the priories had smaller communities or cells dependent on them. Durham led the way, with seven of these so-called handmaids as well as a college at Oxford. The largest and most flourishing of the Durham cells, Finchale, was only three miles north of Durham and by the late middle ages had come to be a place of rest and refreshment for monks from the cathedral. (The prior's manor of Bearpark – more correctly called Beaurepaire – was even closer to the cathedral and served a similar function.) Jarrow, Monkwearmouth, Holy Isle and Farne were much smaller and were evidently maintained primarily because of their historical associations with saints of earlier centuries; Farne sometimes housed a single hermit. In addition there were the priories of Lytham on the Lancashire coast and St Leonard's, near Stamford in Lincolnshire, as well as Durham College, Oxford. Of the seventy monks regarded as the normal complement at Durham, forty generally resided in the cathedral priory itself and thirty in the dependencies. Norwich had five such cells and other houses smaller numbers, of which the most important was probably Dover Priory, a daughter of Christ Church, Canterbury. Secular cathedrals sometimes controlled hospitals but otherwise had nothing comparable to these dependent houses.

Monastic cathedrals also differed from their secular counterparts so far as officials and finances were concerned. Monastic cathedrals had no deans, for the chief officer of the monastery ruled the cathedral as well. Despite their size, these houses were called priories, not abbeys. Normally large monasteries were presided over by an abbot, but in the case of the cathedrals the bishops theoretically filled the abbot's place. Since he was seldom a monk, and never resident within the monastic community, the second officer – the prior – assumed the actual rule of the house.

The priors of the great cathedral monasteries were rich, prominent men. For several centuries they had enjoyed their own separate establishments within the walls of the monastery. They had their own dining halls and kitchens, their own living quarters and servants. Generally they held country estates as well and might live there like country gentlemen. The duties of the prior were enormous: he was ultimately responsible for the buildings, the worship and the finance of the cathedral, and for the education, discipline and salvation of the monks under him. He was also drawn into local politics and national affairs, since he was accepted as the equal of the feudal lords of neighbouring lands. The prior of Coventry even had the right of being summoned to the House of Lords in Parliament, a curious tradition since the heads of larger and richer cathedral monasteries did not enjoy that privilege.

Large numbers of subordinate officers assisted the prior. There was always a subprior who could perform the prior's duties when he was absent. Large houses like Durham had a third prior who assumed responsibility when both of his superiors were away, while Canterbury and Winchester even had a fourth prior.

Officers with more specialized duties, placed in charge of specific aspects of monastic life, were called obedientiaries. Simply noting their titles and functions gives one an idea of the complexity of monastic organization. The sacristan or sacrist had custody of all relics, ornaments, vestments and service books; everything that bore on the order and decency of worship was entrusted to his care. The precentor was responsible for music, as in the secular cathedrals. An officer called the *circa* (or, in English, the 'roundabout') patrolled the cathedral cloisters and precincts, admonishing gossiping loiterers or collecting vestments and books that had been left behind. The anniversarian was in charge of obits and annual commemorations of benefactors; he also had to provide wine, beer or other rewards to those who took part in them. The clerk of the works (*custos operum*) was charged with maintenance and repair of the buildings.

The receiver, as his title implies, gathered in revenues from the monastic estates. The hordarian had charge of the 'hoard' of food for the monastic kitchens, while the cellarer (one of the most important officers) actually supplied the monks with food and drink, sometimes assisted by a kitchener (*coquinarius*). The refectorarian or refectorer maintained the dining hall or refectory in decent order. Clothing, shoes and bedding were provided for the monks by the chamberlain. An infirmarer or infirmarian ran the infirmary, where the sick could be nursed, the aged cared for as they awaited death, and the healthy permitted to enjoy special food and a respite from their normal duties as they underwent periodic bleedings. There might be a gardener, a fruiterer, a porter or doorkeeper, a garnerer (in charge of the granary for wheat), a bartoner (responsible for the priory's home farm) and a pittancer (to distribute small gifts and treats on feast days). The almoner, an important officer found everywhere, was generally charged with operating a school for poor boys as well as the distribution of relief.

Finally, the guest master or hosteller provided shelter and hospitality for travelers, for those who needed to transact business with the monastery and for persons who came to attend special services – the consecration of a new bishop, for instance, or an occasional royal wedding or aristocratic funeral. Most of the obedientiaries had assistants, and several had clearly designated subordinates, like the subsacrist or the succentor.

In all, as many as twenty-five men might hold office as obedientiaries. The more important ones came to have separate establishments, like the prior's but less elaborate. At Canterbury we know that the subprior, the sacrist, the cellarer, the infirmarian and the almoner all had private households by the end of the fourteenth century, with servants, cooks and chaplains. Their responsibilities no doubt required that they be free to transact business and to deal with members of the outside world in ways that were forbidden to ordinary cloistered monks, but some loss in spirituality must have gone along with absence from the full round of choir services, and some loss of community inevitably followed departure from the dormitory and refectory.

Numerous lay persons, too, lived within the monastic cathedral precincts. It has been estimated that there were twice as many servants as monks at Canterbury. There were boys being educated in the monastic schools. There were also the so-called corrodians, generally older men who were maintained for life upon nomination by the king, the prior or occasionally the pope. They have been likened to retired civil servants whose stories of court life and adventure came as a welcome relief from the monotony of the monastic routine.

A vivid picture of the life of a prior, if not of an entire cathedral monastery, can be found in the journal maintained for William More of Worcester between 1518 and 1536.[2] More, or Peers as he was originally named, was probably born in the hamlet called le More near Tenbury in Worcestershire. His parents, for whom he provided gifts and care after his advancement, were of middling social status. William took vows at sixteen, served as kitchener while still a young man, was named subprior in the opening years of the sixteenth century, and survived to see his whole way of life threatened by the impending Reformation. The income from fifteen manors (one quarter of the revenue of the entire priory) was assigned to More as prior. He lived most of the year as a country gentleman on his estates at Battenhall, Crowle and Grimley, all within a five-mile ride of the cathedral. More did come to Worcester for the great liturgical festivals of Christmas, Easter and Whitsunday, and he usually spent about a month each year in London, mending political fences and purchasing luxury items not available in the provinces.

More's journal describes some of these in tantalizing detail. He patronized the finest craftsmen in the country, including the vestment maker William Dysse and the goldsmith John Cranks. The latter made him not only a great chalice 'selver and gylt with many stones in ye futt' and a crosier or 'croystaff' but also a lavish mitre embellished with embroidery, pearls and dozens of jewels, costing in all nearly £50. Dysse was responsible for 'a sewte of vestaments of clothe of Golde' purchased in 1521 for £90; this included two copes, a chasuble, two tunicles, albs, stoles and maniples. He probably provided the cope of blue velvet with ostrich feathers mentioned in an inventory of More's household stuff as well.

Other disbursements recorded in Prior More's journal are equally fascinating. The young Princess Mary Tudor visited him at Worcester and at his manor of Battenhall for long periods in 1525 and 1526, possibly attracted to the cathedral because her uncle, Prince Arthur, was entombed there; she gave More a half-noble in gold (3s. 4d.) for singing mass at the high altar and he gave her servants £7 13s. 4d. when they departed. Singers, jugglers, tumblers, players and minstrels were also rewarded, as was the messenger who brought news of Anne Boleyn's coronation in 1533. The bailiffs and citizens of Worcester were treated to wine after evensong on Christmas Day 1524; on New Year's Day 1525 More received gifts himself, including a peacock from the almoner. When a monk was granted his divinity degree at Oxford he was sent a present of 40s., and later £4 was paid for his expenses in London, while another monk, William Wolverley, was given 3s. 4d. for 'pricking' (writing out: presumably composing) an *Exultavit* in five parts.

More also spent considerable sums on books, generally acquired during his visits to London. In his earlier years these were mainly the works of the church fathers (Jerome, Gregory and Ambrose) or literary and historical writers (Bede, Cyprian, Seneca and Philo). In 1527 More bought Henry VIII's conservative defence of the seven sacraments, *Assertio septem sacramentorum*. Once the Reformation Parliament began its sessions More invested in several volumes of statutes and records of General Councils. He also bought a 'pointed' mass book (a missal with chant settings), and he paid a maker of illuminated manuscripts, Arthur of Evesham, for 'lymyng and flourusshyng of grete letters in my grayle', another service manual. More acquired at least thirty printed volumes, probably intended less for his own use than for the cathedral library, which was already rich in manuscripts.

Cathedrals organized as Benedictine monasteries maintained the full round of monastic offices that had been sung in houses of the Black Monks since the time of Lanfranc. In organization these differed little from the services celebrated in the secular cathedrals – the mass and eight daily offices.

Monastic cathedrals generally had three great masses each day: the morning mass, the chapter mass and the mass honouring the Blessed Virgin Mary, sung in the Lady chapel with more elaborate music than was thought appropriate for other monastic liturgies. Services sung by the Augustinian canons at Carlisle were similar. Chantry masses and obits were celebrated as well.

Shrines and services held at their altars were even more important in the monastic cathedrals than in their secular counterparts. In part this is true simply because the greatest shrines, especially those at Canterbury and Durham, happened to be in cathedral priories. It is probable, too, that the larger population of monks made services at monastic shrines more impressive than those celebrated by smaller numbers of canons in secular cathedrals. The best description of a monastic shrine comes from the so-called *Rites of Durham*. This volume was not written until 1593, but its author was obviously present at the cathedral in the 1530s, perhaps attending a monastic school if not himself a monk, and his picture may be trusted as one drawn by an original observer. His tone makes it clear that he loved the beauty of Durham's ancient shrines and that he deplored the reforms and spoliation of later years.[3]

Some of the most moving services at Durham took place at the shrine of St Cuthbert, erected between the choir and the chapel of the Nine Altars. The author of the *Rites* describes this in some detail.

> His sacred shrine was exalted with most curious workmanship of fine and costly green marble all limned and gilded with gold, having four seats or places convenient under the shrine for the pilgrims or lame men sitting on their knees to lean and rest on, in time of their devout offerings and fervent prayers to God and holy St Cuthbert, for his miraculous relief and succour which being never wanting made the shrine to be so richly invested, that it was estimated to be one of the most sumptuous monuments in all England, so great were the offerings and jewels that were bestowed upon it, and no less the miracles that were done by it, even in these latter days.

Pilgrims visiting St Cuthbert's shrine, or those merely travelling in the north, could be accommodated in the guest hall, 'a famous house of hospitality' where no one was turned away.

Beautiful as St Cuthbert's shrine must have been, it was far less imposing than Thomas Becket's tomb at Canterbury. Here a golden reliquary was concealed beneath a wooden cover, which was itself hidden under an elaborate canopy. As at Durham there were ropes and a pulley, so that the shrine could be uncovered once or twice a day for viewing by pilgrims. Henry VIII, Catherine of Aragon and Charles V paid homage at the shrine during Charles's first visit to England in 1520. The emperor's reaction is not recorded, but we do have the comments of the Venetian ambassador, who wrote the doge about 1500 that 'the magnificence of the tomb of St Thomas the martyr surpasses all belief. This, notwithstanding its great size, is entirely covered over with plates of pure gold, but the gold is scarcely visible from the variety of precious stones with which it is studded, such as sapphires, diamonds, rubies, balas-rubies and emeralds, and on every side that the eye turns, something more beautiful than the other appears'. It was said that one of the rubies was a gift of the king of France, and that it had miraculously leaped from Louis XII's finger to its place on the shrine.

Other cathedrals had their own shrines, not of course as famous as that which drew pilgrims to Canterbury but regional sites of veneration, prayer and oblation. St Swithun's shrine at Winchester, St Wulftstan's at Worcester and St Ætheldreda's at Ely were among the best known. There was also the peculiar case of St William, a baker from Perth, said to be so pious that he attended mass daily and so charitable that he gave every tenth loaf to the poor. He resolved to visit the Holy Land and set out in 1201, accompanied by a young companion whom he had adopted as a foundling. After he had spent the night at the priory of Rochester, William was found dead by the roadside, presumably murdered by his foster son. His body was brought back to the cathedral for burial, miracles began to occur at his tomb, and soon the poor priory had its own martyr's shrine and offerings to swell its coffers. The gifts of pious pilgrims seem to have reached their peak in the fourteenth century. Canterbury took in more than £800 in 1350 and as much as £644 in 1420. But this was exceptional – 1420 was a year of jubilee attended with a general pardon. In 1455 offerings amounted to only £25, and in 1532 to a mere £13. Inadequate evidence suggests that belief in miracles had declined by the early Tudor period, although pilgrimages to some shrines remained popular. Those who still made trips to see cathedral treasures may have resembled modern tourists more than medieval suppliants.

All the monastic cathedrals maintained schools. These were of three sorts. Internal schools for young monks must have existed since the beginning of the houses; by the later middle ages these had become grammar schools, which could fit the brightest young men for study at the universities and their less academically inclined brethren for service within the monastery. Almonry schools had been founded, many in the early fourteenth century, to provide an elementary education for younger boys, generally orphans or other poor children who were entrusted to the case of the monks. Almonry boys were expected to assist the monks at their private masses, much like the secondaries or poor clerks who served the chantry priests in the secular cathedrals. Their presence was so essential that it was occasionally necessary to reduce the number of private masses for want of boys to serve. Many of the almonry boys must have gone on to become monks themselves, although surviving documentation is meagre.

The third type of school, the song school, was for choristers and paralleled the choristers' houses in the secular cathedrals. No doubt these boys were taught some Latin – one hopes that they understood the meaning of the liturgical texts they had to sing – but their training was chiefly musical, and it must have been quite advanced, since the elaborate polyphonic masses of the late fifteenth century, such as those by Robert Fairfax and John Taverner, are demanding works. We know that the master of the song school at Durham was required to teach the boys 'pleynsange, priknot, faburden, dischaunte et countre'. Here six children were instructed in a building adjacent to the chapel of the nine altars, 'fynely bourded within' for warmth; they had their meals with the children of the almonry school, while their master dined in the prior's hall. Eight boys who were taught music by one Edward Pyngbrygge and his assistant, Thomas Goodman, are recorded at Winchester in 1482. It is said that these choristers, together with boys from Hyde Abbey, presented a religious drama called 'Christ's Descent into Hell' for the entertainment of Henry VII when he visited Winchester for Prince Arthur's baptism in 1486. Other cathedrals had comparable establishments.

Not all young monks, of course, aspired to the priesthood, and not all priests could boast a university education. But the monastic cathedrals did send a significant number of students to Oxford and Cambridge during the later middle ages. We read of monks from Durham and Worcester at Oxford as early as 1290 and of three men from Canterbury studying there in 1331. For a time these students were attached to what came to be called Gloucester College, which accepted young men from all of the Benedictine houses. In 1363, however, Canterbury College, Oxford, was founded, with a warden and fellows who were monks of Christ Church, Canterbury, and varying numbers of 'sojourners', including some secular persons as well as monks. Several of the monastic cathedrals sent scholars to Canterbury College, with stipends from the monastery and the expectation that these more highly educated monks would return to provide intellectual and administrative leadership within their communities. At the time of the Dissolution the site of Canterbury College was absorbed into Christ Church – an appropriate carrying over of the name of the priory – and the connexion is still reflected in Canterbury Quad there.

The most important monastic establishment at Oxford, however, was Durham College. Originally small and loosely organized, this had been turned into a full-fledged college on the site still occupied by its successor, Trinity College, in 1381. In addition to a legacy from Bishop Hatfield,

Durham College enjoyed the revenues from four churches and had, from the fifteenth century, a stable annual income of about £175. Its grounds were large, including a grove of three thousand trees, and its buildings included a chapel, residential quarters, and an exceptionally attractive library, furnished with a good collection of books. Most students read philosophy or theology, not canon law, and only a few, mainly those who remained at the college as fellows, proceeded to the doctorate. Throughout the fifteenth century there were usually about twenty monks of Durham who had experience at Oxford. Fourteen members of the community in 1485 had attended the university; three held bachelors' degrees in theology and one had received the doctorate. In the early sixteenth century these numbers rose: by 1520 twenty-four monks had been to Oxford, of whom four had been granted bachelors' degrees and four doctorates. It seems appropriate to stress the importance that the monks of Durham attached to university education in general and to the holding of a degree in particular; it was the graduates who were called to positions of leadership within the monastery, and they were also in demand at Convocation and at Benedictine gatherings. In all, as many as 350 monks and friars are known to have studied at Oxford in the thirty years before the Dissolution.

The other priories seem to have been less committed to higher education than Durham and Canterbury. Fewer students went to Cambridge than to Oxford, and there was no Cambridge college comparable to Durham or Canterbury. Ely, it is true, had established a hostel at Cambridge under Prior Crauden (d. 1341). Originally located on the site of what is now Trinity Hall, it housed two students from Ely and possibly a few monks from other Benedictine houses. But the monastic cathedrals in eastern England, which would normally send young men to Cambridge rather than Oxford, seem in fact to have sent few monks anywhere. Norwich had at one time been distinguished for theological study, but this enthusiasm had vanished by 1492, when Bishop Goldwell complained that the cathedral had failed to support students at the university. He ordered that two were to go immediately – rather surprisingly, they were sent to Gloucester College, Oxford, rather than to Cambridge. In 1538 there were two students at Cambridge, each receiving a yearly allowance of 26s. 8d.

The libraries of the cathedral priories generally surpassed those of the secular cathedrals.[4] Because of the Dissolution, one might have supposed that fewer of the books from the monastic libraries would remain in place. In fact the reverse is true: the largest collection of medieval books and manuscripts to be found in any English cathedral is at Durham, where over three hundred medieval works survive. In addition, more than two hundred manuscripts and printed books from the monastic library at Durham have found their way into other collections; curiously enough, these appear to have been alienated in the seventeenth century rather than in the 1540s. It is interesting to note that many of the books at Durham were given by individual monks, generally at their death, rather than purchased for the library directly. We know of twenty-three monks who donated books during the years between 1485 and 1540; eight of these men left more than a single volume. Most of the donors had studied at Oxford and had probably acquired their books there.

The second largest holdings – more than one hundred fifty volumes – are to be found at Worcester. A few of these books are among those purchased by Prior More. Only twenty-one books from the library of Christ Church are still at Canterbury, but nearly three hundred more survive, scattered among thirty modern libraries. We know that the monastic library at Canterbury held nearly two thousand volumes, and that there were nearly three hundred more at Canterbury College; surviving catalogues and lists of books to be repaired enable us to know the titles of most of the volumes. The other cathedral libraries were probably smaller, but they too must have held impressive collections of theological, literary and historical manuscripts and early printed books.

The existence of these libraries, which were rivalled only by the combined collections of the colleges at Oxford and Cambridge, points up the important role played by cathedrals as homes of learning. It may be true that the books were not actually used very much in the later middle ages: library resources, like fields, sometimes lie fallow. Nevertheless they were there, and a handful of scholars able to interpret them was also present in the cathedrals. Especially in parts of England distant from London, Oxford, and Cambridge, the cathedrals were significant centres of learning. It is unsafe to accept the conventional view that the monks of Durham lived in an intellectual backwater.

What, generally, was the condition of the cathedrals on the eve of the Reformation? The answer is not easy, and the verdict must be mixed. The secular cathedrals faced many problems. Some of them simply reflected human frailty and lack of devotion. Chapter records charge the vicars choral with incontinence, quarrelling, living outside their assigned quarters and absence from services with what may seem shocking frequency. Secondaries were found wandering in the streets rather than attending the grammar schools; chantry priests neglected their duties; canons were non-resident; services were sometimes perfunctory and slipshod; buildings were occasionally allowed to decay. On the other hand, there are numerous instances of cathedrals that were being adorned and enriched even as Henry VIII was severing

England's ties with the papacy – a good example is Hereford, where the magnificent north porch, including a Lady chapel above the covered entrance, was added by Bishop Booth – and of chantries that were founded only months before an Act of Parliament ordered their suppression. The famous Italian humanist Polydore Vergil included a favourable account of the cathedrals in his *Anglica Historia*. At Wells, he wrote, 'there flourished a famous college of priests, men of honest behaviour and well learned, wherefore I account it no small worship that I myself, fourteen years archdeacon of Wells, was elected one of that college'. Travellers came, even from abroad, to marvel at the size and beauty of the great buildings, and pilgrims thronged to their shrines, laden with offerings and intercessions.

A judgment about the state of the monastic cathedrals must also be subtly drawn; an unbiased observer will see varying shades of grey rather than pure black and white. It is easy enough to agree with the reformers that some of the old rites were superstitious, and many will share Erasmus's distaste for dubious relics and over-rich shrines. We should be more sceptical of modern critiques which exaggerate the extent of conflict between monks and townspeople, and we should exercise caution in accepting the view that contrasts the genuine spirituality of monks in the high middle ages with the worldliness of their successors in the fifteen and early sixteenth centuries. The evidence for such inward matters is never adequate, and most of the historians of monasticism have themselves been medievalists who were more likely to see good in their own favourite centuries than in other periods.

Whatever can be said against the rites and shrines of the cathedrals in pre-Reformation England should be balanced by an acknowledgment that they brought warmth, colour and drama into the otherwise cold and drab lives of many people.

9

The Reformation

The earliest stages of the Reformation affected the cathedrals relatively little. Some of the clergy may have read the writings of Martin Luther or the biblical translations of William Tyndale, which were denounced as heretical and prohibited in England as early as 1528. A few may have been included among the heretics, like those within the diocese of Lincoln ('no small number', according to Henry VIII) whom Bishop Longland was ordered to suppress. But the surviving records of the cathedrals themselves contain no trace of the coming religious upheaval.[1]

As is well known, the issue that precipitated the crisis in relations between church and state was Henry VIII's wish to divorce his first wife, Catherine of Aragon, a daughter of Ferdinand and Isabella, the rulers of Spain. Henry was intent on ensuring the continuity of the Tudor dynasty, and he did not believe that the English people would accept Catherine's only surviving child, a daughter named Mary, as their ruler. By 1527 there was no likelihood that Catherine would bear further children, so if Henry were to father a son it would have to be by another wife. Henry came to believe that his union with Catherine was invalid, since it contradicted a biblical prohibition of marriage to a brother's widow – Catherine had earlier been married to Prince Arthur, Henry's elder brother, who had died in 1502. Cardinal Thomas Wolsey, the king's chief minister, sought a papal annulment in 1527, but the pope, Clement VII, was not able to grant this because the Emperor Charles V supported his aunt Catherine in opposing it, and as it happened Spanish forces had just sacked the city of Rome. After several years of fruitless negotiation, Henry finally took affairs into his own hands. In 1529, following the failure of a divorce trial at Blackfriars in London, the king dismissed Wolsey and summoned the famous Reformation Parliament into session.

Parliament's initial meetings had little direct impact on the cathedrals.[2] The cathedral clergy were affected by the limitation of pluralism and non-residency demanded by the Commons in 1529. Like other clerics, they were charged in 1531 with violating the Statute of Praemunire, enacted in the fourteenth century to limit papal jurisdiction during the years of the Babylonian captivity of the pope, and they were forced to pay large sums of money for

their pardon. They were included in the Supplication against the Ordinar-
ies, which was discussed by Parliament and Convocation in 1532, and they
were affected by the Submission of the Clergy, in which the whole English
church lost its power to make canon law without reference to the monarch.
The long-range implications of these Acts were enormous, for through them
the English clergy were stripped of their independence and their ability to
resist changes ordered by the king. At the time, however, they were little felt
and perhaps little understood.

In 1533 Henry allowed his new minister, Thomas Cromwell, to take drastic action. By this time William Warham, the archbishop of Canterbury who
had opposed the divorce, had died and been replaced by Thomas Cranmer,
a Cambridge theologian who had made it clear that he would accommodate
the ruler. In January 1533 the king, confident in his own mind that his union
with Catherine was invalid, secretly married Anne Boleyn. (Their daughter,
Elizabeth, was born in September.) Cromwell now drafted legislation that
not only permitted the English church to grant the divorce without reference to Rome but also totally extinguished papal jurisdiction in England.
The resulting Act in Restraint of Appeals passed with little debate in the
spring of 1533. The most important statute in the entire constitutional history of the church within England, it marks the beginning of the English
Reformation.

Although the cathedrals were not singled out or sent individual direc-
tives, they were included in the royal proclamation that made it illegal to
pray for Catherine of Aragon as queen or give her any title other than that
of princess dowager, to which she was entitled as Arthur's widow. New
Praemunire charges, with their accompanying confiscation of all property,
could be brought against those who refused to comply or denied the style
of queen to Anne. The Act of Supremacy passed in 1534 carried with it an
oath, to be sworn by all clergy, acknowledging royal supremacy over the
church and renouncing the jurisdiction of the papacy. We know that
the clergy of Worcester were notified of the Acts of Supremacy and Succession; presumably similar statements were sent to the other cathedrals.
The submission of the dean and chapter of St Paul's is duly recorded in a
document signed by the minor canons, vicars choral, and chantry priests
as well as the canons. At Chichester the cathedral clergy renounced the
pope and affirmed their support of Supremacy and Queen Anne in July
1535. A circular letter addressed to all sheriffs and justices of the peace in
the same year urged these secular officials to see that the bishops enforced
the king's order that prayers invoking the name of the pope cease and that
all references to him be erased from service books. The dean and chapter
of Wells even asked the king to give them new statutes in 1536. Evidently

they believed their existing constitution was invalidated by the break with Rome. The government does not seem to have agreed, for their request was ignored.

Cathedral finance was affected by parliamentary action of 1534 ordering that clerical annates (first fruits and tenths) be paid to the king rather than the pope. This annual tax was supposed to equal the entire first year's profits from church offices and a tenth of the income received subsequently. A royal order of 1535 commanded all churches to reveal the true value of their possessions to the king's commissioners, who then compiled the so-called *Valor Ecclesiasticus* to form the basis for assessment and collection. In fact the clergy paid considerably larger sums to the king than they had previously remitted to the pope, for papal collections had been based on low, outdated valuations. Few laymen seem to have regretted the beginning of the government's attack on the wealth of the church; when there were rumours of even more drastic action against the clergy, an English observer wrote to Lord Lisle, the king's deputy in Calais, that 'many be glad and fewe bemone them'.

The first actual attack on the cathedrals themselves was motivated by theological and political considerations as well as the government's greed. This was the campaign against shrines and images. Both sceptical humanists and early Protestant reformers had denounced belief in shrines and miracles. In 1536 they were joined by Thomas Cromwell, whose injunctions ordered the clergy not to 'extol any images, relics, or miracles, ... nor allure the people to the pilgrimage of any saint'. His injunctions of 1538 went further; a section condemning 'feigned images ... abused with pilgrimages or offerings' ordered that such objects of idolatry be taken down without delay. No candles or lights might be set before images or pictures, although some images might be allowed to remain if the people were instructed that they 'serve for no purpose but as to be books of unlearned men' and reminders of the lives of the saints. Should clergy have 'heretofore declared to [their] parishioners anything to the extolling or setting forth of pilgrimages, feigned relics, or images or any such superstition', they shall 'now openly recant and reprove the same', showing them to be abuses that had crept into the church through the 'avarice of such as felt profit by the same'.

This attack on images was paralleled by a denunciation of Thomas Becket. A ludicrous process began in April 1538, when a citation ordering Becket to appear before the king's council was read at his tomb. As prescribed by law, thirty days were allowed to elapse, but the 'holy blissful martyr' failed to materialize at the judicial proceedings and sentence was duly pronounced against him. During his life, it was said, he had disturbed the realm, and his own crimes were the cause of his death. He was therefore declared to be no martyr. His bones were to be taken up and burned publicly, and the treasures of his shrine confiscated by the king. Continuing the same line, a proclamation of November 1538 insisted that Becket was a stubborn clerk who had stuck against 'the king's highness' most noble progenitor, King Henry II'. His death, which resulted from a scuffle, was 'untruly called martyrdom; and further his canonization was made only by the bishop of Rome because he had been a champion to maintain his usurped authority'. Since all this was now acknowledged, Becket should no longer be reckoned a saint, and his images and pictures were to be torn down throughout the realm. His name was to be erased from all service books and his feast day (29 December) no longer celebrated. Before the end of the year the great shrine at Canterbury had been demolished. It produced nearly three hundredweight of gold, the same amount of silver, almost twice as much silver gilt, and innumerable precious stones. This spoil filled two great chests, so heavy that six or seven strong men could hardly carry one of them out of the church.

Other shrines soon met the same fate, even though they were dedicated to saints who could not be charged with having opposed the monarchy. Thomas Wriothesley, who with Richard Pollard had supervised the spoliation at Canterbury, reported that Bishop Gardiner approved of the destruction of Becket's tomb and would welcome similar action at the shrine of St Swithun in his own cathedral at Winchester. In fact the royal agents were already on their way; St Swithun's shrine was demolished at 3 a.m. on Saturday, 21 September 1538. Pollard and Wriothesley complained that there was 'no gold, nor ring, nor true stone in it, but all great counterfeits', but they exaggerated. The silver alone amounted to 2000 marks (£1333), and there were also several great chalices and crosses, one studded with emeralds. The commissioners seem to have gone beyond their instructions, for they took down part of the high altar as well as the shrine; its lower stage was covered with gold plates garnished with stones, while the upper section was ornamented with embroidery incorporating numerous pearls. The mayor, eight or nine of his brethren and the bishop's chancellor are said to have assisted in this work and praised the king for it.

On 14 December the king issued a commission to Sir William Goring and-William Ernley ordering them to demolish the shrine of St Richard at Chichester and destroy any other idolatrous images in the cathedral. They did their work on the twentieth, carting off a ship's coffer filled with fifty-five images of silver and gilt, St Richard's coffin full of fifty-seven more pieces of gold and silver, three chests of broken silver, thirty-one rings, fifty-one jewels and other treasures, all destined for the Tower.

John Whitgift, archbishop of Canterbury, 1577–83.

Comparable information about the despoiling of other cathedrals in 1538 does not exist. If there were more royal commissions, they do not survive, and local documents, such as the act books of the dean and chapter, seldom mention such things. They are more likely to record routine business, such as the leasing of lands, than truly momentous matters. Tangential evidence is tantalizing but imprecise. In London, for instance, Sir Richard Gresham heard of the campaign against images from Dr Robert Barnes, a friend of Cromwell's whose views were much influenced by Luther. Since Gresham was already dining with Bishop Sampson of Chichester, he took the cleric with him; they notified the dean of St Paul's, and the three of them together removed the images that same night (23 August). Just what they removed, we cannot tell. Most likely they concentrated on a famous statue of St Wilgefort, popularly called St Uncumber because she could dispose of unwanted husbands if wives offered prayers and, according to one version of the tradition, oats at her shrine. If St Erkenwald's shrine was not sacked then, it must have gone soon thereafter; we know that an image of the saint, probably from his shrine, was delivered to the master of the king's jewels in October.

The image of Our Lady of Worcester, according to the chronicler Edward Hall, disappeared in September, along with other idolatrous statues in monasteries that were not cathedrals. Hugh Latimer, the bishop of Worcester, praised this removal in a letter to Cromwell and revealed his reforming spirit when he attributed the idleness of local people to excessive veneration of the Virgin: 'Now that she is gone, they be turned to laboriousness, and so from ladyness to godliness'. Were the shrines of St Oswald and St Wulfstan sacked at the same time, or were they allowed to remain until the monastery was dissolved two years later? We cannot be sure. An undated list of articles removed from Hereford Cathedral probably belongs in 1538; it includes chalices, censers, a pax, a holy water stoup and an intriguing 'image of the Trinity, of gold with a diadem on his head'. It may have been at this time that a sixteenth-century processional cross, several small crucifixes, fragments of alabaster carvings and remnants of an elaborate fourteenth-century shrine were hidden in the groined vault of the central tower. These were discovered by the dean during a survey of the fabric in 1841.

It was probably in 1538 that the shrine of St Chad at Lichfield was demolished. According to an earlier sacrist's roll, the relics here included bits of Golgotha, Calvary and the rock on which Jesus wept over Jerusalem, as well as part of the bones of the eleven thousand virgins. Some of these objects were surreptitiously carried away by a conservative canon, Arthur Dudley; eventually they found their way to St Chad's Roman Catholic cathedral in Birmingham.

Documentation about the destruction of St Cuthbert's shrine at Durham is unsatisfactory. It may have taken place late in 1537, when Thomas Legh is known to have been demolishing shrines at Selby and William Blythman, another commissioner, was doing the same at York, or it may have been delayed until December 1539, when Legh and other officials came to Durham to receive the surrender of the cathedral priory. When the visitors opened the shrine they expected to find dust and bones, but instead they saw the saint 'lyinge hole uncorrupt with his vestmentes upon him as he was accustomed to say mess withall'. The bystanders could not believe their eyes; they placed the body in an inner chamber until the king's pleasure could be known. Eventually it was buried below ground where the shrine had stood. Bede's shrine in the galilee was defaced at the same time, and his body, too, was reinterred at the site of the shrine. Gold weighing 344 ounces and 5081 ounces of silver were confiscated from Ely in 1539. Much if not all of this must have come from Ætheldreda's shrine.

It was not until 1540 that a royal commission was issued for Lincoln. Here the king's agents were to demolish St Hugh's shrine, sending the jewels to the Tower, and take down other monuments of superstition. More than 2620 ounces of gold and 4280 ounces of silver from Lincoln, together with numerous pearls and precious stones, were in the king's jewel house by June 1540, as were Becket's staff from Canterbury and miscellaneous items from churches and cathedrals in the west country. There is a persistent story that Henry Litherland, the treasurer of Lincoln Cathedral, threw down his keys and resigned his office when the commissioners carried off his precious articles, saying angrily, 'Now that the treasure is seized, the duties of treasurer have come to an end'. This cannot be literally true, for Litherland had been executed in August 1538 on charges that he was involved in the Pilgrimage of Grace and had preached favouring the pope, the veneration of the Virgin Mary and the continued use of images. The dean and chapter of Lincoln, however, did not replace Litherland; ever since his death the cathedral has been without a treasurer, the remaining duties of that office being performed by the sacrist.

At Norwich the dean and chapter paid a mason named Robert Grene for his work in taking down St William's tomb. More positively, they found room to install eleven altars that had been removed from the dissolved church of the Black Friars. The destruction of St William's shrine at York was supervised by Richard Layton, the notorious commissioner for the suppression of the monasteries, who was named dean of the Minster in 1539. At Exeter the issue of images became enmeshed in a dispute between the chapter and the dean, the irascible reformer Simon Heynes, who had taken office in 1537 upon the resignation of Reginald Pole. An initial agreement about the dean's powers was settled by compromise, but the feud erupted again in September 1540, when ten of the canons framed an indictment against Heynes. He was charged with destroying beautiful images of saints that for centuries had ornamented the church and had called the faithful to devotion. He had also lacerated the choir books and had extinguished the sanctuary lamp, a great scandal because it had burned without ceasing for two hundred years. Heynes departed from the cathedral in December 1541 and seldom resided thereafter, but his absence did not prevent his continued quarrelling with the chapter, which lasted until his ouster under Queen Mary in 1554.

One of the bitter ironies of this period is that Henry VIII himself appears to have admired some of the confiscated images, since he ordered a payment of £28 to his goldsmith, named Barnes, for 'newe trymyng and garnishing' a dozen of them, including one of the Father of Heaven. Evidently things that were thought to inspire idolatry in ordinary people were acceptable when viewed by the sophisticated eyes of the king and his courtiers.

It is particularly unfortunate that we do not know the exact circumstances in which the great reredoses at Winchester and Durham lost their statues. The beautiful Perpendicular Gothic screen behind the high altar at Winchester was nearly new, for it had been erected by Bishop Fox shortly before his death in 1528; it contained dozens of statues of saints. The Neville screen at Durham was earlier, a gift of Lord Neville about 1380. Before the Reformation it supported 107 statues, some surrounding the high altar, facing the choir, and some facing east toward St Cuthbert's shrine, which was behind the altar. All these were richly painted and gilded; none survive, and the screen has held empty niches ever since the sixteenth century, probably since 1538. York Minster was more fortunate. Here the stone screen divides the nave and choir rather than standing behind the high altar. Built between 1475 and 1500, and adorned with fifteen statues, it was allowed to remain, presumably because these depicted the kings of England from William the Conqueror to Henry VI rather than saints. We know that the reredos at Lichfield, which may have survived intact because it did not contain images, was regilded in 1543, and that the 'mappe' of the Crucifixion that hung in the middle of the high altar at Chichester was repainted in the same year.

For some of the secular cathedrals, the destruction of the shrines and images was the heaviest blow of Henry VIII's reign. For the monastic cathedrals, however, it was of far less importance than the dissolution of the religious houses. There were precedents, both within England and on the Continent, for the closure of religious houses and the assignment of their resources to other uses. At home, the most notable instances were Bishop Alcock's conversion of St Radegund's nunnery at Cambridge into Jesus College at the end of the fifteenth century; and Cardinal Wolsey's later suppression of St Frideswide's at Oxford and some twenty further monasteries for the endowment of his new colleges at Oxford and Ipswich. On the Continent, parallel events that seem to be less well known to English historians include the dissolution of religious houses in Lutheran parts of Germany and Scandinavia (including the convent of Wittenberg itself), beginning in the 1520s. Acting on this base, and armed with a finely tuned sense of public opinion and political opportunism, Thomas Cromwell conceived his plans for a far more thorough attack. While the evidence is inconclusive, it seems probable that he had decided as early as the beginning of 1535 to seek the dissolution of all religious houses – the extinction of monasticism in England.

It was no doubt in order to justify such drastic action that Cromwell sent commissioners – Richard Layton, Thomas Legh, John ap Rice and John Tregonwell – to visit the religious houses, compiling descriptions of their condition and lists of any failings that might exist. Unfortunately for us, the commissioners did not examine all of the monastic cathedrals, and their comments on those priories they did visit are not especially revealing. At Carlisle, for instance, they found seven monks guilty of sodomy and three, including the prior, incontinent. (Sexual lapses take up a large part of the commissioners' *comperta*, or findings, and the validity of their charges has been questioned for centuries.) Carlisle also had some dubious relics: a fragment of the True Cross, the sword with which Thomas Becket was martyred, and the girdle of St Bride. At York the visitors complained only of pilgrimages to St William's shrine, at Lichfield of the veneration of St Chad. Further sexual irregularities were noted at Norwich.

During the weeks before the Reformation Parliament met for its final session in February 1536, Cromwell and his helpers were busy drafting an Act for the Dissolution of the Monasteries. By this time he had decided on a gradual approach to the suppression, probably in the conviction that this would arouse less opposition than immediate closure of all the houses. There was talk of shutting down only those monasteries and nunneries housing fewer than twelve persons, but the statute as finally framed used a financial criterion, ordering the suppression of all houses with annual incomes of £200 or less. Monks and nuns from such small houses were allowed to transfer to other, larger institutions that would survive, or, if they preferred, to renounce their vows and receive pensions from the government. The property of the dissolved houses was turned over to the king, to be managed by a new financial bureau, the Court of Augmentations.

Since all the monastic cathedrals had revenues substantially greater than

£200, they were not affected by the first Dissolution statute. They were soon caught up, however, in the second stage of Cromwell's campaign, which involved the negotiated surrender of the larger houses. Within the next several years two of the monastic cathedrals were dissolved altogether, the remaining eight transformed into secular institutions, and six new cathedrals founded in order to utilize some of the greatest of the monastic buildings.

The first monastic cathedral to be converted into a secular cathedral, or (as they were called) a cathedral of the New Foundation, was Norwich. Surviving records do not tell exactly why it received special treatment, but there is reason to think that it was the least well run of the cathedral priories, and we know that Bishop Repps (or Rugg), originally a monk himself, was a timeserver who acceded to every demand of the government, finally having to resign his see in 1549 because he had given away too much and was no longer able to manage diocesan finance. A royal charter dated 2 May 1538 converted Norwich into a secular cathedral. The last prior, William Castleton, became the first dean; five monks were named prebendaries, with a sixth stall assigned to John Salisbury, the suffragan bishop of Thetford. Sixteen more monks were named canons. This was a peculiar arrangement, for the terms prebendary and canon were ordinarily used interchangeably, and these men were not referred to as minor canons. When these canons died they were not replaced, and it seems likely that the category of canon as used here was created for temporary use as a way of giving former monks a life office and stipend. The dean and chapter were authorized to make their own statutes (they did not get around to doing so until the seventeenth century) and were allowed to allocate revenues for the support of the clergy and singers as they saw fit.

The government's hand fell next on the cathedral priories at Coventry and Bath. These were special cases, for both of them were co-cathedrals for bishops who enjoyed a seat in a secular cathedral as well as a place in these monastic houses. They were therefore not needed as diocesan centres and (to use modern terminology) could be considered redundant. After 1539 the bishop of Coventry and Lichfield had to be content with his cathedral at Lichfield, although he still used the dual title, and the bishop of Bath and Wells had to be satisfied with Wells Cathedral. The priory of Coventry surrendered to the king's commissioner John London on 15 January 1539, with Bath following suit on the twenty-seventh. The building at Coventry was demolished; the cathedral that was destroyed by bombing in the Second World War was not that building but a medieval parish church which had been raised to cathedral status in 1918. The church at Bath, which was the only cathedral building erected primarily in the Tudor period, became the principal parish church of the city, no doubt an indication that it was already the chief place of worship for the laity there.

The remaining monastic cathedrals were destined to survive as secular establishments, but they were not actually refounded until 1541 or January 1542. Winchester received royal letters patent establishing its secular status on 28 March 1541, with Canterbury following in April, Carlisle and Durham in May, Rochester in June and Ely in September. The last of these cathedrals to be dealt with was Worcester, re-established by a document issued on 24 January 1542. While it is not entirely clear what happened at these places during the interim (usually more than a year) between the dissolution and the new foundation, it looks as if some members of the monastic community at Worcester stayed on, acting as caretakers of the fabric and probably maintaining services as well. At Carlisle the last prior was guardian of the buildings until a new cathedral chapter was formed. Similar provisions, perhaps informal, were probably made elsewhere.

The royal letters patent appoint the dean and prebendaries by name. Generally the last prior became the first dean. This arrangement, obviously a convenience and one that helped overcome any opposition that the monks might have expressed at the Dissolution, was followed at Durham, Ely, Rochester, Winchester, Worcester and Carlisle as well as at Norwich. The only outsider appointed to head a refounded cathedral was Nicholas Wotton, a learned courtier and diplomat, later secretary of state under Edward VI. He was named dean of Canterbury in 1541. Three years later he was made dean of York as well. Generally non-resident in both places, he continued to hold these offices through all the religious changes down to his death in 1567.

Not all the monks were so fortunate as their priors, for the new foundations were smaller than the old and many of the religious had to be satisfied with pensions. At Durham, sixty-six of the last monks have been traced. Of these, twenty-seven were given office in 1541, and one more was appointed later. Those who stayed on appear to have been the most articulate and intelligent members of the monastic community. Former monks, however, did not have a monopoly on prebendal posts; secular canons were appointed as well. Some other cathedral functionaries, as well as the monks, were occasionally given pensions; when the monastery at Winchester was dissolved, for instance, provision was made for four singing men, eight choristers and four bell ringers. One imagines that they stayed in place and very likely continued performing their usual duties pending the introduction of new conditions.

Rearrangement of the living quarters associated with the monastic cathedrals was obviously necessary. It was relatively easy to convert the prior's lodgings into a deanery, since these were self-contained apartments of some luxury. This was done at Durham and Worcester, and doubtless in most other places. At Worcester the subprior's house and the home of the master of the guest hall were assigned to prebendaries, while at Durham twelve houses for the canons were formed out of the monastic buildings. Refectories could easily be converted into dining halls for the minor canons and singing men; we know that this was done at Canterbury, Ely and Worcester. After 1560 the monks' refectory at Worcester found a new use as a schoolroom; it is still the college hall of the King's School. Rochester was less fortunate. Here most of the monastic buildings were taken over by the king, who planned to use them as a residence when travelling between London and Dover. There was considerable rebuilding in 1541. In 1551 the property was granted to Lord Cobham, who returned it to the dean and chapter in 1558.

The most positive aspect of the Dissolution of the Monasteries was the accompanying foundation of six new cathedrals. A scheme for creating new bishoprics, probably originally Wolsey's, had been in the king's mind for some time. At one stage it was suggested that there should be a bishop and a cathedral in every county, a logical notion that can be traced back to King Alfred. Such new foundations really became feasible only with the confiscation of monastic endowments, which could be used to support the work of new dioceses, and monastic buildings, some of which were already of cathedral proportions.

The government toyed with the idea of establishing as many as fifteen new cathedrals. They also considered a plan to create sixteen bishoprics with their cathedral churches, each diocese being allocated £1000 out of the revenues of the dissolved religious houses.[3] Exact arrangements had not yet been decided when Parliament met in 1539; nonetheless, Cromwell was determined to introduce a Bill giving the king authority to create an indefinite number of new bishoprics, altering diocesan boundaries as necessary and of course naming the new bishops himself. An aspect of the measure that is interesting constitutionally is the clause stating that royal letters patent naming bishops shall have the force of statute. Even more fascinating is the preamble, written by Henry VIII himself and of importance because it is the only extant example of such royal drafting. This notes the 'slothful and ungodly life which hath been used among all those sorts which have borne the name religious folk'. Now that the religious houses were dissolved, their endowments could be 'turned to better use ... whereby God's word might better be set forth, children brought up in learning, clerks nourished in the universities, old servants decayed to have livings,

1. Canterbury Cathedral, with Bell Harry Tower. (*Woodmansterne*)

2. Durham Cathedral from the River Wear. (*Woodmansterne*)

6. Lincoln Cathedral, South Transept and Bishop's Eye. (*Woodmansterne*)

5. Lincoln Cathedral, Chapter House. (*Woodmansterne*)

4. Exeter Cathedral, Nave looking west. (*Woodmansterne*)

3. Salisbury Cathedral from the south west. (*Woodmansterne*)

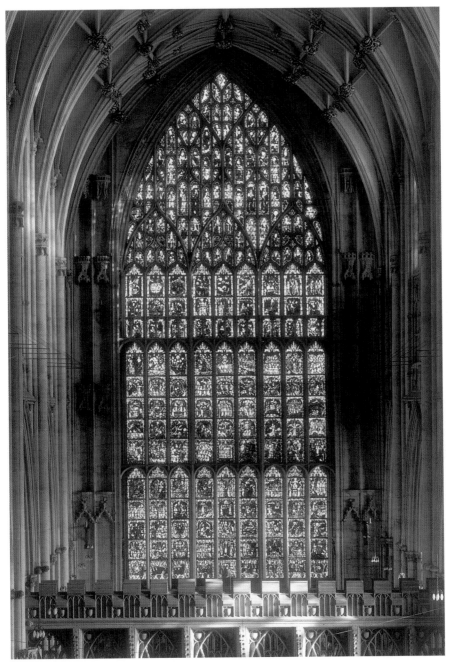

7. York Minster, Great East Window. (*Woodmansterne*)

8. Canterbury Cathedral, Becket window. (*Woodmansterne*)

almshouses [provided] for poor folk to be sustained in, Readers of Greek, Hebrew, and Latin to have good stipends, [and] daily alms to be administered'. All of these responsibilities (and even the maintenance of highways) could be assigned to the new bishops and cathedrals.

In the end, the early grand designs were abandoned and only six new cathedrals were founded. No doubt the first thoughts were too expansive – too costly and too disruptive of the existing order. We do not know what sort of discussions took place behind the scenes, but it may well be that bishops whose jurisdiction and revenues would have been reduced if new dioceses were carved out of their territories joined the king's financial advisers in opposing truly drastic change. New Henrician cathedrals were created only at Bristol, Chester, Gloucester, Oxford, Peterborough and Westminster.

All of these were based on great monasteries, four of them Benedictine and two (Bristol and Osney, which was to serve as the cathedral for Oxford) houses of Augustinian canons, as at Carlisle. Several of them made possible the continuing use of monastic churches that were among the finest buildings in the realm. Indeed the government probably paid too much attention to the available structures and too little to the size and shape of the dioceses created. Gloucester and Oxford formed adequate sites for the administration of a diocese, but Peterborough was too far from the centre of its long, narrow diocese, while Chester became the cathedral church of a huge territory that was calculated to provide an income for the bishop with little regard for the fact that personal oversight of such a diocese was virtually impossible. Even more absurd geographically was the arrangement that created the diocese of Bristol out of the city and a few parishes as far away as Dorset.

Westminster presented still greater difficulties. It was obvious that such a wealthy foundation, long associated with the monarchy and containing many royal tombs, could not be allowed to fall into ruin, and conversion of the abbey into a cathedral must have seemed the easiest way of preserving it. But the division of greater London into two dioceses did not work well and did not last long. The position of bishop of Westminster was apparently offered to Bishop Richard Sampson, but in the end he was translated from Chichester to Coventry and Lichfield rather than Westminster, and another conservative, Thomas Thirlby, was appointed to the new see. He has the distinction of being the only bishop of Westminster in Anglican history. No successor was appointed when he was translated to Norwich in 1550, to pick up the pieces left in disarray by Repps, and for six years the diocese of London had two cathedrals, St Paul's, in the City of London, and St Peter's Westminster. (Their rival claims for donations led to the saying 'To rob Peter to pay Paul'.) In 1556 Queen Mary restored monastic life at the abbey;

when Elizabeth finally dissolved the monastery three years later Westminster assumed its present status as a 'royal peculiar', operating much like a
cathedral but not attached to a bishop or diocese. An anonymous writer,
offering suggestions for reforms to be enacted by the Elizabethan Parliaments, proposed the creation of a bishop to serve the queen's court out of
the merged deaneries of Westminster and Windsor – an interesting idea, but
abortive.

The diocese of Oxford, originally named Osney and Thame, may have
been viable, but Osney, across the river west of Oxford, proved an unsatisfactory site for its cathedral. In 1546 the cathedral was transferred to its
present location, as an integral part of Christ Church within Oxford itself.
A fine historic structure, in part Norman, was available here too, for Wolsey
had dissolved St Frideswide's, another house of Augustinian canons, in 1524
and incorporated its buildings into those of his new college. The last abbot
of Osney, Robert King, was the first bishop of Oxford, while John London,
who had been the government's chief agent in the suppression of monasteries in Oxfordshire, was the first dean of the cathedral at Osney. When he
died in 1544 he was succeeded by Richard Cox, who may have been instru-
mental in suggesting the move to Christ Church. Four canons from the
Osney chapter came to Oxford with him.

The most successful of the new dioceses, and the possessor of the finest
building other than Westminster, was Gloucester; it is hard to believe that
this magnificent church, with one of the largest and most beautiful east
windows in the land, was not always a cathedral. Bristol, too, inherited a
marvelous edifice: as we have seen, the choir, with its tall aisles and unique
vaulting pattern, is one of the masterpieces of the Decorated style, and
the fine Perpendicular tower had been completed only at the beginning
of the sixteenth century. The Norman nave was being rebuilt at the time of
the Dissolution, but this project was abandoned and whatever had been
done was torn down. The present nave, which copies the style of the choir,
is Victorian.

Financial arrangements for the new cathedrals, and for the secularized
monastic cathedrals as well, were quite generous. The former income of
Westminster Abbey had been £3470, while the revenue from the new
endowment was £2598. Gloucester, Peterborough and Chester were given
less than previously; Bristol remained about the same; the allocation for
Oxford (£825) was about equal to the combined income of both Osney and
St Frideswide's. It is evident that some levelling of resources was thought
desirable; the revenues of Durham, like those of Canterbury, were reduced,
while those of the poorest houses (Rochester and Carlisle) were increased.

This was appropriate in view of the fact that large numbers of monks had been supported at Canterbury and Westminster, while the staff required in a refounded secular cathedral was considerably smaller.

It is of some interest to note the numbers of positions and the specific stipends allocated to these cathedrals. Westminster and Canterbury may be taken as examples (admittedly not typical) of a new cathedral and a refounded cathedral priory. At Westminster the proposed allocations can be traced through two government drafts and two 'erection books', the last representing the final establishment. The dean, whose salary as originally proposed would have been far lower than that in the old secular cathedrals, was actually given an income comparable to that of deans at Salisbury, Wells and St Paul's. The number of scholars to be supported while studying in the cathedral school was set at forty, each being allowed £3 a year. Choristers received the same amount. Minor canons were to be paid £10 a year, singing men £8, almsmen £6 13s. 4d. each. Twenty students were to be maintained at Oxford and Cambridge, each receiving a bit more than £8. There was also provision for readers in Greek, Hebrew, Latin, civil law and physic at the universities; for porters, butlers, cooks and an auditor; and for alms and repairs to the buildings.

The situation at Canterbury was similar. Here the first refoundation proposal allowed for a dean (called provost), twelve prebendaries, six preachers (an office peculiar to Canterbury, probably indicating that the prebendaries could not be trusted to preach reformed doctrine), eight minor canons, twelve lay clerks or singing men, ten choristers, sixty scholars to be taught Latin and Greek in the grammar school, twenty students at Oxford and Cambridge, five readers of divinity, physic and civil law, a master of the choristers and two masters of the grammar school. The dean was to be paid £300 a year, the canons £40 each, the preachers £24 2s. 2½d., minor canons £10, singers £8 and university scholars £6 or £8 depending on their status.

As noted already, the dean and chapter of Norwich were given authority to make their own statutes. The other cathedrals of the new foundation, however, had statutes imposed on them from without; the letters patent creating these new institutions stated that they were to be operated 'according to the ordinances, rules and statutes to be specified hereafter'. These were delivered in 1544.

We are fortunate in knowing who the actual compilers of the statutes were. Thomas Cromwell was not involved, since he had been executed in 1540. Cranmer and Gardiner, who led the reforming and conservative wings of the church respectively, may have been consulted, but the detailed work was left to Nicholas Heath, bishop of Worcester, George Day, bishop of

Chichester, and Richard Cox, archdeacon of Ely. It is possible that the three were chosen to represent divergent factions in the church, for Heath and Day were staunch conservatives, destined to be deprived of their sees under Edward VI but restored by Mary, whereas Cox was a leading Protestant, later to be dean of both Westminster and Oxford, theological tutor to Edward, a Marian exile, and finally the Elizabethan bishop of Ely.

Although there were some local variations in the wording of the statutes, they shared a basic common text. This was divided into chapters (the number of these ranges from thirty-eight to forty), beginning with provisions for the election and duties of the dean and canons. Then followed clauses regulating the choice and responsibilities of the subdean, receiver and treasurer. These, together with the dean, were the only statutory officers drawn from the cathedral chapter. Several sections of the statutes related to the minor canons, vicars choral, choristers, precentor, sacrist, almsmen and servants. The statutes concluded with general comments on order and discipline. The dean and canons were to have separate houses within the cathedral precinct and were to maintain hospitality, although there was no demand that they incur the heavy burdens of entertaining laid earlier on some residentiaries. The minor canons, singing men, choristers and grammar masters might live separately but were supposed to dine together in the common hall, the precentor presiding: minor canons, the master of the choristers and the headmaster of the school were to sit at the high table, lay clerks and the undermaster at the second, and the choristers at the third.

The statutes contained only brief references to the services of the church. What was said was conservative. Masses were still to be celebrated daily at the altars, and the obits of founders and benefactors were to be observed. Midnight matins, however, were dispensed with – quite understandably, these had always presented problems, and permission for absence from them was often granted long before they were abandoned altogether.

The old secular cathedrals had no need for new statutes. There was at least one proposal, however, that they too might be reformed along more Protestant lines. This emanated from the troublesome dean of Exeter, Simon Heynes. The chief officer in a cathedral, he suggested, should be called its pastor, not dean. The prebendaries should be renamed preachers, while the chancellor might be translated into a lecturer in theology. These advanced notions did not receive a favourable hearing.

Carlisle Cathedral possesses a fascinating artistic monument to its refoundation. This is the wooden screen, enclosing part of the choir, erected about 1541 by Lancelot Salkeld, the last prior and first dean. The carving, of superb quality, incorporates early Renaissance motifs such as those in the screen made for the chapel of King's College, Cambridge, a few years earlier. The designs at the top of the side facing the choir are ecclesiastical, with the shield of Carlisle priory and the initials LSDK (Lancelot Salkeld Decanus Karleolensis). All of the devices on the outer side of the screen are secular. The royal arms, flanked by Tudor symbols, are placed on the cresting. Below, the centre compartment has the feathers of the Prince of Wales and the inscription GSPE, presumably meaning 'God Save Prince Edward'. Panels at the bottom of the screen contain finely carved profiles of human heads; the significance of these is uncertain. Salkeld must have wished to celebrate his own continuing appointment and his success in converting the cathedral to its new status. In addition he may have hoped to curry favour with the king, who had so greatly desired a male heir, and with Prince Edward, whose accession to the throne could not be far off.

As the reign of Henry VIII drew to a close there were some signs that liturgical and theological reforms were coming soon. Sensitive observers, especially those committed to Protestant views, may have understood the implications of the proclamation issued in 1541 ordering the English Bible to be set up, available to lay persons, in every church as well as the king's order that Cranmer's English Litany – a foretaste of the English Prayer Book – be used beginning in 1544. The English Primer, which included the Litany as well as other vernacular prayers, was authorized in 1545 and carried the movement toward worship in the vernacular a step further.

In the main, however, the services of the English church and its cathedrals remained traditional so long as Henry lived. A proclamation of 1538 tried to end the 'difference, strife and contention' regarding such old ceremonies as creeping to the Cross on Good Friday or bearing candles on the feast of the Purification (popularly called Candlemas) by ordering that they remain in use as good and laudable customs, even though one ought not to place trust of salvation in them. Three years later another proclamation insisted that the feasts of St Luke, St Mark and St Mary Magdalene should continue to be celebrated – some people had argued that they should be abrogated because the first two fell within the law terms at Westminster, while the last came during the busy harvest season. St Mark's day was clearly identified as a feast, not a fast day, thus ending local variations; perhaps as a sop to the reformers, the 'superstitious and childish observances' of special days for St Nicholas, St Catherine, St Clement and the Holy Innocents were abolished. Account books kept by the cathedrals themselves confirm that age-old customs continued. At Chester, four men were paid a penny apiece for carrying the canopy for the Palm Sunday procession in 1545, and almonds, raisins, spiced cake, spiced ale and wine were provided for the Maundy Thursday supper. The bells were rung on Christmas and Corpus Christi Day, and new altar cloths were still being provided. Shortly before Henry VIII's death a new gilt candelabrum was purchased at Worcester.

When the king died in January 1547 a solemn dirge must have been sung in all the cathedrals. Occasionally there is a specific reference to this in the accounts: at Chester, for instance, 12*d.* was paid to the singers who helped honour the king's memory. The obsequies would have included the Latin mass that Henry had long known and loved. For the cathedrals, as for the church generally, the reign of Henry VIII had brought profound constitutional and financial changes. The Henrician Reformation, however, had been almost entirely a political one. The adoption of Protestant theology and an English liturgy remained ahead.

10

Protestant Ascendancy
and Catholic Reaction

The death of Henry VIII removed the chief obstacle to further reform in the church. His successor Edward VI, the nine-year-old male heir whose birth he had so greatly desired, had been taught by evangelical Protestant tutors, including Richard Cox, and had become convinced that he was divinely destined to bring true religion to the land, sweeping away the last vestiges of popery and superstition. Surrounded by Protestant churchmen such as Archbishop Cranmer and led by Protestant ministers such as his uncle, Protector Somerset, Edward VI supported a Protestant ascendancy that soon ushered in the most drastic changes of the century for the cathedrals.[1]

The new regime started with the promulgation in July 1547 of royal injunctions concerning religious reform. In the main these echoed Henry VIII's orders, emphasizing royal supremacy and the extirpation of papal jurisdiction. Images, relics, shrines and pilgrimages were denounced in several of the injunctions, with preachers commanded to instruct the people that there is 'no promise of reward in Scripture' for honouring them. But the new orders went beyond the old in directing deans to destroy all shrines, tables, candlesticks, pictures, paintings and other monuments of idolatry and superstition, even images found in stained-glass windows. No torches or other lights were allowed except for two candles on the altar, 'for the signification that Christ is the very true light of the world'. The Bible and Erasmus's *Paraphrases* were to be set up in all churches; sermons were to be preached regularly, and one of Cranmer's newly issued homilies was to be read each week if no authorized preacher was available. 'To avoid all contention and strife which heretofore' had arisen during processions, the new English Litany was not to be said as the clergy and choir processed, but rather as they knelt 'in the midst of the church'. It was to be used more frequently than before: under Henry the Litany was to be sung on Wednesdays and Fridays, but the Edwardian injunctions mandated its regular use before high mass. The Epistle and Gospel of the mass were to be read in English rather than in Latin, and the portions of Scripture for matins and evensong were also to be in the vernacular. But the 'laudable ceremonies of the church as yet not abrogated' still had to be observed without dissension, and chantry priests remained in place, now exhorted to be diligent in teaching the young to read and write.

These general orders were supplemented by a set of royal injunctions aimed specifically at the cathedrals. The most interesting of these directed all cathedrals to fit up a library containing the standard patristic works together with the writings of Erasmus and other good, presumably modern, writers; to make yearly inventories of all their vestments, ornaments, jewels and plate; to establish free grammar schools if these did not already exist; and to support former choristers studying at a grammar school with an annual stipend of £3 6s. 8d. Further injunctions were given to some cathedrals individually. Those for Canterbury attempted to clarify some ambiguities in the constitutional position of the dean by reiterating his authority to make appointments so long as he is within the realm, just as if he were physically present at the cathedral. They also mandated the creation of a common garden and the allocation of suitable chambers to minor canons and vicars choral. The wearing of copes was forbidden at Winchester, while at Lincoln ministers below the degree of prebendaries were ordered not to wear habits or black hoods, but only surplices. At York Minster there was to be but one mass each day, celebrated at the high altar at 9 a.m., and the singing of dirges and some other services was discontinued so that the clergy might spend their time in study and contemplation of God's Holy Word.

These injunctions were to be enforced by a general visitation of the church. Cranmer and Somerset evidently did not trust the bishops to see that the reforming orders were actually obeyed – indeed their fear was justified, for at least one-third of the bishops were conservatives who felt no enthusiasm for enforcing change. So normal episcopal powers of visitation were inhibited while visitors named by the government made their way throughout the realm. For this purpose, the kingdom was divided into six sections; thirty visitors were appointed, of whom two-thirds were laymen, generally lawyers of staunch Protestant or Erasmian views. When Gardiner and Bonner, the chief of the conservative bishops, opposed this infringement of their authority, they were packed off to prison. Both were deprived later in the reign.

The visitors were given a set of seventy-four articles that were to serve as the basis for interrogation of appropriate clergymen and lay people. None of the articles related solely to cathedrals, but several had an impact there. The campaign against images and shrines continued, as clergy were asked whether they knew of any shrines 'or other monuments of idolatry, superstition and hypocrisy' that had not been destroyed and whether they had taught the people the true use of images, 'which is only to put them in remembrance of the godly and virtuous lives of them that they do represent: and if [they] use the images for any other purpose, they commit idolatry to the great danger of their souls'.

Another set of articles reveals the growing concern for the use of English in the services of the church. Priests were asked 'whether they have counseled or moved their parishioners rather to pray in a tongue not known than in English', and they were interrogated about their use of the English Litany. It is interesting to find lay persons asked whether matins and evensong, as well as the mass, are kept at due hours in the church, for these were to be the main non-eucharistic services set forth in the Prayer Book which Cranmer was preparing but which had not yet been published or put into use. In view of the movement to dissolve chantries that would shortly be the focus of governmental activity, it is interesting, too, to find five articles for chantry priests. The visitors were to ascertain whether they were resident, what benefices they held in addition to their chantries, whether they assisted in the administration of the sacraments, whether they were of honest conversation and behaviour, and whether they performed all the deeds of charity mandated by their chantry foundations.

Local sources confirm the effects of these policies. At Hereford, the chapter act books record the receipt in March 1547 of a letter requiring that any remaining images be pulled down. Some further jewels and plate from Canterbury were sent to their way to the mint in July. Despite Bonner's opposition, all the images of St Paul's were demolished in September, and the rood, crucifix, tombs and even altars followed in November. Those who still sympathized with the old religion did not fail to note that two of the workmen engaged in these sacrilegious acts were killed. It is likely that the tragic defacement of the fourteenth-century statues in the Lady chapel at Ely occurred at about the same time. The order to clear away all images was received at Lichfield in March 1548 and was honoured by the removal of statues from the high altar and throughout the church. To prevent further losses, the resident canons divided the altar ornaments, copes and other vestments among themselves in October. In 1549 the chapter of Westminster agreed to sell two lecterns of brass and several candlesticks adorned with gilt angels 'by cause they be monymentes of Idolatre and supersticyon'; the proceeds of the sale were to be spent on books for the cathedral library. The conservative dean of Wells, John Goodman, offered up four large brass candlesticks and two brass images of bishops but seems to have been able to avert any thoroughgoing iconoclastic activity there for the time being.

What threatened to be one of the heaviest blows of the century to cathedral finance came late in 1547 with the act for the Dissolution of the Chantries.

After a stormy session, this was finally passed by Edward's first Parliament on Christmas Eve. The chantries had been very important, especially in the old secular cathedrals, where many of the vicars choral gained supplementary employment and badly needed income as chantry priests. The confiscation of chantry endowments severely reduced the revenues available to singing men just at the time when they were being allowed to marry; many of them were already experiencing financial pressures as they attempted to support families in an era of rising prices on stipends that had been barely adequate for celibate clerics. There was even a threat to the continued existence of the colleges of vicars choral, which might be suppressed along with the colleges of chantry priests.

Theologically the movement against chantries, indeed against all prayers for the dead, can be traced back to Martin Luther's doctrine of Justification by Faith, which had been accepted by many of the English reformers. If salvation did depend solely upon one's faith, prayers for the departed were of no avail; indeed they might be worse than useless, since they created the illusion that salvation could be purchased. Most of the reformers came to reject the doctrine of purgatory as being a popish invention, devised purely as a means of extracting money from the faithful. That some laymen, too, had come to reject prayers for the dead was made clear in a visitation at Gloucester in 1540, when one Humphrey Grynshall had affirmed 'that there is no moo places wherein christen soules departed maye be, but only hell and heven, and therefore he sayde that he wolde have no prayers sayde for his sowle when so ever he shall dye, [for] suche prayers & suffragyes did nothinge prevayle nor helpe soules departed'.

The attack on chantries had begun in the last year of Henry VIII's reign, when an Act passed by Parliament in 1545 gave the government authority to dissolve chantries, colleges, hospitals and guilds, just as it had done in the case of monasteries. This act, which was justified in terms of financial necessity rather than theology, was applied selectively, only a few chantries actually being suppressed in 1547. Because the power to appoint commissioners and confiscate properties was thought to lapse with the old king's death, a new Bill was put before Parliament in 1547, this time adorned with a preamble alleging that 'a great part of superstition and errors in Christian religion hath ben brought into the minds and estimation of men by reason of the ignorance of their very true and perfect salvation through the death of Jesus Christ, and by devising and phantasying vain opinions of purgatory and masses satisfactory to be done for them which be departed'. The Act then speaks of the king's desire to convert chantry endowments to more suitable educational and charitable purposes.

Armed with this legislation, commissioners were once again sent around

The ship of the Romish Church.

Shippe ouer your trinkets and be packing ye Papistes.

Burning of images.

The Temple well purged.

The Papistes packing away their paultrye.

The Communion Table

John Foxe's *Book of Martyrs* (1570). The illustration sets out the virtues of the Edwardian church, with its emphasis on the Bible and on preaching, its reduction of the sacraments and its purging of popish images.

the country, this time to list all chantry foundations, set valuations on their endowments and fixed properties, and state whether the incumbent priests served any purpose other than that of memorializing the departed. The certificates of these commissioners were returned to two young financial administrators, Sir Walter Mildmay and Robert Keilway, who made the final decisions about confiscation, continuation or reassignment of revenues. Acting through the Court of Augmentations, they also handled pensions for displaced priests.

Although surviving documentation is incomplete and ambiguous, it appears that in fact some cathedrals succeeded in retaining chantry endowments, now turning the revenues to the support of cathedral services rather than prayers for the dead. The commissioners who reported on the situation at York in 1546 had been very generous, even recommending that the college of St William, which housed twenty-four chantry priests, should be allowed to continue as a residence for the petty canons who would still minister in the choir and say mass at their several altars. A second set of reports, submitted in 1548, also proposes the exemption of many cathedral properties. In the end, St William's College was confiscated and the property sold in 1549. But the Bedern, or college of the vicars choral, was allowed to remain; its continuation was ratified by the government in 1552. Some chantry properties 'annexyd to the same vicares choralles, and alwayes used and taken for parcell of th'augmentacion of theyre lyvyng' may have been retained as well. The total revenues of the chantries at York, after some deductions were allowed, were given by the commissioners as £627. Even if all of these were confiscated, the sum was not large in comparison to the real income of the cathedral, which had been stated as £2455 in the *Valor Ecclesiasticus.*

At Chichester there is an Elizabethan list of the cathedral chantries that did not suffer expropriation, together with a note that states that the Edwardian statute did not apply to the endowments of chantries within the cathedrals so long as these were used for the maintenance of services. Ironically, the vicars choral of Lichfield had sought a charter of incorporation in 1528, but without success. Had it been granted, their college might have been dissolved. As it was, the Court of Augmentations ruled that the vicars choral were not independent but part of the cathedral community and they escaped. At Hereford, too, the vicars choral were able to claim that their endowments (and those of the choristers) formed an integral part of the cathedral establishment. This was later confirmed by a royal charter granted in 1587.

At Lincoln the number of senior or priest vicars seems to have fallen from twenty-five to twelve at about this time, although there is no mention of such a reduction in the chapter acts. Four vicars choral were granted annuities and presumably pensioned off in 1549. But it is not certain that these changes had anything to do with the dissolution of the chantries; the number of young men who sought ordination had been declining since the 1530s and a general movement toward lay vicars is a more likely explanation.

One suspects that a number of the cathedrals found themselves in the same situation as Exeter. Here it was held that the cathedral's chantry properties did fall within the scope of the Chantries Act, so they were seized by the crown. All the chantry priests, or annuellars, were pensioned off. But little of the property was actually alienated during Edward's reign, and most of the endowments were eventually returned to the cathedral in exchange for an annual payment of £145. Queen Elizabeth confirmed such a grant in 1585.

In the end, it seems that most cathedrals survived the Dissolution of the Chantries without catastrophic blows to their revenues or disastrous losses of personnel. Nowhere were the vicars choral forced to vacate their courts or closes. Chantry priests in the cathedrals were less likely to be involved in teaching than those attached to parish churches, so the grammar schools associated with the cathedrals do not seem to have suffered. Obviously there were changes, often quite visible: the chantry chapels, many of them great architectural monuments, stood empty, despoiled of their ornaments. Cathedrals came to operate with smaller staffs, as those chantry priests who held no other office departed. Many of their young assistants, the poor clerks or secondaries, also disappeared from the scene, although a number of them received stipends to remain as students in the cathedral schools. Prayers for the departed no longer formed one of the reasons for the existence of the cathedrals or one of their ties to local families that had founded chantries or endowed obits. Even those who applauded the end of belief in purgatory and 'masses satisfactory' may have felt sad at the thought that great men and women of earlier ages now had no memorial.

A renewed campaign of iconoclasm was ushered in by the Dissolution of the Chantries. In virtually every cathedral one can find a chantry chapel that suffered mutilation. Dates are seldom recorded, but spoliation at the time of the Dissolution seems most likely. There was considerable local variation in the timing and the severity of the destruction.

One of the most interesting instances, and one that is important because of its royal connections, is provided by Prince Arthur's chantry at Worcester. Here the body of Henry VIII's elder brother had been entombed soon after Arthur's death at Ludlow in 1502. The chantry chapel, which stands to the right of the high altar, was erected by Henry VII; its exterior is decorated with heraldic devices illustrating the union of the houses of Lancaster and York. In addition, there are symbols of Arthur's wife, Catherine of Aragon: the bunch of arrows emblematic of Catherine's mother, Isabella, and the pomegranate of Granada, Catherine's former home. The arms of England and France are supported by the greyhound and the Welsh dragon of Cadwallader. The Garter, the Tudor rose and portcullis, and the ostrich feathers of the Prince of Wales are also represented in stone.

Inside the small chapel itself, an altar is surmounted by a reredos bearing five large statues. The central figure is a Christ of pity, supported by angels. St George and the Dragon are depicted at the south end, and the two crowned figures are probably Edward the Confessor and Edmund, King and Martyr. The figure at the extreme north, carrying a long scroll, remains unidentified. Between these large statues are four small representations of saints; the upper pair are bishops, one of them probably Becket, while the lower two are ladies, undoubtedly St Margaret and possibly either St Catherine or Elizabeth of Hungary. All of these exquisite carvings were defaced, probably in 1548. It may be that animosity against Catherine of Aragon as a staunch Catholic was coupled with distaste for chantries as a motive for this work. Many of the eighty-eight small statues, however, escaped the hammer and chisel and remain as beautiful examples of the Tudor mason's craft. Prior to Queen Elizabeth's visit in 1575 the east wall of the chapel was plastered over to conceal the mutilated statues, and the royal arms and 'Vivat Regina' were painted there. Only in 1788 was the plaster removed.

At Wells the enormous cruciform Lady chapel that had been built by Bishop Stillington less than a century earlier was demolished. It had lost its revenues to the chantry commissioners, and in 1552 it was made over to Sir John Gate, the king's collector of lead, who not only stripped off the roof but took down the entire building. According to John Harington, 'such was their thirst after lead (I would they had drunke it scalding) that they tooke the dead bodies of Bishops out of their leaden coffins, and cast abroad the carkases skarce throughly putrified'. A bit earlier the chronicler John Stowe recorded a peculiar bit of demolition at St Paul's, the destruction of a cloister that must have resembled the famous Campo Santo of Pisa. In 1549

the cloister of Paul's church in London, called pardon churchyard, with the dance of death, commonly called the dance of Paul's about the same cloister costly and cunningly wrought, and the chapel in the midst of the same churchyard were begun to be pulled down. Also the charnel-house of Paul's with the chapel there (after the tombs and other monuments of the dead were pulled down, and the dead men's bones buried in the fields) were converted into dwelling houses and shops.[2]

The most positive aspect of religious change under Edward VI was the introduction of the Book of Common Prayer. As has been noted, Cranmer wished to have the people worship in their own tongue, not in an ancient language that only the learned could understand. His English Litany had foreshadowed a liturgical revolution even before the death of Henry VIII. With the accession of Edward VI, and with the political leadership of Protector Somerset, who shared his desire for reform, the archbishop was free to proceed rapidly. He was probably already at work on the first Book of Common Prayer in 1547 and was able to see it though the press and into use throughout the church by 1549.

There had been some experimentation with the use of English in services other than the Litany ever since the beginning of the new reign. On Easter Monday 1547 compline was sung in English at the Chapel Royal. Westminster Abbey, no doubt because of its close connection with Parliament and the crown, was a centre for trial usages. We know that the *Gloria in Excelsis*, the *Credo, Sanctus, Benedictus* and *Agnus Dei* were all sung in English at the mass that marked the beginning of Parliament in November 1547. A similar polyglot service was held to celebrate Henry VIII's obit in May 1548. The musical settings used for these sung portions of the mass may survive in the so-called Wanley Part Books, where a few of the texts clearly antedate the Prayer Book versions.

At St Paul's, the Epistle and Gospel, as well as the Litany, were read in English in February 1548; the Chronicle of the Grey Friars says that 'after Easter beganne the servis in Ynglyche at Powles at the commandment of the dene at the tyme, William May'. At Lincoln the injunctions of 1548 directed that 'They shall from hensforthe synge or say no Anthemes off our lady or other saynts but only of our lorde, And them not in laten but choseying owte the beste and moste soundyng to cristen religion they shall turne the same into Englishe, settyng therupon a playn and distincte note, for every sillable one, they shall singe them and none other'.

The legal basis for the use of the English Prayer Book was laid by the Act of Uniformity passed early in 1549 by Edward's second Parliament. Here the preamble noted that the medieval English church had not possessed a common liturgy, for there were local variations, including the uses of York, Bangor and Lincoln, as well as Salisbury, home of the Sarum rite, which enjoyed the greatest popularity. Further alternate forms had crept in during recent years, as reformers began to use new liturgies despite the government's warning that these should not be introduced until a common order was provided. Now, to end these differences and divisions, the Book of Common Prayer was to be published and to be used uniformly throughout the realm.

The Act of Uniformity mandated the introduction of the Prayer Book by the Feast of Pentecost, which in 1549 fell on 9 June. But copies of the book seem to have been available earlier, at least in London, and in some places the new services came into use before Easter. The last Latin mass at St Paul's was sung on the second Sunday in Lent; Coverdale preached, and after the service the dean 'commandyd the sacrament at the hye autre to be pullyd downe'.

Once the Prayer Book was in use the continued performance of Latin services became illegal, except in cases where people were familiar with the tongue. (This allowed the continued use of Latin in college chapels, since a knowledge of Latin was an entrance requirement at Oxford and Cambridge until the twentieth century.) To ensure that old service books were abandoned, the government ordered their destruction; a proclamation issued on Christmas Day 1549 commanded subjects to give up any hope that the Latin services would be brought back, for they were 'but a preferring of ignorance to knowledge and darkness to light'. The old books, including 'all antiphoners, missales, grayles, processionales, manuelles, legendes, pies, portiases, journalles and ordinalles', were to be delivered into the hands of the bishops, who were directed to destroy or deface them.

The relatively small number of service books that survives testifies to the success of this campaign. Among the lost volumes were many that included illuminated initials and musical settings. In a few cases manuscripts were sold, not for their contents but for the parchment that could be used in stiffening bindings. The books that remain were probably hidden away in 1549; these include the famous Worcester Antiphoner, which contains the music for a whole range of services, another manuscript antiphoner from Gloucester, the Winchester Troper, an antiphoner and a gradual from Salisbury, and a missal according to the use of Hereford, printed in 1502.

There must have been an urgent scramble to provide suitable musical settings for the new English services. Occasionally this is reflected in the financial records of the cathedrals. At Canterbury, for instance, twenty-six 'psalters of the gretter sort for the quere' were purchased in 1550. Psalters were also bought at Chester. At Wells the organist, William Parsons, was given 16s. 4d. 'for divers songs and books by him made and to be made'. Expenses at Christ Church, Oxford, included 12s. 8d. for ten psalters as well as 2s. 8d. 'for pryckyng of the buriall service eight tymes in sundry places', while the dean and chapter of York paid 4s. 4d. for a service book in 1551.

In 1550 John Marbeck, the firmly Protestant organist of St George's, Windsor, published his Boke of Common Prayer Noted, in which simplified plainsong – unison and monosyllabic – was set to the new English texts. The Edwardian church was fortunate in its composers; among those setting

English texts at this time were Christopher Tye, Thomas Tallis, William Mundy, John Sheppard, Richard Farrant and Osbert Parsley, all of whom are still represented in the repertory of cathedral choirs. Nevertheless it must have been difficult throughout Edward's reign to perform the new services with dignity and artistic integrity; not until the Elizabethan church became firmly established would adequate musical settings be readily available. Despite proclamations and injunctions to the contrary, Latin anthems, if not Latin settings of the mass or of the canticles for morning and evening prayer, must still have been used in many cathedrals, particularly those with conservative deans and bishops, located in remote areas. Even in London there may have been diversity in musical practice, just as there was about holy days – the Grey Friars' Chronicle testifies that 'at the Assumpcion of our Lady was soche devision thorrow alle London that some kepte holy day and some none. Almyghty God helpe it when hys wylle ys! For this was the second yere, and also the same devision was at the fest of the Nativitie of our Lady'.

Although the 1549 Prayer Book still referred to altars, the movement to demolish stone altars because of their association with the popish doctrines of transubstantiation and the mass as a sacrifice started almost immediately after its introduction. So began a further round of iconoclasm. In May 1550, less than a month after his installation as bishop of London, the reformer Nicholas Ridley ordered his clergy to remove their old altars, arguing that a table was 'more meet' for the Lord's Supper. The required change was made at St Paul's in June. Later, in 1552, 'alle the goodly stoneworke that stode behynde the hye alter', together with the seats of the priests and the dean and subdean, was hacked away. Only a command from the council saved John of Gaunt's tomb from similar treatment.

In November the council ordered all the bishops to follow Ridley's example. Most of them must have complied rapidly; we know that the removal of the altar at Hereford was undertaken in December 1550. The Chester accounts for this year record the payment of 5s. 6½d. for taking down the stone altars and 2s. 9d. for making a wooden communion table. The bishop of Chichester, George Day, refused to enforce the removal of altars or to preach against them, although he would have been willing to see their form changed. He explained his precise position in a letter to William Cecil:

> I stick not at the alteration either of the usual form of the altar, either at the situation thereof, either of the matter (as stone or wood) whereof the altar was made, [for] I take these things to be indifferent, and to be ordered by them that have authority. But the commandment which was given to me to take down all

altars within my diocese and in lieu of them to set up a table, implying in itself (as I take it) plain abolishment of the altar (both the name and the thing) from the use and ministration of the holy communion, I could not with my conscience then execute.[3]

When Day remained adamant, he was summoned to appear before the council, imprisoned in Fleet Prison, and ultimately deprived. At Worcester the choir stalls and bishop's throne were taken down in 1551, and further clearing out was undertaken by John Hooper, the zealous reformer who became bishop when the conservative Nicholas Heath was deprived. 'Our Churche ys greatly defaced', the dean and chapter were later to write Cardinal Pole, 'owr quear pulled down, our belles and organns be broken, our Altars and Chapelles are by Hoper violated and overthrowne'. Westminster Abbey, evidently suffering from the pressures of inflation, was forced to sell plate and ornaments in 1550 and again in 1552 in order to pay salaries. Whole shiploads of religious statuary were exported to France in the 1550s, and one of the illustrations in the 1570 edition of Foxe's *Book of Martyrs* depicts just such a scene (see p. 125).

The financial crisis in which the Edwardian government found itself was responsible for further losses and confiscations. In March 1550, 'forasmuche as the Kinges Majestie had need presently of a masse of mooney', it was ordered that commissioners be sent into every county to take into the king's hands such church plate as remained in the parishes and cathedrals. In general the policy seems to have been to allow parish churches to retain a single chalice and paten, cathedrals being permitted to keep two. In many cases actual expropriation did not take place until the last months of the young king's life and was in fact incomplete at the time of Mary's accession.

Often the commissioners did not limit themselves to removal of plate; it was common for them to carry off vestments and other ornaments in addition. At Lichfield the royal agents removed a large number of vestments in January 1553, selling them for the meanest price (*'pro vilissimo pretio'*). Later, in May, one of the commissioners returned with a wagon and carried off the best copes and mitrers as well as all the silver vessels, pouring the consecrated oil from three cruets on the ground before the eyes of two horrified canons.

The losses recorded at York are staggering, and must be typical of those suffered at the greater cathedrals. Among the articles taken away were chalices of gold and silver, bread boxes, censers, gold and silver basins, sconces, cruets, paxes, pectoral crosses set with precious stones, candlesticks, standing cups, and holy-water pots; silver basins, ewers, goblets, and ale pots belonging to the individual canons; nearly fifty red and purple copes, dozens of green, blue, black, and white copes and sets of vestments, altar cloths and curtains, fringes, hangings, canopies, cloths of tissue, turkey carpets, and mitrers decorated with diamonds, sapphires and pearls.

At Chester, an example of a much poorer cathedral, the commissioners sent the best vestments to the king's wardrobe and sold the rest for £5 11s. 3d. They left two chalices and patens, a pair of organs and five bells. The government was distressed to hear that the dean and chapter had already sold another great bell and applied the money to their stipends, and that income from the sale of a cross and two silver censers had been used to pay for repairs to their houses. It is tragic to think of the finest artistry of medieval goldsmiths and silversmiths, now melted down and lost forever, and of the gorgeous embroidered vestments that might have been saved as a part of the country's artistic heritage, even if there was no desire to have them worn by clergy in the reformed church.

The last great religious measure of Edward VI's reign was the introduction of the second Book of Common Prayer in 1552. By this time Protector Somerset had fallen and his place as chief minister had been taken by John Dudley, duke of Northumberland. Whatever Northumberland's religious views may have been – he used to be pictured as a politique but was probably a convinced evangelical Protestant – Archbishop Cranmer retained his primacy in determining ecclesiastical policy, urged on more and more by the young king himself as Edward grew in years and in understanding of politics.

Cranmer seems to have been dissatisfied with his first Prayer Book soon after its introduction.[4] Perhaps it never really represented his own theological convictions; he may well have introduced a more conservative and more ambiguous book than he wanted in the hope of avoiding dissension. Such zealous English reformers as Ridley and Hooper, as well as Protestant émigrés from the Continent, among them Martin Bucer and Peter Martyr, soon convinced him that ambiguity was unacceptable in any cause as vital as religious belief. Hence the Prayer Book had to be revised to eliminate any hint of popish superstition and to make clear the Protestant complexion of the English church.

While there are numerous differences between the 1549 volume and its successor, the most significant can be found in the communion service and in the funeral liturgy. Communion, no longer called the mass, was now celebrated in remembrance of the Last Supper, not because of Christ's sacrifice on the Cross, and belief in the Real Presence was no longer appropriate. All prayers for the dead were deleted from the burial office despite their acknowledged antiquity, a final acceptance of the logic behind Justification by Faith and the Dissolution of the Chantries.

Use of the new Prayer Book beginning in November 1552 was ordered by a new Act of Uniformity. This was carefully drafted so as to make it appear that the 1549 book had merely been revised, not supplanted because of inherent defects; the revision had been intended to remove 'divers doubts for the fashion and manner of administration of the authorized worship' that had arisen, due to which 'a great number of people, following their own sensuality and living without knowledge or due fear of God, do wilfully and damnable refuse to come to their parish churches'. Penalties were now prescribed for any who persisted in worshipping according to other rites.

St Paul's was one of the first cathedrals to bring in the new liturgy. The account in the Grey Friars' Chronicle emphasizes the simplified vestments that were required by a rubric in the new book – no albs or copes, but plain white surplices for priests and rochets for bishops.

> Item on Alhallon day began the boke of the new service of bred and wyne in Powlles, and the bysshoppe [Ridley] dyd the servis hymselfe, and prechyd in the qwere at the mornynge servis, and dyd it in a rochet and nothynge elles on hym. And the dene with alle the resydew of the prebentes went but in their surples and left of[f] their [h]abbet of the university [hoods]; and the byshope prechyd at afternone at Powelles crosse, and stode there tyll it was nere honde v. a cloke, and the mayer and aldermen came not within Powlles church nor the crafftes as they were wonte to doo, for because they were soo w[e]ary of hys longe stondynge.

Morning and evening prayer were now more important than the eucharist, which was celebrated only on Sundays, and preaching more vital than the sacraments.

Local sources tell little about the reception of the second Prayer Book. Several of its rubrics may have proved as important as its changes in wording. The destruction of altars was recognized by a rubric directing that the Lord's Supper be administered at a table covered with a fair white linen cloth, placed in the body of the church (the nave) or in the chancel, not necessarily where the old altar had been. The priest was directed to stand at the north side of the table, which would have been positioned with its longer dimension east and west, not 'altar-wise' north and south; the priest's eastward stance, with his back to the congregation, was ruled out.

The order for simplified vestments reflected the reformers' dislike of the old elaborate 'popish rags' as well as the fact that most of these had already been confiscated or destroyed. Two more rubrics of some interest regulated the administration of the communion. This was not to be celebrated unless four persons, or at least three, were present to communicate with the priest

– there could be no more private masses, and there was obviously no expectation that every priest would celebrate daily. In cathedrals all priests and deacons were to receive communion each Sunday unless they had reasonable excuses; lay persons were to communicate at least three times a year, always including Easter. The famous Black Rubric, added by the council after the other rubrics had already been printed in red ink, stated that communicants should still kneel but that this was done for the preservation of order, not because anyone should adore or venerate the bread and wine.

As Edward's brief reign drew to its end, the cathedrals, like the rest of the English church, reached the most Protestant point in their long history. The sweeping reforms of these six years must have been bewildering in their rapidity and variety. No area was left untouched, as change affected liturgy, theology, finance, staffing, living conditions, music, vestments, images and ornaments, even the very altars at which the sacred services of the church had been celebrated time out of mind. It would have taken years for most people to digest the changes and to gain an appreciation of the new manner of worship and belief. Alas for the reformers, this time was not theirs. Edward was already ill when the new Prayer Book came into use; he died on 6 July 1553, three months short of his seventeenth birthday. With him died the radical Protestant experiment in the Anglican church and its cathedrals.

As he lay dying, Edward VI had accepted the so-called Device for the Succession, presented to him by Northumberland and Cranmer. This would have guaranteed the continuation of Protestant practices by excluding both of Edward's half-sisters, Mary and Elizabeth, from the succession and passing the throne instead to his cousin, Lady Jane Grey. But Lady Jane was scarcely known outside the closed circle of ministers and courtiers, while Mary was remembered as the elder daughter of Henry VIII and the next in line for the crown according to Henry's will and an Act of Parliament, as well as normal hereditary right. That she was an ardent Catholic who would be bound to rescind all the reforms of Edward's reign must have been generally understood, but evidently seemed less important than adherence to the accepted order. Jane found few supporters, and Mary was acknowledged to be the lawful sovereign on 19 July, less than two weeks after Edward's death. Seldom has a change on the throne implied such a profound reaction for the church.

Mary's reign appeared to begin mildly, with a proclamation issued on 18 August acknowledging that she could not 'hide that religion which God and the world knoweth she hath ever professed from her infancy hitherto'. She would 'be glad the same were of all her subjects quietly and charitably embraced', and yet 'she mindeth not to compel any her said subjects there-unto unto such time as further order by common assent may be taken'. For the time being existing laws should be obeyed, and subjects should leave 'those new-found devilish terms of papist or heretic, and such like; and live in the fear of God'.

Despite these conciliatory words, the work of replacing Protestant leaders with those loyal to the old faith began almost immediately. Indeed it had already started, for Edmund Bonner, the former bishop of London, was released from prison on 5 August; he made his way to St Paul's dressed in full pontifical vestments, and (according to the Grey Friars' Chronicle) all the people bade him welcome. As many women as could kissed him. The cathedral's bells were rung for joy as the bishop knelt on its steps to pray. His place in prison was taken by Richard Cox, the Protestant dean of Westminster, who was thus barred from officiating at Edward VI's funeral three days later. Bishops Gardiner, Tunstall, Day and Heath were shortly freed, as was the duke of Norfolk. Northumberland was beheaded, while Cranmer, Ridley, Latimer and Barlow were sent to the Tower.

A revolution in personnel had thus taken place well before Mary's coronation, which was celebrated in Westminster Abbey on 1 October. Gardiner officiated, joined by a large choir and as full a procession of mitred bishops as could be gathered; services at St Paul's were suspended so that all might be present at the great event. The bishops of Lincoln and Hereford, John Taylor and John Harley, withdrew at the beginning of the mass, which they felt in conscience they could not attend.

Mary's first Parliament convened on 5 October. The Convocation of the Clergy, always held concurrently, began on the seventh with a solemn mass of the Holy Ghost sung in St Paul's by Bishop Bonner. This was the first mass (the former Grey Friar noted) to be celebrated there since 1549, and the high altar was set up again for the occasion. Parliament's main business was the passage of Mary's first Act of Repeal, which extinguished all the religious legislation of Edward's reign, thus disposing of the Prayer Book and officially bringing back the Latin services of the old church. The change was to become effective on 20 December, prior to Christmas but allowing some time for the gathering of missals and music books.

One of the Edwardian statutes now abrogated was that which permitted the marriage of the clergy. Since one of the queen's most firmly held beliefs demanded celibacy, the campaign against those who had taken wives was fast and probably thorough. A few examples will illustrate the magnitude of the issue for the cathedrals. At Lichfield the dean, two prebendaries and two vicars choral were deprived. The married dean of Bangor was ejected. The dean of York remained in office, but seven married canons and three vicars choral were turned out. At Hereford the precentor and three prebendaries were deprived, and there was trouble about the proposed admission of a chorister and, later, a vicar choral who acknowledged that they were the sons of priests. The succentor of Salisbury was ousted in 1554, probably because of his marriage, and six prebendaries of Canterbury were deprived for this reason in 1553.

A set of royal injunctions promulgated by proclamation in March 1554 ordered bishops and other appropriate officers to proceed 'with all celerity and speed' in depriving those 'who contrary to the state of their order and the laudable custom of the Church have married and used women as their wives, or otherwise notably and slanderously disordered or abused themselves'. Moving on to ceremonies, the injunctions commanded the restoration of processions, holy days and fasting days, and in general the 'laudable and honest ceremonies which were wont to be used' in the church.

Many of the cathedral clergy and musicians – those who had reluctantly acquiesced in the changes of Edward's reign as well as the conservatives once ejected and now restored – must have welcomed the return of traditional forms of worship. We know, for instance, that a splendid procession was held in 1554 at St Paul's to honour St Paul's Day, 25 January. Fifty priests were clad in copes of cloth of gold, somehow found for the occasion; all sang the traditional processional hymn 'Salve Festa Dies'.

Even grander ceremonial marked the queen's marriage to Prince Philip of Spain. This was solemnized by Bishop Gardiner in his own cathedral at Winchester, not at Westminster Abbey; it may have been that disruptions were feared in London, which had already been the scene of a rebellion protesting against the Spanish alliance, but it is also possible that Winchester was thought to be more convenient because of its proximity to Southampton, where Philip landed, and because of its association with Gardiner. Philip was initially welcomed in Winchester on 23 July 1554: there was a procession of civic and ecclesiastical dignitaries, and the choir sang a *Te Deum*. The wedding itself was held two days later, on St James's Day, a date chosen to honour the patron saint of Spain.

The cathedral had been prepared most elaborately for the event. A scaffold had been erected, three feet high, running down the length of the nave. Flanking this, twelve Flemish tapestries were suspended from hooks on the nave pillars; these had just been woven to commemorate the victory of Philip's father, Charles V, over the infidel at Tunis in 1535. Five bishops in full pontificals and the combined choirs of the English and Spanish royal chapels as well as the cathedral choir helped lend splendour to the occasion. There were also trumpeters. Just before the ceremony began a herald announced that Philip had been created king of Naples (he had not yet inherited the Spanish crown), so that the marriage could unite sovereigns of equal rank. As well as the Englishmen, large numbers of Spanish grandees attended.

In London, bells were rung and bonfires lighted to celebrate the union. A few days later the king and queen made their ceremonial entry into the capital, where pageants and displays had been prepared along the royal route. This was the famous occasion on which a painter depicted Henry VIII holding a volume inscribed *Verbum Dei* (the Word of God); when some functionary realised that the Catholic rulers might be distressed by this reference to Henry's religion, the sign painter was summoned, interrogated, and finally made to paint a pair of gloves over the offending book. A *Te Deum* was again sung at St Paul's. On St Luke's Day (18 October) Philip returned to the cathedral to hear mass sung by a Spanish priest. By this time the rood had been reinstated.

With Philip at her side, Mary was ready for the final stages in the restoration of the Catholic faith. The Parliament that met in November 1554 passed a second Act of Revocation, annulling all the religious legislation of Henry VIII's reign, back to the beginning of the Reformation Parliament in 1529. This very long Bill confirmed the confiscations of Henry and Edward, so that persons who had acquired church lands need not fear that they would lose their property. It also acknowledged the existence of Henry VIII's new bishoprics. The charge of treason that had been laid by Henry against his Catholic kinsman Cardinal Pole was now lifted, in order that Pole could enter England again after his long exile in Italy and assume the post of archbishop of Canterbury to which Mary intended to name him once Cranmer had been deprived.

Pole's arrival and his ceremonial absolution of the entire realm from the sins of heresy and schism that had been committed in the years since 1533 provided the occasion for what must have been the most splendid and, for some, the most moving event of the century at St Paul's. On 2 December, the second Sunday in Advent, the king and cardinal attended high mass. The mayor, aldermen and members of the City guilds were present in their finest liveries, as were a hundred English, a hundred Spanish and a hundred German guards of honour. The choir of the Chapel Royal joined the musicians from the cathedral in singing the service. It is said that such a audience was never before seen at St Paul's and that all listened in profound silence as Gardiner preached on the text, 'Brethren, now is the time to awake out of sleep'.

The work of refurbishing cathedrals, providing ornaments appropriate for Catholic worship and restoring old customs proceeded rapidly and has left traces in most of the surviving accounts and chapter act books. The queen herself gave jewels for a new screen at Westminster Abbey. Eight stops were added to the organ there, new music was written for the coronation, and old service books were bought back from singing men who had taken them away during Edward's reign. Five quarts of muscatel were provided 'accordyng to the old custome' for the choir and readers of the Passion on Palm Sunday 1555, when candles, incense and baskets of flowers to be strewn by the choristers were also purchased.

The accounts for Canterbury list an exceptionally large number of expenses associated with the revival of traditional worship. Missals, psalters, antiphoners, ordinals, pontificals and other service books were acquired. John Marden, a singing man, was paid for 'pricking' a *Gloria in Excelsis, Sanctus* and *Agnus Dei*. His colleague, Robert Colman, received 5s. 'for prycking of four bookes to set forthe the olde Service', while a priest, George Frevell, was given 12d. for writing out a legend of St Thomas. A new organ was erected in the Lady chapel, and other organs were repaired with calf skins and glue for their bellows. A chalice and paten, cruet, pax, monstrance and sanctus bell were provided. Among the new vestments and hangings were copes, tunicles, albs and frontals (with fringe). A new rood was made, with statues of Mary and John as well as Christ on the Cross, all painted and gilded. The Easter sepulchre and paschal candle were reinstated.

Some of the refurbishing at Canterbury was probably undertaken in preparation for a visit by the queen and Cardinal Pole in 1557. Additional organs appear to have been borrowed for this great occasion, since four labourers were paid 8d. 'for feching and carydg of a paire of organs from St Georges and thether againe'. When the queen departed she was given £10 in a purse of crimson velvet ornamented with gold and lace. Perhaps it was at this time that Pole presented a gold and silver mitre to his cathedral church. He also fitted up the old almonry chapel for his private use.

York was fortunate in receiving ornaments as gifts. In 1556 an alderman, George Gale, provided money for an altar frontal of purple, red and blue velvet with the Resurrection embroidered on it in gold, and a year later Sir Leonard Beckwith presented a red and green canopy under which the sacrament might be carried in procession. The cathedral's own funds paid for repainting the high altar and replacing statues of the Virgin and St John, presumably as a rood loft. The fabric rolls record the payment of 4s. 8d. for old glass, probably panels which had been removed from the windows because they contained images that had been hidden away to avoid destruction. Some of the windows were releaded, and 4d. was paid 'for setting uppe of an ymage'. Other expenses include making a tabernacle and scouring candlesticks.

At Wells fourteen great tapers were supplied for the Easter sepulchre at a cost of 2s. 8d., while £18 was paid to Richard Roberts of London, probably an embroiderer, for twelve silk copes and six dalmatics and tunicles. The dean and chapter of Chichester bought copes, tunicles, albs, antiphoners, processionals, hymnals and books of music for the Lady chapel; they paid for repairing bells and raising and lowering the great paschal candle. Although no local records provide proof, it may be that some cathedrals were able to take back gold copes and other vestments that were still stored at Whitehall, for a contemporary diary says that 'good qwyne Mare' ordered them to be returned to churches which could identify their former property.

It appears that some service books, a chasuble, two tunicles of blue velvet and a needlework cushion had been hidden away at Lichfield; they were restored to the cathedral. The dean of Hereford presented a new cope to his church – probably quite a plain one, since it cost only 40s. At Chester, a conservative cathedral where the return of the old religion was generally welcomed, twelve pounds of wax was provided for tapers at Candlemas and wine and ale were allowed on Maundy Thursday; a painted cloth with velvet embroideries and silk fringe was placed on the Jesus altar (presumably the high altar), and a pax and censer were purchased for the altar dedicated to Our Lady. At Durham, where the reconciliation with Rome was celebrated with feasting, bonfires and minstrels, repairs were made to the bells and windows, wainscot was placed around the altar, and a 'cayse' of ironwork was made for the Sacrament reserved there.

Monastic life in Westminster Abbey was revived in 1556. For the first three years of Mary's reign the abbey had continued to operate as a cathedral, sharing that status in the diocese of London with St Paul's. But Mary was personally devoted to the idea of monastic orders; while recognizing that it was impossible to reestablish all the monasteries or to return the endowments confiscated from them, she was eager to see the institution of monasticism reborn and to provide for the restoration of at least a few religious houses.

On 7 September letters patent for the dissolution of the existing foundation at Westminster and the erection of the new abbey were issued. The dean and chapter resigned on 26 September and the monastery received its endowments on 10 November. Additional chalices, bells and vestments were purchased, together with £40 worth of choir books and £13 in missals and service manuals. The singing men and choristers remained, now probably performing services at the high altar, although they had sung only in the Lady chapel prior to the dissolution.

By the end of November 1556 about twenty-six monks had returned to the abbey. Only two of them were from the old community at Westminster; the others came from different Benedictine houses. There were also at least two Cistercians and two Augustinian canons. By the end of the reign some fifty men had come to the abbey, and several had died while wearing the habit. The Marian abbot, John Feckenham, was a sincere and able man who had been sent to the Tower during Edward's reign. Freed by Mary, he was dean of St Paul's during her earlier years on the throne and was well qualified to oversee the refounding of the monastery. But he was realistic and worldly, not a fanatic about monkish observances; many years later a writer who had known some of Feckenham's monks wrote that he did 'not insist much upon monastick regularities, but contented himself to have sett up there a disciplin much like to that he saw observed in cathedral churches, as for the Divine Office; and as for other things he brought them to the laws and customs of colledges and inns of court'.

Some of the records for this period have been lost (or perhaps they were never generated by the monks), so we know relatively little about the exact state of affairs at the abbey during the Marian restoration. It is probable the church was little affected by the changeover from secular to monastic status and that most of the officials remained in place during the later years of Mary's reign. It does appear, however, that the choir saw its worst days under Mary. There were only eight boys in 1553, and the allocation for choristers' expenses was reduced from £33 6s. 8d. to £27 18s. 4d. It was suggested that the number of lay singing men be cut in half, with only eight men and five boys at the time of Mary's death. It would be interesting to know just how the polyphony of these trained singers was mixed with the plainsong chanted by the monks themselves, but the surviving sources do not say.

A significant number of Protestants fled to the Continent during Mary's reign. Some, no doubt, feared persecution and possible death if they remained in England; others were moved by conscience and the determination to worship according to the dictates of a reformed church. In either case, their motives must have been strong, for the dislocation of family life and the distress of financial uncertainty would have been enough to stay the fainthearted.

Nearly eight hundred Marian exiles can be traced.[5] Of these, a number were wives, children and servants; we have the names of 472 adult males, of whom sixty-seven were priests. In 1553 or shortly thereafter thirty persons who had served the cathedrals in some capacity left England for Frankfurt, Strasbourg, Geneva, Zurich or some other refuge.

The exiles included six deans: Bartholomew Traheron and Thomas Sampson, successive deans of Chichester, Robert Horne of Durham, Thomas Cole of Salisbury, William Turner of Wells, and Richard Cox, who had held both Westminster and Oxford. Several of these, most notably Horne and Turner, were such radical Protestants that they had been involved in disputes with the own chapters prior to Mary's accession. The five exiled archdeacons included Thomas Cranmer's brother Edmund (who took the archbishop's son under his care), John Aylmer and Thomas Bullingham from the diocese of Lincoln, the future bishop John Jewel of Chichester, and Guy Heton of Gloucester.

Four of the eighteen exiled canons or prebendaries had held positions at Westminster (the group included a future archbishop, Edmund Grindal); there were also men from Canterbury, Lichfield, Oxford, Peterborough (Edwin Sandys, the future archbishop of York), St David's (Thomas Young, the precentor and effective head of the cathedral), St Paul's, Salisbury, Wells (William Thynne, brother of Sir John, the builder of Longleat), and York. Two of the six preachers who had been appointed according to the statutes at Canterbury fled (they were Richard Beeley and John Joseph). The roster of exiles was completed by Alexander Nowell, headmaster of Westminster School and a future dean of St Paul's, and, rather surprisingly, a former chantry priest, John Staunton from Hereford.

Pathetic as the plight of the exiles often was, the sufferings of those who were imprisoned and martyred were infinitely greater. In all, about three hundred men and women were executed between February 1555 and November 1558, and others died in custody, sometimes of starvation. Although most of the martyrs were husbandmen or artisans – weavers, glovers or shoemakers, for instance – a significant minority were priests, several of whom had held office in one of the cathedrals.

The best-known Marian martyrs were of course the bishops, especially the Oxford martyrs, Ridley and Latimer (who were burned together) and Cranmer. Curiously enough, these three had no special connection with Oxford; all had been educated at Cambridge, and they had held other bishoprics. No doubt many who witnessed the emotional scenes of fervour and distress as these men went to the stake were moved, but it was not because they had known the victims.

The burning of John Hooper at Gloucester may have been different, for he had been a zealous and controversial leader there. He had also served as bishop of Worcester, for the two sees were amalgamated in 1552, only to be separated again when Hooper was deprived in 1555. Hooper was the only bishop to be executed in the precincts of his own cathedral; he was sent to the stake under a great elm tree near the college of priests at Gloucester in 1555. The priests are said to have watched his execution from a chamber over the gatehouse.

Robert Ferrar, who had been named to the Welsh see of St David's when his friend William Barlow was translated to Bath and Wells, met his death in 1555 at Carmarthen, the market town to which Barlow had tried to move the cathedral. Like Barlow, Ferrar had quarrelled bitterly with the chapter of St David's; indeed, they had brought a suit against him and he had been imprisoned in 1552, partly because he had no friend at court after the fall of Protector Somerset. According to John Foxe he died well, but since he did not speak Welsh there were probably few who understood his last words, and there may have been some gloating among the conservatives at the fate of their antagonist.

Some of the other bishops survived by going into exile; this group includes Ferrar's patron Barlow, John Ponet of Winchester, Miles Coverdale of Exeter, John Scory of Chichester and Robert King, the first bishop of Oxford. Two others, John Taylor of Lincoln and Robert Holgate, archbishop of York, died before the persecution could touch them.

Among the cathedral canons to meet their deaths by execution, pride of place belongs to John Rogers, the earliest of all the victims of the Marian purge. A prebendary of St Paul's, Rogers was especially disliked because of his association with Tyndale in preparing the English translation of the Bible. He was burned at Smithfield, not far from the cathedral, in 1555. John Bradford of St Paul's was also executed there in 1555. Rowland Taylor, another prebendary of St Paul's who is depicted by Foxe as the 'lively image or pattern of all those virtuous qualities described by St Paul', had spent most of his ministry at Hadleigh in Essex and was executed on a nearby common. John Cardmaker alias Taylor, a former friar who had married and become a prebendary of Wells, was consigned to the fires of Smithfield, while Lawrence Saunders, a reader at Lichfield and prebendary of York, was burned in Coventry.

A number of the burnings of lay people took place in cathedral cities. Generally we do not know exactly where the fires were set, but since cathedral closes provided a suitable open space it may be that many of the martyrs met death in the shade of cathedral towers. The persecution was largely concentrated in south and east England, so it is not surprising that there should have been large numbers of executions in Kent and East Anglia. Foxe tells of twenty-seven persons who were burned at Canterbury, where an additional five perished in prison. Two more were killed at Rochester.

The deans of Ely and Norwich as well as Bishop Thirlby of Ely and his
suffragan Nicholas Shaxton were active in prosecuting laymen and were
responsible for two deaths at Ely and six at Norwich. Perhaps because the
north and north-west were generally conservative areas, they remained relatively quiet. But seventeen Protestants were executed at Chichester, eleven
at Lichfield, five at Bristol, and one (a 'godly woman') at Exeter. Only a few
cathedrals escaped some sort of involvement in the Marian tragedy.

Anyone who has pored over Foxe's *Book of Martyrs*, or looked at the engravings with which most editions are illustrated, will find it hard to hold any
mental image for Mary's reign other than that of persecution and horror. So
far as the cathedrals are concerned, however, there are more positive aspects
of these years which should be put alongside accounts of deprivation and
death.

A number of Marian bishops were able men, dedicated to the restoration
of what they regarded as the true faith. Several of the Marian deans, too,
appear to have been intelligent and constructive, introducing improvements
in the organization and finance of their cathedrals. Among those who stand
out are Thomas Watson of Durham, John Christopherson of Norwich,
Thomas Reynolds of Exeter, John Feckenham of St Paul's and Westminster
Abbey, and Henry Cole, dean of St Paul's after Feckenham's departure. One
of the achievements of these leaders was a great increase in the number of
young men ordained to the priesthood and to lesser orders, especially in the
dioceses of London, Oxford and Chester. Ordinations, together with matric-
ulations at Oxford and Cambridge, had fallen severely during the unsettled
decade of the 1540s. Now, at Oxford, ordination lists for Mary's reign contain nearly five times as many names as those for Edward's, while the
increase at Chester was even more dramatic, as many as seventy priests
being ordained in Mary's last year alone. This number was far higher than
that for any earlier year in the history of the diocese.

Dean Watson may have been at least partly responsible for new statutes
that were granted to Durham Cathedral in 1555. The issuance of these had
been prompted by unusual circumstances. During Edward's reign, Bishop
Tunstall had been imprisoned and later deprived. No successor was
appointed, and an Act passed by Edward's last Parliament proposed that the
diocese be divided into two halves, with a second cathedral to be established
at Newcastle. The cathedral at Durham was to continue, but with revenues
reduced to 2000 marks a year (£1333), while the dean and chapter of
Newcastle were to be granted 1000 marks.

Edward's advisers had intended to translate Ridley from London to the
diminished bishopric of Durham. But the king died before these plans could

be put into effect, and Mary disliked them. Her first Parliament repealed the Edwardian statute, thus confirming the traditional arrangements. The see was reconstituted by letters patent early in 1554, and a full set of statutes, unusual in being issued under the great seal, was delivered to the cathedral in March 1555. They had been drawn up by Heath (the new archbishop of York), Tunstall (now restored to Durham), Bonner and Thirlby.

While based on the Henrician statutes issued for cathedrals of the new foundation, the Marian code for Durham was carefully reworked. Some of the changes were stylistic, adding clarity or removing superfluous phrases. Others, like that requiring the dean to be of sound Catholic faith, reflected the complexion of the Marian establishment. A new section defined the role of the bishop in relation to the cathedral: in processions and other ceremonies he was to take precedence over the dean and canons, and he was to be allowed to preach in the cathedral whenever he saw fit. He was still, however, not a member of the chapter. Another new section clarified and strengthened the authority of the dean. A statute defining the requirements of residence allowed the dean to spend up to forty days a year at his manor of Bearpark, the old monastic house of rest and recreation. Provision was made for a procession and mass each year on 1 October, celebrating the anniversary of the queen's coronation, and for observance of royal obits.

Further efforts were made to strengthen the church in other parts of the realm. In May 1556 the archdeaconry of Wells, which had been suppressed by an Edwardian statute, was reestablished and reendowed. At Chester and Durham the right of naming the prebendaries, formerly held by the crown, was granted to the bishop, thus bringing these houses in line with the other cathedrals of the old foundation. At Lincoln the poor clerks were revived. They and the junior vicars choral were to be housed in a new college, or school, of thirty poor clerks, within the cathedral close. Here ten scholars between the ages of fifteen and twenty were admitted in 1556, and others probably came later. In 1557 the minster school at York was refounded; fifty boys were to be taught grammar in the former hospital at the Horsefair. Dean Wotton and his colleagues in the chapter were quite specific about their hope that the men educated here would become militant shepherds who could 'put to flight the rapacious wolves, that is devilish men, ill-understanding the Catholic faith, from the sheepfolds of the sheep entrusted to them'.

The melancholy events of Mary's later years held profound implications for the cathedrals. Stephen Gardiner, the greatest conservative statesman of the century, died halfway through the reign, in November 1555. His loss was severe, for he had been Mary's lord chancellor and closest adviser as well as her bishop of Winchester. The queen's isolation and loneliness were made worse by her husband's absence. After Charles V abdicated the Spanish throne, Philip II found it essential to be in Spain, and there was no suggestion that Mary should accompany him. Even the pope abandoned Mary at the end. As part of a campaign against the Habsburgs, he withdrew his legates from all of Philip's territories, including England, denying Reginald Pole's position as archbishop of Canterbury. Mary refused to accept Pole's deprivation or the pope's nomination of the eighty-year-old former friar William Peto in his place, but the idea of quarrelling with the papacy after her struggle to restore papal jurisdiction in England was heartrending.

A further tragedy was more personal and, if possible, even more poignant. On several occasions Mary believed that she was pregnant, bearing the child who would assure the continuation of the true faith in England. There had even been *Te Deums* of rejoicing and peals of bells at St Paul's prompted by rumours that a boy had been born. But 'on the morrow it turned out otherwise'; the queen was not with child, but was suffering from delusion and ultimately from the disease that would end her life. The loss of Calais on 6 January 1558, just as her health failed, was a final bitter blow.

Within the church the absence of leadership became increasingly apparent. It was hard to find new bishops who shared the queen's views, so bishoprics were left vacant, often for a year or more. Among the sees that suffered were Carlisle, Chichester, Lincoln, Peterborough and Winchester. Bangor, Oxford and Salisbury were without bishops at the time of Mary's death. And there were financial problems: in the summer of 1558 Tunstall complained that he did not have enough money to meet his pension obligations at Durham.

Mary's brief reign ended with her death on the morning of 17 November 1558. Cardinal Pole followed her later the same day. The queen's funeral at Westminster Abbey was conducted with all the pomp that such a bastion of Catholicism could muster: the hearse was met by four bishops and the abbot, mitred and in copes, and a procession of a hundred poor men bearing long torches. John White, who had succeeded Gardiner as bishop of Winchester, preached the sermon, after which Mary's officers followed the coffin into Henry VII's chapel, broke their staffs of office, and threw them into the grave. The royal trumpeters blew a blast as the entourage departed. This was the last great Latin requiem mass to be sung in the abbey, an appropriate symbol for the end of an era in the church.

11

The Elizabethan Settlement

Pageants enacted on the eve of Elizabeth's coronation gave dramatic visual form to the realization that her accession would bring a reversal of religious policy. Naturally enough those who prepared the displays favoured change. Thus the queen was greeted, as she rode along the route near St Paul's Cathedral, with a living tableau showing the Virtues trampling on the Vices: 'Pure religion', she was told, 'did tread upon Superstition and Ignoraunce'. Another pageant contrasted Mary's 'ruinous Republic', where the 'decayed common weale' was characterized by 'want of the feare of God', with the 'well instituted Republic' or flourishing common weal, where a wise prince, learned rulers and obedient subjects lived peaceably in awe of the Almighty.[1]

Although religious changes affecting the entire realm had to wait until the assembly of Elizabeth's first Parliament, the queen proceeded to institute limited reforms in her own chapel almost immediately after her accession. According to an unsubstantiated rumour she was using the English Litany as early as 17 December, only a month after her accession. Shortly thereafter, on Christmas Day, she demonstrated that she did not believe in transubstantiation by ordering that the elevation of the host be omitted. When Bishop Oglethorpe, who was celebrating, refused to comply, the queen simply left the chapel prior to the consecration.

Far more important, since they were great public ceremonies, were the coronation and the subsequent opening of the Parliament of 1559. Both involved religious actions that implied a good deal about Elizabeth's own beliefs. There has been some disagreement about just what happened during the celebration of the mass at the coronation in Westminster Abbey, but it appears that Oglethorpe now managed to swallow his misgivings and omit the elevation. The Epistle and Gospel were read in English after they had been sung in Latin, and the consecration was probably intoned in English as well. It is significant that a bishop from the relatively obscure diocese of Carlisle officiated at such an important event. There was no archbishop of Canterbury in office, but one would have expected Archbishop Heath of York or another prominent bishop to participate. It must have been painfully evident that all of them refused to accede to the queen's demands.

The ceremonial opening of Parliament on 25 January 1559 was another opportunity for the queen to manifest her Protestantism. On this occasion the monks of Westminster were rebuffed. When the queen arrived at the abbey,

> the abbot, robed pontifically, with all his monks in procession, each of them having a lighted torch in his hand, received her as usual, giving her first of all incense and holy water; and when her Majesty saw the monks who accompanied her with the torches, she said, 'Away with these torches, for we see very well', and her choristers singing the litany in English, she was accompanied to the high altar under her canopy.

It has usually been assumed that she was protesting about the monastic procession with its smoking lights, but possibly her chief desire was to be accompanied by her young choristers, wearing white surplices and singing the English Litany, rather than elderly monks clad in black, chanting Latin. There could hardly have been a clearer visual symbol of the new order. Richard Cox, newly returned from exile, preached the sermon, inveighing against the monks as authors of the Marian persecution and urging Elizabeth to waste no time in reforming the church.

The Parliament, however, presented serious problems. The new government was caught between the conservative Marian bishops and the abbot of Westminster, who were still members of the House of Lords, and the reformers, including the 'wolves coming out of Germany' and other former exiles, who had a few seats and a larger number of friends in the Commons.

When the long session ended on 8 May the final outcome was clear: the statutes assented to by the queen included an Act of Supremacy, granting her the title Supreme Governor of the Church, and an Act of Uniformity, restoring the Book of Common Prayer to use throughout the realm. Elizabeth's title thus differed from that claimed by her father and brother, who had held Supreme Headship, but it was still to be enforced by an Oath of Supremacy that could be used as a vehicle for depriving papists of their positions in the church. The Prayer Book of 1559 was based on the second, more Protestant version of Edward's reign but with a few changes of considerable significance, all of them tending toward moderation, ambiguity and toleration, probably insisted on by the queen herself. The English services were introduced in the Chapel Royal immediately, on 12 May, and came into compulsory use everywhere on 24 June.

Royal articles and injunctions, together with a royal visitation of the church, were needed to put the Elizabethan Settlement into effect. Elizabeth's visitation articles are based on those set out at the beginning of Edward VI's reign, although the situation was somewhat different: Edward's government was innovating; Elizabeth's was in essence restoring a form of religion that had existed earlier but had been interrupted by Mary's accession.

As under Edward, several of the visitation articles dealt with images, shrines, relics and other forms of 'vain and superstitious religion'. These were to be abandoned once again, both in churches and in private homes. The visitors were to inquire whether any persons 'contemn and abuse priests and other ministers of the church', whether any talked or caused disruption during services, whether any were drunkards, adulterers, brawlers, sorcerers or rumour mongers, and whether any secretly held masses or other services prohibited by law. An article new in Elizabeth's reign inquired whether the English Litany came into use when the queen commanded it by proclamation; another ordered the compilation of lists of those who had died or were imprisoned for the sake of religion.

The injunctions of 1559 begin with the command that deans, archdeacons and parish clergy obey the laws extinguishing all foreign jurisdiction in the church and preach quarterly sermons showing 'that the queen's power within her realms and dominions is the highest power under God, to whom all men, within the same realms and dominions, by God's law owe most loyalty and obedience'. Processions must be abandoned, because they led to quarrels about precedence and because prayers said in procession could not be heard distinctly, but the Litany was retained and, indeed, given greater prominence by the order that it should be said or sung in the midst of the church before the beginning of the communion.

Two injunctions that were to prove of special importance dealt with marriage of the clergy and with church music. In both cases the queen's own tastes and preferences were involved. As is well known, Elizabeth was not enthusiastic about clerical marriage, and Sir William Cecil had to argue as 'stiffly' as he could to keep her from outlawing it altogether. (He realized, perhaps earlier than the queen did, that the reconstructed church would have to rely on ministers who had married under Edward.) If she could not go that far, Elizabeth was determined to place as many obstacles in the path of married clergy as she could. The injunctions of 1559 therefore contained a clause intended to prevent unsuitable marriages by ordering that prospective wives should be examined and approved by the diocesan bishop and two local justices of the peace. Even this demeaning requirement did not satisfy the queen; two years later she issued a supplementary order banning the wives and children of deans, prebendaries and other members of the cathedral and collegiate foundations from living within the precincts of the college or cathedral. It was said that their presence violated the intention of founders and, worse, was a hindrance to study and learning. Copies of the queen's order were written into the act books at several cathedrals, as was a letter from Archbishop Parker to the dean and chapter of Lincoln urging compliance. Fortunately for the married ministers, none of the bishops undertook a drastic campaign to enforce the rule. Many of them must have shared the views of Bishop Cox, who wrote, 'in these vast cathedral churches with their rooms plenty and several, on what ground should this be ordained? I have but one prebendary continually resident in Ely church. Turn him out, and daws and owls may dwell there for any continual housekeeping'.

The famous injunction regarding singing reflects the queen's own love of church music; it must reveal, too, that demands for extreme simplification were already being felt. Elizabeth was clearly thinking of the cathedrals among the places where 'there hath been livings appointed for the maintenance of men and children to use singing in the church, by means whereof the laudable science of music hath been had in estimation, and preserved in knowledge'. This tradition was to continue. In the hope of satisfying the reformers, the queen ordered that the new English services be sung with 'modest and distinct song ... so that the same may be as plainly understanded, as if it were read without singing'; but, 'for the comforting of such as delight in music', she permitted the singing of a more elaborate hymn or song at the end of morning or evening prayer, 'in the best sort of melody and music that may be conveniently devised'. Were it not for this clause, we might be deprived of the glorious anthems of Tudor church music.

Several additional orders were appended to the injunctions. 'An Admonition to Simple Men Deceived by Malicious' was intended to satisfy at least some of the conservatives by putting a broad interpretation on the Oath of Supremacy, indicating that the allegiance required was no greater than that acknowledged to be due to the queen's father or brother. More important for the cathedrals was a statement of policy regarding 'the Tables in the Church'. This commanded that no more altars be destroyed. In cases where they had been taken away, a wooden table might remain, but it should be placed where the altar had stood except during the actual administration of communion, when it might be moved temporarily to a more convenient location, still within the chancel. Here again the queen attempted to define a via media and to introduce that 'mediocrity in religion' which she wished to characterize her reign.

No general set of injunctions for cathedrals was prepared, as had been done earlier in Edward's reign. Instead, the royal visitors delivered separate injunctions to the dean and chapter of each cathedral as they examined them beginning in August 1559. The injunctions for Exeter, Salisbury, Peterborough, Wells and Worcester Peterborough survive, as do the answers made by the clergy of Canterbury to the visitors' queries. The issues are

Title page of the Bishops' Bible (1568). Queen Elizabeth, who represents Hope, is between Faith and Charity.

mainly the same as those dealt with in the earlier royal injunctions. In addition, there are some unique clauses. At Salisbury a divinity lecture was to be read each week, the lecturer being appointed by the chancellor and paid £20 a year; all prebendaries and other ministers of the church were to attend. Provision was made for choristers whose voices broke: formerly employed as altarists, they were now to be given the same stipends but to spend their time studying in the grammar school. Vicars choral, whether married or not, were required to live within the cathedral close or lose their appointments. At Worcester the visitors insisted that the common hall should continue, with all the petty canons, 'inferior ministers', schoolmasters and children being taught grammar or music eating together; a sufficient amount of the produce from cathedral lands was to be reserved for this purpose. The injunctions for Peterborough included a requirement that the scholars admitted to the grammar school be 'apt for learning and the poorest of birth', chosen without regard for friendship, kindred or bribery.

The normal round of services was specified more clearly than usual at Exeter. Here the day was to begin at 6 a.m. with the Litany and a New Testament lesson, followed by morning prayer at 7:45. At 9 a.m. on Monday, Wednesday and Friday the chancellor was to provide a divinity lecture, with one of the vicars choral reading a paraphrase of the Epistle and Gospel on Tuesday, Thursday and Saturday. All the vicars and singing men were expected to participate in the communion at 10 a.m., though we know from other sources that they actually received the bread and wine much less frequently. Interestingly enough the dean and chapter at Canterbury denied that they were required to have a divinity lecture (although they acknowledged that the staff was still to include the six preachers), and therefore said that they could not be bound to attend it.

Some further orders issued between 1560 and 1562 complete the first phase of the Settlement. The Ornaments Rubric printed in the new Prayer Book required ministers to wear the vestments in use during Edward VI's second year. (Evidently the intention was to bring back the vestments prescribed by the Prayer Book of 1549, even though this was not actually issued until Edward's third year; that would include albs, chasubles – commonly referred to simply as 'vestments' during this period – and copes at communion, white linen surplices at other services.) A supplementary royal injunction regulating the outdoor garb of the clergy perhaps added confusion by referring to the garments commonly worn at the end of Edward's reign. An interpretation issued by the bishops said very directly that there was to be 'only one apparel' throughout the land: 'the cope in the ministration of the Lord's Supper, and the surplice at all other ministrations'. Their requirement faced considerable opposition from the Puritans, who refused to don vestments that smacked of popery and superstition, and soon led to one of the most bitter confrontations of Elizabeth's reign.

A proclamation issued in 1560 complained of the destruction or defacing of ancient monuments and tombs in churches and cathedrals. This 'barbarous' practice was to cease, and those who were guilty of it, if they were known and still alive, were to restore the monuments. A royal order of 1561 dealt with rood lofts and related matters. In many places the figures so recently set up under Mary were taken down by overzealous reformers at the beginning of the new reign; the roods, 'with Mares [Marys] and Johns and odur emages', made two great bonfires in London. Elizabeth herself would have been pleased to see the roods remain, but (uncharacteristically) she finally gave ground on the issue, and the order confirmed that they should be removed. Their place could be taken by a 'convenient crest' if desired – this led to occasional taunts that the 'lion and dog' flanking the royal arms had replaced the religious images. Some sort of partition between the nave and the choir, such as that which the old roods had provided, was said to be appropriate. Fonts were not to be moved from their accustomed places, nor was there to be any further damage to bells, steeples or porches. The Ten Commandments were to be displayed on the wall behind communion tables; a printed form was suitable for parish churches, but cathedrals were to have 'the said precepts more largely and costly painted out, to the better shew of the same'. Finally, the linguistic situation in Wales was at last acknowledged in injunctions that provided for the reading of the catechism as well as the Epistle and Gospel in Welsh.

The Elizabethan Oath of Supremacy was used as an instrument for ejecting from the church those ministers who refused to support the Settlement. At the episcopal level the revolution was virtually total; there was a greater break in continuity than at any other time in the history of the English church. Ten sees were vacant in 1559, so only seventeen bishops were required to subscribe. Fifteen of them declined to do so and were deprived. Oglethorpe, having accommodated the queen earlier, now obeyed his conscience and joined his colleagues in refusing submission; he died at the end of December 1559. The only Marian bishop who was not put out was the octogenarian Anthony Kitchin of Llandaff, a weak reed on which to support a church, and even he did not actually swear, merely submitting a curious paper in which he promised conformity to the new course of religion mandated by the government.

In filling the vacancies created by this purge, Elizabeth relied heavily on men who had been Marian exiles and, earlier, scholars and administrators at Cambridge and Oxford. Matthew Parker, the new archbishop of

Canterbury, had been dean of Lincoln and master of Corpus Christi College, Cambridge. He preferred the study of Anglo-Saxon history to involvement in theological controversy; more than any other prominent cleric of the reign he shared the queen's own moderate, generally tolerant views. Many of the other new bishops were dedicated reformers with advanced beliefs. These included Edmund Grindal, who was made bishop of London. Richard Cox was sent to Ely, Edwin Sandys to Worcester and John Jewel to Salisbury. William Barlow, previously bishop of St David's and, later, Bath and Wells, was now given Chichester, while John Scory, the Edwardian bishop of Chichester, was named to Hereford. These men, and others like them, soon came into contact – and often conflict – with the cathedrals.

Most of the cathedrals also witnessed a substantial turnover of clergy. In all, twelve deans, twenty-five archdeacons and just over a hundred prebendaries were deprived or replaced between 1558 and 1564. A few examples will illustrate the situation. At Worcester the Catholic dean, Seth Holland, who had spent Edward's reign on the Continent, was replaced by John Pedder, a Marian exile and intransigent Puritan; five of the ten canons were ejected. John Ramridge, the zealous papist dean of Lichfield, voluntarily left England at the time of Elizabeth's accession, only to be murdered in Flanders. He was succeeded by Laurence Nowell, a Marian exile, eminent antiquarian, and (like Parker) an Anglo-Saxon scholar. Laurence's older brother, Alexander Nowell, who had been master of Westminster School and a prebendary of the abbey before fleeing to Frankfurt, became dean of St Paul's.

Another exile, the learned physician and botanist William Turner, was restored to the deanery at Wells – the Marian dean, John Goodman, was ejected, as he had been once before under Edward VI. Turner was soon in trouble: too much a Calvinist precisian to comply with the moderate Settlement, he was suspended for nonconformity in 1564, and his writings were banned. At Hereford, John Ellys supplanted the Marian dean, William Daniel, and several of the prebends changed hands. One of Queen Mary's secretaries of state, John Boxall, was sent from the deanery of Peterborough to the Tower of London; his place was filled by William Latimer, who was also a prebendary of Westminster.

Religious change was of course especially evident in London. At St Paul's five archdeacons (one of them the notorious John Harpsfield) and perhaps as many as twelve prebendaries were deprived. Harpsfield and his brother Nicholas, who lost his own archdeacon's position at Canterbury, were both imprisoned for strenuous opposition to the Protestant Settlement. Nicholas Wotton, more prominent as a diplomat than as a dean (though he held that post at both Canterbury and York), possessed a pliable conscience that enabled him to retain his preferments from the 1540s until his death in 1567, but about half the members of the chapter at York were displaced at the beginning of Elizabeth's reign. In addition to Nicholas Harpsfield, four prebendaries were deprived at Canterbury.

More remote areas were relatively immune to revolution. At Carlisle, Lancelot Salkeld, the former prior who had presented the screen, took the oath but seems to have been deprived nonetheless. He soon accommodated Elizabeth by dying, and Sir Thomas Smith, the layman who was to be one of her principal secretaries, was restored to the deanery that he had held under Edward. But the chancellor and all four prebendaries (one of them a former monk and all of them probably conservative) remained in office. At Chester two archdeacons were deprived, but the four canons named by Mary stayed in place. Hugh Turnbull, appointed dean of Chichester a few months before Mary's death, retained that position until he died in 1567, but as many as twelve prebendaries of Chichester appear to have been ejected.

Even where there was change, the tone might remain conservative. A good example is provided by Durham, which saw the deprivation of Mary's dean, Thomas Robertson, and the return of his Edwardian predecessor, Robert Horne. Nine of the prebendaries originally refused to subscribe – one of them said quite clearly, 'the Pope hath and ought to have the jurisdiction ecclesiastical and not the Queen' – but several eventually persuaded themselves that accommodation to the new order was possible, and only five were actually deprived. Eight minor canons who originally declined the oath also submitted in the end. The result was a chapter that was dominated by conservatives for a decade or more, a situation common in other cathedrals as well. Although five or six canons were deprived at Lincoln, the dean, Queen Mary's former chaplain Francis Mallet, was allowed to stay on, and that chapter, too, resisted change for several years.

Since so many prominent Protestants had fled from England under Mary, it was not surprising that Elizabeth turned to Marian exiles in staffing her church. In all, we know of nineteen men who had held positions in the cathedrals before 1553 and returned to an office (not necessarily the same one) after 1558. An additional thirty-eight exiles, not previously employed in a cathedral, were given posts under Elizabeth. Most of them became canons, but we can count at least four exiles appointed to deaneries at the beginning of the reign and five more named after 1561.

Changes in the physical appearance of the cathedrals made the coming of the new order clear for all to see. Entries in the account books often tell just what was done, and when. At Salisbury the unusually full fabric account for 1559 includes payments for taking down altars, laying altar stones, setting twenty-three feet of new glass in the chapel on the north side of the church, and procuring a large printed Bible for the choir as well as copies of the Prayer Book and Psalter. The charges for painting and erecting the Ten Commandments are recorded at Winchester ('to Addams for painting upp ye X Commaundyments where the altar stoode', 20s.), Chichester (the purchase of canvas and paint), and Chester (a mere 14d. 'to my Lord Busshops man' who did the work). Three tables of the Commandments were set up at Wells in 1561, at a cost of only 4d., but this was evidently a temporary expedient and a year later a painter from Gloucester received 53s. 4d. 'for writing off the X Commandementes and other thinges upon the wall within the quier'.

Payments for communion cups are found in several places. Probably there was a general order, issued about 1560, commanding that pre-Reformation chalices no longer be used, because of their association with the popish mass. No copy of such an injunction seems to have survived, but local records show its being put into effect nonetheless. It is not clear exactly how the new cup was to differ from the old chalice; no doubt it was to be larger, since it was intended to hold wine for the whole congregation, not just for the priests. Certainly this was the case at Canterbury, where two chalices were melted down to make one communion cup and an additional sum of 39s. 7d. was paid, presumably for more silver. At the same time an hourglass was provided for the pulpit in an obvious attempt to regulate the length of sermons. Communion cups also figure in the accounts at Durham, Carlisle and Chichester, and the bishops ordered that they be provided at Rochester, Norwich, York and Winchester. At Lincoln the holy table was to be covered with 'a comely table cloth'; there were to be two 'handsome Communion cups, and a decent paten of silver to minister the Lord's bread upon, and also two comely pots of pewter to fetch wine to serve the Lord's table, reserved and kept clean to that use, being no tavern pots'.

During a later visitation at Worcester the sexton testified that the plate and jewels had been taken away by the prebendaries at the beginning of Elizabeth's reign and divided among them, 'but to what use they did employ the same he saith that he cannot tell. And the Copes, Vestmentes, and suche ornamentes were converted, some of them to the making of cushens, and to some suche other uses belonging to the Churche, and the rest therof converted, he knoweth not to what uses'. Some years later, Dean Goodwin of Canterbury was accused of dividing and selling £1000 worth of plate and ornaments, but he insisted that the division had occurred at the beginning of the reign, when Wotton was dean, so that 'not a tenth' remained when Goodwin took office. At Peterborough, Bishop Scambler inquired whether any persons had sold vestments, ornaments or plate, or had converted them to their own private uses without his permission. One would have expected the use of incense to disappear after 1559, with thuribles being melted down or hidden away, but the accounts record payments to 'thuriblers' at York as late as 1562. Throughout the 1570s injunctions issued by the bishops and archbishops frequently ordered the destruction of any remaining popish books or articles, and as late as 1581 Bishop Chaderton still thought it necessary to inquire whether such 'monuments of superstition and idolatry' as missals, antiphoners, vestments, paxes, sacring bells, censers or crosses and candlesticks remained in the diocese of Chester.

Account books also record the purchase of books necessary for performing the new services. We know that psalters were bought at Wells, Salisbury, Chester and Canterbury, where a 'table of Psalms' was painted up and erected to remind the vicars which ones were appointed for each service. The treasurer at Chester was evidently not fond of the new English texts, for he recorded the purchase of a considerable quantity of paper 'for prickyng of dyvers strange songs to the quyre'. But at Wells the communar noted the payment of 13*d*. 'to Mr Lyde for a good songe, viz. *Te Deum* in Englishe'.

The cathedral at Durham was deeply involved in the Northern Rising, or Rebellion of the Earls, in 1569. As old aristocrats and adherents to the old faith, the earls of Westmorland and Northumberland were out of step with the Elizabethan government and were ignored by the queen and her council. Thus isolated, they came to believe that many of their neighbours in the north of England shared their convictions and would rise under their banner if they sought to restore Catholicism and gain recognition for Mary, Queen of Scots, as the legitimate ruler. Indeed enough rebels did gather in Yorkshire and the county of Durham to frighten the government badly – their number was said, at its peak, to exceed five thousand.

A force of five hundred horsemen entered the city of Durham on 14 November 1569. Dean Whittingham had suggested that the church mobilize the tenants on its estates to oppose the rebels, but Bishop Pilkington refused to do so and the riders were not challenged. Making straight for the cathedral, they smashed the communion table and destroyed Protestant books, proclaiming in the name of the queen herself that the Catholic faith had been restored. Westmorland's uncle, Cuthbert Neville, was left in charge while the earls and most of their followers moved south. Under his direction labourers re-erected several altars and replaced holy water stoops. The Latin mass was restored in the cathedral; especially splendid services were held on St Andrew's Day (30 November) and the following Sunday, 4 December, when the preacher inveighed against Protestantism and pronounced the reconciliation of the faithful to Rome. This state of affairs continued for a month. Only on 16 December were the rebels driven out of the city. For eight days there were no services in the cathedral. Finally the Prayer Book was brought back into use and the Anglican Settlement was re-established.

Once the rebellion had been suppressed the government set about determining what had happened and fixing punishment. Just over two hundred were executed in the county of Durham, and another eighty in the city itself – a tenth of the adult male population. Depositions were taken from various members of the cathedral staff. A lay clerk admitted that he

> came to masse, matens, evensong, procession, and like idolatrous service, therat knelling [kneeling], bowing, knocking, and shewing such like reverent gesture, used praying on beades, confession or shriving to a priest, toke holy water and holye breade; and did also then and ther heare false and erroneouse doctrine against God and the churche of England preached by one W. Holmes in the pulpit, and, subjecting him selve to the same doctrine, and to the Pope, did, among other like wicked people knowen to him, knell down and received absolution under Pope Pius name, in latin; falsely terming this Godly estate of England to be a schism or heresy.

When the dean attempted to correct three more lay clerks before allowing them to receive communion, they insisted that he had no jurisdiction over them (the dean and chapter might have, but not the dean alone) and that the cathedral was legally bound by its Marian statutes, which commanded the use of the Latin services. George Clyffe, a prebendary, spoke nostalgically about hearing the Advent anthem *Gaude, Virgo Christopara* but denied that he had received 'the Poop's absolution'. A minor canon admitted that he had sung *Ora pro nobis* out of a processioner delivered to him by the chanter, a significant indication that old service books had not been destroyed, and John Brimley, the ageing organist, confessed that he had 'played at orgaines, and dyd dyvers tymes help to singe *salveas* at mattins and evesong, and went in procession, as other dyd, after the Crosse'. At the command of Neville and Northumberland he had also instructed the choristers in the use of the old services, which the boys would of course not have heard before. Several labourers, when examined, stated that they had set up five altars and helped roll and lift two large stones into place for the high altar, but they insisted that they were forced to do so and had acted against their will. This is again interesting evidence, suggesting that pieces of altars had been hidden away in the hope that they would one day be wanted again.

Four conservative minor canons were deprived following the rebellion. Fourteen others known to have been involved were permitted to retain their positions. Protestant members of the chapter complained that they had lost books and furniture, and Dean Whittingham, who had fled south before the rebels arrived, said that his house had been entered and spoiled, his books 'rent in pieces ... in such sort and abundance as was pityfull to beholde', and cattle and corn stolen from his manors.

Conservative rebels, like the earls and their followers, could be dealt with by military action and, if necessary, execution. The reformers who mounted opposition to the Settlement could not be handled in that way, and they proved far more difficult for the queen and her ecclesiastical leaders to manage.

Puritan dissatisfaction with the Elizabethan church hardened around several issues. The first of these to become evident involved music. In December 1559, when the Settlement was less than a year old, a group of townspeople from Exeter, probably urged on by zealots from London, invaded the choir of Exeter Cathedral, usurped the places of the lay clerks, and began singing metrical psalms at the early morning service. In doing so they were attempting to introduce the simplified, unaccompanied congregational singing favoured by Calvin at Geneva and adopted by the more advanced Marian exiles. The clergy tried to drive the singers out, but when an appeal was made to royal visitors, including Bishop Jewel, they lost their case, for the visitors admonished them to permit these 'godly doings' to continue. In a further appeal to the ecclesiastical commissioners the dean and chapter pointed out that they were merely trying to enforce the Act of Uniformity by forbidding liturgical actions not sanctioned by the Prayer Book, but this, too, was unsuccessful, and the Puritan singers won the day.

The issue came to a head in the Convocation of 1563. In preparation for this the Puritan leaders had drafted a set of 'General Notes' that proposed, among other things, that 'the use of organs and curious singing be removed'. An expansion of this demand, found in the more detailed 'Seven Articles', said that the psalms should be sung 'distinctly by the whole congregation', or, if that were not convenient, be said by the minister alone. Had such a petition prevailed, the long tradition of church music in the English cathedrals would have been terminated, the organs silenced and the choirs disbanded. Several prominent churchmen, including Dean Nowell of St Paul's, supported the radical position, which came close to gaining the endorsement of the Lower House. In the end a more tolerant view prevailed, and the deputies of the clergy merely requested that organs be removed but that otherwise the queen's broad-minded injunction regarding music be put in execution. Vicars choral throughout the land, if they knew what was going on in London, must have rejoiced when the Genevan propositions failed. Most organists, too, probably realized that their positions were safe enough so long as they enjoyed the support of the dean or bishop.

Local sources make it abundantly clear that the traditional sung services continued everywhere, and that organs were repaired, tuned and in some cases enlarged or rebuilt. Choral singing of the traditional Prayer Book canticles was confirmed in an agreement with the new organist appointed at Lincoln after William Byrd left the cathedral to take up duties in the Chapel Royal: the *Te Deum* and *Canticum Zacharie* (the *Benedictus*) were to be used at matins, with *Magnificat* and *Nunc Dimittis* at evensong, and the services were to include 'Le anthem'.

Still, there were occasional Puritan outbursts. In 1570 the queen, obviously distressed at rumours emanating from Norwich, ordered Bishop Parkhurst to inquire into the activities of certain prebendaries who were said to have broken down the organs and committed other outrages in the choir. Parkhurst's reply does not exist, but his injunctions for the cathedral, issued in 1571, suggest that he was in two minds about the matter: he said that 'no ditties nor notes of psalms' were to be used without authority but betrayed his sympathy by referring to them as 'godly songs'. Troubles at Norwich may well have continued, however, for George Gardiner, who was probably one of the offending prebendaries, was named dean in 1573.

The Puritan dean of Durham, William Whittingham, wrote metrical versions of several of the psalms, and also of the Ten Commandments, but his love of music led him to support the continued use of organs and anthems. While he was dean of York, Matthew Hutton regularly purchased additional copies of the Genevan psalter. Bishop Horne's injunctions for Winchester Cathedral (1571) suggest that he, too, favoured the Puritan position on music, for he commanded 'that in the choir no note shall be used in song that shall drown any word or syllable, or draw out in length or shorten any word or syllable otherwise than by the nature of the word it is pronounced in common speech, whereby the sentence cannot well be perceived by the hearers'. This was clearly more restrictive than the queen's order.

For the church at large, although not for the cathedrals, the issue of vestments gave rise to more bitter division than the matter of music. The Ornaments Rubric and the bishops' interpretation of it – copes for communion, surplices for all other services – had never pleased the reformers, whose 'gloss upon this text' was 'that we shall not be forced to use them'. We know that copes were used in some places; a statement of custom at Canterbury made in 1563, for instance, says that the epistler and gospeller, in addition to the celebrant, wore them. But practice varied, and if there was one thing that the queen could not tolerate it was outward, visible lack of uniformity in her church.

The surprisingly moderate Puritan proposals regarding copes made in the

Convocation of 1563 would have softened the requirements by allowing the surplice for all services. These failed to pass in the Lower House by a single vote; even if they had been adopted, they would have been rejected by the queen as going too far and by the real reformers as not going far enough. Parker seems to have been able to persuade Elizabeth not to give ground, by agreeing that she would not oppose some relaxation of the order even though she would not give it her official sanction. Thus the archbishop's 'Advertisements' of 1566 make a distinction between cathedrals, where copes should continue to be worn by the chief ministers at communion, with surplices for all other services and hoods for preachers, and parish churches, where 'a comely surplice with sleeves, to be provided at the charges of the parish', is to be the attire for all services. With this lower standard as the basis on which uniformity was to be enforced, the issue was joined between those ministers who flatly refused to wear the surplice, for them an important symbol of continued belief in popery and darkness, and those whose consciences permitted them to satisfy the queen and acquiesce in the archbishop's command.

The first confrontation between these opposing forces came at Oxford, where two leading Protestant divines, Thomas Sampson, the dean of Christ Church, and Laurence Humphrey, president of Magdalen College, continued their long-standing campaign against the surplice. As early as 1549, when Sampson had been ordained by Bishop Ridley, he had refused to wear the popish garb and had been granted a dispensation. Appointed dean of Chichester shortly before Edward's death, Sampson had spent Mary's reign imbibing the pure Protestant waters of Geneva and Zurich. He was offered the bishopric of Norwich in 1560 but turned it down, accepting instead a canonry at Durham and, in 1561, his appointment at Oxford. Here he made a bonfire of popish articles that a diarist called 'great riches' which might have been turned to other uses. For a time Sampson was permitted to preach in a doctoral gown rather than a surplice, but in March 1565 he was called before the Ecclesiastical High Commission; when he refused to conform he was deprived. He thus has the distinction of being the first man ejected from the English church for nonconformity.

Humphrey's case was similar. A great scholar and linguist, educated at both Cambridge and Oxford, he was a Marian exile but on his return was named regius professor of divinity at Oxford and president of Magdalen College. He too was deprived in 1564.

The Vestiarian Controversy reached its climax a year later, when Archbishop Parker, on the queen's order, required the clergy to promise that they would wear the surplice. A petition signed by twenty leading churchmen, including deans Nowell of St Paul's and Whittingham of Durham, requested the ecclesiastical commissioners to renounce any attempt at enforcement, but this plea did not gain acceptance. The campaign against nonconformity was now centred primarily in London. Some ministers simply feigned illness and absented themselves from gatherings at which they would be asked to subscribe, but quite a number had the courage of their convictions and were driven out of the church for their refusal to comply. This episode marks the real beginning of organized nonconformity in England.

So far as we know, the cathedrals were relatively little affected, for many of their officers were either conservative or Erastian. Grindal said that he disliked the order but would comply – he was willing to wear a surplice at St Paul's but did not promise to do so everywhere. Bishops Cox, Guest, Horne and Jewel, though they might have private scruples, conformed publicly and encouraged others to do the same. At Durham both Bishop Pilkington and Dean Whittingham abhorred the surplice – with fine literary flair Whittingham wrote to Leicester, 'How can God's glory be advanced by those garments which superstitious men and Antichrist have invented for the maintaining and beautifying of idolatry?' – and both were brought before the High Commission on charges of failing to wear it. In the end they promised to conform and doubtless did so on occasion, but Whittingham may well have continued to conduct services in a black gown rather than a surplice, and it is said that he did not celebrate communion after 1563 in order to avoid putting on a cope. In 1567 three of the Durham prebendaries were brought before the High Commission for vestiarian offences and two of them were deprived. Documentary sources do not reveal exactly what the normal practice was, but several paintings show the surplice being worn at Durham, and one may assume that this was the custom in the 1570s.

Elsewhere a few adamant Protestants were deprived. The irrepressible William Turner of Wells, who supposedly trained his dog to snatch the square cap off the head of a bishop dining with him, lost a lectureship in Middlesex but was allowed to retain the profits of his deanery. Robert Crowley, perhaps the most vocal of all the recalcitrant clerics, whose appointments had included an archdeaconry at Hereford and a canonry at St Paul's, was imprisoned and forced to beg the Privy Council for mercy. A conciliatory line was taken by Bishop Horne in his injunctions of 1571 for Winchester, which stipulated that copes worn in the cathedral should be plain, 'without any images', but this cannot have made much difference; if Horne imagined that the opposition was limited to the embroidered orphreys on the copes, he did not understand his adversaries very well.

In the later years of the queen's reign the issue of vestments generated less heat, and the government tacitly permitted black Geneva gowns in place of the white surplices. Sampson, for instance, was allowed to officiate outside

Oxford without wearing offensive vestments, a practice he continued at St Paul's after being named a prebendary there in 1570. Humphrey became dean of Winchester in 1580, evidently still adhering to his earlier views. But in 1589 Bishop Freake exhorted the dean and prebendaries of Worcester to wear surplices and hoods. We will never know precisely what the situation was in all the cathedrals, but the chances are that they presented a motley sight: the choristers and singing men probably wore surplices, but a number of the higher officials may have succeeded in officiating without them.

Another issue that separated the Puritans from their more conservative colleagues was the relative importance of preaching and sacraments. Zealous Protestants had always set great store by sermons, through which the people could be instructed in religion and exhorted to godly living, while the more conservative wing of the church continued to believe in the importance and efficacy of the eucharist. On this matter the reformers' point of view prevailed more and more as the sixteenth century wore on, with frequent sermons and infrequent communions becoming the rule, even in the cathedrals.

One can follow the decline of the frequency of eucharistic celebrations in episcopal injunctions and in the record books of the cathedrals themselves. The Royal Injunctions of 1559 for Exeter Cathedral seem to anticipate a daily communion, but this was unusual. At Winchester a weekly celebration was required. One set of orders for Rochester mentions communion every Sunday and on holy days, but another speaks of celebration every three weeks. That was in 1565; by 1571 monthly communion was the norm. At Wells the queen's visitors required one of the residentiary canons to celebrate communion on the first Sunday of each month, with all the canons and vicars receiving the elements. Similar orders refer to monthly celebrations at St Paul's, Canterbury, Salisbury and York. The matter should have been settled by Parker's Advertisements of 1566, which required that communion be administered in cathedrals and colleges on the first or second Sunday of each month; the dean, prebendaries and other clerks were to receive monthly, and other members of the cathedral staff at least four times a year. This was a significant decline from the standard weekly celebrations anticipated by the rubrics in the 1559 Prayer Book. But even this modest requirement was not always observed. Archbishop Grindal's injunctions for cathedrals in the province of Canterbury, issued in 1576, refer merely to a yearly reception, as do Bishop Howland's for Peterborough (about 1584). At Wells two vicars choral were suspended in 1581 because they had not communicated in four years. In 1596 the vicars there were admonished to receive communion at least three times a year, but not all complied and two vicars had to be threatened with deprivation in 1599 if they continued to fail to communicate.

Preaching, on the other hand, grew in importance. Weekly sermons were required almost everywhere. The orders for Winchester, set out in 1562 and 1571, were especially clear; they charged the prebendaries with providing sermons each Sunday, either preaching in person or by deputy. Each prebendary had to preach at least one sermon a year himself. Fines of 20s., to be used for poor relief, were to be levied for any failure to deliver the sermons, which were to deal with such topics as royal supremacy, the end of the pope's usurpation and the 'enormities' of private masses. The dean, prebendaries, and other ministers are to attend all of these sermons, unless they are prevented from doing so by a 'just, urgent, and lawful cause'. Grindal's injunctions for York Minster (1572) include a schedule showing clearly which officer was responsible for preaching week by week. A rota for Bangor Cathedral was established by Grindal in 1576, and in 1577 Bishop Whitgift ordered a 'table' of preachers to be set up at Worcester. When Bishop Barnes visited Carlisle Cathedral in 157 he 'urged the importance of preaching and the need for a fuller provision of sermons in the cathedral church', and he agreed to a scheme by which the bishop and dean would each contribute four sermons a year, the archdeacon two, and every major canon six.

At Hereford the chapter ordered that all twenty-eight prebendaries, not just the residentiaries, should preach in order, so that there would be a sermon each Sunday. The dean was to preach on Christmas and Easter. A later fabric roll recorded the payment of £1 13s. 9d. to a carpenter 'for making a backe for a new seate for the gentlemen of the citie, on promise that he make it lower, that the people may see the pulpit and heare the better'. The prebendaries of Peterborough were responsible for preaching once a quarter, but since this did not produce a weekly sermon it was agreed that one of them, William Hills, would preach every second Sunday and receive an additional payment of £10.

By the mid 1570s the chapter at Durham had changed character and, surprisingly, had become the most Puritan group of cathedral clergy in the land. Much of the change was the work of two Protestant deans, William Whittingham and his successor Tobie Matthew. Both were zealous preachers; we know that Dean Matthew personally preached twenty-eight sermons in the cathedral during 1585, nineteen in 1586 and twenty-seven in 1587.

Divinity lectures, as noted above, were mandated by statute at many of the cathedrals. Even more than sermons, they provided an opportunity for Puritan teaching in the cathedrals. In 1562 Bishop Horne commanded the dean and chapter of Winchester to appoint a virtuous man, learned in divinity, to lecture twice a week at a stipend of £1 per lecture. At Durham one of the prebendaries read a divinity lecture two or three times a week in the chapter house for an additional salary of £20. Hugh Brougham, the lecturer in the late 1570s, was especially popular and is said to have attracted large crowds. A lecturer named Thomas Hitchins was active at Chester in the 1580s, while at Peterborough Walter Baker was hired in 1588 to read a weekly lecture as well as to preach on alternate Sundays. His stipend was £20, to be taken from the wages formerly paid to two petty canons. Bishop Scambler required the dean and prebendaries of Peterborough to lecture themselves, in turn, on Wednesday mornings; at Rochester the singing men were to be fined if they failed to attend lectures. We know that a number of parish churches where Puritan feeling ran strong fulfilled the letter of the Anglican law by having Prayer Book services on Sunday mornings and Puritan lectures in the afternoons. The evidence for the cathedrals is not so clear, but it may be that some of them, too, used lectures as a means of satisfying the more zealous Protestants or inculcating reformed theology.

A final sign of Puritan influence, significant as a symbol rather than for its own sake, may be found in the contribution of £5 sent in 1590 by the dean and chapter of Ely to the city of Geneva, presumably a token of appreciation for spiritual leadership given at a time of need.

The later years of Elizabeth's reign were calmer than those at its beginning. Some accommodation with the Puritans had gradually been worked out, often tacitly rather than by official action. Years of familiarity with the Prayer Book produced acceptance and, for some at least, affection. Cathedral services settled comfortably into a routine; more and more they were enriched by new musical settings of unsurpassed beauty written by such masters as Thomas Tallis and William Byrd. As preaching grew in importance it became clearer that cathedral churches were places of instruction for the laity, not merely houses where isolated clerics sang the praises of God or offered intercessions for the dead. To some extent the quiet was deceptive, as the events of the seventeenth century were to prove. The Puritans had gone underground, not died out, while on the other side there remained a few – they would eventually find a leader in William Laud – who felt that the church had abandoned too much of its medieval tradition, its 'beauty of holiness' in ceremony and sacrament. But in 1603 the Puritan Revolution lay decades in the future. As the Tudor age closed, the cathedrals appeared to have weathered the storm of the Reformation and to have adjusted to new circumstances without compromising their essential character.

12

The Early Seventeenth Century

The cathedrals of England entered the seventeenth century under relatively quiet conditions.[1] Unlike the monasteries, they had survived the Reformation and had adapted to new conditions successfully. But it is clear that many of the buildings suffered from neglect and dilapidation. Lack of attention from non-resident deans and canons is one reason for such decay, coupled in many cases with financial problems which made proper maintenance difficult. The condition of Carlisle Cathedral was so bad that Charles I was prompted to order the dean and chapter to inaugurate a plan for repair. 'We have been informed', he wrote in 1639, 'both at our being in the North and since, that our Cathedrall Church of Carlisle is fallen exceedingly into decay, and indeed soe farr that if there be not present care taken for the repaire theiroff it cannot be long upheld'. The king blamed both the 'long continued absence' of the dean and the negligence of his predecessors. In 1612 there was concern about the ruinous and dilapidated state of the church, ornaments and bells at Wells, and the chapter ordered all prebendaries to contribute a tenth of their income for the next three years. The dean and chapter of Worcester, having found 'the church in debte and the fabricke much in decay' in 1635, agreed to reduce the expenses of the audit feast accordingly (hardly a heroic measure). At Lincoln the cathedral itself seems to have been sound, but the houses of the vicars choral were found to be 'greatly ruinated and decayed'; the dean and chapter told the vicars to allocate £10 a year out of their rents for repairs. Even at Canterbury houses in the precinct were deteriorating. In 1605 the dean and chapter required residents to undertake repairs and agreed to give the petty canons 40s. a year for this purpose. Some revenues normally paid to non-resident clerics were allocated to the fabric of the cathedral itself, but in 1612 the chapter was able to note that 'the church is now in better state', so the funds reverted to their customary use. Oaks felled on cathedral estates were used for the repair of Hereford Cathedral and the canons' houses there. In 1642 Charles I allowed the dean and chapter of Winchester to lease lands for three lives rather than for the twenty-one year period normally stipulated, in view of the great charges for repairing the church. This practice yielded large entry fines for immediate use but prevented the chapter from raising rents for long periods of time.

With the possible exception of Carlisle, no cathedral was in such dangerous condition as St Paul's in London. During Elizabeth's reign the steeple
had fallen and never been rebuilt, and the roof had been damaged by lightning. It was said to be a scandal to the nation. In 1608 King James wrote
Bishop Ravis complaining that such decay would not have occurred if the
church had allocated its revenues properly. A detailed estimate of the repairs
needed was prepared. Its main items included:

The Quier and Iles to the same, £1619 4s. 1d.

The Steeple, £21,015 15s. 0d.

The Bodie of the Church and the two Iles thereof, £6891 19s. 4d.

The retourne Isles north and south, £1647 4s. 5d.

The Chapter House, £361 19s. 5d.

Each of these sections was subdivided; work on the steeple, for instance,
would involve payments of £8821 to masons, £1585 to carpenters, £1133 to
bricklayers, £370 to smiths, £74 to plumbers and £31 to glaziers. There is also
a list of the materials required and the chief workmen to be employed. The
total was a staggering £22,537 2s. 3d. Although a commission was appointed,
nothing was done, perhaps because no one could imagine raising such a sum
of money. In 1620 a new estimate was prepared. Less complete, it is mainly
a calculation of the amount of stone which would be needed (about 12,000
feet) and its cost (about £6400). Once again, the work was postponed.

Less daunting projects were undertaken in most of the cathedrals. The
bishop of Bristol, Robert Wright, was responsible for some significant
improvements made to his cathedral about 1630. These included a new
organ, built by Thomas Dallam at a cost of £258 2s. 7d., a new clock and a
new window in the west wall. As we have seen, the cathedral, formerly an
Augustinian priory, was a truncated building consisting only of the choir.
The west end had been sealed with a solid wall in the sixteenth century, but
Wright ordered it opened up with a 'great' expanse of glass. Since the window cost only £20 it may not have contained painted subjects; it disappeared
when the Victorian nave was constructed. Wright also tried to beautify the
choir with statues of the four Evangelists and twelve Prophets, but the work
'was hindered', perhaps by iconoclasts, and he may have had to settle for a
new table of the Ten Commandments. At Wells, too, the choir was
reordered; the vicars choral were removed to the higher stalls and desks were
placed at the lower seats for the use of the choristers. The choir vault was
repaired in 1620.

During James's reign a new pulpit, incorporating the arms of Scotland, was erected at Worcester. The 'Peter Bell' at Exeter, which crazed during the ringing on Guy Fawkes Day in 1611, had to be recast in 1612. Four years later all the bells in the south tower were 'new cast and made tuneable' at a cost of £38 6s. 6d., but they must not have been satisfactory since three of them – the 'Grandisson bell', the nine o'clock bell and the third bell of the ring – were recast again in 1625. There were frequent small payments for work on the steeple and for gilding the 'cock' at its top. Doors were provided for the stalls set aside for the dean, dignitaries and resident canons; new seats were installed for singing men and choristers, 'somewhat neere to my Lord Bishops seat in the quire'; and considerable sums were spent on refurbishing Edward the Confessor's seat, the sedilla near the high altar which was reputed to contain a relic of the saint. In addition, the choristers' school was repaired and their privy cleaned.

In 1633 the steeple at Norwich required attention, for its top was found to have decayed. A new weathercock installed at Chichester in 1638 remained in place until 1978, when it was moved to the cathedral treasury and replaced by a modern copy. The interior walls of Chester cathedral were whitewashed in 1642 – we know of the work because it was necessary to spend 3s. 4d. cleaning seats which had been spotted in the process. The library at Durham, having allegedly fallen into ruin, was refurbished in 1629 with 'fair shelves and stalls', but there were no funds for books: the dean and prebendaries were ordered to make contributions at the time of their installation, and a tenth of a year's profit on each lease granted by the chapter was set aside for buying 'choyce and faire' volumes. At Salisbury there were continual expenses for the maintenance of the bells, gutters and glass; a thousand tiles were purchased in 1617. A fine new prebendary's house was built at Norwich in 1626. With some later additions, it survives as No. 71 the Close.

Financial records provide considerable detail regarding repairs to the deanery at Lichfield in 1623. Without this work, it was said, several buildings would have fallen down. The workers included a chief carpenter, Robert Gladwin, who was paid 14d. a day; four other carpenters at 1s. a day; a free mason (16d.) and his man (10d.); a tiler and mason (1s.); a plumber (2s.); and unspecified numbers of additional masons (10d.) and day labourers (6d.). Materials used included 14,300 bricks at 14s. per thousand, sixty-four feet of glass at 5d. a foot, six loads of timber, lime, nails, gutter tiles, sand, hinges, planks, 'a skuttle 6d., a hodd 4d., a piggin 4d., and a riddle 3d'. The expenses of carriage included bread and beer for the workers; in all the undertaking cost about £38. An entirely new deanery was built for Henry King at Rochester about 1640, but that rising cleric did not enjoy it long since he was elevated to the bishopric of Chichester in 1642.

Relatively little iconoclasm occurred in these years. Virtually the only references in the surviving records come from Chester, where in 1602 6s. 8d. was paid to a man named Holmes 'for disfiguring of Moyses face & making the place in some good order agayne'. This probably refers to a likeness of Moses painted on the table of the Ten Commandments. Later, on the eve of the Civil War, the Puritan subdean ordered an image at the east end of the choir to be defaced and the area plastered over.

The early Stuart cathedrals were not immune from bickering among members of the clergy, but the matters in dispute did not represent major theological differences. In 1608, for example, the canons of Exeter drafted a petition charging the dean, Matthew Sutcliffe, with 'molestations and grevances offered unto us and injuries and misgovernmentes in our Churche'. This complaint was to be sent to the Privy Council, in the hope of forestalling further trouble and scandal, but nothing seems to have come of it. Sutcliffe held controversial, strongly anti-Catholic views, but it is not certain that these lay behind the quarrel. A pettier matter dragged on for years at Salisbury, where the treasurer insisted that he was entitled to have two vergers precede him when he attended services. The dean and bishop, who were content with a single verger apiece, had ordered that the treasurer also be satisfied with one, but he appealed to the Court of Arches, citing the testimony of two octogenarian women who supported his traditional claims. The matter was still not resolved when Laud conducted a visitation of the cathedral in 1634.

Norwich Cathedral was unique in receiving new statutes during the reign of James I. These were needed because Norwich lacked a set of Tudor statutes: as we have seen, Norwich was the first monastic cathedral to be secularized and a royal charter gave the dean and chapter authority to make their own statutes, but they had never done so. When the bishop called the matter to the king's attention, James issued the statutes in 1620, and they were accepted by members of the cathedral establishment on 5 September. Similar to the statutes of the other refounded cathedrals, they remained in force until 1941.

All in all, life in the cathedrals ran its usual course during the first decade or two of the century. The accession of James I had a minimal impact on the church. Buildings decayed and were repaired, and the clergy occasionally quarrelled, but there was little sign of change in liturgy, theology, or administrative policy.

The rise of William Laud changed all this. Born in 1573, the son of a clothier of Reading, Laud was educated at Oxford, where he was elected president of St John's College in 1611. His first major appointment in the church came in 1616, when James I named him dean of Gloucester. Laud had been angling for such an office for half a decade, but the king admitted that it was no political plum: 'His Majesty was graciously pleased to tell me', Laud wrote to the bishop of Gloucester, 'that there was scarce ever a church in England so ill governed, and so much out of order and withal, required me in general to reform and set in order what there I found amiss'. After spending Christmas at court and being installed in the cathedral by proxy, Laud rode to Gloucestershire and held his first chapter meeting on 25 January 1617. He immediately undertook (as he said) 'the repair of somne parts of the edifice of the Church and [the] redress of other things amiss'. Most notably, he persuaded the chapter to pass an act moving the communion table from the middle of the building to the east end, where it was to be placed 'altar wise', that is, north and south, 'at the upper ende of the quier close under the walle'.

In itself the order presented no novelty; Laud may have believed that he was merely enforcing existing policy. As we have seen, stone altars had been removed from cathedrals and other churches during the reign of Edward VI on the grounds that they were superstitious reminders of the mass as a sacrifice, a Catholic doctrine no longer acceptable in the reformed Church of England. Instead, 'honest wooden tables' had been set 'table-wise' (east and west) in the body of the church, either in the nave or at the foot of the chancel but not against the east end, so that communicants might see the actions of the minister and participate more directly in the service. In the injunctions of 1559 the more moderate Elizabethan Settlement returned the holy table to its traditional position against the east wall, though it might be moved to a more central position during communion. Stone altars reappeared in some places where they had been preserved by the more conservative churchmen. Canons issued in 1604 reiterated that the altar should stand 'within the church or chancel' so that the minister might be 'heard of the communicants in his prayer and ministration'. Another clause expressed the hope that 'convenient and decent tables' had been provided already 'in sufficient and seemly manner, and covered in time of divine service with a carpet of silk or other decent stuff, thought meet by the ordinary of the place'.

Some of the cathedrals complied with the canons of 1604, anticipating Laud's concerns in part. In 1615, so far as we know without outside pressure, a new communion table was ordered to be erected at Exeter 'with all convenient speed'. Richard Neile, who shared Laud's views about the significance of the sacrament, probably demanded compliance in his successive bishoprics of Rochester (1608), Lichfield (1610) and Lincoln (1614). Certainly Neile prevailed upon Francis Burgoyne, a prebendary of Durham, to move the communion table to the east end of the chancel in that cathedral shortly after Neile's translation to the see of Durham in 1617.

At Gloucester and Durham Laud and Neile ran into trouble immediately. Laud had not reckoned with the Puritan sympathies of Gloucester's citizens, municipal corporation and bishop, Miles Smith. The bishop's chaplain, John White, complained of the dean's arbitrary actions and accused him of favoring popery. Members of the chapter were deeply divided. Some suggested that Laud have the Court of High Commission consider whether he had been libelled by his enemies. The subdean expelled two choristers, probably because they had maligned the dean. The bishop was so greatly antagonized that he vowed never to set foot in the cathedral again, and so far as we know he never did. But Laud won in the end; 'Reason', he wrote, began 'to take the place of Passion', and 'the Rabble began to be more sensible of the errors that they had committed'.

Neile was less successful at Durham. Here he encountered the animosity of Robert Hutton, son of the former bishop, and Peter Smart, a Puritan prebendary. The chapter was split between Puritans – reformers who generally accepted the theological views of John Calvin – and Arminians – traditionalists who sought to reintroduce certain practices of the medieval church which they believed had wrongfully been dropped as part of the break with Rome.

Hutton preached against Arminianism at Durham Cathedral in 1621. Smart's grievances festered and finally came to a head on 27 July 1628, when he delivered a blistering sermon attacking the alterations of the past decade. Drawing his text from Psalm 31 – 'I have hated them that hold of superstitious vanities' – he used such inflammatory phrases as 'spiritual fornication' in denouncing the 'presumptuous boldnesse of him, or them, [who] alter[ed] the situation of the communion table about eleven years ago'. Later the same day (Sunday afternoon) the High Commission for the northern province met in the deanery to initiate proceedings against Smart; the case was transferred to Lambeth in 1629 but revoked to York the next year. Finally Smart, who was charged with contumacy, was deprived and degraded. He was also fined £500 and when he refused to pay it he was imprisoned in the King's Bench prison for more than a decade. Not until the Long Parliament considered his case was he released. His friends raised funds to support him and his family during his years of imprisonment, and he was restored to his preferments during the Interregnum. He lived to gain vengeance against Laud, since he gave evidence against him during the trial which preceded the archbishop's execution in 1645.

One of Smart's special enemies was John Cosin, the later bishop of Durham, who became a canon of the cathedral in 1624. Under Cosin's

Winchester Cathedral, marble screen by Inigo Jones (1640).

leadership the chapter became dominated by the Arminians and remained so until the Civil War; Smart was the odd man out, and until his imprisonment he did all he could to disrupt the activities of the chapter. In 1631, for instance, the dean and canons were so 'hindered and disturbed by Mr Peter Smart' that they 'were forced to surcease and departe' from a chapter meeting. But in the short term Neile won at Durham, just as Laud had at Gloucester, and Arminianism triumphed. So great was its hold that Cosin was able to introduce embroidered copes, images, incense and candles: it was said, tongue in cheek, that 'Mr Cosin was so blind at evensong on Candlemas day that he could not see to read prayers in the minster with less than 340 candles, whereof 60 he caused to be placed round the high altar'.

In his *Short Treatise of Altars* published in 1629 Peter Smart charged Neile with 'the setting up of altars and images, with a multitude of superstitious ceremonies, changing of services, and corruptions of sacraments; which, beginning in Durham, have since that time spread themselves over all the cathedrall, collegiate churches, and colledges in this realme'. What Neile began, Laud continued. In 1621 he was advanced from the deanery of Gloucester to the bishopric of St David's. Here, in his visitation of 1622, he merely required the communion table to be placed in the chancel (not necessarily against the east end), decently covered with fair linen and a 'carpet of silk'; he emphasized that it should not be profaned by 'sitting on it, throwing hats on it, [or] writing on it'. Since many Welsh bishops were English absentees, it is worth noting that Laud actually did visit Wales: in 1625 he spent three months there and built a new chapel in his house at Aberguilly. But a Welsh diocese offered inadequate scope for Laud's talents and ambitions. In 1626 he was promoted to the English see of Bath and Wells; in 1628 he succeeded his friend George Monteigne as bishop of London. At Wells Laud was non-resident and, as far as the records reveal, made little impact. His hand can be seen, however, in a letter which the king ordered to be sent to the dean and chapter in June 1632. 'His majesty is informed', it began, 'that the communion table in your church is not furnished with such decent ornaments as ar prerequistite and as in other cathedrall churches ar supplied. He therefore expecteth from you a spedy redrese on that behalf that he may not have cause to charge you withe the neglect of your dewtie, which he will not forbeare to doe if he doe not receive a better accompt of your care heerein'.

Things were different in London. The placing and adornment of the altar at St Paul's was not a matter of concern – suitable arrangements had been made some years earlier – but Laud had long been distressed about the cathedral fabric and was determined to sweep away some houses and shops which abutted the church, then initiate a major campaign of rebuilding.

His episcopate coincided with the last years of John Donne's tenure as dean (a mere decade, 1621–31) and with the height of Inigo Jones's career as England's purest classical architect. Funds for repairs and new work to be supervised by Jones were raised from the court and the City, and an order of the Privy Council (doubtless drafted by Laud) asked for voluntary contributions from all the clergy and laity. After he became archbishop of Canterbury, Laud retained a great interest in the work, and very large sums of money were raised in the 1630s – more than £10,000 a year between 1633 and 1638, and a total of £101,330 by 1643. Laud asked all the bishops to pity the ruinous state of the realm's 'mother church', and we know that some of the clergy did heed the appeal. In 1640, for instance, the dean and chapter of Exeter made a free gift of £500 to St Paul's (it was part of the fine for renewing a lease, and the chapter wished to devote it to some pious use).

Inigo Jones repaired the decaying nave of St Paul's, generally doing a poor job of it, but his chief delight lay in providing a new western portico with fourteen large fluted columns in the Roman style and a triangular pediment. Observers agreed that the work was splendid, nobly proportioned and of great beauty, although there was an obvious clash of style between the Gothic cathedral and its Classical entrance, while the funds consumed by the portico might better have been spent renewing the walls of the church itself.

Laud's concern for St Paul's went far beyond his desire to enrich the fabric, and other aspects of his work bear more directly on his ecclesiastical policy. Like Donne (and John Colet before him), he was offended by the use of St Paul's for secular purposes, and he issued orders against 'profanation', prohibiting all persons from walking about the cathedral during services, transacting business or allowing children to play there.

The death of Archbishop Abbot in 1633 made it possible for Charles I to promote Laud from London to Canterbury. Politically, Laud's advancement made little difference, for he had been the king's chief adviser in matters religious since the beginning of Charles's reign. But his position as primate gave Laud new powers to conduct visitations outside his own diocese and to see that his policies were more broadly enforced. He was now able to demand adherence to his fully developed policy regarding altars: they were to stand against the east wall of the chancel at all times, including celebrations of the eucharist; they were to be railed in to prevent their being defiled by dogs or irreverent humans; and communicants were to kneel at the altar rail when receiving communion, to eliminate the inconvenience of the minister having to come to them as they sat in their pews.

Beginning in 1634 commissioners acting on Laud's behalf visited all the dioceses and cathedrals in the province of Canterbury. At the same time Neile, now archbishop of York, instituted a visitation of the northern province. Local inquiries were based on visitation articles written by the archbishops. Individual sets of articles for the various cathedrals survive, all containing essentially the same points but with occasional specific variations. As might be expected, the commissioners were to report on communion tables, fonts and vestments, and on the condition of buildings; sermons, leases, the keeping of residence and the due filling of vacant places were additional concerns. Occasionally there was a unique query, such as 'whether the quire of Canterbury 'be strewed with rushes, or suffered to lie in any unfitting or nasty manner'.

The report of Laud's vicar general, Sir Nathaniel Brent, includes comments on a number of the cathedrals and provides further evidence of neglect and decay. Brent found Norwich Cathedral 'much out of order. The hangings of the choir are naught, the pavement not good, the spire of the steeple is quite down, the copes are fair, but want mending. The churchyard is very ill kept'. Peterborough was better, 'very fair and strong', and Lichfield was generally 'very fair', although the east end, where the communion table stood, was 'undecent in many respects'. Worcester had beeen 'much in decay' before William Juxon became dean, but he 'put it in so good a way that they have gone on ever since', although Juxon himself had gone on to be bishop of London. Still, there were no copes at Worcester, and there was much walking about during services. Many things were amiss at Gloucester: 'no cope; the fabric in decay; the churchyard much pestered with buildings; the [puritanical] schoolmaster refused to take his oath'. Chichester was somewhat out of repair; Winchester very much in decay, but 'of late they have bestowed much money, and are bestowing more'. In several places Brent complained of failure to bow at the name of Jesus or when entering the church, as ordered by the archbishop; at Chichester he formally admonished one of the 'puritanically addicted' aldermen for putting his hat on during divine service.

In 1635 Laud issued orders for a number of the cathedrals, directing the correction of faults discovered by the visitors. These commands were quite specific; they dealt, for instance, with encroachments on the churchyard at Gloucester, the need to erect a consistory court within Peterborough Cathedral, and the urgency of repairing the bell frame at Lichfield. The chapter act book at Wells records Laud's command that they provide 'suitable ornaments for the church' and pay for them out of the dividend – the annual surplus of receipts over disbursements which was ordinarily divided among the dean and members of the chapter. Chichester was told to 'provide copes fitting for the service of your cathedrall, one a yeare untill you be sufficiently furnished with them', and the ministers were reminded that they should wear surplices, square caps and hoods to all services.

Laud's relations with his own diocesan cathedral at Canterbury were strained. Shortly after his elevation the archbishop heard that some members of the chapter had 'been a little too bold' with him, refusing to honour his orders and resisting his right of visitation. Laud reminded the canons that nine of the twelve prebends were in the king's gift, so that he could alter the composition of the chapter if he were ill used. Specific matters which concerned Laud included buildings which encroached on the church, the fair which was held in the churchyard, and the necessity of multiple locks to the muniment room, as specified in the statutes. 'One peevish difference or another' always seemed to be arising, caused, Laud believed, by mere 'spleen'. In 1637, allegedly at the command of Charles I, Laud drafted new statutes for the cathedral. While these did not represent significant changes in governance, they did emphasize the authority of the monarch and his archbishop.

Since Laud's interest in church music has not been the subject of much discussion – except among the Puritans, who deplored it – it is interesting to note that the visitation articles include the requirement that the cathedrals maintain 'a skilful organist and able singers' as well as the full number of well-trained choristers. Laud complained about the 'meanness'of the choir at Canterbury, which was inexcusable in a church so well endowed, and he was involved in a dispute about the 'insufficiency' of a man appointed by the dean to a petty canon's place. The weakness of the choir at Norwich was also a matter of concern. Again Laud told the dean and chapter to provide better support and to give small benefices only to petty canons who sang in the choir, as was the custom elsewhere. Failure to do so would 'utterly overthrow the quire service, and you will not be able to retain either skill or voices amongst you'. Better accommodation for the choirmen at Bristol was also recommended by the archbishop; he thought the marsh 'lying under the college walls' should not be leased but used for suitable housing. During the metropolitical visitation Laud's vicar general noted that the choir at Winchester was 'ill served, because some of the chiefest (Mr Frost, &c.) are now of the king's chapel'. Following the visitation, Laud reminded the chapter at Worcester that they should admit no one to the choir 'before he be first approved for his voice and skill in singing', and he suggested that the two defective organs at Lichfield be repaired and put together in one new instrument, 'if it will stand with the grace of your church, and be more convenient and useful for your quire (as we conceive it will)'.

An article in Laud's memoranda for his vicar general required him 'to look to the seats in all cathedral and collegiate churches, and remove all that are inconvenient'. The question of seating was in fact one of the most vexed issues in the cathedrals. Stalls in the choir were assigned to the cathedral clergy and musicians, whose wives might have customary places. Special seating for civic authorities was generally provided, but there were occasional disputes about this, especially when the townsmen tried to erect their own seats. There seem to have been no instances of pews being installed in either the choir or the nave by prominent lay families, as was common in the parish churches, but seats were sometimes reserved for frequent worshippers, who might pay a verger for their use.

The increasing frequency of sermons preached in the cathedral naves had led, during the years following the Reformation, to the provision of seats there. These bothered Laud, who believed that they interfered with the architecture and were contrary to medieval practice. The king himself was involved, for Charles had expressly ordered 'that the bodies of cathedral church should not be pestered with standing seats, contrary to the course of cathedrals, and the dignity of those goodly piles of building'. Hence Laud charged the dean and chapter of Gloucester to remove all fixed seats, including those where the wives of the mayor and aldermen usually sat, and replace them with moveable ones. A letter from the archbishop's vicar was written into the act book at Worcester. Again it commanded the removal of some 'mean seats' in the nave, 'which did not become so faire a ffabricke'. 'My Lord knoweth', Brent continued, 'that the mayor & his brethren, and verie many from everie parish of your towne doe resorte to your sermons, and is desirous that they should be well provided for, but withall doth believe that by handsome seates made with backs to be removed att pleasure, and by a convenient number of formes, they may all be fitted verie well'. But the mayor and citizens did not agree; in 1639 they petitioned the king for more convenient arrangements which would prevent the 'extraordinary thronging and uneasiness of continued standing both of men and women'. Laud agreed to restore the pulpit at the west end (it had been moved to the choir), with adequate but moveable seating.

At Durham, York and Salisbury Laud ordered seats removed from the choir, despite the fact that they were used by members of the corporation and the wives of prebendaries, and he became involved in a long-standing dispute over seating at Chester. Some further problems arose locally, not at the instigation of the archbishop. At Wells galleries had been set up in the choir, although they were unattractive and unusual in other cathedrals, but since some improper persons presumed to sit in them the doors were to be nailed shut. (It was especially unsuitable for 'men and women to sitt together in so eminent a place in the view of the choyre'.) Perhaps in place of these galleries the chapter had agreed to provide seats for the wives of the

vicars choral, but 'since the ereccion of them some of the same woemen cannot agree about their places therein'. Hence it was necessary to order that
the women 'shall sitt in the respective sides of the said choyre, by seniority
as their husbandes places are in, without any disturbance'. Notices had to be
placed on the upper stalls at Winchester, reserving them for clergymen and
graduate scholars, not 'servingmen, tradesmen, and ordinary people'. At
York long-standing antagonism between the minster and the civic corporation, originating in clashes over jurisdiction, came to a head in 1633 when
the archdeacon dared to sit in a higher stall than that occupied by the lord
mayor. The corporation boycotted the minster until the archdeacon was
forced to apologize. Charles I intervened in that dispute, and he did so again
at Winchester in 1640. Here too he ordered that the mayor be allowed to
occupy his accustomed seat in the choir, which the archdeacon had tried
to usurp.

Some miscellaneous improvements which can be thought of as being Lau-
dian, even though a few of them antedate Laud's appointment as
archbishop, may be noted briefly. Exeter acquired new communion plate in
1627 and spent 24s. 6d. repairing the altar rail in 1639. A new painted reredos was also commissioned, executed by William Cavell, 'lymner'. It
included depictions of Moses and Aaron flanking the tablet of the Ten Commandments as well as pictures of St Peter, St Paul and angels. One of the
canons of Canterbury, John Warner, gave the cathedral a new font in 1639
to commemorate his elevation to the see of Rochester two years earlier.
Figures of the four Evangelists adorn the black and white stem which supports a fluted marble bowl, while above a two-storey wooden cover bears
images of the Twelve Apostles. The font was smashed by Puritan soldier in
1642 but the pieces were saved and the restored font returned to its place in
the nave in 1662. A new cover was placed on the Saxon font at Wells. York
Minster acquired new plate and paid for adorning the altar: special gifts and
revenues from fines were used for frontals, canopies and a carpet. Bishop
John Bridgeman was mainly responsible for some fine Jacobean work at
Chester, including a new pulpit (now converted to pew fronts), raised steps
to the altar and stained glass in the east window. As early as 1621 new plate
was ordered at Durham. More communion plate was purchased in 1626, and
the dean and chapter sent vestments to London 'to be altered and changed
into faire and large copes'. Cushions and maces were also provided, and a
'great lantern' imported from Antwerp was hung between the altar and the
choir.

Exeter, which had already installed a proper communion table in 1615,
ordered a new one in 1622, adding rails 'for keping of it decently and handsomely', cushions, hangings and flagons in subsequent years; some of

the old plate was 'changed' into new chalices. A gift of £100 was spent 'for furnishing and adorning the quire of the church with a suite of new hangings and a faire new covering for the communion table'. Salisbury spent petty sums mending the pulpit and communion table cloths in 1619 and 1622. Here the responses to Laud's visitation inquiries included the comments that 'there are no coapes in our church, [for] most of them were sould away about 66 yeares since', and 'there is a great defect of ornaments about the altar'. But sumptuous copes, adorned by a London embroiderer whose bill ran to £44, were soon provided, along with communion vessels. The old communion table at Worcester was replaced by a stone altar in 1634, with an azure cloth hung behind it and a frontal divided into upper and lower panels. There were new copes and cushions at Hereford. An inventory prepared at Gloucester in 1637 lists 'one crimson velvett alltar cloth imbrodered with a faire oval with gleames issuinge from it and large letters vizt: I.H.S.', as well as other hangings, carpets, cushions, flagons and communion cups.

Inigo Jones worked at Winchester as well as at St Paul's. His contribution to Winchester was a marble screen (see p. 173). This appears to have been motivated by concerns expressed by Laud's visitor Brent as well as by comments from the king himself. The severely classical screen was adorned with life-size brass statues of James I and Charles I made by Hubert Le Sueur at a charge of £340. The screen itself, completed in 1640, cost somewhat less, about £234; the dean and chapter originally hoped that the king would pay for it, but in the end they had to do so themselves. In 1662 a Dutch visitor was greatly impressed by this 'screen of white stone, with niches on both sides, in which stand the life-size statues of King James and King Charles, very artistically cast in copper and above in the front two recumbent angels'. The screen was indeed one of the finest examples of Inigo Jones's work. The statues remain in the cathedral – they are now placed inside the west door – but the dean and chapter had the screen removed in 1820, since they thought it blocked the view.[2] Wooden busts of James and Charles, and a stone boss depicting Charles I and Queen Henrietta Maria, were also set up when the tower at Winchester was revaulted in the 1630s. The boss is still there, but the statues (originally corbels) have been moved to a display area in the triforium.

Laud enriched Canterbury. He refitted the choir with a high altar adorned with candlesticks and a rich carpet. Above it he placed a 'Glory-cloth' on which golden rays emanated from the name Jehovah. Finally, in 1639, he caused four large iron 'flags' or weathervanes to be erected on the pinnacles for the central tower, which housed Bell Harry. Each flag was emblazoned:

the arms depicted severally were those of the king, Prince Charles, the cathedral church and Laud himself. It was an act of uncommon presumption.

Laud himself, together with Neile and such followers as John Cosin at Durham and Accepted Frewen at Gloucester, cared greatly for the beauty of holiness and the solemnity of church buildings and liturgies. The overriding tragedy of Laud's life, indeed a tragedy for the entire church, lay in his inability to appreciate the genuine piety of those who disagreed with his elevated views. Instead, he regarded his opponents as rabble and dismissed them with the famous comment, ''tis superstition now-a-days for any man to come with more reverence into a church, than a tinker and his bitch come into an alehouse'. Sir William Dugdale expressed the same view more elegantly when he wrote that 'all cost and care bestowed and had of the Church, wherein God is to be served and worshipped, was accounted, by those people, a kinde of Popery; so that time would soon bring it to passe, if it were not resisted, that God would be turned out of Churches into Barnes'. Laud left the cathedrals of England more beautiful but less popular than he found them.

Although the minute books of the cathedral chapters continue to be filled with the routine of leases, appointments and disciplines until the mid 1640s, there are occasional signs of the approach of war. An attempt was made to collect Ship Money from several cathedrals during the eleven-year Personal Rule of Charles I (1629–40). At Winchester the dean and chapter had willingly paid Ship Money when the sheriff requested it, but after the city asked for another payment in 1636 they concluded that the demand ran contrary to the privileges of the cathedral and decided to petition the king and Privy Council. The mayor meanwhile imprisoned two of the cathedral's singing men, threatening to keep them in gaol until the charge was paid. In May 1637 there was a hearing in London; the dean displayed the cathedral's statutes, which confirmed the claim to immunity from the city, but the king complained that he had never seen 'so muche good counsaile come so ill prepared' and postponed a decision. Finally it was determined that the cathedral need not pay the city but was nevertheless responsible itself for a contribution, which was reduced from £31 to £20. There was a similar dispute over Ship Money assessments at Chichester; here too the cathedral did pay a minimal amount (£2 10s.).

When the First Bishops' War between England and Scotland broke out in 1639, Laud wrote to all the bishops requesting contributions towards the cost of the king's army. The cause of the conflict, he asserted, was 'not religion, but sedition', and bishops needed to be vigilant against 'pretenders of that kind'. A personal letter to the bishop of Durham warned him (unnecessarily) of the danger in those parts, against which he should use all possible care and industry. We know that the cathedrals of Exeter and Chichester did contribute £100 each, and other chapters probably followed suit.

The royalist cause was clearly popular at many of the cathedrals. The overly optimistic dean and chapter of Exeter ordered the bells to be rung on 19 February 1641 'in token of joye for the good accord of the king and the Parliament' – the Long Parliament had just granted the king a subsidy in exchange for his acquiescence in the Triennial Bill, which guaranteed that there could never by another long period of personal rule – and on 8 July they celebrated 'a day of Thanks-giving for peace settled between England and Scotland'. On 27 November the bells were rung at Chester and a bonfire was lit to celebrate Charles's safe return from Scotland, where he had gone to open the Scottish Parliament.

But the year 1641 produced ominous signs as well. In May confiscation of the lands of the deans and chapters was discussed as a possible way out of the realm's financial woes – Sir Symonds D'Ewes referred to the cathedrals as the 'new abbies' whose resources could be tapped – and in September a group of London Puritans threatened to tear down the organ in St Paul's and deface ornaments there. It was then that the images adoring the font at Canterbury were smashed by iconoclasts. Meric Casaubon, one of the canons, took the precaution of removing the 'Glory' over the altar and taking it to his own home, safely wrapped in brown paper and placed in a locked box. As treasurer of the cathedral he also paid 15s. to a watchman 'for attendance of three weekes or upward to keepe ye churches windowes from defacinge'.

After the failure of his attempt in January 1642 to arrest the Five Members of the Commons whom he blamed for leading the opposition, the king decided to send his wife and a daughter to safety in the Netherlands. He accompanied them to Dover. The usual ringing welcomed him to Canterbury on 12 February, and a broken staff of the royal canopy was repaired. The bells were rung again for the king's return from Dover on the twenty-fifth.

By this time there was a general perception that the realm was moving toward civil war. In August 1642 the mayor and aldermen of Exeter asked the chapter to leave the gate to the close open all night 'in this tyme of feare and danger', so that the watchmen might have free passage and see that all was kept in peace and good order. Four months later Dean Young recorded several payments for guarding Chichester Cathedral and concealing its plate. The prebendaries of Wells were well enough informed to be fearful that it might 'heare after happen that the Corporation of the Dean & Chapter be dissolved by Act of Parliament or by [some] other lawful meanes'. Should that occur, each canon (or his executor) was to be paid back the caution money which he had deposited.

An event of 1639 was interpreted by some as a sign of Archbishop Laud's impending fall. A great storm erupted at Canterbury on the morning of Holy Innocents' Day (26 December); the pinnacle containing Laud's arms was blown down from the cathedral tower and crashed into the cloister. This in turn brought down a boss containing the armorial symbols of the arch-bishopric itself, so that 'the Arms of the present Artch-Bishop of Canterburie brake down the Armes of the Arch-Bishopric, or Sea of Canterbury'. A popular verse ran:

> Cathedrall Church of Canterbury,
>   Hath taken mortall harmes;
> The Quire and Cloister do want a plaister,
>   And so doe the Arch-Bishops Armes.
> The heavens just stroake the Prelates Armes broke
>   And did the cathedrall maule:
> 1.6.3.9. Brought forth this signe,
>   Heaven foretells Prelates fall.

In 1641 Laud was committed to the Tower, at the insistence of Parliament, and bishops were excluded from the House of Lords. For several years radical leaders had been calling for the extirpation of episcopacy and the reform of the church 'root and branch'. If bishops went, so would the cathedrals; for several decades they had been prime targets of Puritan animosity. They had few friends in Parliament and were destined to be fought over and despoiled.

13

Civil War and Interregnum

The English Civil War began with a symbolic act, Charles I's order to raise the battle standard at Nottingham on 22 August 1642. The causes of the war have been hotly debated by historians from that day to this. Some have pointed to constitutional conflicts separating the king and the House of Commons. Others have noted social and economic dislocations. For a time it was fashionable to consider the war as one aspect of a general European crisis of the seventeenth century. Another view emphasized regional differences and local animosities. Most recently it has been argued that there was no adequate reason for a war – the king must have begun it in the mistaken hope that he could quickly teach his critics a lesson – or, if there was, it arose from a conjunction of crises in Scotland and Ireland as well as England, and from Charles I's inability to handle the problem of a multiple monarchy.[1]

Members of the cathedral chapters themselves would have had no difficulty identifying the issues at stake, which so far as they were concerned were religious. The king and his royalist followers were fighting to preserve the Church of England with its bishops, cathedrals, art, music and Book of Common Prayer. Their Puritan opponents, if victorious, would smash statues and windows, destroy organs, turn out canons, choristers and choirmen, confiscate endowments, put an end to the centuries-old tradition of cathedral services and sacraments, possibly even pull down the cathedral buildings themselves. Never had the king's title 'Defender of the Faith', inherited from Henry VIII, been so literally true. It is not surprising that those who cared for cathedrals or served in them were among the staunchest royalists in the realm.

The spoliation of cathedrals, or, as the Puritans would have put it, the removal of popish ornaments from them, began during the later months of 1642. Accounts of the destruction at several of the cathedrals were collected by Bruno Ryves, a royal chaplain who later became dean of Chichester, and published anonymously as *Mercurius Rusticus: or The Countries Complaint of the Barbarous Outrages Committed by the Sectaries of this Late Flourishing Kingdom*. Ryves's title makes his bias clear, as does his comment that 'God in his good time will, we doubt not, pour down his Judgments upon the Actors of these horrid Profanations'. His narratives may exaggerate, but documents in the cathedral archives, and even the condition of the cathedral buildings today, testify to the basic truth of his story.

The relevant section of *Mercurius Rusticus* starts at Canterbury with a letter written on 30 August 1642 by Thomas Paske, the subdean. On the previous Sunday Colonel Sandys and his parliamentary troops had prevented the clergy from entering the cathedral and had demanded its keys. Then

> the Soldiers entering the Church and Quire, Giant-like, began a fight with God himself, overthrew the Communion Table, tore the velvet cloth from before it, defaced the goodly Screen, or Tabernacle-work, violated the Monuments of the Dead, spoyled the Organs, brake down the ancient Rails, and Seats, with the brazen Eagle which did support the Bible, forced open the Cupboords of the Singing-men, rent some of their Surplices, Gowns and Bibles, and carried away others, mangled all our Service-books and Books of Common Prayer; bestrewing the Pavement with the leaves thereof: a miserable spectacle to all good eyes.

Later the zealots attacked an arras containing figures of the Saviour. 'One said here is Christ, and swore that hee would stab him: another said here is Christ, and swore he would rip up his Bowels, which they did accordingly'. Many of the soldiers, Paske admitted, abhorred what was done; Colonel Sandys finally stopped the violence, and his men departed for Dover.

The chapter ordered that the organ and eagle be repaired. They might just as well have saved their money, for a 'more thorough Reformation' at Canterbury began on 13 December, when commissioners arrived to execute a parliamentary order against idolatrous images. According to another contemporary account (not in Ryves) they hardly knew where to start, since the cathedral seemed to have been built for no other end but to be a 'stable for idolls'. Finally they set to work on the great east window, demolishing the likeness of St Augustine, the first archbishop of Canterbury. Thirteen stone statues of Christ and the apostles were hewed down, 'and 12 more at the North doore of the Quire, and 12 Mytred Saints ... aloft over the West doore of the Quire'. A prebendary's wife 'pleaded for the images there, and jeered the Commissioners viragiously', but they continued. Turning to the 'great idolatrous window' in the north transept, which was 'the superstitious glory of [the] Cathedrall', they attacked pictures of God the Father embracing a crucifix, the Holy Ghost in the form of a dove, and the Virgin Mary being transported by angels into heaven. Richard Culmer, a Puritan minister, undertook to demolish the depiction of Thomas Becket at the top of the window; when others were afraid to ascend so high, he climbed to the top of a ladder, sixty steps up, with a pike in his hand and commenced 'rattling down proud Beckets glassy bones'. Someone said "'tis a shame for a Minister to be seen there; the Minister replyed, Sir, I count it no shame, but an honour ... these are dead Idylls, which defile the worship of God here'. Some wished he would break his neck, 'but he finished the worke and came downe well, and was in very good health when this was written'. Archbishop Morton's cardinal's hat was also 'rattled down' from a high window. It took a hundred men with ropes to dislodge the stone angel that stood on the central tower, and when it fell it was so heavy that it buried itself in the ground. The image of Jesus on Christ Church gate was also pulled down, but not without difficulty: the head nodded to and fro, then fell two hours before it was possible to dislodge the rest of the statue, which was riveted to the wall with iron bars.

The royalist city of Worcester was besieged on 25 September 1642. During the strife the soldiers pulled down the altar and destroyed it, along with some vestments and ecclesiastical furniture, but the cathedral survived relatively unhurt for the time being. The parliamentary Sergeant Nehemiah Wharton, formerly a London apprentice, described an incident which occurred a few days later at Hereford. On 'Sabbath day [7 October 1642] we went to the Minster, where the pipes played and the puppets sang so sweetly that some of our soldiers could not forbeare dauncinge in the holy quire; whereat the Baalists were sore displeased'. Following the prayers for the king one of the soldiers said loudly, '"What! Never a bit for the Parliament?" which offended them much more'. The troops then went to hear a Puritan preacher, Mr Sedgwick, whose sermons so affected the poor inhabitants that they said they had never heard the like before. 'The Lord move your hearts to send them faithfull and painfull ministers', the sergeant concluded, 'for the revenues of the Collige will maintain many of them'. The earl of Stamford held Hereford for Parliament throughout the autumn of 1642 and Waller occupied it for a month in 1643, but the royalists were generally in control and the cathedral escaped serious damage.

Rochester was also relatively fortunate. Here parliamentary soldiers 'brake down the rail about the Lords Table, seized upon the Velvet Covering of the holy Table, and in contempt of those holy Mysteries which were Celebrated on the Table, removed the Table itself into a lower place of the Church'. They strewed the pavement with torn leaves from the Prayer Book, and, hearing the organ, cried, 'A Devil on those Bag-Pipes'.

The parliamentary general Sir William Waller entered Winchester on Tuesday, 12 December 1642. His men fell immediately on the close, seizing the prebendaries' horses and plundering their homes. On Thursday the foot soldiers broke open the cathedral and marched in

> with Colours flying, their Drums beatinge, their Matches fired ... Some of the Troops of Horse also accompanied them in their march, and rode up through the body of the Church, and Quire, until they came to the Altar; there they begin their work, they rudely pluck down the Table and break the Rail: and afterwards carrying it to an Alehouse, they set it one fire, and in the fire burnt the Books of Common Prayer, and all the Singing Books belonging to the Quire; they throw down the Organ, and break the Stories of the Old and New Testament, curiously cut out in carved work, beautified with Colours and set round about the top of the Stalls of the Quire: from hence they turn to the Monuments of the Dead, some they utterly demolish, others they deface.

They scattered the bones from these tombs, even those of Edward the Confessor, William Rufus and Queen Emma. Some bones were thrown at the windows in order to break glass that could not easily be reached otherwise. Documents torn up included deeds and charters. Finally the troops rode though the streets in surplices and tippets, some brandishing organ pipes or pieces of carved wood to boast of their glorious victory.

Having completed this work, Waller's army marched on to Chichester, arriving the day after Christmas. Here the sympathies of most townspeople were with Parliament; the burden of defence fell to the royalist gentry, who surrendered after a brief siege. The first business of Waller's victorious troops was to plunder the cathedral. Once again they seized vestments, ornaments and plate, leaving no cushion or chalice behind. Then the troops 'brake down the Organs, and dashing the Pipes with their Pole-axes, scoffingly said, *hark how the Organs go*'. They smashed the communion table and rail. Disliking the pictures of Moses and Aaron flanking the tablet of the Ten Commandments, they broke it 'into small Slivers'. The music books of the singing men were torn up and the leaves scattered over the whole church. Finding a portrait of Edward VI, the men plucked out its eyes, saying that 'all this mischief came from him, when he established the Book of Common Prayer'. The following day the soldiers held a service of thanksgiving in the cathedral, followed by a 'Bachanalian fury' in which they 'ran up and down the Church, with their swords drawn, defacing the Monuments of the dead, hacking and hewing the Seats and Stalls, scratching and scraping the painted Walls'. Waller and the other officers made no effort to stop the onslaught. When the troops were informed that the plate was stored in the chapter house, they demanded its keys, broke down the wainscot and seized a chalice. Sir Arthur Haselrig, 'dancing and skipping' as the holy vessel was tossed about, cried, 'there Boys, there Boys, heark, heark, it Rattles, it Rattles'.

Severall

LETTERS

FROM

Colonell Morgan

Governour of G L O U C E S T E R,

AND

Colonell Birch.

Fully relating the maner of the taking
of the City and Garrifon of H E R E F O R D,
with the number flain on both fides, and the
particular circumftances at the gaining thereof.

With a perfect Lift of the names of the prifoners
taken therein.

Die Martis 23. *Decemb.* 1645.

ORdered by the Lords in Parliament affembled, That
thefe Letters, with the Lift, be forthwith printed and
publifhed.

Joh. Brown Cler. Parliamentorum.

Imprinted at *London* for *John Wright* at the
Kings Head in the old Bayley.
24. Decemb. 1645.

Title page of a Civil War pamphlet giving an account of the taking of Hereford by
Colonel John Birch and the Parliamentary army, 18 December 1645. Hereford
Cathedral Library, X.13.2/16. (*Dean and Chapter of Hereford*)

When someone asked them to leave a communion cup, a Scotsman said they should use a wooden dish.

The final account printed in *Mercurius Rusticus* concerns Exeter. Here the cathedral remained in the custody of the rebels for nine months, during which time 'the *Holy Liturgy* lay totally silenced'. The cathedral became 'a common Jakes for the Exonerations of Nature, sparing no place, neither the *Altar* nor the *Pulpit*, though this last finds a better place in their estimation'. The soldiers were 'tippling and taking tobacco' as they broke the windows and defaced the bishops' tombs, 'leaving one without a *Head*, another without a *Nose*, one without a *Hand*, and another without an *Arm*'. Next they broke down the organ, 'and taking two or three hundred Pipes with them in a most scornful, contemptuous manner, went up and down the street, Piping with them: and meeting some of the Choristers of the Church, whose surplesses they had stoln before, and imployed them to base, servile Offices, scoffingly told them, *Boys we have spoiled your trade, you must go and sing hot Pudding Pies*'. Such stories may well be royalist gossip rather than historical fact, but once again physical evidence confirms that the organ and tombs were disturbed.

Other sources tell of events in other places – chapter act books, of course, rarely exist for this period. Anonymous notes written on and opposite the title page of a life of Christ by Ludolphus de Saxonia in the library at Wells give a short description of what happened there. Wells cathedral was vandalized twice in 1643. On 15 April 'divers pictures and crusifixes in the church and our lady chapel' were destroyed, and 'on Wednesdaie 10 May 1643 beging Ascension yestreve Mr Alexander Pophams souldiers he being a coll [colonel] in or for the Parliament after dynner rusht into the church, broke downe the windowes, organs, fonte, seates in the quire, [and] the busshops see[t] besides many other villanies'.

Information about contemporaneous looting at Peterborough comes from a history of the cathedral written by Symon Gunton. A Peterborough native, graduate of Magdalene College, Cambridge, and prebendary from 1646 until his death thirty years later, Gunton lamented that 'the Records of the Church, out of which a more compleat History might have been gathered, are never to be recovered: being torn in pieces, or burnt, by the more than Gothish Barbarity of those ignorant people, who took upon them the glorious name of *Reformers*'. But one book was saved by the precentor, Humfrey Austin, who 'first hid it (in *February* 1642) under a Seat in the Quire; and when it was found by a Souldier on the 22 April 1643 (when all the seats were pulled down) rescued it again, by the offer of ten Shillings for that old Latine Bible, as he called it'. Thus it was purchased from Henry Topclyffe, 'Souldier under Captain Cromwell, Colonel Cromwell's Son'.

Gunton's further account must be based on what he saw himself, or what he was told by eyewitnesses like Humfrey Austin, rather than on what was written in the old book. According to Gunton, parliamentary troops came to Peterborough on 18 April 1643.

> They fell to execute fury upon the Cathedral, destroying all things as the malicious Eye of each Sectarian Varlet prompted him to do mischief, beating down the Windows, defacing the Monuments, tearing the Brass from Grave-stones, plundering of Vestments, Records, and whatsoever else came to hand, which nothing could resist; Their Commanders, of whom *Cromwell* was one, if not acting, yet not restraining the Souldiers in this heat of their fury.

One of the monuments defaced in 1643 had been erected earlier in the century to honour members of the Orme family. Sir Humphrey Orme had commissioned this in his own lifetime, 'to save his heirs that charge and trouble'. A classical surround remains, but only one small panel of figures is left.

While lodging in a house in the close, Oliver Cromwell suffered an accident: his horse stumbled on some stone steps leading up to the cathedral, then rising suddenly dashed Cromwell's head against the lintel of the gateway door. 'He fell to the ground as dead, was so carried into the house, and it was about a fortnight ere he recovered'.

A second account tells how the organ at Peterborough was 'thrown down upon the ground, and there stamped and trampeled on, and broke in pieces, with such a strange furious and frantick zeal, as can't be well conceived, but by those that saw it'. The altar was also torn down and the rails cut in pieces. One of the officers did prevent the great Bible and Prayer Book from being carried off. The reredos was beautifully wrought, with three pinnacles rising almost to the roof of the cathedral. 'This had no imagery work on it, or any thing else that might justly give offence, and yet because it bore the name of the High Altar, was pulled down with Ropes, laid low and level with the ground'. A picture of the Last Judgment, including Christ and the four Evangelists, was painted on the ceiling above the altar; since it was out of reach, the soldiers 'defaced and spoiled' it with musket shot. Eventually the army marched on to Stamford, leaving 'the *abomination of desolation* in this Church behind them'.

Such activities were justified by an ordinance passed by the House of Commons on 26 August 1643, ordering 'the utter demolishing, removing and taking away of all Monuments of Superstition or Idolatry'. According to the ordinance, stone altars were to be demolished, communion tables moved from the east end to the body of the church, rails taken away, candlesticks, basons, crucifixes, images, pictures, and superstitious inscriptions removed or defaced. A proviso exempted images, pictures, and coats of arms in glass or stone which had been set up 'onely for a Monument of any King, Prince, or Nobleman, or other dead Person which had not been commonly reputed or taken for a Saint', but in practice eager iconoclasts continued to ignore the fine distinction between ornaments which were superstitious and those which were merely decorative.

Lincoln was one of the first cathedrals to be purged as required by the ordinance. The city was besieged in May 1644 by forces of the Eastern Association commanded by Manchester and Cromwell. It was difficult for them to gain control of the upper city, where the cathedral stood opposite the castle, for it was strongly defended by royalists who hurled great stones at the attackers. But the parliamentary army triumphed; Sir Francis Fane, the governor, and 650 royalist soldiers were taken prisoner, and the parliamentary troops were allowed to pillage the cathedral. It suffered severely. The greatest damage was to the windows, but tombs and monuments were attacked as well. When the diarist John Evelyn visited the minster in 1654 he was told that 'the Souldiers had lately knocked off all or most of the Brasses which were on the Gravestones, so as few inscriptions were left: They told us they went in with axes & hammers, & shut themselves in, till they had rent & torne of[f] some barges full of Mettal; not sparing the monuments of the dead, so helish an avarice possess'd them'. Most of this activity must have been contrary to the ordinance and proviso. It is often said that Cromwell stabled his horses in the minster, but this story comes from an unreliable source and should be dismissed. So should the tale that Cromwell (who was not the actual commander of the army) contemplated total destruction of the cathedral.

The neighbouring cathedral of Norwich came under attack at about the same time. Joseph Hall, recently consecrated bishop of Norwich, recounted the event.

Lord, what work was here! What clattering of glasses! What beating down of walls! What tearing up of monuments! What pulling down of seats! What wresting out of irons and brass from the window and graves! What defacing of arms! What demolishing of curious stonework, that had not any representation in the world, but only of the cost of the founder, and skill of the mason! What tooting and piping upon the destroyed organ pipes! And what a hideous triumph on the market day before all the country, when in a kind of sacrilegeous and profane procession, all the organ pipes, vestments, both copes and surplices, together with the leaden cross which had been newly sawn down from over the Green Yard pulpit, and the service books and singing-books that could be had, were carried to the fire in the public market-place, a lewd wretch walking before the train, in his cope training in the dirt, with a service-book in his hand, imitating in an impious scorn the tune, and usurping the words of the Litany used formerly in the Church!

An amusing if half-crazed set of royalist reminiscences describes what happened to some of the soldiers who desecrated the cathedral. 'Their Captain was Major Sherwood who hanged himselfe, their Lieutenant was one Craske ye was smitten with sudden death at Mr Ben Bakers, their Ensign was one Heath yt formerly lived in great splendor, but dyed very poore, one of the Serjeants name was Brathwayte who hanged himself next door to St Johns of Maddermarket Church, another Serjeants name was Downing who hanged himselfe in Racky wood, and had hanged there about 14 dayes and was full of flyes and vermin'. Several years later the aldermen of Great Yarmouth, a nearby port, asked Parliament if they might take part of the lead and other materials from the 'vast and altogether useless Cathedral in Norwich' so that they could build a workhouse and repair the pier, but it does not appear that this was ever done.

York Minster was less heavily damaged during the eleven-week siege of York in 1644. Here (according to the musician Thomas Mace, writing some years after the event) 'an abundance of people of the best rank and quality', and also 'the souldiers and citizens, or most of them', came to the minster every Sunday for prayers, preaching, and psalm singing. The church was battered, even during services, 'so much that sometimes a canon bullet, has come in at the windows and bounc'd about from pillar to pillar, (even like some furious fiend or evil spirit) backwards and forwards, and all manner of side ways, as it has happened to meet with square or round opposition amongst the pillars, in its returns or rebounds, until its force has been spent'. But 'in the whole time of the siege, there was not any one person (that I could hear of) did (in the Church) receive the least harm by any of their devilish canon shot: and I verily believe, there were constantly many more then a thousand persons at that service every Sunday, during the whole time of that siege'. Nevertheless the organ was taken down, although it required several orders from the Commonwealth committee to have the work completed. Other articles taken away included candlesticks, copes, a great iron chest, a brass statue, and all the brasses from gravestones. Damage to the windows was minimal, possibly because Sir Thomas Fairfax, a scion of a wealthy Yorkshire family and himself commander of the parliamentary armies, ordered them to be taken down and preserved.

At Exeter, now again in the hands of the king's friends, the dean and chapter ordered the cathedral bells to be rung celebrating several royalist triumphs in 1644: the relief of Newark, Waller's defeat near Banbury, Prince

Rupert's victory over the Scots in the North, and 'the greate victory his Majestie had over the Rebeles in Cornwall'. There was a bonfire when the king and queen visited Exeter in May (Henrietta Maria had returned from her trip to the Netherlands the previous February), as well as ringing to commemorate the anniversary of the king's coronation. A pedestal costing £5 3s. 3d. was erected for the christening of Princess Henrietta, the king's fifth daughter, who was born in Exeter on 16 June, and 3s. was later spent mending seats which had been broken at the baptism. There were also gifts to the king's servants.

At the time of Henrietta's birth the king was in Worcester; we know that he attended a service in Worcester Cathedral that very day. Six thousand royalist soldiers were lodged in the city, the royal party itself occupying the bishop's palace for most of a week. Charles knighted the mayor and persuaded the city to advance him £1000.

Although the king's forces had been relatively successful in 1644, their hopes were dashed by the disastrous defeat of the royalists at Naseby on 14 June 1645. This was the final great battle of the Civil War; subsequent events were not likely to alter the outcome. Following the debacle at Naseby, the king again spent some time at Worcester. Early in September his forces, almost miraculously, had been able to end the Scots' siege of Hereford. Heartened by this success, Charles undertook to raise another siege at Chester. On 23 September the king watched from the tower of Chester Cathedral (and narrowly escaped being shot there) as his troops were defeated in the battle of Rowton Heath. The city was then starved into submission and capitulated on 3 February 1646. It is uncertain how much the cathedral suffered. The articles of surrender stated that it should be spared, and it was clearly more fortunate than many others. The victors did pull down the High Cross which stood outside the cathedral, and they sold the furniture from the bishop's palace. Meanwhile Hereford had capitulated in December to a parliamentary army led by Colonel Birch, despite the brave opposition of the dean, Herbert Croft.

One of the last royalist strongholds, Worcester itself was besieged by a parliamentary army in May 1646. Despite the shortage of food and other supplies, the citizens held out for two months. Articles of surrender were accepted on 19 July and the organ was taken down the next day. According to a local diary, 'Some parliamentarians, hearing the music of the church at service, walking in the aisle, fell a skipping about and dancing as it were in derision. Others, seeing the workmen taking them down, said, "You might have spared that labour, we would have done it for you". "No", said a merry lad (about ten years old), "for when the Earl of Essex was here, the first man of yours that plucked down and spoiled the organs broke his neck here, and they will prevent the like misfortune"'. The last Anglican service in the cathedral was held at 6 a.m. on 12 July. The cathedral's detached bell tower, called the Leaden Steeple or clocherium, was demolished in February 1647; its lead and other materials were sold and the proceeds used to repair almshouses that had been damaged in the fighting.

The city of Carlisle suffered what was perhaps the most horrible siege of the war. In 1643 the cathedral chapter had suspended payments to inferior members of the staff 'considering the hard condition of theis times and fore-seeing great losse in our rents and revenues, and alsoe great charge and burthen to be imposed upon us for His Majesties service'. The siege itself, which took place in 1644 and 1645, was chronicled by an eighteen-year-old, Isaac Tullie. In May 1645 the townsmen were butchering horses and coining silver plate into three-shilling pieces; by June they were reduced to eating dogs and rats. 'Now were Gentlemen and others so shrunk', Tullie wrote, 'that they could not chuse but laugh one at another to see their close [clothes] hang as upon men on gibbets, for one might have put theire head and fists between the doublet and the shirts of many of them'. As soon as news of the king's defeat at Naseby reached the city the defenders realized that they would have to yield, but they did insist on articles intended to protect the cathedral. Every member of the cathedral foundation was to be allowed a livelihood out of church revenues until Parliament ordered otherwise, and it was agreed that no church should be defaced.

This pledge, however, was not honoured. The city was garrisoned by Scottish soldiers under the command of Alexander Leslie – at this time the Scots were still allied with the English Parliament – and in 1646 the Scots pulled down the west front of the cathedral and six bays of the Norman nave, which had been used as a parish church. They used the stone to repair the castle and construct additional fortifications. The nave was never rebuilt. One bay remains and gives testimony to the quality of the original Norman architecture. The modest façade which seals the west end of the existing truncated building is Victorian, designed by Ewan Christian; the cathedral stands as a visual monument to the war's destruction.

Even this was not the end of the troubles at Carlisle. In 1648, when the king had allied with the Scots in the so-called Second Civil War, the Scottish garrison held the city against the parliamentary armies. Once again royalist hopes were dashed; the Scots were defeated in the battle of Preston, and Oliver Cromwell demanded that they surrender their border garrisons at Berwick and Carlisle. 'If you deny me herein, I must make our appeal to God, and call on Him for assistance', Cromwell wrote. Needless to say the Scots were in no position to refuse his terms.

The Scots were also responsible for damage to the cathedral at Durham. After the battle of Dunbar in September 1650 Cromwell took 10,000 Scots prisoners. Nearly half of these were sent to Durham, where about 3000 were housed in the cathedral for two years. In a letter to the authorities at London Sir Arthur Haselrig insisted that the captives were well treated, fed with oatmeal, beef and cabbage. But there was no heat in the cathedral, so the prisoners broke down the choir stalls, font and anything else that could be burned to keep themselves warm. Since the Scots had a special hatred for members of the Neville family, they defaced the fourteenth-century tombs in the Neville chantry, even though they were not combustible. It is said that an English gaoler robbed the Scots of any valuables they still possessed and also sold the cathedral lectern, in the shape of a pelican, for his own profit. The sick were sent to be lodged in the adjacent castle; as many as 1600 died. More than a thousand books from the great library at Durham were entrusted to the librarian of Peterhouse, Cambridge, but were safely returned to the cathedral in 1660.

Lichfield was besieged more often than any other cathedral city, and the cathedral suffered greater damage than any other, except perhaps Carlisle. Lichfield close was walled and moated so that it could be occupied and defended; the city was strongly royalist and it lay in the midlands where much of the fighting took place. Following the battle of Edgehill in 1642 Lichfield was garrisoned by the royalists. Parliamentary troops arrived to besiege the close in March. Their leader, Lord Brooke, was killed by a deaf-and-dumb man firing a fowling piece from the cathedral tower, but the parliamentary army was so strong that the king's followers realized they had no hope of holding out and shortly laid down their arms. Puritan soldiers then set about ridding the cathedral of objects which they regarded as superstitious. They destroyed the choir stalls, smashed 12,000 feet of painted glass in the windows, broke up images, crucifixes and tombs, and burned most of the books in the cathedral library. (A few of the more precious volumes, including the manuscript known as St Chad's Gospels, had been hidden by the precentor William Higgins.) Both organs were broken in pieces. The west front of the cathedral was famous for its image screen adorned with 113 statues of kings, prophets, martyrs and saints. This was an obvious target for the iconoclasts; the figures low enough to be reached were pulled down with ropes, while those higher up were battered with gunfire. Sir William Dugdale, in his *Short View of the Late Troubles in England*, wrote that they 'hunted a cat with hounds through the church, delighting themselves with the echoe from the goodly vaulted roof; and to add to their wickedness brought a calf into it, wrapt in linen, carried it to the font, sprinkled it with water and gave it a name in scorn and derision of the holy sacrament of baptism'.

In March 1634 Prince Rupert, the king's nephew and royalist commander, received orders to retake the city of Lichfield. His troops surrounded the close and, when the parliamentarians refused to surrender, proceeded to blow up part of the walls which enclosed it. Fierce fighting took place on 20 April; Colonel Russell and his parliamentary soldiers finally capitulated and were allowed to march out of the city, taking with them the linens and communion plate from the cathedral.

Lichfield remained in royalist hands for three years. Following his defeat at Naseby the king took shelter in the loyal city twice, lodging at the bishop's palace. The plague struck Lichfield early in 1646 and was soon followed by a third siege. The cathedral and close were bombarded by parliamentary forces for five days in May. Heavy guns were brought in and aimed at the church's central spire – Lichfield was famous for its three spires, unique among English cathedrals, which reminded some Puritans of the pope's triple crown – and when a cannon ball hit the base of the tallest spire it collapsed, part of it falling into the choir and part into the nave. By this time it was obvious that the king had lost the war. Charles surrendered to the Scots in May, and his wartime headquarters at Oxford fell to the New Model Army in June. The royalists abandoned Lichfield on 10 July. In the end 'the church was so totally demolished An. 1646 that it may be truly said there is not now remaining the least piece of Brass, Glass, Iron, Armes &c. but what appear to have been put up Since 1661'.

Several cathedrals survived the war relatively unscathed, since they were located in cities that were not fought over. London was one of these. As early as May 1642 the committee 'for pulling down and abolishing all monuments of superstition and idolatry' was ordered to take all the copes from St Paul's and have them burned, so that the fire might separate out the gold in the embroidery. This was to be sold and the revenue used for poor relief in Ireland. Money remaining in the fund raised by subscription for repairs to the church was confiscated, and the scaffolding that still enclosed the tower was taken down and assigned to military uses. Later, in 1645, the cathedral's plate was sold to pay for supplies for a train of artillery. Statues of the Stuart monarchs were removed from Inigo Jones's portico and smashed, but the classical colonnade and the Gothic cathedral which it masked remained intact.

In 1644 Oliver Cromwell, while still only a colonel leading troops from the Eastern Association, ordered Canon Hitch of Ely 'to forbear altogether your Choir service, so unedifying and offensive', lest the soldiers should take it upon themselves to reform matters in a 'tumultuary or disorderly way'. When Hitch refused, Cromwell came himself to a service (with his hat on) and, laying his hand on his sword, ordered the canon to 'leave off his fooling and come down' from the communion table. Oliver is said to have locked the cathedral and put the key in his pocket. Four years later a committee was asked to consider whether materials from the 'ruinous' building might be sold for the relief of sick and maimed soldiers, widows and orphans, but no looting actually occurred. The demolition of the medieval chapter house and cloister is not well documented and is sometimes attributed to this period, but Cromwell himself can be exonerated. Possibly he was willing to tolerate the cathedral because he had lived in Ely himself and had been a tithe farmer for the dean and chapter.

Although both royalist and parliamentary forces occupied Salisbury at various times during the war, the cathedral there escaped serious damage. No doubt the organ would have been knocked about, but the chapter had the foresight to have it dismantled and stored before the outbreak of hostilities. There was little if any loss of glass. The detached bell tower (now demolished) was occupied as a parliamentary observation post in 1645 and some royalist prisoners were later housed there – they were freed when the royalists set fire to the tower door and smoked the parliamentary garrison out. Bristol, too, changed hands, but two Members of Parliament asked to report on conditions there in 1645 wrote that 'the collegiate [cathedral] men were still chanting out the Common Prayer to the wonted height'. As late as 1646 there was a sermon commemorating the anniversary of the king's coronation; use of the Prayer Book was not abandoned until it was prohibited by parliamentary order in 1645. Exeter surrendered quietly in April 1646. Scottish soldiers may have broken some windows at Gloucester, but on the whole it was (as Thomas Fuller wrote) 'decently preserved'; there is a tradition that Charles forbade his artillery to be directed against the cathedral and that the upper part of the tower was protected with wool sacks.

Until 1645 Oxford was spared a siege although it served as the king's headquarters throughout the war. The restored royalist garrison surrendered on the king's command following a second siege in 1646. Charles lived in the deanery at Christ Church (the queen had rooms at Merton) and frequently attended services in the cathedral, sitting in the vice-chancellor's stall. We have a list of those who preached before the king during August and September 1645, together with an intriguing reference to musicians from the Chapel Royal being in residence at the college. (One wonders whether they ever sang with the cathedral choir, which uniquely remained in existence throughout the entire period of the Civil War and Interregnum – if so, the melancholy king may have heard some marvellous music.) In 1649 the organs were taken down, but perhaps not destroyed, and in 1651 the dean and chapter issued an interesting order 'that all Pictures representing god, good or bad Angelles or Saintes shall be forthwith taken downe out of our

Church windowes, and shall be disposed for the mending of the Glasse that is out of repair in any part of the Colledg'. In fact only minimal damage was inflicted; heads and faces were removed (one may still see the blank spots today), but the windows remained structurally intact.

Contemporary accounts generally leave the impression that damage to the cathedrals was the work of soldiers operating under the influence of zealous enthusiasm or, perhaps, drink. Some visual evidence, however, makes it clear that this was not always the case. A picture of Canterbury Cathedral painted by the minor artist Thomas Johnson shows a group of men, presumably a parliamentary committee, seated at a table in the nave calmly supervising further destruction. At the left, a single workman swings what looks like a scythe at the choir stalls; at the right, another stands on a window sill to smash stained glass. Planned activities of this sort no doubt occurred elsewhere.

Following his surrender, Charles was held prisoner in various places until January 1649, when he was put on trial. After he was found guilty of subverting the constitution and making war on his subjects the king was executed outside the Banqueting House in Whitehall on 30 January. The House of Lords was also abolished. England was now to be governed as a Commonwealth, with supreme authority residing in the 'Rump' House of Commons, the small number of radical Members left following Pride's Purge in December.

The Rump shortly turned its attention to the cathedrals. On 30 April it passed a long Act abolishing 'Deans, Deans and Chapters, Canons, Prebends and other offices and titles of or belonging to any Cathedral or Collegiate Church or Chappel within England and Wales'. The primary justification cited was the necessity of raising money, and the fact that lenders would not yield it without sufficient securities, such as the lands of the deans and chapters. The Act confiscated 'all their Honors, Manors, Lands, &c. and Hereditaments whatsoever', placing the administration of these estates in the hands of trustees. Surveys of this property were to be made. Leases granted after 1 December 1641 were declared void. Colleges within the universities were exempted, as were revenues devoted to the maintenance of grammar schools, highways and almshouses. If lands were sold, the price was to be at least twelve times the annual income. In all, £300,000 was to be borrowed on the security of dean and chapter lands; it was later agreed that a third of this should go to the navy and a third to the forces in Ireland, while the final third should be reserved for exigencies. Late in October the Council of State was informed that £170,832 had been collected and £167,213 disbursed; £129,167 remained due. The State Papers contain many warrants for payments out of dean and chapter lands. A typical entry, dated 26 October 1649, authorizes the payment of £1429 to Colonel Pride (earlier the leader of Pride's Purge of the Commons), to cover his own expenses and those of two majors, eight captains, two lieutenants, forty sergeants, twenty drummers and two thousand recruits.[2]

Because of subsequent Acts of Parliament the sum raised on the security of these lands through the end of 1657 was actually £455,621; additional rents, profits, and money borrowed at interest raised the total to more than £516,913. Of this amount £15,628 had been spent on stipends for those ministers and lecturers approved by the Commonwealth, and £428 for schoolmasters. Far more had gone to the army (£169,298) and the navy (£164,000), or for the expenses of the council (£48,033).

Parliamentary surveys of the property of the deans and chapters (and in some cases related institutions, notably the colleges of vicars choral) survive in most of the cathedral archives or in the record offices to which their papers have been transferred. These elaborate documents were compiled in 1649 and 1650. Not surprisingly, the cost of preparing them was high: the total was £40,418, of which £13,419 was still owed to the surveyors, clerks and messengers in November 1650. Two copies of each survey were made, one for use locally and the other for the central government.[3]

Fascinating detailed information about cathedral properties is included in the surveys, which (so far as the cathedrals are concerned) can be regarded as a seventeenth-century version of the *Valor Ecclesiasticus* prepared under Henry VIII. The cathedral buildings themselves are generally not described, presumably because there was no intention of demolishing them. Lichfield is the exception. Here the survey notes:

> Nothing about the Cathedrall Church valued. The whole ffabrick of it is exceedingly ruinated; much Leade and iron was taken away whilst it was a Garrison. And much lead and other materialls is taken away since And is continually by evill persons stolne away in the night. A great part of the roofe uncovered. If some course bee not taken to preserve it, within a little time the leade wilbe all gone and the whole ffabricke fall to the Ground.

Materials from the dean's house, which was ruined, were thought to be worth £120. The demolished library could yield £60, some canons' houses £110 each, the rooms of vicars choral as little as £4 10s. apiece. In all, the materials which could be salvaged from ruined buildings amounted to £722. The gardens near the great pool had been 'Spoyled by digging trenches of fortification', and the trees were 'now all cutt downe'.

At Carlisle too the deanery was in great decay; its stone, timber, lead and slate were valued at £120. There is no mention of the cathedral. The governor intended to repair several neighbouring buildings for the storage of 'Coale, turfe, and other fewell needfull for the Garrison'. He planned to take down the singingmen's house and move it to the grounds of the castle, where it could provide accommodation for the troops, 'forasmuche as the Ruines of the Cittie are soe great as at present hee is fforced to quarter neere about halfe of the souldiers without the Cittie'. Concluding memoranda note that 'all the houses and buildings in Cattcoates, Stone Cross gate, and Calden gate were all burnt downe to the ground in the time of the Leager [siege] and very few Rebuilt; ... the Burgage houses and Buildings held by Lease of the late Dean and Chapter within the City of Carlisle are all together very Ruinous and not Tenantable Scarse to live in'.

Norwich, as has been seen, was more fortunate. Here, according to the survey, 'the Close, wherein the Cathedral Church standeth, is a place of very large extent, encompassed parte with the common river on the east thereof, and the residue with a highe stone wall. It containeth many faire houses & buildings hereafter particularly mentioned, & wee are informed is accounted as the scite of the mannor of Amners, and hath some privileges mentioned after the end of this survey'. The dean's house, 'a faire stone built house', was in good condition, occupied by Mistress Wright, widow, tenant to the former dean, for an annual rent of £14. Should it be decided to strip the lead from the deanery roof, it could be sold for £341 8s. The total yearly rent from houses in the close was £390 – plus, in some cases, a stated number of capons, hens and eggs.

The most amazing entry comes from Wells, where the commissioners actually suggested taking down the fourteenth-century chapter house. One of the glories of medieval English architecture, it was described as containing 'Severall Roomes below stayres with a fayre Spatial Roome over them together with a large Stayre Case leadinge up to the said Roome. The materials of all which, the Charge of takeing downe being deducted, we value at £160'. The deanery, 'Consisting of a faire gate house at the south entrance thereof with Lodgings over the same together with one large hall, two fayre Parlors, a large Kitchen, Buttery, Larders, and Cellars, with Divers other nessisary rooms below stayres, a fayre dineing roome and many fayer Lodging roomes with a large gallery over the same, a large stable, a coach house, together with many other houses', could be demolished at a profit of £210. This vicars' hall, if taken down, might yield £110. Fortunately none of this destruction actually took place. The small houses in Vicars' Close were still in good condition, and the commissioners planned to let them at annual rents of about £1 each.

The survey for Worcester provides another good description of the deanery. Still in sound condition, it was a fine residence which included the

Gestenhall (64 feet x 34 feet), a large parlour (40 feet x 20 feet) with the dining room of the same size over it, the 'Queen's Chamber', a chapel, gardens and stables. It was let for £3 6s. 8d. a year. Thomas Tomkins, the organist, still held the lease of two new houses, one of which contained a hall, kitchen, buttery, five sleeping chambers and a high turret or study. The most valuable property of the dean and chapter was the manor of Wimbledon, near London, rather than any holdings in Worcester itself.

The deanery at Rochester had been let by the Sequestrators for Kent for £22 a year. The list of its rooms reads like a modern real estate advertisement:

> The House consisteth of a Low Roome by the Entry, a Hall, an entering Roome, a Parlor wainscotted, a Closett and Convenient Kitchin, a back Chamber, a back house & two back roomes over it, Two sellers and divers ould houses for wood & coals and other necessary uses. A Stayre Case about Six foote square Leading to a very faire dyning roome being about ffortie five foott long & about Twentie four foott broad, Eight Chambers of which six have Chimneys and five have Closetts, A gallery of about Thirtie-five foott Long and about Thirteene foott broad, Garretts unfinished over.

Canon Row, 'That long Rowe off buildings within the Colledge Wall Commonly called or knowne by the Name of the Pettye Canons', contained eighteen lower rooms with five more over them; it was inhabited by 'ould and decrepitt poore People ... that did belong to the Cathedrall Church' rather than the singingmen for whom it was intended. In all it was valued at £14. The organist's house was worth £6 a year, the prebendaries' homes £10, £8 or (if decayed) £5.

Some of the houses in the close at Lincoln had been pulled down or 'fired' during the fighting, but the former precentor, Hamlett Marshall, still lived in his house 'with a Hall open to the Roofe 52 foot long 20 broad, a dyning Parlor partly wainscoated with a Roome adjoyninge, Also another Lodging Parlor adjoyninge partly wainscoated now used as a kitchen. In the second Story a dyning Roome with five Lodgings and a Clossett, and also a little Chapple with a Study'. The house was built of stone and covered with tiles; an orchard and garden adjoined it. There were fourteen dwellings in the College of the Old and New Vicars, some of them still 'fair' buildings but others 'much out of repair'; the ancient hall was 'very ruinous and unfitt for use'. The annual income from the vicars' houses was £60 10s. 8d., but if they were taken down the materials could fetch £525 6s. 8d. Timber from the Minster Wood was valued at £731 15s.

Other sources tell us of a proposal to demolish the cathedral at Winchester. This was countered by a petition drafted by the city's recorder,

Cornelius Hooker; in the end the building was spared and funds were raised for its repair. The Survey for Winchester recorded that the 'very faire' deanery was 'for the most part in very good repaire, very pleasantly situated, neer the said Cathedrall Church, the passage leading thither through the Cloisters, on the south parte thereof there is a very faire Court adorned with nine very great Trees'. The close survived less well. All but three of the houses were totally or partly demolished following the war. One of the survivors, No. 2, was given a new roof of five thousand tiles; originally the home of a prebendary, it was occupied by three lawyers during the Interregnum, after 1660 by the dean while his own house was being repaired, then by the cantankerous Canon Thomas Gumble and later by the saintly Thomas Ken.

At Gloucester the Survey included the bishop's palace, probably because it lay within the cathedral close. It was 'very ruinous and not habitable soe that nobody will rent itt of us butt att a very low rate'; it was valued at £200 but actually sold, together with some additional land, for £913. The bishop's stable was occupied by 'certaine poore People put in by ye Maior of the Citty of Glocester'.

In most of the surveys the commissioners list both the present rent received from properties and the 'improved' higher rent which they believed could be charged. Often the 'improvements' are many times the existing sums. The survey for Canterbury bears this out dramatically. The present rents of dean and chapter properties in the parish of St Andrew, for instance, were £50 18s. 8d., but the total of 'improvements with the rent included' was £449 17s. The figures for the parish of St Mary Magdalene were £18 18s. 9d. and £143 11s. 8d.; for St George's £4 19s. 4d. and £35; for St Alphege £9 2s. 8d. and £86. The usher's house and other buildings of the Latin School now yielded £53 4s. 4d. but with improvement could produce £117 1s. 4d.

Because the cathedral archives themselves contain no record of the years between 1649 and 1660, it is difficult to ascertain just how the cathedral buildings were used during the Interregnum. A proposal to pull them all down and use the proceeds for poor relief was debated by Parliament in 1651, but fortunately it was not adopted. In some cases we know that the cathedrals continued to provide a space for sermons and services (no longer based on the Prayer Book); in others they are said to have housed troops and horses.

The reformed religion was perhaps most successful at York. Here the municipal corporation turned the Minster into a preaching centre for the whole city. Four ministers were employed, maintained by a parliamentary grant of £600 a year out of the property of the former dean and chapter. These preachers were learned men, 'painful and pious', and their work was highly regarded by the mayor and aldermen. The Minster seems to have been more fully integrated in the life of the city than before the war.[4] Certainly the corporation maintained the fabric of the Minster, authorizing repairs and installing new seating; when they ordered that the organ be taken down they were careful to prevent unapproved looting.

Oxford Cathedral remained a special case, since it served as the chapel for Christ Church. Services continued to be held throughout the Interregnum, although the hours were changed from 10 a.m. and 3 p.m. to 5 or 6 in the morning and 5 o'clock in the afternoon. The choir remained in existence, now presumably leading the singing of psalms, and disputations and sermons (by acceptable Puritans like John Owen) continued as well. Since the cathedral was an integral part of the college, its endowments seem to have escaped confiscation.

Parliament allocated £300 a year from the former revenues of the dean and chapter of Gloucester for the maintenance of preachers in that city. For a time Thomas Jackson was the minister at the cathedral and was well received by the city council; the town clerk referred to him as 'a worthy Minister [who supplied] the room of the Bishop, Dean, and Chapter to the College'. Two lesser men filled the place after Jackson's death in 1647. A reference to rooms set aside for storing the cushions used by the mayor and aldermen on sermon days confirms their attendance. In 1656 Cromwell (now Lord Protector) and his council granted the cathedral '& the Utensills thereof with the Cloysters' to the burgesses 'for the preaching & hearing of Gods word & other publique uses'. Such uses presumably included the assizes and quarter sessions, which were held in the nave. The city fathers raised subscriptions for the restoration of the cathedral, 'now very ruinous and in great decay', and ordered that 'such [things] as are most needfull be speedily repaired and amended'. A public library was established in the chapter house, largely as a result of efforts by Thomas Purdy, a gentleman who gave both money and books. When he visited Gloucester in 1654, John Evelyn commented especially on this 'new Librarie, very noble though a private designe'. The cathedral grammar school continued in operation, with a headmaster paid £40 a year out of the former revenues of the dean and chapter. Almsmen received their accustomed allowances from the Trustees for the Maintenance of Ministers.

Peterborough Cathedral remained in use as a parish church. The choir was restored and made 'pretty decent for the Congregation to meet in'. Samuel Wilson, a schoolmaster from the Charterhouse in London, was sent by the Committee of Plundered Ministers to be the preacher, at a salary of £160 a year. The south transept of Chester Cathedral had functioned as St Oswald's parish for centuries and was screened off with a separate entrance; the parish continued to operate throughout the Interregnum and, surprisingly, used the organ, which was undamaged. In 1645 the citizens of Chichester asked Parliament for £600 from the former cathedral revenues so that they could maintain three men who were providing a learned and godly ministry there. Two new ministers, Leonard Cooke and Humphrey Ellis, were appointed to preach in Winchester Cathedral and were allotted houses in the close. At Worcester the Presbyterians and Independents shared the use of the cathedral, and four of the prebendal houses were allocated to ministers. The 'strenuous' Puritan Hugh Peter preached there occasionally; Richard Baxter, pastor of the church at Kidderminster, also delivered sermons in which he tried, vainly, to bring all parties together. One of the regular preachers at the cathedral was the old Independent Simon Moore, but according to Baxter 'he somewhat lost the people's love'. Edward Reyner and George Scotereth were appointed ministers at Lincoln Cathedral; although a staunch Puritan, Reyner had been a prebendary of Lincoln since 1635 and had been paid by the city to lecture in the cathedral as well as his own parish church, St Peter at Arches. At Bristol members of the corporation continued to attend Sunday sermons in the cathedral and to pay for keeping their seats in repair. Three Puritan ministers preached regularly in the cathedral at Hereford, which also served as St John's parish church. It is believed that the famous 'Mappa Mundi' was hidden under the floor of a chantry chapel throughout the Interregnum. Similarly, the remaining part of Carlisle Cathedral was evidently patched up to serve as a parish church: the fact that one of the bells is dated 1657 certainly suggests continued use.

Presbyterians and Independents shared the building at Exeter; Robert Atkins was the Presbyterian minister and Cromwell sent his own personal chaplain, Lewis Stukeley, to serve the Independent congregation. Conflicts arose because both groups wished to use the building at the same time. These were resolved in 1657 when the city fathers ordered the construction of a brick wall across the cathedral, dividing the choir from the nave. The wall itself cost £150, but it was necessary to provide a new entry into the choir, removing a window from one of the chantry chapels in the process, and to make a new 'Avenue through the Garden Hall and outrooms of the late Treasurer's house'; a total of £800 had to be raised to pay for the alterations. The Presbyterians also had the bishop's seat removed (perhaps as a symbolic gesture), and they took down the fourteenth-century timber screens backing the choir stalls, fortunately storing them away rather than destroying them. This action made possible their later re-erection.

The cathedral at Norwich, too, was used by the Independents. The choir was rearranged to suit the convenience of the mayor and aldermen, whose seats were placed at the east end, the mayor sitting where the high altar had been. Sir Thomas Browne, who visited the cathedral during the Interregnum, tells us that the tall tomb of the Norman bishop Herbert de Losinga, which stood in front of the altar, proved inconvenient and had to be 'taken down into such a lowness as it now remaineth'. Considerable sums were spent on repairs during the 1650s; payments included the cost of 15,000 tiles laid in the north and south aisles, probably in areas where memorial brasses had been removed.

In London the east end of St Paul's was walled up and turned into a preaching house. For a time the eminent Presbyterian Cornelius Burges filled the pulpit; he was given the title lecturer and granted the use of the deanery. There is a legend that Cromwell contemplated selling St Paul's cathedral to the Jews. This can hardly be true – neither the Puritans nor the Jews would have welcomed the idea. In fact we have Sir William Dugdale's word that the body of the cathedral was 'frequently converted into a *Horse quarters* for Souldiers' and fell into a 'lamentable condition'. He feared that the vaults would fall and not one stone be left on another. Inigo Jones's noble portico was hacked up for rental as a series of mean shops for 'Seamstresses and other Trades', with makeshift stairways leading to lofts over them. The outdoor pulpit known as Paul's Cross, which might have been used by Independent preachers, was also pulled down and never re-erected. In 1651 there was a complaint that the soldiers were playing nine pins noisily in the churchyard, disturbing those who wished to sleep nearby; they were ordered to end their sport by 9 o'clock.

Preaching at Canterbury took place in the chapter house, which was now styled the sermon house. The cathedral stood idle and empty except when it was used as a stable or armoury, but minimal repairs were made to the roof and masonry. A visitor to Wells found the cathedral 'much ruined and leaky', because thieves were stripping the lead off the roof. There was some preaching by Cornelius Burges, who retired to Wells after finding life in London too difficult, but he was 'uneasily listened to'; citizens walked up and down in the cloister during his sermons, and the constables had to be called in. Lead (a valuable commodity in the seventeenth century) had been removed from the roof of the nave and cloisters at Bristol Cathedral as well; in 1656 the chamber said it regretted this action and ordered the lead to be sold, the resulting £77 8s. 6d. to be used for repairs to the church. The choir, where sermons were heard, remained intact, and payments were still made for looking after the seats occupied by members of the corporation. If God's word continued to be heard in the other cathedrals, it made little impact in the records. At Rochester we read only of abuse and dereliction; in 1651 the mayor reported that lead had been stolen there too. It is said (improbably) that Ely Cathedral remained locked for seventeen years after Oliver Cromwell took off the key.

Virtually all of the cathedral clergy lost their positions and homes as a result of the Puritan victory. Most of them were turned out under the Act of 1649 providing for the appropriation of the property of the deans and chapters, since it abolished all 'offices and titles of and belonging to any Cathedral'. Cathedral clergy who also held parish livings (about three-fourths of them did) were permitted to retain one such benefice provided that they agreed to conform to the religious policies of the government. Some of them later lost these positions too as a result of the ordinance 'for ejecting Scandalous, Ignorant and Insufficient Ministers and Schoolmasters', passed in 1654. Under that Act charges could be directed against the politics, churchmanship and moral character of the clergy, and a number were found wanting.

We know a good deal about the ejected Anglicans because of the labours of John Walker, who published his account of the *Sufferings of the Clergy during the Grand Rebellion* in 1714. Walker was a member of a prominent Exeter family, born in 1674 and educated at Oxford. After ordination he served as rector of the parishes of St Mary Major in Exeter and Upton Pyne, near the city; following the publication of his work he was given a prebend at Exeter Cathedral and a D.D. from Oxford.

Walker was prompted to compile his catalogue of displaced Anglican clergy because of his antipathy toward Edmund Calamy's *Abridgment of Mr Baxter's History of his Life and Times: With an Account of Many Others of Those Worthy Ministers who were Ejected after the Restauration of King Charles the Second* (1702), followed by Calamy's *Account of the Ministers, Lecturers, Masters and Fellows of Colleges and Schoolmasters who were Ejected or Silenced after the Restoration in 1660* (1713). While Calamy attempted to arouse sympathy for nonconformists who were ejected from the Restoration Church of England, Walker believed that the sufferings of the Anglicans displaced during the Interregnum were greater, and he set out to document his case. It was his contention that the episcopalians affected far outnumbered the nonconformists who suffered, and that their lot was far worse.[5]

Walker thought that about 10,000 men were deprived under the Commonwealth and Protectorate. Thirty-two deans and sixty-six archdeacons were deprived. Nearly 400 prebends and canonries were vacated, and 130 minor canons (priests who sang in the choir) lost their positions. Since laymen are not included in Walker's count, we have no record here of the number of organists, singingmen or choristers whose positions disappeared, nor is there any account of sextons, almsmen, bell ringers, organ blowers or schoolmasters. Taken altogether the number of persons who were dismissed from the cathedrals probably approached a thousand.

The ejected clergy had a very limited range of career opportunities open to them. Some became chaplains or tutors in the houses of gentlemen or members of the aristocracy, while others obtained posts as schoolmasters. The Act against scandalous ministers and teachers was responsible for loyal Anglicans losing even these posts. A few clergymen obtained vacant parishes – this could happen only if both the clergy and the local authorities showed some flexibility in their views. Some found employment overseas, or, if they had private incomes, simply lived as exiles until the Restoration.

Examination of some individual cases may help flesh out these generalizations. One may take as a sample the dean and chapter of St Paul's. Richard Steward had served as dean of the Chapel Royal and Westminster Abbey as well as the cathedral and was in addition provost of Eton; he was a leading figure among the English exiles in Paris until his death in 1651. One of the prebendaries, Joseph Crowther, also lived in France as chaplain to the duke of York and a preacher at the English church in Paris. Three prebendaries – Alexander Strange, Robert Thompson and Samuel Hoard – were able to retain parish appointments since they held Puritan or Presbyterian views. At least five members of the chapter (Thomas Soame, William Haywood, Thomas Wilson, Benjamin Stone and John Montfort) were imprisoned, mainly early in the war. After his release Haywood kept a school in Wiltshire under his son's name; Soame, whose parishioners at Staines sought in vain to keep him as their minister, retired to a life of poverty in Oxford. Richard Bayly, the former president of St John's College, Oxford, compounded and lived on at the university, as did John Tolson (former provost of Oriel). At least eight of the prebendaries died during the war or Interregnum. The estate of Isaac Singleton, whose death came soon after the war began, was forfeited for treason. The parish formerly served by Samuel Baker sent him financial assistance shortly before his death in 1658 because he was living 'in great necessity and sickness'. In several cases wives or widows of prebendaries were granted allowances (fifths, not tenths) out of the revenues of their husband's former parishes. The minor canons and singingmen probably continued to receive their usual small stipends, since the Committee for Sequestrations ordered the mayor and corporation to pay inferior officers the same amounts the dean and chapter had allowed them.

Similar fates awaited members of the chapter at Durham. The dean, Walter Balcanqual, died in 1645, before he could be removed. His successor, Christopher Potter, left Durham to become dean of Winchester in 1646, but he died later that year. He was followed, at least in theory, by William Fuller, previously the dean of Ely. Fuller was imprisoned for a time at Ely House in

London; he was vicar of St Giles, Cripplegate, and may have continued to minister there. An archdeacon, Isaac Basire, had also been a royal chaplain and had been imprisoned following the siege of Carlisle; he spent the Interregnum travelling in Europe and the Near East and was in Hungary at the time of the Restoration. The most interesting of the prebendaries is perhaps Eleazar Duncan, who went abroad after narrowly escaping arrest and served as chaplain to the Levant Company at Leghorn. He died in Italy while preparing to return to England after the Restoration. John Cosin spent the Interregnum in Paris as chaplain to Protestants in the queen's household. Thomas Triplet taught briefly in Dublin but after 1656 was a resident teacher at the Dutch embassy in London. John Barwick was imprisoned in the Tower for two years on a treason charge; after his release he continued to organize royalist sympathizers. Elias Smith, a minor canon and precentor, was allowed to stay on as master of the Durham grammar school and curate of one of the churches in Durham. Thomas Wanlesse, another minor canon who had been master of the cathedral song school, was imprisoned for a time at Hull and remained there after his release, dying about 1653.

Turning to the experiences of other deans we find that John Young, dean of Winchester, owned a farm at Exton, in the Meon valley of Hampshire, and retired there when he was turned out of his cathedral. He died at Exton in 1654. Herbert Croft, dean of Hereford, inherited a substantial estate on the death of his brother, Sir William; during most of the Interregnum he lived in the home of Sir Rowland Berkeley near Worcester. Samuel Fell, dean of Christ Church, Oxford, and a prebendary of St Paul's, held the rectories of Sunningwell and Longworth in Berkshire. The Committee on Plundered Ministers sequestered him from the latter, since he was allowed to hold only one rectory and had ignored their demand that he make a choice. He died at Sunningwell on 1 February 1649, supposedly of shock upon hearing of the execution of the king. His wife Margaret had joined him in vigorous resistance to the parliamentary visitation at Oxford; his son John, who later followed in his father's footsteps as dean of Christ Church, lived quietly in Oxford and continued to hold Prayer Book services in his house throughout the Interregnum. The dean of Wells, Walter Raleigh (a nephew of the famous Sir Walter), was captured by parliamentary troops following the fall of Bridgwater in 1645. After periods of imprisonment he was brought back to Wells and confined in the deanery, but in 1646 he was stabbed (probably by his keeper) and died shortly thereafter.

Some cases involving prebendaries are interesting. There was perhaps more justification for action against Nicholas Andrews, a prebendary of Salisbury, than in many other instances, for he was accused of tippling in taverns, neglecting to preach and refusing to remove idolatrous images.

Still, his treatment was severe. According to Walker, he was 'hurried from Jayl to Jayl, some time Imprisoned on Shipboard and Died under this barbarous Treatment'. Henry Ancketyll, a prebendary of Wells, was the royalist governor of Corfe Castle in Dorset, so once again there was ample reason for his sequestration, but he too died under suspicious circumstances; Walker was not sure whether he succumbed to wounds in Taunton Castle or to poison while incarcerated in London. John Arnway, a prebendary of Lichfield, was taken prisoner at the surrender of Shrewsbury. He fled to Oxford, then to the Hague, and finally (most unusually) to Virginia, where he died in 1653.

More is known about Robert Creyghtone, whose fate was somewhat happier. A residentiary at Wells and prebendary of Lincoln, Creyghtone spent the earlier years of the war at Oxford as a royal chaplain. When that city fell to Parliament he escaped to Cornwall, disguised as a labourer. From Cornwall he made his way to the Continent. Since he was distantly related to the royal family (his mother was from Scotland, descended from the Stewarts) it was natural for him to join the court of the exiled Stuarts, where John Evelyn heard him preach in 1649. During the 1650s he found a livelihood in the Hague as tutor to the son of Sir Ralph Verney. His wife remained in Wells throughout these unsettled times. Creyghton was named dean of Wells in 1660 and served as bishop of Bath and Wells for two years before dying in 1672, at the age of seventy-nine.

We have no way of knowing how the cathedrals would have fared had the new system of government lasted longer. Perhaps accommodations of the sort experienced at York, Exeter and Oxford might have become acceptable in other places. As it was, political events continued to determine religious practices. In 1653 government without an executive head proved unworkable and England was transformed from a Commonwealth into a Protectorate. A satisfactory constitution had still not been found when the Lord Protector, Oliver Cromwell, died on 3 September 1658, the anniversary of his great military victories at Dunbar and Worcester. Although his son succeed him, Richard Cromwell was manifestly unable to govern or even to get along with the army, which had become the most powerful force in the country. Ironically it was an army leader, General George Monck, who neutralized that force and made possible the restoration of the monarchy by the Convention Parliament. Charles II returned to his native land on 25 May 1660, and was welcomed to London with a triumphant celebration, 'the wayes straw'd with flowers, the bells ringing, the streetes hung with Tapissry, fountaines running with wine'.

The diarist John Evelyn 'stood in the Strand, & beheld it, & blessed God'.

He was convinced that 'it was the Lords doing, *et mirabile in oculis nostris* [and marvelous in our eyes]: for such a Restauration was never seene in the mention of any history, antient or modern, since the returne of the *Babylonian* Captivity, nor so joyful a day, & so bright, ever seene in this nation: this happening when to expect or effect it, was past all humane policy'. Many of the cathedral clergy, especially those who had spent years in exile, must have shared his belief in divine intervention.

14

The Restoration

The Restoration of the monarchy was greeted with rejoicing at the cathedrals. At Winchester, for example, Charles II was proclaimed by the mayor in a ceremony at the High Cross and there was a service in the cathedral. Evidently none of the former cathedral clergy were available, so Henry Complin, the rector of Avington, Hampshire, and a fellow of New College, Oxford, was chosen to preach a 'loyal and eloquent sermon'. Such members of the choir as could be gathered sang the anthem 'Lord, Make thy Servant Charles Our Gracious King to Rejoice in thy Strength'; they were directed by William Burt, an octogenarian lay clerk. There was a festive service on Coronation Day at Gloucester, with preaching and singing, a bonfire which cost £3 and a peal on the bells (6s. 9d.). At Wells there was ringing, and £5 was distributed to the poor at the almshouse. Virtually the only recorded expression of discontent occurred at Oxford, where some Presbyterians took the surplices that had come back into use at Christ Church Cathedral, put them in the privy for Peckwater Quad, and 'with long sticks thrust them downe into the excrements'. In general, however, 'the happy return of the church', as the chapter clerk at Salisbury called it, was an occasion for general celebration.[1]

The cathedrals were not significantly involved in debates about the character of the Restoration church – in the abortive movement for a broader establishment and the final passage of the Clarendon Code. Instead, the cathedral clergy were concerned with the restoration of their buildings and services. The discussion recorded at Durham Cathedral in November 1660 reflects the common position.

> The Deane and Chapter aforesaid takeing into their serious Consideration the great mercy and gracious providence of Almighty God in Restoring his Majestie to his Throne, The kingdome to peace, And the Church to the Exercise of Religion, & Enjoyment of her Rights & Lybertyes, did unanimously resolve as a fruit of their Thankfullnesse to God to Resettle this Cathedrall upon the Antient Bottome of her Statutes & laudable customes by all prudentiall meanes, and with all possible Expedition, And in order hereunto, did decree and Enact as followeth.

Their first goal was to preserve the fabric of the church, which was

'Exceeding Ruinous, the leads much decayed, the Windowes almost Totally broken, and no seates in the Quire, but such as have been made since his Majesties happy Restauracion'.

A survey of the decay at Durham was compiled by workmen and presented to the chapter in April 1661. The accounting begins with the spires, an interesting reminder that the western towers, which today have square tops, were still capped with lead spires in the seventeenth century. It was said that their rebuilding would require a thousand tons of timber at a cost of £1800. Lead work for the roof was estimated at £1600, stone work for the church at £1000. The reconstruction of the minor canons' lodgings and hall would cost £1270, the school house only £110. In addition the deanery required £520 in repairs. Work on the twelve canons' houses, at charges ranging from £50 to £450, would account for £2480. The system of piping bringing water to the cathedral and close needed £400 in lead work. The expense of restoration at Bearpark, the former monastic cell now used for retreats, was estimated at £2000. The total cost of repairing all the 'dilapidations of the Church and College' at Durham was set at £14,120.

Work was obviously incomplete when John Cosin held a visitation of the cathedral in 1662. The new bishop asked generally whether 'order [had been] taken for renewing and repairing the fabric of the Church, where it hath bin in the late violent, impious and rebellious tymes, either destroyed [or] decayed'. More specifically he inquired: 'Is the Communion table or altar recovered out of their hands that tooke it lately away and is it now ready to be sett up where it was before? What has become of the lead and wood of the two great Broaches [spires] that stood upon the square towers at ye west end?' Somewhat vindictively, he suggested that the dean and chapter should search out those who had destroyed the fabric and ornaments and demand restitution, or at least 'have their Sacrilegious violence recorded for all posterity'.

One of the finest pieces of Restoration wood carving is the new font at Durham, provided by Bishop Cosin. On close examination it proves to be a curiously successful combination of styles: the lower portion is Classical or Baroque, with Corinthian capitals, but higher up the work turns Gothic, with ogee arches and pinnacles. The choir stalls, made by an unknown local carver, are less elaborate but include elegant benchends topped by fleurs-de-lys. Some medieval misericords survived, but new ones had to be added.

As we have seen, the damage at Lichfield was worse that at Durham. When services were resumed, on 16 June 1660, they had to be held in the chapter house, since that and the vestry were the only parts of the church that had roofs. John Hacket, the Restoration bishop of Lichfield and

Coventry, deserves the chief credit for reviving the cathedral. His early biographer wrote, 'Bishop Hacket at his first coming to Lichfield found his Cathedral most desolate, & ruined almost to ye ground, the Roof of Stone, ye Timber, Lead & Iron, Glass, Stalls, Organs, Utensils of rich value, all were embezzled, 2000 shot of great Ordinance & 1500 Granadoes discharged against it, which had quite battered down ye Spire, & most of ye Fabric'. The next morning after his arrival Hacket set his own coach horses to work carrying away rubble. The initial phase of restoration took eight years – there was a service celebrating its completion on Christmas Eve 1669 – and cost £9092 1s. 7½d., of which Hacket contributed £1683 12s. himself and the residentiary canons at least £1035. Hacket died in 1671, shortly after hearing the first of the new bells rung: his own passing bell, he called it. A modern stained glass window in the choir depicts the bishop overseeing the work of the builders. A statue of Charles II, who contributed one hundred trees to the construction, was erected above the new west window; this is still in the cathedral, but a figure of Christ has taken its place on the façade.

At Exeter the cathedral chapter gathered on 18 September 1660 and demanded possession of the church. They ordered that the chapter house be 'glased' immediately and that the wall which had been erected to separate the nave from the choir be pulled down. The demolition cost £82 7s., and a further £8 8s. 10d. had to be paid for carting away the rubbish. A sermon referred to 'the monstrous Babylonish wall' as a symbol of 'the church-rending schisms and confusions of those times'. The canons did not wish to have the new door into the north-east corner of the building closed up, as it provided convenient access to their houses, so it remained until Gilbert Scott's restoration of the cathedral in the 1870s. Some items which had been taken away for safekeeping were recovered; these included four organ pipes, the king's arms as painted on the organ case, gilt flagons and chalices, a crimson carpet and hangings. Cushions, gowns and surplices were ordered, new seats were fitted in the nave and chapter house, the interior of the cathedral was whitewashed, and (as at Durham) a survey of the defects of the church was put in hand. This does not survive, but we do have a later paper which lists 'What hath been donne by the Dean and Chapter of Exeter since the Restoration'. It begins with the statement that 'they have repaired the Church and brought it into a comely forme, which hath and will cost at least £5000'. They had agreed to devote a tenth of the income from the fines charged for sealing leases to such repairs. They had also augmented the stipends of the lecturers, schoolmasters and prebendaries and had converted the cloisters ('which were made a market place' during the Interregnum) into a hospital for persons who 'formerly lived in good estate and now are fallen into distresse chiefly for their loyaltie to his Majesty'. In 1661 Charles

II wrote to the dean and chapter commending them for their good work. Further adornments were added in the later years of the century. These included a brass eagle lectern given by a local physician and a new font presented by Dean Annesley in 1684: its Sicilian marble bowl is ornamented with angels' heads, while the oak cover has eight inlaid figures of apostles.

At Lincoln the chapter considered a general appeal for financial assistance. 'Most of the cathedrals', they noted, had 'escaped totall destruction, yet many of them [were] miserably rent, torn, and defaced. And particularly the Cathedral Church of the Blessed Virgin Mary of Lincoln, and not only that, but the dwelling houses & habitations of the churchmen, the Vicars, the Singingmen, and other officers belonging to that Cathedral [were] pulled down, and the materials sold, and converted to profane uses'. An account prepared for Dean Honywood in 1664 records the expenditure of £3054 1s. 5d. in repairs to the fabric, as well as £1100 spent for ornaments, £600 for rebuilding the canons' houses, and £453 for refurbishing the dwellings of the vicars choral. These charges had actually been met out of ordinary revenue rather than through an attempt to enlist support from the lay community; in 1661 the dean and chapter authorized a special allocation of £1000 for the fabric, and they occasionally made loans to the fabric fund. Individual members of the chapter also made gifts to the vicars choral, who handled their own funds separately.

When the dean and chapter of Worcester held their first meeting following the Restoration, they lamented that 'the service of god of late years hath bin neglected in the said Church'. They ordered that services begin immediately in the nave, 'and in the Quire alsoe soe soone as itt can be repaired and fitted for that purpose'. Five hundred pounds was borrowed for urgent repairs, 'in regard that the said Church is very ruinous and some partes thereof in verie great danger of falling yf not timely prevented'. Mattins was first said on 31 August 1660. On 2 September 'there was a very great assembly at morning prayer by six in the morn, and at 9 of the Clock there appeared again at prayers all the gentry, many citizens, and others numerous, and after prayers Dr Doddeswell, a new prebend, did preach the first sermon'. Choral worship in the choir was resumed the following April. It was at first thought that '£10,000 will put the whole fabric in that order it was before the barbarous civil wars', but a later detailed statement of damage prepared by Barnabas Oley, the cathedral treasurer, ran to £16,354. This included repairs to the cloister, the dormitory and individual houses, as well as to the church itself; the largest single items were lead for the roof and timber for the great spire. Six masons came from Gloucester to assist those available locally. When a workman named Robert Prior hurt his shoulder 'in Raising the Chapter House Roof', a 'Chirurgeon' had to be summoned

The entry of Charles II into London, 1660.

to care for him. Large subscriptions were given by the second duke of Buckingham (George Villiers) and the duchess of York (Clarendon's daughter) as well as the bishop, George Morley. Actual expenditures amounted to £1507 13s. 2d. in 1661 and £1303 14s. 5d. in 1662. Among the items which had to be provided was a new font, completed in 1668.

The dean and chapter of Wells spent £1084 on repairs in 1661 and a further £300 in 1662. Timber, glass and tiles are the principal items in the sketchy accounts left by the master of the fabric. In addition, the chapter purchased six vases for the communion table, fourteen new Prayer Books and a 'whirlygig' for the clock. Dean Creyghtone gave the large brass lectern which now stands at the entrance to the Lady chapel. When the restoration was finished, the residentiary canons, who had paid £3080 5s. 10d. in all, complained that the non-resident prebendaries, who received substantial incomes from the cathedral, had not contributed a farthing; they were ordered to 'beautify' their stalls at their own charge. The bishop paid £5000 for the rebuilding of his palace, and he joined with the dean in giving the cathedral ornaments valued at £820. A tablet still visible in the north transept at Chichester records contributions toward the restoration there: £1010 was given by clerics, including the bishops of Winchester, Oxford and Peterborough as well as Chichester, and £770 by laymen, led by the earl of Northumberland. The fabric accounts document substantial expenditures over a period of several years, mostly for lead, stonemasonry and plumbing. A joiner was paid £10 7s. for the rails and boards around the communion table.

The cathedral at Winchester had not been severely damaged in the war, so most of the work there involved either adornments or normal maintenance. Shortly after the Restoration the bishop, Brian Duppa, paid £100 to retrieve Le Sueur's statues of James I and Charles I, which had been buried in a garden on the Isle of Wight. Some plate was also returned. When Archbishop Juxon visited Winchester in 1663 he was able to record that 'the Cathedral Church is well repayred'. More than £1100 had been spent by the end of 1667, but the chapter found that additional work was needed. After this was completed, revenues were to be allocated for rebuilding the deanery and the houses of the canons, in due succession; if any of them insisted on reconstructing their houses earlier, they would have to bear the charges themselves.

The principal expense at Canterbury was the reinstallation of stained glass: although Becket's 'glassy bones' were gone forever, a great deal of the medieval glass had been removed from the windows and stored safely throughout the Interregnum. Surviving memoranda list the glass in Richard Hornsby's workhouse, glass delivered to his father, 'old Hornsby', and glass in the hands of another craftsman, John Railton. In all there were at least eleven chests of glass, each containing about 230 feet, and several hundred pounds of lead. Everything was reinstalled by September 1662, apparently at the very reasonable cost of £60. Fine new doors, carved with the cathedral arms, were installed at Christ Church gate, and a curious painting showing Charles I exchanging an earthly crown for a heavenly one was placed in the north choir aisle.

At Gloucester, too, restoration of the glass proved the main expense. The craftsmen (William Lane, a glazier from Evesham, and John Painter, a former chorister) estimated the charges at £362, the most expensive item being the large window in the Lady chapel. A great deal of new glass had to be made for the famous Crécy window, and nearly nine thousand bricks were purchased for repaving the nave. Candlesticks, flagons, maces, cushions, altar cloths and a new font were also required. In July 1662 William Schellinks, a Dutch traveller, noted that the war had left the cathedral in bad condition but that it was 'now being assiduously repaired and rebuilt'.

The damage to organs during the Civil War meant that almost every cathedral needed a new or rebuilt instrument. Some of the builders rank among the finest in English history. Renatus Harris built large new organs for Chichester (1678), Bristol (1685), and Hereford (1686). His great rival was Bernard Smith, often known as 'Father' Smith because of his eminence (not because he was in holy orders or a Roman Catholic). Smith rebuilt the organ at Rochester and provided new instruments at York, Oxford, and St Paul's. John Loosemore installed a fine organ with an unusually beautiful case at Exeter in 1665.

At Hereford the dean and chapter made special contributions for the fabric, and Lord Scudamore (earlier a friend of Buckingham and admirer of Laud) gave £100. The worst problem seems to have been the spire: funds were borrowed from St Katherine's hospital in Ledbury to pay for the work, but it was not undertaken until 1673. During the 1660s chapter meetings were held in the library because the chapter house had fallen into decay after its lead roof was melted down for ammunition. The chapter house at Carlisle, too, had been 'utterly ruinated in the late time of troubles', so the chapter met in the upper room of the new fratry. Records of the bishop's visitation in 1666 state that the cathedral had been brought into good repair, with the walls firm, the windows glazed, and the lead roof sound. The floor still needed to be repaired and made even, and the remaining portion of the nave had to be fitted out for use by St Mary's parish. We do not know what the repairs cost, but they must have been partly responsible for the financial troubles of the dean and chapter, who had to borrow £400 in 1670 to meet their necessary expenses.

In 1664 the dean of St Paul's, John Barwick, wrote to the lord mayor of

London describing his problems in returning that cathedral to good condition. The chapter would gladly have paid for 'adorning and beautifying' the seats of the civic dignitaries, but the mayor and aldermen had ordered it 'done in [their] owne way (different from all former practice) and by [their] owne Workmen'. The dean sought to repay the City, lest the incident establish a precedent that outsiders could have work done in the church.

The greatest catastrophe to befall any of the cathedrals was the Great Fire of London, which left St Paul's a smoking ruin. The flames which spread from a baker's oven on Sunday, 2 September 1666, reached the cathedral on Tuesday morning. The king had commanded the lord mayor to pull down houses in order to stop the fire, but (as the diarist Samuel Pepys reported) people would not obey him; 'the fire overtakes us faster than we can do it.' Pepys spent the evening watching the conflagration from an alehouse on the south side of the Thames and saw 'one entire arch of fire from this to the other side of the bridge and in a bow up the hill above a mile long.' The next morning he sent his most important possessions from the Navy Office, where he lived as secretary, to the country; he buried the naval records and his wine in the garden.[2] St Paul's was engulfed by fire for two days; molten lead ran down the streets, splinters of stone shot off in all directions, and finally the roofs of the choir, nave and transepts collapsed with a thunderous roar. On 7 September Pepys wrote that he had gone to see the 'miserable sight of Paul's church, with all the roofs fallen and the body of the quire fallen into St Fayth's', an adjacent church. The problem of rebuilding will concern us later.

In other places the cost of repairing cathedral buildings was not substantial or, if it was, we have no record of it: in several cases there is no proper documentation for the first few years after 1660. A small notebook describing the repairs at Norwich survives; it names workmen and lists the quantities of nails and boards used but has no cost figures. In 1662 an unusually large fine, £500 paid by Sir Jacob Astley for a new lease, was designated for the fabric rather than being divided among members of the chapter, as usual, and gifts were received from a number of lay people, including the widow Thomasine Brooke, Lady Pettus, Sir Thomas Browne (the famous physician and author) and alderman Robert Bendish. Such donations totalled nearly £300. At Salisbury nothing seems to have been done until 1668, but in that year members of the chapter agreed to pay a fifth of their income for repairs to the cathedral. When this proved insufficient, the dean wrote all the non-resident prebendaries seeking further contributions 'of your owne good minde' to remedy the 'great decayes and ruynes of this church, and ye absolute necessitie of speedy repaires, to which we are quickned by his

Majesties peronsall observation, & speciall commandes'. Christopher Wren had been summoned to survey the cathedral and prescribe a suitable strategy for its preservation. The prebendaries of Ely loaned £860 for repairs there, and £400 was borrowed on at least two occasions. The east and of the cathedral was restored first, but the 'steeple' (presumably the great octagon) required the most expensive attention; £1066 was spent on it in 1669.

It was said that £1000 had been spent at York between 1660 and 1662, and that a further £1000 was needed, but in fact the minster survived the war in good condition and did not require any major reconstruction. Relatively small sums were spent repairing the south-west tower, which was damaged in a storm rather than a siege, and on 'Ballasters and postes for the Rayles of the Communion Table'. The lead roofs were still a matter of concern in 1685, when the cost of repairing them was estimated at £3500. There was major work on the roof of the north transept in 1695; new gates were installed at about the same time. The chapter at Rochester worried about the condition of the central tower but seems to have done little: we cannot be sure, because the chapter books do not begin until 1678. Apparently nothing but routine maintenance was done at Chester until 1677, when the chapter borrowed £100 to repair the 'ruinous' roof. There were no unusual major expenses at Peterborough.

Two new windows were installed at Bristol in the 1600s, but the cathedral had suffered little in the war and there is no indication that they were needed as replacements. Instead the dean and donor, Henry Glemham, simply wished to beautify the building. Each window contained six large biblical scenes as well as heraldry relating to the Glemham family. One of the windows is still in its original position, at the east end of the north choir aisle; its twin was shattered in the bombing of 24 November 1940 and only fragments remain.

The reconstruction of cathedral staffs was as difficult as the renovation of cathedral buildings. A number of the clergy had died during the Interregnum, as had some cathedral musicians. Many of the singing men who survived had been forced to find other occupations and might not choose to return to their choirs. All of the choristers who sang in the 1640s would have had their voices change by 1660, so they could no longer serve in their old posts. Indeed the years of the Interregnum form the only decisive break in the entire history of English cathedral choirs. In 1660 there was not a prospective chorister in all of England who could remember the old sung services – a serious matter, considering that boys need the apprenticeship of attending rehearsals and hearing sung services before they are ready to take a full part themselves.

Chapter act books for the second half of 1660 record the installation of large numbers of new canons and other officers. The earliest entry comes from St Paul's, where an archdeacon and two prebendaries were admitted on 6 July. Fifteen more prebendaries and the new precentor were appointed in August, and a further four prebendaries in September. Matthew Nicholas was named dean; before the war he had been a canon of Salisbury and dean of Bristol. Singing men (minor canons and vicars choral) were not admitted until the summer of 1661, when sung services were probably resumed; no record of the choristers survives. It is said that Dean Cosin had returned from exile by the end of July and 'settled the Church and Quire' at Peterborough. The chapter of Canterbury Cathedral held a session in mid July. There was also a chapter meeting at Chichester in July, but only one prebendary was present. Here Bruno Ryves, the author of *Mercurius Rusticus*, had been named dean by Charles I but was never installed. Although he was officially recognized in 1660, he did not serve at Chichester, for Charles II made him dean of Windsor. Joseph Henshaw followed Ryves. When Henshaw was elected bishop of Peterborough in 1663 Joseph Gulston succeeded him. Once again the choir was not reestablished until 1661. Three vacant positions for lay clerks were filled in September 1661, and the full complement of eight choristers was appointed at the same time.

Chapter meetings at York, Norwich, Hereford and Exeter began in August 1660. York, like Chichester, recognized a dean nominated by Charles I fifteen years earlier. A contemporary letter commented that 'Dean [Richard] Marsh has carried things in order to a settlement of the church very high, the singingmen and organs are preparing'. The houses in the Bedern normally occupied by the vicars choral had been rented out during the Interregnum, but the vicars endeavoured (allegedly 'at great cost') to recover them for their own use. Several prebendaries nominated by Charles II were installed at Norwich before the end of August. The master of the choristers and the organ blower were appointed in March 1661, probably a sign that music returned then. Some of the new prebendaries at Hereford were also royal nominees. Here the first vicars choral were designated in September, the first choristers the following January. The dean and chapter gave the choristers a reward of 2s. 6d. 'when they began to sing alone in ye chore, for their Incouragement'.

Choral services at Winchester must have been among the earliest to be resumed, since a personnel list, dated 10 September 1660, records a full complement of ten lay clerks (including the organist, Christopher Gibbons) and six choristers. Eight members of the chapter were present at a meeting held that day, although the former dean, chapter clerk and seven prebendaries had died during the war or Interregnum. The chapter at

Worcester ordered, also in September 1660, that 'the Quire-men as soon as conveniently may be shall be provided with houses for their habitacions within the Precinctes or Sanctuary of this Church'. By October 1661 all positions had been filled except for two vacant petty canonries. The unusually large staff included ten prebendaries, eight petty canons and ten lay clerks (thus a total of eighteen singing men), and ten choristers, in addition to schoolmasters and almsmen.

Eight of the twelve canons of Durham had been named by 5 November 1660, and eight of the full complement of ten lay clerks were sworn in on 8 December. No choristers are listed in the financial records for 1660–61, but ten are named the following year. Both vicars choral and choristers were elected at Lincoln in November 1660. At Lincoln, Lichfield and Salisbury – all cathedrals with large numbers of prebendaries – the chapter was built up speedily in the autumn of 1660, partly with royal nominees. Some problems persisted: in 1665 Chester had only five choristers (the full number of eight was not reached until 1678), and there were still fewer petty canons than there should have been; in 1666 there were vacancies at Carlisle, because 'we want fit men'. But most of the cathedrals were fully staffed by 1662, and services had returned to something approximating the prewar standards.

As a result of the Civil War and Interregnum the cathedrals were more closely aligned with the monarchy than they had been earlier in the century. Royal patronage, always important in the cathedrals, was now exercised to the full. Charles II was particularly active in nominating canons, prebendaries and deans in the years immediately following the Restoration. Lists preserved among the papers of Sir Edward Nicholas, Charles's secretary of state, show that the exiled court had kept track of vacant positions and persons deemed suitable to fill them. Following the return of the monarchy, Charles II received a spate of petitions from men seeking preferment. More than one hundred such requests were dated between May and September 1660; others flowed in later, and in the end the king made about two hundred presentations to positions in cathedral chapters. Many of those who benefited from royal patronage had been deprived of positions in the church during the Interregnum, but a number had conformed and may have held Presbyterian sympathies. The king seems to have responded to petitions in haste, without being sure that loyal supporters were cared for and perhaps without having full information about the background of the petitioners.

Under the circumstances it is not surprising that Charles and his advisers occasionally became confused and named several men for the same position. At Wells, for instance, Charles nominated John Selleck for the canonry made vacant by the death of James Dugdale early in 1661, then (only two days later) recommended the appointment of Grindal Sheafe. After the problem became apparent, Secretary Nicholas wrote to Dean Creyghtone to apologize and to reiterate royal support for the original nominee. The king subsequently put forward Sheafe's name for the next vacancy, whenever it might occur. In 1679 Charles again named two men to the same canonry at Wells. In September 1660 he wrote to the dean and chapter of Exeter admitting that his nominations exceeded the number of places available. The chapter was permitted to choose among those commended by the king but was told to appoint no others.

Royal intervention in affairs at Durham was particularly notable. Here, as usual, Charles II nominated residentiaries who had been 'loyal and faithful to the royal interest in the time of the late usurpation', almsmen, including one who had lost a hand during service at sea, and even a lighthouse keeper for Farne Island. In addition, Charles used his influence to see that a number of non-resident canons received full financial allowances. As early as November 1660 he asked that Thomas Triplett, a prebendary, not be required to reside owing to his infirmity and inability to undertake the long journey north. In 1661 he sought a dispensation for the former prebendary Isaac Basire, who had been forced into exile in Hungary and could not take up residence immediately. (According to the act book, Basire voluntarily gave up this privilege for the peace of the church, but in 1667 the king was still seeking an exemption for him on the grounds that he was involved in an Exchequer suit and needed to remain in London.) William Sancroft was occupied with the revision of the Prayer Book, then with royal business, and after 1670 with his position as dean of St Paul's. Daniel Brevint had been sent on a mission to France. John Durrell was needed at Windsor, where he was dean of St George's chapel. Although it was customary for prebendaries to resign upon being promoted to bishoprics, Charles insisted on continued payments to Thomas Wood following his appointment as bishop of Lichfield and Guy Carleton after he became bishop of Bristol.

Three cases of royal intervention at Durham are of special interest. One involved the king's attempt to name Robert Collingwood as the chapter registrar. Evidently Charles accepted the argument that such an appointment belonged to the dean and chapter themselves, since he rescinded his nomination and allowed the chapter to designate the person they believed best qualified. Charles also tried to appoint the chancellor of the diocese, only to be told that the chancellor was an officer of the bishop; since the bishopric was vacant, the dean and chapter were guardians of the spiritualities, and they had already made an interim appointment. Finally there was the case of Denis Grenville (sometimes spelled Greville or Granville), son of the royalist general Sir Bevil Grenville who had been killed in action in 1643.

Through royal patronage the younger Grenville became an archdeacon of Durham in 1662, but 'extraordinary concerns' – possibly his role as a royal chaplain – kept him in London. In 1674, while he was in residence at Durham, he was arrested in the cloisters and gaoled for a 'small pretended debt'. Since this was a breach of the privileges of both church and monarchy, he was soon released. Grenville then went overseas 'to improve his health', the king again dispensing him from the residency requirements. In 1684 Grenville was named dean.

The issue of residency aroused different concerns at Norwich, where the king agreed to alter the statutes in 1674 at the request of the dean and chapter. Previously canons had been required to be in residence four months out of the year but during that time actually needed to be present at the cathedral only once a day, four days a week. The new arrangement cut the term of residence in half, to two months, but insisted on regular attendance during that period. The bishop of Norwich and Lord Keeper Finch, who often advised the king about religious issues, supported this relaxation, which (it was said) would allow canons who also held parish positions to devote more time to the cure of souls there.

At Hereford the king asked the dean and chapter to elect Thomas Wootton their lecturer in divinity, for his lectures gave 'great satisfaction [to] the Auditors', thereby overlooking the usual requirement that lecturers be chosen from among the prebendaries. Because of his loyalty and sufferings in the 'late unhappy differences', the royal chaplain Raphael Throckmorton was to be admitted as a residentiary at Lincoln, where he was archdeacon. Here Secretary Nicholas sought a favourable lease for Sir Edward Rossiter, while a whole group of prominent politicians (Clarendon, Albemarle, Manchester and Portland, as well as Nicholas) supported special treatment for Sir Robert Knight, who had allegedly been influential in bringing about the restoration of the monarchy. In 1666 there was such competition for almsmen's places that Charles had to order his secretaries not to prepare nominations except for persons who have been maimed by naval service in the Dutch wars.

Sometimes the cathedral chapters favoured royalists on their own volition, without outside pressure. The dean and chapter of Worcester, for instance, made small gifts to Mr Underhill and Captain Digby, both described in 1676 as 'distressed Royalists', while the little houses in the cloister at Exeter were assigned to poor men who 'have been ruined by the late unhappy wars for their loyalty to ye king'. At Durham the dean and chapter acted in 1661 to void a lease to one Henry Rawlings, who had supported the 'horrid murder' of Charles I.

Royal intervention continued under James II. In 1688 he ordered the dean and chapter of Peterborough to give a bedesman's place to Hammond Thornton, 'who was an officer in the Army of our Royal Father of Blessed Memory from the first setting up of his standard at Nottingham to the end of the war, and is now very aged and reduced to great want'.

Political involvement became increasingly important after 1680, when the desire to ensure that no Roman Catholic became king led to the creation of the 'country' or Whig party. Charles II and his court of Tory followers opposed the exclusion of Catholics, believing that it was improper to inter- fere with the divine right of hereditary succession even if the heir adhered to Rome. The issue became acute as it was apparent that Charles would have no legitimate offspring; he would be followed by his Catholic brother, James, duke of York, or Charles's illegitimate Protestant son, James, duke of Mon- mouth. In August 1682 Monmouth visited Chester Cathedral during one of his progresses through sympathetic parts of the country. He was well treated by the mayor and aldermen, but one of the canons (Lawrence Fogg, later to be dean) preached against disobedience, angering the duke. A mob of Monmouth's supporters later made bonfires outside the cathedral, broke into the building, damaged stained glass, the organ and the font, and tore up surplices, hoods and other vestments.

Monmouth came to Chichester in February 1683. Amongst the accounts of his visit we have a letter from Guy Carleton, bishop of Chichester, to Archbishop Sancroft. According to Carleton, many of the townspeople and cathedral clergy welcomed Monmouth 'with bells and bonfires', even though the king and council ordered that he not be given a public recep- tion. The precentor, Dr Edes, acted as the duke's chaplain and brought him to a Sunday service in the cathedral, where he was given the dean's stall. The psalm selected for the occasion predicted that 'He shall be like a tree that grows, Fast by the River side'. Those who opposed Monmouth had their turn the following Sunday, when the duke was present again. The bishop's chaplain preached on a text from I Samuel, likening rebellion to witchcraft and concluding, 'Because thou hast rejected the word of the Lord, he hath also rejected thee from being king'. The incensed duke and some of his followers walked out during the sermon, and others jeered the preacher at the end of the service. The bishop himself disapproved of Monmouth, but the mob called him 'an old Popish rogue' and showered his house with stones.

By 1685 support for Monmouth had dwindled and James succeeded with- out incident. Unwisely, Monmouth picked that summer to mount a rebellion, landing at Lyme Regis on 11 June. On 1 July the rebels reached Wells and turned their attention to the cathedral, where the dean and chapter had already pledged their loyalty to James II. One of Monmouth's commanders, Lord Grey, tried to prevent any theft or sacrilege at the cathedral, but without success. The only member of the chapter in residence was the eighty-nine-year-old chancellor, Thomas Holt, who wrote a long Latin description of the day's events in the chapter act book. 'This cathedral church', he lamented, 'has much, alas! over much experienced the barbarity of the rebel fanatics, who early this very morning profaned the whole furniture thereof, almost ruined the organ, and transformed the sacred edifice into stalls for their horses'. A few days later the rebellion was crushed at the battle of Sedgemoor, and Holt was able to add, 'it is now possible to return in safety to the care of the church, which stands firm against treason, arms, and hatred, and against the gates of hell. *Deus, Deus nobis haec otia fecit*'.

This entry probably exaggerates the damage, but subsequent notes in the act book confirm that there were loses. A new verger's wand had to be purchased, 'the old [silver] Verge having been stollen out of the Church by the late Rebells on the 1ˢᵗ day of July last'. The sacrist was given £10 in appreciation of his 'very honest service to the Church, in the preservation of the Ornaments & Plate belonging to it, when the late Rebells were in this place'. The precentor's wife (and dean's daughter-in-law), Frideswide Creyghtone, paid £20 to Monmouth's army to dissuade them from plundering the canons' houses; had she not done so, 'not only this Cathedral Church but the Canons houses also would have suffered the violence of those Rebells'. The *London Gazette* reported that the rebels were drunk, even 'drinking their villanous healths at the altar', and it is likely that some of the damage to the lowest tier of statues on the cathedral's great façade occurred during Monmouth's Rebellion rather than in the Civil War, since an engraving in Dugdale's *Monasticon Anglicanum* shows them still in place in 1655.

Other cathedrals were involved less directly. The dean and chapter of Exeter – near enough to fear the rebels – borrowed £1000 and sent it to the king to help him repel 'the invasion now made by the Rebells'. The bells at Salisbury were rung in rejoicing on several occasions: 'on the taking of [Monmouth's ally] Argyle in Scotland', 'on the Rowting of Monmouth in the West', and 'on the taking of Monmouth at Ringwood'. Similarly, the bells of Worcester Cathedral rang out 'at ye news of ye victory over ye Westerne Rebells' and 'at Munmouthes being taken'.

Despite his Catholicism, James II was generally accepted by the cathedral clergy during the earlier years of his reign. The common attitude was reflected in a letter which the bishop and clergy of Wells sent the king in March 1685. Noting the 'Auspicious Promise Your Majesty has made us of Protecting Our Established Religion, the Greatest Concern Wee have in ye

World' and the 'Dying Benediction, His late Majesty gave to His Kingdom', they promised 'to inculcate Allegiance, both in Our Discourses, & by Our Examples'. James visited Worcester in 1686; he conducted the ancient ceremony of touching for the King's Evil in the cathedral but worshipped in a Catholic chapel. When he was at Chichester in 1687 he stayed with Bishop Cartwright but did not attend a service in the cathedral, again having a private mass instead.

Opinion began to turn against the king as a result of his disregard of the Test Act and other pieces of anti-Catholic legislation passed by Parliament. Churchmen who quarrelled with him included John Sharp, the dean of Norwich, and Henry Compton, the bishop of London. In 1686 James ordered that Bishop Compton should be suspended from office. Notice of this action was duly written into the act book of St Paul's, with the further note that the bishopric was not considered to be vacant. If Compton were actually removed, the dean and chapter proposed to send the archbishop the names of two or three canons, from whom the archbishop should choose an official to exercise jurisdiction in London during the vacancy: this was said to be in accord with an agreement made by Archbishop Boniface in the thirteenth century.

The king's popularity declined further in 1688. His imprisonment of seven bishops (including Compton and Archbishop Sancroft) because they opposed his Declaration of Indulgence aroused uncommon sympathy for the prelates, and the birth of a son to Mary of Modena, James's second wife and like him a Roman Catholic, suggested that unless James was forced off the throne England might be ruled by an unending succession of papists. Both Mary and Anne, the king's daughters by his first wife, Anne Hyde, had been raised as Anglicans; Mary had wed William of Orange, the ruler of the Netherlands, and Anne had taken a Danish Protestant husband, so if either succeeded the Anglican monarchy would be restored. On 30 June, the very day on which the populace celebrated the acquittal of the seven bishops, another group of seven eminent political leaders wrote William inviting him to come to England, take the throne, and maintain the Protestant succession.

Initially these events did not involve the cathedrals and their clergy directly. But high politics did lie behind a feud at Durham, where Dean Grenville was at odds with the minor canons in March 1688 (after the arrest of the seven bishops but before the birth of James's son). In a long letter to the precentor Grenville complained of the 'undecent and indiscreet forwardness' of a petty canon and advised his brethren to 'beware how you do that which will be much more scandalous, I mean to oppose both King, Bishop, & Dean'. At St Paul's note was taken of the relaxation of Compton's suspension, a step in James's unsuccessful attempt to regain support. Otherwise the chapter act books are devoid of references to the progress of the Glorious Revolution.

On 5 November, the anniversary of the Gunpowder Plot, William's army landed at Torbay. A few days later the Prince of Orange came to Exeter. Not wishing to be associated with William's cause, the bishop and dean carefully removed themselves from the scene, but ordinary people thronged to welcome the Dutch deliverer. Lord Macaulay's description of events at the cathedral can hardly be bettered.

> The members of the chapter at Exeter were the first who were called upon to declare their sentiments. [Gilbert] Burnet informed the Canons, now left without a head by the flight of the Dean, that they could not be permitted to use the prayer book for the Prince of Wales, and that a solemn service must be performed in honour of the safe arrival of the Prince. The Canons did not choose to appear in their stalls; but some of the choristers and prebendaries attended. William repaired in military state to the Cathedral. As he passed under the gorgeous screen, that renowned organ, scarcely surpassed by any of those which are the boast of his native Holland, gave out a peal of triumph. He mounted the Bishop's seat, a stately throne rich with the carving of the fifteenth century [sic]. Burnet stood below; and a crowd of warriors and nobles appeared on the right hand and on the left. The singers, robed in white, sang the *Te Deum*. When the chaunt was over, Burnet read the Prince's Declaration: but, as soon as the first words were uttered, prebendaries and singers crowded in all haste out of the choir. At the close Burnet cried in a loud voice, 'God save the Prince of Orange!' and many fervent voices answered, 'Amen.' On Sunday, the eleventh of November, Burnet preached before the Prince in the Cathedral, and dilated on the signal mercy vouchsafed by God to the English Church and nation.

After the Revolution became an accomplished fact it was generally accepted in the cathedrals, which joined in public celebrations of the coronation of William and Mary. The list of payments for making bonfires and ringing bells at York minster provides a typical guide to the changes of heart and opinion.

> 1688. June 19. A bonfire upon ye news of ye birth of a Young Prince, 14s.

> Ringing on ye day of thanksgiving for ye Queen's delivery of a Young Prince, 17s.

> 1689. To Danby's agent for delivering the pastoral staff formerly belonging to the popish Bishop Smith for the use of the cathedral, £1 1s. 8d.

> To the verger for a bonfire on Thanksgiving Day for deliverance from Popery &c by Prince of Orange, February 14, 12s. 6d.; more for bonfire when King William

and Queen Mary were proclaimed, February 17, 12s. 6d. A bonfire when they were crowned, 12s. 6d.

A great crowd attended the special service held in the minster following the proclamation of William and Mary and applauded the sermon improvised by Canon Thomas Comber.

At Durham a minor canon became 'scandalously drunke' as he greeted the Revolution. He was later charged with 'drinkinge undecent healths', including 'Confusion to ye first Obstructors of ye Reading ye King's Declaration'. There were bonfires in 'thanksgiving for our deliverance from popery' (14 February, as at York) and 'for the proclaiming of the King' (21 February).

Irreconcilable principles left the English clergy deeply divided about the Glorious Revolution. Some took the Tory view that hereditary monarchy existed by divine right and could not be interfered with by mortal men, while others believed, with the Whigs, that the Protestant cause outweighed all other considerations. Most churchmen came to support the Revolution, if only grudgingly, but when Members of both Houses of Parliament were asked to swear an oath of allegiance to William and Mary, Archbishop Sancroft and six other bishops felt compelled to refuse. The first of the Non-Jurors, they were promptly suspended from office.

All ecclesiastical persons were subsequently required by statute to take the oath before the beginning of August 1689. If they did not do so they were subject to immediate suspension and if they still did not comply they were to be deprived on 1 February 1690. A larger number of clergy who felt that they could not in good conscience abandon their belief in the hereditary monarchy thus joined the Non-Jurors. Since they had little reason to quarrel with other aspects of the theology of Anglicanism and only gradually drifted away from it liturgically, they formed what was essentially a small separate branch of the Church of England, which continued to exist alongside the legally established body for a century.

Most cathedral chapters had members who agonized over the oath, but relatively few of them became Non-Jurors. A few examples will indicate the scope of personnel change. The new archbishop of Canterbury, appointed following Sancroft's deprivation, was John Tillotson, formerly the dean of both St Paul's and Canterbury. John Sharp, who as dean of Norwich had joined Bishop Compton in opposing the policies of James II, was rewarded with the deanery at Canterbury, and later with the archbishopric of York. Following this promotion, William and Mary named George Hooper dean of Canterbury, allowing him to retain a prebend at Exeter.

Aside from Sancroft, the best known of the Non-Jurors was Thomas Ken, the bishop of Bath and Wells. When Ken was deprived, the king nominated William Beveridge to the bishopric and Samuel Freeman to the canonry at Canterbury which Beveridge would vacate, but Beveridge refused to take the see during Ken's lifetime and the monarchy eventually named Richard Kidder, formerly dean of Peterborough. Although Edwin Sandys and some of the other clergy at Wells sympathized with Ken, none of the residentiary canons there, and only three of the numerous non-resident prebendaries, followed him into spiritual exile. Despite qualms and reservations, the aged Dean Bathurst complied with the statutory requirements, but he too declined a bishopric when offered Bristol.

Thomas Comber, who had preached in favour of William at York, was given the deanery of Durham when (not surprisingly) Denis Grenville refused the oath and was removed. One of the handful of Non-Jurors who became active Jacobites, Grenville was made titular archbishop of York by the exiled James II. He died at Paris in 1703. The prickly Grenville had never been popular at Durham; few followed him or missed him.

Bishop Lake of Chichester was one of the initial Non-Jurors but died the day before he would have been deprived. His chaplain and biographer, precentor Robert Jenkin, joined him in refusing the oath and was removed from office, but later he swore and became master of St John's College, Cambridge. One other prebendary of Chichester, William Snatt, was deprived in 1690. Although Dean Francis Hawkins had been appointed by James II in 1688, he demonstrated his flexibility by swearing allegiance to William III and thus was able to continue in office until his death. George Hickes, dean of Worcester, and a minor canon, Thomas Morris, were deprived. Three of the minor canons at Norwich became Non-Jurors and were removed in 1690; the records note that one of them, John Connold, had refused to pray for William when he first landed in England. Three or four prebendaries (out of fifty-two) were deprived at Salisbury. The situation elsewhere was similar.

Cathedral buildings continued to be embellished and repaired during the later decades of the seventeenth century. A 'good and substantial altar piece' – probably an altar and reredos – was commissioned by the dean and chapter of Lichfield in 1677. The artisans chosen were Thomas Kinward, a joiner of London, and Henry Phillips, a carver who had previously done work for the royal chapel at Windsor under the supervision of Christopher Wren and was sometimes referred to as His Majesty's carver. Financial arrangements were troublesome; the craftsmen originally agreed to do the work for £120 but later insisted that no absolute bargain had been made and that the charges would have to be higher. Phillips finally lamented, 'My only profitt and advantage by ye work is, that I hope I have given you all content in the honest and well performance thereof'. Elaborate painting and gilding, including work on the royal coat of arms, was done by Robert Streeter, who had also served the king. Streeter's bill for £113 5s. had not been paid at the time of his death in 1679; his son and widow had to write Dean Smallwood several times seeking the full sum. The altar at Chester was also refurbished, but it cost much less: in 1697 a Mr Crane did some painting above the altar, the altar cloth was dyed, and the 'tabernacle work' and tapestry were cleaned. 'Turkeywork' cushions were added the following year.

Work at Lichfield continued though the 1680s. An iron cross was placed atop the central spire, the north-west steeple was repaired, and steps were taken to correct worrisome shifting of the walls. 'The North side of the Church [has] gone out 14 inches and halfe from its place, by Line, & the South, 15 inches & quarter', a report noted. The solution proposed was to drill holes through the walls above the capitals and insert iron tie rods and bolts. At the end of the century the 'waterwork' required expensive repairs as well.

On 29 March the north-west corner of the north transept of Ely cathedral fell down. Sir Christopher Wren was called in, perhaps because he was a nephew of the late Bishop Matthew Wren, and the area was rebuilt to his specifications; the work was supervised by Wren's assistant Robert Grumbold, a mason from Cambridge. Initially the dean and chapter hoped that the construction could be completed for £1000 and agreed to pay £250 a year for four years out of their own revenues. When costs rose (the final total exceeded £2500) they sent a request to the provost of King's and the heads of several other colleges at Cambridge asking for help. They had already erected a new bishop's throne, perhaps paid for by Bishop Wren, and spent £400 repaving the choir.

At Wells one of the bells fell in January 1686; the sacrist was ordered to have it hung as before, the cost being borne by the master of the fabric. Lead work and glazing were done as well, the total charge for repairs that year being listed as £500. In 1674 there were said to be 'great breaches' in the east window at Winchester. These were repaired and some plastering and whitewashing was undertaken. 'Inrichments and Ornaments' provided at Lincoln in the 1670s included wainscot behind the altar; cornices, pilasters, and pillars; new rails for the altar and the choir; a bishop's throne; rails about the eagle lectern; and 'Pyramids or Capitalls over the Stalls of the Dignitaries & Prebends'. A local builder, William Evison, contracted to provide these for £270.

Four new brick houses for the residentiary canons of Winchester were put up in the 1660s, to replace buildings 'demolished in the late rebellion'. The initial residents provided their own fittings, including wainscotting. The deanery was also restored, but work on it proceeded slowly, possibly because Dean Clark lived mainly in London and did not urgently require housing in Winchester. Three of the canons' houses at Hereford were repaired by 1679.

Libraries were rebuilt or refurbished at several places. The most notable of these is the Wren Library which forms the north side of the cloister at Lincoln. In 1674 Dean Honywood contracted with William Evison to erect the library at a cost of £780. The exterior reflects Wren's usual Baroque style, with a ground-floor loggia reminiscent of Wren's library at Trinity College, Cambridge; the elegant interior has beautifully carved bookcases and panelling, splendidly refurbished in the 1980s. A new library was created at Canterbury in 1669. At Ely a library was fitted up in the room where the dean and canons had kept their surplices and paid for by a bequest of £100 from the late Dean Robert Mapiltoft. The existing library at Worcester was given new furnishings in 1681. In 1686 it was decreed 'that the Library [at Wells] shall be repaired, with Dr Busby's benefaction, & so Thomas Wood of the University of Oxford shall do it, by contract, for £50'.

The rebuilding of St Paul's Cathedral following the Great Fire proved slow and controversial. At first it was thought that the existing building could be restored. Bishop Henchman was among those who held this view. But a careful survey made it clear that the remaining walls, which had caused problems earlier in the century, could not be made sound. The collapse of part of the roofless nave in 1668 confirmed the decision that all of the existing building, including Inigo Jones's portico, had to be demolished.

It was the dean of St Paul's, William Sancroft, and the archbishop of Canterbury, Gilbert Sheldon, who chose Christopher Wren as the architect of the new cathedral. His appointment was confirmed by a royal warrant and he began to draw plans. A First Design, presented late in 1669, was for a relatively small building with a domed space for assembly, entrances on the north and south as well as the west, and a flight of steps leading up to the choir. This did not prove popular, and an Act providing revenue from a levy on coal transported to London from northern England by sea suggested that funds for a larger structure might be available. Wren then produced his Great Design, a model of which can be seen in the crypt of the present cathedral. This was essentially a Greek cross pattern with a central dome and four façades, the western arm being somewhat longer than the others. This plan too attracted criticism: the nave was not long enough for great services or processions, and the Baroque style was too popish and reminiscent of St Peter's in Rome. Finally, in 1675, Wren submitted his final scheme, which reverted to the traditional Latin cross shape with a long nave, transepts, and a full choir for daily services. The crossing was to be capped by a small dome which would support a spire – spires were thought to be typical of English or Anglican architecture. This came to be known as the Warrant Design because the king issued a royal warrant ordering that work begin according to its specifications.

Wren saw to it that the warrant gave him the right to make such modifications as might prove necessary during the course of the construction. It seems probable that he never intended to erect the spire and that the great dome which crowns the cathedral was always his dream. Certainly the lower stages of the piers which support the dome were built with it in mind, and when they were completed erection of the dome was inevitable. There were problems, however, about its exact structure. The final resolution actually provided for the construction of three domes – a shallow saucer-shaped dome which was attractive when viewed from below, a much taller external dome which would dominate the landscape for miles around, and between them an invisible wooden structure to give support to the outer stonework. The choir was brought into use in 1697 and the building completed in 1710. One of the last problems involved the columns for the west portico. Wren had hoped to have a single giant order of columns, but the Portland stone quarries were unable to supply stones of the size required and in the end it was necessary to have smaller coupled columns. The upper stages of the towers show the influence of the Italian architect Francesco Borromini and are the most clearly Baroque elements in the cathedral.[3]

Although most of the funding for the construction of St Paul's came from the levy on sea coal, there were also a number of gifts from the other cathedral chapters. An incomplete list, based on the local sources, includes £120 from Worcester (1679), £150 from Winchester (1681), £100 from Ely (1681), £20 a year for seven years from Canterbury (1679), and £10 a year for five years from Norwich (1678). In addition, the dean and chapter of Worcester sent £60 for relief of the poor of London, and the communar of Wells was directed to give 40s. to persons who had lost their homes in the fire. While such contributions may be taken as a sign of concern, it is obvious that their monetary value was negligible.

Some entries in the minute book of the dean and chapter of St Paul's itself bring home the effect of the fire on the lives of those who served the cathedral. In November 1666 the organist, Randall Jewett, sought permission to go to Winchester, where he would act as organist 'untill it shall please God to make St Paules Cathedrall in a condition for him to discharge his duety there'. Leave was granted, and all the petty canons were allowed to be absent 'until there may be cause to summon them again to the service of the church'. The vicars choral sought allowance for the stipends which would normally be paid for services in the church and were granted some help. In May 1669 Jewett was ordered to resume residence in London and instruct the boys, but when he asked for all the rents usually due him the dean and chapter declined on the grounds that there were 'no boyes now kept'. In the end Jewett submitted to the judgment of the chapter and was given £24, half of the £48 which he was accustomed to receive out of the revenue from houses in Aldersgate, but he retained his position as organist at Winchester and died there in 1675. In 1678 it was said that three of the vicars choral had died and only three remained in office; in 1685 the chapter ordered that absolutely no more petty canons and vicars were to be appointed until they could be put to work. Although some services were held elsewhere, there was a gap of thirty-one years before organ and singers were heard again in the choir of St Paul's, at a service of thanksgiving held in 1697 to celebrate William III's return from the Netherlands following the Peace of Ryswick.

As the seventeenth century ended the reconstruction of St Paul's was well under way. The other cathedrals had made good the damage inflicted by the Civil War and had added embellishments and improvements to their buildings. In terms of personnel, too, rebuilding was complete, with chapters and choirs at full strength.

15

Houses of Praise and Prayer

What was the actual role of cathedrals during the sixteenth and seventeenth centuries? Were they important parts of society in England and Wales, interacting in significant ways with the lives of lay people, or were they isolated pockets of privilege, havens for lazy rich clerics who had little concern for outsiders? If they did have a valuable contribution to make, where did it lie and what were its dimensions? What difference would it have made if the cathedrals, like the monasteries, had been dissolved at the time of the Reformation?

Fundamental questions of this sort are the ultimate ones that a history of the cathedrals ought to answer, but paradoxically they are the most difficult ones to attack. None of the sources created during the period itself relate to them directly, for such queries were never clearly posed. They can be tackled only by using inadequate materials that were originally intended to serve other purposes. Only through a combination of tangential approaches can one hope to penetrate to the heart of the matter.

Criticisms of the cathedrals and their clergy were common in the sixteenth century, and many of them were voiced by bishops or other knowledgeable observers sympathetic to the church. Their comments deserve to be taken seriously.[1]

Late in life Bishop Sherburne wrote of the 'ancient squalor' that he had found early in the sixteenth century at Chichester Cathedral, so great that eminent men would be deterred from residing there. Shortly after the break with Rome, Bishop Latimer visited the cathedral at Worcester (still monastic) and wrote, 'I evydentlye perceve the ignorance and neglygance of dyverse relygiouse persons in this monasterye to be intollerable and not to be sufferyde, for that therby dothe reign Idolatre and many kindes of supersticions and other Enormyties'. When he was considering constitutional arrangements for cathedrals of the new foundation, Archbishop Cranmer concluded that the 'sect of prebendaries' was not 'a convenient state or degree to be maintained and established', for 'commonly a prebendary is neither a learner, nor teacher, but a good viander. I would wish that not only the name of prebendary were exiled [from] his Grace's foundations but also the superfluous conditions of such persons'. It would be no great loss if they perished altogether, along with the monks, for in the days of the Apostle Paul there had been no prebendaries in the Church of Christ. A third Marian martyr, Bishop Hooper, voiced similar sentiments in 1552. 'Ah, Mr Secretary', he wrote to Cecil, 'that there were good men in the cathedral churches, God then should have much more honour than he hath, the king's majesty more obedience, and the poor people more knowledge. But the realm wanteth light in such churches where as of right it ought most to be'.

Some of the Elizabethan bishops penned similar laments. In a letter to Peter Martyr, written in 1559, John Jewel described a visitation in which he had found that 'the cathedral churches were nothing else but dens of thieves, or worse, if anything worse or more foul can be mentioned'. Three years later, prescribing reforms for Salisbury, Jewel began with a mixed metaphor, saying that the cathedral should shine brightly among other churches like a city set on a hill, while instead 'we found in our late ordinary visitation that there were not only elsewhere on every side but even in the close itself many things amiss, a fact which we took much and grievously to heart'. At about the same time John Scory found the cathedral at Hereford 'a very nursery of blasphemy, whoredom, pride, superstition, and ignorance'.

Writing to Grindal regarding the prophesyings in 1576, Richard Cox thought that 'if the bysshopps earnestly see to the ministers' there was little need of new orders, 'savinge that the cathedrall churches would be brought to some better frame touching exercise of learninge'. At Durham, Bishop Barnes found 'an Augean stable whose stink is grievous in the nose of God and of men and which to purge far passeth Hercules' labours'. This was in 1578. When examined the prebendaries admitted the partial truth of the charges: 'It hath been cast in our teeth', they said, 'that we teach others but amend not ourselves, that we speak of charity but live in hatred, talk of concord but sow discord. We are ashamed to hear it, but the accusation is true in some part, we cannot deny it'.

One of the fullest critiques comes from John Field's tract *A View of Popish Abuses*. It is worth quoting at some length.

We should be too long to tell your honours of cathedral churches: the dens afore-said of all loitering lubbers, where master Dean, master Vicedean, master Canons or Prebendaries the greater, master petty Canons or Canons the lesser, master Chancellor of the church, master treasurer (otherwise called Judas the purse-bearer), the chief chanter, singing men (special favours of religion), squeaking choristers, organ players, gospellers, pistelers, pensioners, readers, vergers, etc., live in great idleness, and have their abiding. If you would know whence all these came, we can easily answer you: that they came from the pope, as out of the Trojan horse's belly, to the destruction of God's kingdom. The church of God never knew them; neither doth any reformed church in the world know them.

Field was probably also the author of the 'Petition to Parliament for the succession and restoring of Christ to his full regiment', dating from about 1587; it refers once again to the cathedrals as 'dens of lazy, loitering lubbards, the very harbours of all deceitful and timeserving hypocrites'.

Each of these complaints needs to be understood in its context. Bishop Sherburne was explaining why he had founded the four 'Wiccamical' prebends and instituted other reforms at Chichester; he believed that the situation there improved greatly under his leadership. Latimer, Hooper and Cranmer were in the vanguard of reformers and often felt that their work was hampered by conservative cathedral clergy. Jewel, Cox and Scory, writing early in Elizabeth's reign, were troubled by men who had held office under Mary and still adhered to popish views. Barnes, on the other hand, found himself in opposition to the extreme Protestantism that developed in the chapter at Durham under Dean Whittingham. Field was one of the most radical of the Elizabethan Puritans; he could see little that was good in the established church. The petitioners were also advanced Protestants, leaders of the movement that introduced abortive Puritan Bills into virtually every session of Parliament during the 1570s and 1580s. One can explain the reasons for their positions and discount their views accordingly. Sometimes one can refute their comments directly: a study of the prebendaries would show that they were not 'dumb dogs' and their income did not reach the sums alleged. Still, such views were too common and too sincerely held to be ignored.

Disputes between cathedral authorities and bishops occurred less frequently in the seventeenth century, although something less than cordial relations was common enough. At Oxford there was a quarrel in 1629. The bishop claimed the right to confirm children and ordain priests in the cathedral, but the dean and chapter insisted that this was an infringement of their privileges: the dean was to investigate the matter. In 1681 the dean and chapter of Norwich complained that the petty canons had been publishing excommunications sent to them by the bishop's court; they insisted that the bishop had no jurisdiction within the cathedral, except as visitor, and that his excommunications were not to be received there. A number of cathedrals housed consistory courts in which the chancellor of the diocese heard cases under the jurisdiction of the bishop. These led to occasional conflicts, and the courts were eventually removed everywhere except at Chester.

There were also a number of disputes between cathedrals and the cities in which they were located. These grew more common during the seventeenth century. Jurisdiction was often an issue, since cathedrals commonly claimed exemption from municipal authority within their liberties and closes. At Norwich, for instance, it had been agreed in 1524 that the cathedral liberty included a substantial area – Tombland, Raton Row, Holme Street, St Paul's parish, and Magdalen hospital or Spittalland – but there were still disagreements in the 1630s. In some places questions of jurisdiction were resolved by a Privy Council order of 1638 which made deans and residentiary canons members of the appropriate commission of the peace. In others troubles persisted. At Bristol the grassy plot adjoining the cathedral, known as College Green, belonged to the dean and chapter, but in the 1670s the city council allowed residents to encroach on it and kept the gates open at all hours, contrary to the rights of the cathedral; the chapter was eager to find a compromise solution so that they could 'still enjoy peace and friendship' with the aldermen.

In 1665 the dean and chapter of Lincoln complained of a breach of their privileges when the sheriff of Lincoln made an arrest within the close. The issue was still simmering in 1668, when the sheriffs were fined 50s. and made to submit to the church. When the clerk of the works at Exeter was summoned to appear before the sheriff of the city in 1616 he refused to go, on the grounds that he lived in the close and was immune from secular jurisdiction. Similar disputes between the cathedral and the city continued; an appeal was made to the Privy Council and referred by Charles I to a small panel headed by Archbishop Laud. A quarrel at Lichfield was settled in 1635 by a Star Chamber ruling that the cathedral close was part of the county of Stafford but not of the city of Lichfield itself. As already seen, a particularly notorious case arose at Durham in 1674 when three bailiffs arrested Denis Grenville, a prebendary and later dean, within the cloister because of a small debt. The undersheriff went so far as to order Grenville gaoled, 'to the great dishonour of the church and its privileges'. Again the issue was appealed to the Privy Council; the bailiffs and undersheriff made their submissions and the king pardoned them.

Liability to taxation was a related issue. The collection of Ship Money during Charles I's personal rule raised problems in many places. Winchester Cathedral voluntarily paid the amount requested by the county sheriff but refused to contribute to the city's assessment. This position was ratified by the Privy Council in 1637, when the cathedral's independence was reasserted and the city's apportionment reduced accordingly. At Chichester there was also a dispute about the city's right to charge the cathedral. In the end, despite traditional claims of exemption, Chichester and several other cathedrals did pay Ship Money, perhaps because they sympathised with the monarchy, and many cathedral chapters later contributed money for the campaigns against the 'rebel Scots' and parliamentary armies. Tax payments were more common after the Restoration, when the clergy gave up their financial independence in exchange for the privilege of voting for Members of Parliament. At Hereford, for instance, the justices of assize agreed in 1662 that the college of vicars choral was not subject to taxation, but two years later the vicars agreed to pay the hearth tax levied on their houses. Cathedral foundations had always paid tenths to the king and were now included in national taxes, but they remained immune from local levies; thus in 1678 the liberties of Worcester cathedral, including freedom from such taxation, were reasserted.

There is some evidence that cathedral chapters regarded services as their own corporate offering to God, which lay men and women were not encouraged to attend and at which they were not entirely welcome. At Chichester, Bishop Story had ordered in 1481 that the great doors to the choir should be kept shut on festival days so that strangers could not come in and disturb the celebrations, as they had been doing. In 1486 the dean and chapter of Lichfield emphasized that the cathedral was not a parish church and that they did not hold the cure of souls by ordering that such sacraments as marriage, extreme unction and burial not be given to any lay persons save members of the choir and relatives of the canons.

At Exeter the clergy tried to drive some townspeople out early in Elizabeth's reign, for they had disturbed the ministers by singing 'certain vernacular ryming songs', probably metrical Psalms. After some controversy Archbishop Parker ruled that lay persons should be admitted, provided that they were willing to worship according to the lawfully established services of the church. At both Worcester and Carlisle there were orders that the doors to the cathedral should be kept locked except during services, a two-edged regulation suggesting that visitors were to be discouraged but worshippers allowed. In 1595 the chancellor of Norwich commanded 'that in tyme of devine service the officers attendant, viz. the twoe Sextens and verger, shold see that the noyse made and used in the church in the tyme of devine service maye be herafter appeased, wherby the service may be the more quietly performed'. This again implies that laymen frequented the building, but without much devotion or piety.

Although most cathedrals were open to all visitors during the daytime, some problems of access arose. The Jacobean statutes for Norwich stated very precisely that doors were to be opened at seven o'clock each morning and closed following evening prayer in the winter; during the summer the cathedral was to be open from sunrise to sunset. In some places certain entryways were closed – at Canterbury, for instance, a postern gate on the south side of the cathedral was shut up early in the century because of its 'clapping', and following the Restoration an 'inconvenient' door to the cloister was bricked up – but these changes did not prevent men and women from entering the building.

In 1637 the dean and chapter of Exeter decided to shut the doors each day following evening prayer, a move which would exclude visitors on long summer afternoons and evenings. Three years later they introduced stricter measures. 'Whereas wee find daily the Church much abused and prophaned by the standing open of the doores all dayes, wee therefor decree that the Church and Cloisters shalbe kept shutt and not opened, but in the tyme of divine service and sermons'. Such drastic measures, although rare, seem to have become more common after the Restoration. They were reiterated at Exeter in 1680: 'by reason of some rudenes laterly committed in the Cathedral Church by children's playing, they ordered ye Church doores to be shutt up between the tymes of Prayers for a month'. Even during services the doorkeepers were charged to keep the people quiet and prevent their walking up and down. In 1669 the sacrist of Wells was told to keep the cathedral doors closed except at service times and during sessions of the ecclesiastical courts; even then only one door was to be opened. Earlier there had been problems with schoolboys playing in the cloisters and with 'improper persons' sitting in the galleries, which were to be nailed shut. At York one of the archbishop's injunctions of 1690 ordered that a verger should be present in the nave between 8 a.m. and 6 p.m. 'to prevent the tumultuous playing of boyes in the bodye of the church'.

Disturbances and annoyances also plagued cathedral closes. Following a visitation in 1611 the chapter of Chichester ordered that the churchyard be purged of 'hogs, dogs, and other trespassers'; the verger was to 'scourge out the ungracious boys with their tops'. Dog-whippers were commonly employed to keep dogs out of the church itself as well as the close. One can be seen in a painting of Paul's Cross.[2] Others are recorded at Durham and Wells. One of the arguments against lowering the altar rails at Wells was that dogs would jump over them. It was the responsibility of vergers to keep dogs out of the choir at Ely. Hogs and jackdaws had to be driven from the churchyard or killed at Peterborough. At Hereford the chapter complained that the churchyard was 'too often made a Common thoroughfare for carts to pass yt way'. At Canterbury it was necessary to order that shops within the churchyard not be open on Sundays.

Despite all these problems, most of the cathedrals were open most of the time and extended a welcome to serious visitors. At Peterborough there is the reassuring comment that 'many straungers doe come to towne on purpose' to hear the services, with the implication that they were happily admitted.

Although the English cathedrals themselves did not serve as parishes, parts of their buildings were often set aside for parochial use. At Chichester the nave was used in this way; since the subdean of the cathedral served as vicar this was referred to as the subdeanery parish. A portion of the abbey at Chester was designated as St Oswald's parish church. Probably one of the chapels served until the 1530s, when the monks, sensing that the end was near, gave the parishioners the large south transept. At Carlisle the parish used the nave, the dean and chapter the choir. St Luke's chapel at Norwich functioned as a parish church. At Ely the beautiful Lady chapel was given to the parishioners of St Cross in 1562, when their own building was so decrepit that it could no longer be occupied. This arrangement continued until 1938. Three of the Welsh cathedrals were also parishes. Christ Church cathedral at Oxford never housed a parish but served as a college chapel, this function perhaps making its outreach to the non-academic community more difficult. In many other places small parish churches were located within cathedral closes, sometimes nestling against the cathedral building itself. These were usually staffed by priests from the cathedral, and it was here that vicars choral and other persons employed by the cathedrals were often baptized, married and buried. The situation at Exeter was unique, for here the parish churches did not possess cemeteries. Funerals for all lay men and women were conducted in the cathedral, with burial in the cathedral close. When space limitations made it necessary to reuse graves, older bones were taken to a charnel house that remained in existence until the 1550s.

Some services did take place in the cathedrals themselves, perhaps more often in the seventeenth century than earlier. Registers survive in many places. That kept at Durham lists 143 baptisms, 306 marriages and 330 burials during the period from 1609 to the end of the seventeenth century. Many of the persons baptized were children of members of the cathedral establishment – deans, prebendaries, organists, singing men, divinity lecturers, bellringers and the like – but, especially later in the century, there was a good sprinkling of gentry, attorneys and nobility (the Nevilles). As unusual case was recorded at length in 1666:

Elias Turvill, a Greek by nation, born in Constantinople, a Jew by religion, having been instructed, and being desirous of Christian Baptisme, on the thirtieth day of November, which was St Andrewe's day, was presented to the font by Daniell Brevent, doctor in divinitye, and Dennis Greenvill, master of Arts and

Archdeacon of Durham, Prebendaries of the Church of Durham, godfathers, and by Frances Basiere, wife to Isaac Basiere, doctor in divinitye, godmother; and was in this Cathedrall Church solemnly babtized by the same Isaac Basiere, prebendary of the same church, by the name of Andrew; and afterwards did solemnly receive the confirmation by the hands of the Right Reverend father in God John, Lord Bishop of Duresme, and on the 2 day of December following did also receive the holy sacrament of the lord's supper at the hands of the above named doctor Basiere.

The fees charged for baptism were perhaps similar to those set at Ely in 1695: registering the event cost 2s. 6d.; the subsacrist was paid 1s. as clerk and 1s. for providing the water and the church sweeper received 6d.

In most cases the register of marriages at Durham gives only names. Where we can identify the status of the individuals we again find clergy and gentry: in 1642, for instance, Sir Thomas Thynne, a younger son of the squire of Longleat, was married to Stuarta Balcanquall, daughter of the dean of Durham, while in 1662 a minor canon was married to the daughter of another minor canon. Most of the persons buried during the period before the Civil War were members of the cathedral family, but in the later years of the century one finds not only gentry but also a glazier, an apothecary, a plumber, a joiner, the dean's steward, the bishop's cook and one Christopher Mickleton, described as an attorney skilled in the law and learned in all sorts of science.

An unpublished register at Bristol, to take another example, begins only in 1670. For the remaining years of the seventeenth century it records only four baptisms and eight burials (including a sea captain, John Ivy) but as many as sixty marriages. Most of the persons being married appear to have no special connection with the cathedral; many were parishioners of other churches in the city, including St Mary Redcliffe, but others came from towns and villages in Gloucestershire and Somerset.

In fact it appears that the cathedral clergy, mainly minor canons, had a thriving trade in marriages, which they often performed by special licence rather than after having the banns read normally in a parish church. This enabled the ceremonies to be performed more speedily, and in some cases without the knowledge of family members who might oppose the union. An example of such a situation arose in 1606 at Wells, where a marriage had been solemnized without banns and at an unlawful hour. In 1638 one of the clergy at Wells refused to marry a couple who had the dean's licence unless they paid him 10s.; when the dean objected to his refusal, he threw down the licence and went away 'in a grumbling manner'. In 1672 a priest vicar or minor canon of Exeter admitted that he had married the daughter of Sir

George Chidleigh, Bart, without the father's consent and submitted himself to penance. Four years later one of the minor canons of Worcester, Daniel Kendrick, clandestinely married a couple 'without banns thrice asked', to the great dishonour and scandal of the church and the 'unspeakable grief' of the bride's parent. The groom appears to have been another minor canon and was perhaps not thought to be of sufficient social standing. When Kendrick replied contumaceously to inquiries, he was suspended for three years and his stipend given to a deputy who would perform his services during that interim. In the 1680s the clergy of St Paul's were warned not to perform clandestine marriages in several so-called exempt parishes near the cathedral. Marriages there were said to require licences, as they did elsewhere. Earlier, in 1608, a petty canon of Norwich was warned not to publish banns of matrimony for a couple until the prospective groom was cleared of a previous contract.

Most of the people who came to the cathedrals heard sermons. Preaching was regarded as important long before the Reformation, and it came to be thought of as even more essential once Protestant views prevailed. In London crowds resorted to Paul's Cross, the outdoor pulpit adjoining the cathedral. Worcester also had a tall stone cross where sermons were delivered in the open air, with seats for the principal citizens near the church wall. In other places preaching normally took place indoors, often in the cathedral nave.

When establishing his new prebends at Chichester, Bishop Sherburne laid down statutes that mandated preaching. The prebendaries were ordered to preach regularly and were given guidance about the subjects to be covered: their sermons were to deal mainly with the vices of detraction, perjury, neglect of the duty of educating children, and murmuring against God whenever things did not turn out prosperously. At Lincoln special arrangements were made for sermons during Lent and Advent, 1505. Those in Lent were to be delivered in the nave, the Advent sermons being preached in the chapter house. It is said that Ralph Collingwood, dean of Lichfield from 1512 to 1521, preached for half an hour every Sunday, and that he was the first to do so. The act book for Westminster Abbey records that when the church became a cathedral it was 'decreyd yt sermondes shuld be mayd every sonday'. The statutes given to cathedrals of the new foundation generally require that each canon deliver at least four sermons a year and that the dean preach himself, or by sufficient deputy, on the principal feast days. The importance attached to preaching is underscored in statements like that for Durham: 'Because the Word of God is a lamp unto our feet, we therefore appoint and will, nay by the mercy of God we implore, that the Dean and all the Canons be diligent in season and out of season in sowing the Word of God both in the country and especially in this Cathedral Church'. Elizabethan injunctions often contain similar passages.

Members of the chapter at Durham can hardly be accused of shirking this responsibility. During Elizabeth's reign there were at least 170 sermons and lectures a year, generally of high quality. In 1585 the dean, Toby Matthew, preached twenty-eight sermons in the cathedral. He delivered nineteen in 1586 and twenty-seven in 1587. During his eleven years in office, Matthew is said to have preached 721 sermons, most of them in the cathedral but fifteen or twenty a year in parish churches. Initially Dean Whittingham was disappointed that relatively few of the 'stiff' townspeople came to hear the preaching, but in 1563 he thought that 'now of late they begin to resort more diligently to the sermons and service'. The situation was quite different at Chester, where for some years the subdean, John Nutter, was the only member of the chapter actually in residence. Yet even here he was said to preach often, 'godly and sincerely'.

Theology lectures, often given by Puritans, frequently supplemented the sermons. Divinity lectures at Durham began in 1559; they were delivered in the chapter house two or three mornings a week. Attendance by both major and minor canons was supposed to be compulsory. Hugh Broughton, the lecturer in the 1580s, was especially popular and attracted large crowds. Among the various lecturers referred to in the records of other cathedrals is Thomas Thackham, a former prebendary of York, who was appointed at Hereford in 1581.

Sunday afternoon sermons were more common in the seventeenth century than they had been earlier. They were instituted at Canterbury in 1620, the preaching to be undertaken in rotation by the dean, canons and six preachers. Earlier, in 1610, it was agreed that the divinity lecturer should preach in the choir on Christmas, Easter and Whitsunday, and should deliver lectures on Wednesdays. Sermons on thirteen of the chief holy days were to be supplied by members of the chapter. In the 1690s, possibly as a precaution against the Non-Jurors, outsiders were prohibited from preaching in the cathedral unless they obtained prior approval from the dean or a senior prebendary. Sunday afternoon sermons were also preached at Worcester (by members of the chapter or others holding the M.A. and wearing surplices and hoods), Exeter (where a preacher was paid £40 a year), and Norwich (where a gift from several laymen, including Sir John Suckling, provided the stipend). The corporation of Bristol, which had established a stipend for a preacher as early as 1585, brought in Edward Chetwynd from Oxford to fill the position in 1606; he subsequently became dean of the cathedral. In 1616 one of the prebendaries of Worcester was fined

20s. because he failed to preach or provide a substitute on a Sunday afternoon in October, 'to the dishonour and discredit of the said church'. Immediately after the Restoration the chapter lamented the lack of sermons which should have been preached on Sunday afternoons in place of the lectures which had been provided during the Interregnum by appointees of the city. During the years between 1660 and 1667 as much as £280 was paid to outside preachers, but the prebendaries and properly qualified minor canons undertook to fill the pulpit themselves in the future. 'Catechistical lectures' on Sunday afternoons were introduced at Winchester in the 1660s; the lecturer, Thomas White of St Mary at Hill, London, was allowed £52 a year. In 1661 the accounts for Lincoln record £10 'payed to Mr Winstanley for ten sermons preached in ye absence of soe manie prebends'.

The canons of Durham evidently supplied the Sunday sermons there without additional compensation, but fees were paid for sermons on saints' days and other special occasions. In 1685 £30 was allocated for twenty-seven sermons. Among the dates celebrated by sermons early in the century were 5 November (Guy Fawkes Day), 24 March (the day of James I's accession), and 5 August (the anniversary of James's deliverance from the Gowrie conspiracy). 29 May (Charles II's birthday and accession day, known as Royal Oak Day) was added after the Restoration. In addition to sermons the cathedral at Exeter offered Thursday lectures after 1660 – the term suggests a Puritan flavour as well as didactic content. 'Because of his great abilities in performing that duty' the lecturer's stipend was increased from 20 marks to £40. In 1630 the mayor and aldermen of Carlisle spoke appreciatively of the cathedral's efforts to provide a divinity lecturer for them, at a cost of £20 a year. Following the Restoration the chancellor of the diocese agreed in 1670 to serve as lecturer, the city paying him £6 13s. 4d. and the chapter making up the rest of a stipend of £60. In 1672 Charles II directed the dean and chapter of Hereford to name Thomas Wootton their lecturer in divinity, despite the fact that he was not a prebendary, for he had been discharging the office 'to the great Satisfaction of the Auditors'.

Despite these favourable comments there are some signs of disenchantment with preaching. In 1683 the chapter of Worcester found it necessary to order that no one leave a service without hearing it through to the end and that no one walk or loiter in the choir while preaching was underway. A longer entry in the act book for 1685 notes that

the Congregation at the Sermons on Sundays in the Afternoon in very inconsiderable, and is a pretence for many people, children and servants of the City to be absent from their parish Churches (where there is constant preaching, and is, or ought to be Catechizing too) and yet never come to the College, but loyter and

Spend the time profanely elsewhere, whereas if they were at their own parish Churches their Parents or Masters would see them engaged in the parochial religious duties.

Sunday sermons in the cathedral were therefore discontinued, and the minor canons were allowed £10 in place of the fees they had received for preaching.

More theoretical or theological reservations had been voiced by Bishop Neile during his visitation of Lincoln in 1614. He believed that the benefits of lecturing and preaching were widely exaggerated.

This lecturing [he wrote] hath brought many of gods holy and good ordinances into contempt, as publike prayer, Reading of ye Scriptures and receiving of the blessed Sacraments, for ye multitude is drawne to this conceit, That the preaching of the word is not only a *principall*, but even the *sole and only meanes* of mans salvation and that all religious worship consists only in speaking and in hearing.

Neile realized that extinguishing lectures, both in the cathedral and in parish churches, would raise a clamour, but he ordered that no 'factious men' or those without university degrees should fill the pulpits.

The cathedral clergy frequently preached in parish churches, especially those in which the dean and chapter held the tithes. In 1578 the canons of Durham delivered more than three hundred sermons in parishes, 215 within County Durham and eighty-eight in Northumberland. Worcester paid members of the chapter 3s. 4d. for each sermon delivered in a parish church, or twice that sum if it was more than twenty miles distant. At Chester the fee was always 6s. 8d.

Throughout these centuries cathedrals were involved in civic ceremonies and celebrations. Some of these were associated with visits by the monarch or other members of the royal family. Coronations of course took place in Westminster Abbey; Edward VI and Mary were crowned there during its brief incarnation as a cathedral. Coronation processions often stopped near St Paul's. During the pageantry held in 1533 to honour Anne Boleyn, for instance, two hundred children, including those from St Paul's School, declaimed translations of Latin poetry from a platform erected at the east end of the churchyard. Royal marriages, baptisms and funerals might occur in cathedrals outside of London. We do not know exactly where the union between Henry VII and Elizabeth of York was celebrated. The couple's elder son, Prince Arthur, was born in Winchester and baptized in the cathedral there. As a boy, Arthur visited the cathedral at Worcester, accompanied by his parents and his grandmother, Lady Margaret Beaufort. A few years later he was buried there, and a chantry chapel was built in his honour. His marriage to Catherine of Aragon had been solemnized at St Paul's. Henry VII and Elizabeth of York were interred at Westminster Abbey in the lofty fan-vaulted chapel added east of the shrine of Edward the Confessor.

Catherine of Aragon had visited Exeter Cathedral in 1501, spending several days at the deanery shortly after her initial landing at Plymouth. She married Henry VIII in the Franciscan church at Greenwich, not in Westminster Abbey or a cathedral, and Henry was buried at Windsor rather than Westminster. The marriage of Philip II and Mary took place at Winchester. In 1554 Philip attended a great service at St Paul's honouring the arrival in England of Cardinal Pole. Mary and Pole visited Canterbury in 1557, when the chapter had to make special payments for cleaning the chapter house, carrying away rubbish, and preparing the library and tombs for royal inspection. During her father's reign Mary had paid several visits to Worcester, where she was entertained by Prior More, both in Worcester itself and at his manor of Battenhall. Perhaps she was especially attracted by Prince Arthur's chantry, with its armorial references to her mother, Catherine of Aragon. In 1526 she stayed from 7 January until Easter, leaving only on 15 April. She returned again in August for the Feast of the Assumption of the Virgin. Mary's funeral took place in Westminster Abbey and she is buried there.

Elizabeth's progresses took her to several of the cathedrals. Her visit to Canterbury in 1573 is described in a letter sent by Archbishop Parker to Grindal, then archbishop of York.

I met her Highness, as she was coming to Dover, upon Folkston Down. The which I rather did, with all my men, to shew my duty to her, and mine affection to the Shire, who likewise there met her. And I left her at Dover, and came home to Bekesborne that night: and after that, went to Canterbury to receive Her Majesty there. Which I did, with the Bishops of Lincoln and Rochester, and my Suffragan, at the West dorr: where, after the Grammarian had made his Oration to her upon her horseback, she alighted. We then kneeled down, and said the Psalm *Deus misereatur* in English, with certain other Collects briefly; and that in our chimers and rochets. The Quire, with the Dean and Prebendaries, stood on either side of the Church, and brought Her Majesty up with a Square-song, she going under a canopy, born by four of her Temporal Knights, to the traverse place by the Communion board, where she heard Evensong, and after departed to her lodging at St Austin's, whither I waited on her ... And so Her Majesty came every Sunday to Church, to hear the Sermon; and upon one Monday it pleased Her Highness to dine in my great Hall, thoroughly furnished, with the Council, Frenchmen, Ladies, Gentlemen, and Mayor of the Town, with her Brethren, &c.

Her Highness sitting in the midst, having two French Ambassadors at one end of the table, and four Ladies of Honour at the other end.

After staying fourteen days at Canterbury the queen returned to her palace at Greenwich, stopping on the way to attend a Sunday service at Rochester Cathedral and hear a sermon there.

In 1575 Elizabeth visited Lichfield, where she stayed from 20 July to 3 August, and then journeyed to Worcester, arriving on Saturday, 15 August. The next day she attended a service in the cathedral. This included 'a great and solem noyse of syngyng of service in the Quier, both by note and also plaing with cornetts and sackbutts'; the bishop preached, and she lodged in his palace. Three years later, in 1578, her progress into East Anglia took her to the cathedral at Norwich.

The queen attended services at St Paul's on numerous occasions. An amusing episode occurred on New Year's Day 1562. Dean Nowell had obtained from a foreigner some fine engravings or woodcuts depicting saints and martyrs, and he had these bound into a copy of the Prayer Book that he laid at the queen's place, intending to give it to her for a New Year's gift. When she saw it she was displeased. 'She opened the book, and perused it, and saw the pictures; but frowned and blushed, and then shut it (of which several took notice); and, calling for the verger, had him bring her the old book, wherein she was formerly wont to read'. After the service she interrogated the dean, who admitted that he was responsible for the volume. 'Have you forgotten our Proclamation against images, pictures, and Romish reliques?' Elizabeth asked. Nowell insisted that he meant no harm and had hoped to please her. After some further interchange the queen left with the parting command, 'Let no more of these mistakes ... be committed within the Churches of our Realm'.

During his progress from Edinburgh to London in 1603 James I paused at Durham. Here he stayed with the bishop. The records do not say that he toured the cathedral, but it is hard to believe that he could have ignored it. Festivities at York were much more elaborate. Here the civic authorities met the king three miles outside the city and escorted him to the cathedral, four knights carrying a canopy of cloth of gold over his head. When the entourage reached the minster, the king was 'royally received, by the Deane and Prebends, and the whole quyer of singing menne of that Cathedrall Church, in their richest coapes'. James sat on a throne specially prepared for him. On the following day – Sunday, 17 April – he went again to the minster, 'and heard a Sermon made by the Deane, who was Byshoppe of Limericke in Ireland; the Lord Maior, Aldermen, the Sheriffes, and foure and twentie, attended upon the King, the Earle still bearing the sword, the

Lord Maior the mace, and the Sheriffes bearing up their rodds, as well within the Church as in the streets'.

Shortly after his coronation James visited Salisbury, where he was entertained by the bishop for three days. The cathedral authorities went to considerable trouble and expense to prepare for his coming: payments were made to repair the bell-wheels, whitewash the church, carry away thirty loads of dung from the churchyard and set up the king's arms on the gate. A second visit in 1615 was also costly. The cloister was cleaned and weeded, flowers were provided to 'dresse his Majesties seat', five additional singing-men and two boys were engaged, and payments were made to the king's own musicians. Bells were rung as the king went in and out.

In 1606 King James, Queen Anne and her brother Christian, the king of Denmark, attended a service at Rochester and heard a sermon preached in Latin for the benefit of the Danish king, who did not speak English. Prince Henry accompanied Christian when he toured St Paul's later in the year. Here the Danish monarch 'ascended the top of the steeple, and when he had survayed the Citie, hee held his foote still whilest Edward Soper, keeper of the steeple, with his knife cutte the length and breadth thereof in the lead; and for a lasting remembrance thereof, the said Soper, within few dayes after, made the King's character in gilded copper, and fixed it in the middest of the print of the King's foote'.

James's return to Scotland in 1617 gave him opportunity to visit several cathedral cities. In March he was at Lincoln, where the mayor, aldermen, sheriffs and other citizens 'in their ranks, youngest first', escorted him to the minster. After being met by the dean and chapter as well as the bishop, Richard Neile, he knelt at the west end for a short prayer 'and so, under a canopy which was held over him by four or six Prebends in surplices, went into the Quire, the Mayor still bearing the Sword, the Aldermen and other Citizens in their gowns going before him into the Quire, and there sate by the Bishop's pue hanged about with rich hangings in a Chair all prayer-time'. Following the service the king viewed the ancient monuments and the chapter house. On a second visit to the cathedral James touched for the King's Evil and supposedly healed fifty persons.

In April the royal entourage came again to York. 'On the 15th, being Sunday, his Majesty went to the Cathedral, where the Archbishop preached a learned Sermon before him'. After the sermon James touched about seventy persons. The following Sunday he celebrated Easter Day at Durham Cathedral, where Lancelot Andrewes, who was accompanying the king as royal chaplain, delivered one of his famous Resurrection sermons. After revisiting his spawning grounds in Scotland (like a salmon, the king said), James passed through Chester on his way back to London.

One of the grandest ceremonies in early Stuart London took place on 26 March 1620, when James went in great state to St Paul's in order to give his support to the work of restoration which was in progress. It is possible that the bishop and dean had been trying to engage the king's interest in St Paul's for several years, but in the end James gave the civic authorities only a week's notice that he was coming, so the mayor and alderman had to scramble to arrange all the details.

In his journey from Whitehall the king was accompanied by peers and bishops as well as gentlemen and esquires, great officers of state, ambassadors and sons of noblemen. This entourage was met at Temple Bar by a concourse of civic dignitaries; members of the livery companies, in ceremonial attire, stood behind railings along the route of the procession, with tapestry hanging from the windows above their heads. Following evening prayer in the cathedral the king heard a sermon preached at Paul's Cross by the bishop of London; 'the Sermon being ended, the King observed the greatnesse and state of that Church, and three new windowes newly glazed, in rich colours, with the story of Saint Paul'. The scene is easy to visualize because just such a procession to old St Paul's is depicted in a well-known painting of the cathedral.[3] The several panels of this triptych show not only the procession itself but also the cathedral (with an imaginary celestial spire), the preaching place at Paul's Cross, and some of the embellishments completed in recent years.

We know that Charles I heard a sermon at Paul's Cross in 1630. Three years later he visited several of the cathedrals while travelling to Scotland. In May 1633 he was at York. Here there had been some trouble: members of the chapter had been ordered to attend a meeting on 22 May, presumably to prepare for the king's coming, but only John Cosin (then the archdeacon) appeared and the other clergy were pronounced contumacious. Nevertheless the visit went off well enough. On 24 May the civic leaders met Charles at Micklegate and accompanied him to the minster, where one of the canons welcomed him with a Latin oration. The king then solemnly examined the choir and nave, his canopy being held aloft by the dean and some canons. It was not a Sunday and it does not appear that a service was held.

Affairs at Durham were more elaborate. The royal party visited the cathedral on Sunday afternoon, 1 June. Here again an elaborate canopy of cloth of gold was held over the king throughout his stay. The *Te Deum* was performed by the choir, accompanied by the organ and other instruments. After suitable versicles and responses were sung, prayers were offered by William Laud, the king's chaplain (still bishop of London though soon to become archbishop). Charles toured the whole building, noting especially the tombs of St Cuthbert and the Venerable Bede; when leaving he was presented with a cope of red velvet, sumptuously embroidered (at a cost of £300) with a scene showing the decapitation of John the Baptist. The next day he returned to hear morning prayer, which included Psalm 150 and the anthem 'Canite tuba in Sion'.

At both York and Durham Charles was disturbed by the presence of houses which abutted on the cathedral, detracting from its beauty, and – within the cathedrals – distressed by problems involving seating. At York, he wrote, 'wee sawe meane tenementes in many places, which gave us cause to enforme our selfe of that great abuse in buildeing houses and stables with their uncleane passages a great deale too neare to the house of God'. At Durham, too, there were 'certaine meane tenements uppon the Church-yard, and some of them adjoyninge to the walls of the Church'. In both cases the king ordered the dean and chapter to allow no more such houses to be built, to renew none of the existing leases when they expired, and to pull down the houses as soon as possible. The notion that cathedrals needed to be freestanding, not hemmed in by subordinate structures, seems to be one of the new ideas of the seventeenth century. Earlier, it was common for parish churches and libraries, and even dwellings and shops, to adjoin cathedrals and nestle between their buttresses.

Charles II's interest in cathedrals was minimal. After landing at Dover in 1660 he passed through Canterbury, where he attended a Sunday service, and Rochester, where he appears to have ignored the church. In September 1665 he was in Salisbury, and the ringers were paid 10s. 'when the king desyred to heare the bells', but he was more concerned with racing than religion. In 1670 the queen went to Canterbury and the bell ringers there had to be rewarded. During the last years of his life Charles II was fascinated with the prospect of building a new royal palace at Winchester, surrounded by a park and connected to the cathedral by a 'stately street'. For a time members of the court flocked to the ancient city, making it difficult to obtain lodging: when Bishop Ken refused to house Nell Gwynn she had to make do with rooms at the deanery. But only a shell of the palace, designed by Sir Christopher Wren, was ever built, and the project died with the king.

James II visited Salisbury and Worcester in 1686, Chester in 1687, and Salisbury again in 1688. On each occasion the cathedrals paid for ringing in his honour, but there is no record that he entered the buildings. William III, although a Calvinist, did attend a service and hear a sermon at Chester Cathedral in June 1690.

Cathedrals were naturally involved in many non-royal civic occasions as well. It was common for the installation of new mayors and aldermen to be solemnized at the cathedral. Some seventeenth-century accounts describe these ceremonies in detail. A journal written by the Dutch traveller William Schellinks provides details of the lord mayor's installation and show at London in October 1662, and one of Schellinks's earlier entries mentions a more ordinary occurrence in which he happened to see 'the Lord Mayor coming out of St Paul's Church magnificently attired, with a heavy golden chain hanging back and front over his tabard down to the ground, and mounting his horse, which was very preciously and elegantly decked out in the old fashion with gold, velvet, and jewels. The sword was carried before him'. The dean and chapter of Hereford gave £2 to the mayor there 'at his second feast' in 1666 – presumably this was a civic banquet to which the cathedral dignitaries were invited. The visit of the assize judges was often marked by a sermon in the cathedral attended by legal and civic dignitaries; at Durham it was ordered that the dean should preach, or in his absence one of the prebendaries. The worsted weavers of Norwich obtained the chapter's permission to name their own preacher for a service held annually on Whit Monday. This is merely one example of guild ceremonies which were common throughout the realm. Prominent lay persons were often invited to the audit feasts held yearly in many places. We know that £9 17s. was spent on this dinner at Chester in 1614 and that a musician engaged to provide entertainment was paid 2s. Richer cathedrals could afford more elaborate celebrations: Durham hired the local waits and gave them 5s. Bishops' visitations, too, provided opportunities for special gatherings and the need (as at Salisbury) for additional coals and perfumes as well as food and wine. The visitation dinner held at Bristol in 1677 cost £6 'besides ye wine'. In 1668 the dean and chapter of Exeter invited the bishop and his wife together with some other dignitaries to a dinner on 29 May celebrating the anniversary of the Restoration.

Additional entertainment was provided by deans and, occasionally, by prebendaries. At Durham the dean was allowed forty marks in 1622 for 'keeping hospitality in the country'. In 1660 members of the chapter were absolved from the usual requirements of hospitality because of the ruinous nature of their houses, but in 1661 it was noted that they experienced unusual expenses because 'a greater measure of hospitality was expected upon return from so long an exile'. The following year they set limits to their entertaining, in order to 'prevent scandal to prudent and sober men': they would not (except once a week) invite more than six persons to dinner, 'besides such strangers as they shall occasionally meet', and they promised to avoid the 'extremes of parsimony and profuseness'. At Peterborough there were differences of opinion about the hospitality required of the dean, and in 1621 it was agreed to consult Lord Burghley about the matter. A chapter act of 1671 specifically required the dean of Worcester to maintain hospitality during his four months in residence. An ambiguous item in the accounts for Hereford refers to 'ye Church' being invited to dinner, perhaps by the dean and perhaps by the vicars choral. In any case 5s. 8d. was spent for wine.

The relationship that existed between the cathedrals and ordinary members of the laity is much less well documented than that which involved the royal family and civic officials. One way of approaching it is to examine artifacts rather than documents, in this case the tombs and monuments of lay people erected within the cathedrals. These can surely be read as proof of interaction between the cathedrals and the laity, a sign that prestige was associated with burial in a cathedral or lasting commemoration there. It seems certain, too, that the funerals of civic leaders and aristocrats commemorated in the cathedrals were attended by throngs of laymen.

During the centuries before the Reformation, chantry chapels were memorials as well as locations for requiems and obits. All the cathedrals had chantries, and most of them had elaborate chantry chapels. Some of these, like Sir John Speke's chantry at Exeter, were erected during the sixteenth century, and some of them include iconography suggesting friendship and mutual respect between laymen and clerics.

After the Reformation and the dissolution of the chantries, monuments took over the role of memorializing lay men and women, though they were not of course sites for the prayers and masses that had existed earlier. There are extraordinary collections of monuments at both Canterbury and York. One of the most haunting monuments at Canterbury depicts the tragic death of two generations of the Hales family: a painted panel shows the suicide by drowning of Sir James Hales in 1554, after his mind had been unsettled by the rapid religious changes, while a relief pictures the burial at sea of his son, the younger Sir James, who died aboard a disease-stricken warship in 1589. Two of the finest Jacobean effigies depict members of the Boys family: Sir John Boys, who died in 1612 after serving as recorder of the city and steward to five successive archbishops, reclines on a tomb chest in the nave, while his nephew Dr John Boys, a notable scholar who was dean of the cathedral from 1619 to 1625, is shown at his writing table surrounded by walls of marble books. St Michael's chapel, dedicated to military men, has tombs of Sir Thomas Thornhurst, who was killed at La Rochelle in 1627, and William Prudde, who died at Maastricht in 1632. Two great ladies have memorial statues in the same chapel: Lady Thornhurst (d. 1609), who married Sir Richard Baker of Sissinghurst, is shown reclining, wearing a large ruff, while Dame Dorothy Thornhurst (d. 1620) appears more severe as she kneels at her priedieu. A double monument captures Dean Thomas Neville

(d. 1615) in clerical garb and his brother Alexander in armour, both kneeling in prayer. All of these monuments precede the Civil War; the years following the Restoration left little of interest beside a large Baroque tablet commemorating Dean Thomas Turner (d. 1672), who had shared Charles II's exile and returned to preside over the renewal of the cathedral.

York Minster was never the chosen burial place for civic dignitaries, who preferred one or another of the parish churches; most monuments memorialize bishops or members of aristocratic landowning families. Many of the smaller tombstones and brasses were removed when the nave was refloored in the eighteenth century. What remains is nevertheless impressive. For the early seventeenth century we have the tombs of archbishops Matthew Hutton (d. 1606) and Tobie Matthew (d. 1628); a large monument to Sir William Gee (d. 1611), secretary to the Council of the North, flanked by his two wives and attended by his six children; a similar memorial to Sir Henry Belasyse (d. 1630), who ordered the monument from the sculptor Nicholas Stone some years before his death; simple likenesses of Anne Bennett (d. 1601), widow of an ecclesiastical lawyer, and Frances Matthews (d. 1629), wife of the archbishop; and a naive statue, now lacking its hands, of Nicholas Wanton (d. 1617). The monuments erected at York following the Restoration are more imposing and of higher quality as works of art. The grandest depict archbishops: Accepted Frewen (d. 1664), Richard Sterne (d. 1683), John Dolben (d. 1688) and Thomas Lamplugh (d. 1691). The standing figure of Lamplugh, perhaps the finest piece of seventeenth-century sculpture in any of the cathedrals, was carved by the famous woodworker Grinling Gibbons. John van Nost the elder, another leading sculptor, is represented by a pretentious monument to William Wentworth, second earl of Strafford (d. 1695) and his wife; the figures are larger than life-size and the style is that of the early eighteenth century.

A few monuments from old St Paul's remain in the crypt of the present cathedral. The haunting figure of John Donne in his shroud, carved by Nicholas Stone, fits the poet perfectly. It survived the Great Fire unharmed. The same cannot be said of the effigies of William Hewitt (d. 1599), a City merchant, and Sir William Cokayne (d. 1626), the famous lord mayor. Two post-fire plaques memorialise members of Sir Christopher Wren's family. Wren's sister Susanna (d. 1688) has her qualities praised in English while her husband William Holder (d. 1697), a canon of the cathedral, is lauded in Latin; a particularly attractive monument to Wren's daughter Jane (d. 1702 aged twenty-six), carved by Francis Bird, shows a young women playing the organ to the evident delight of angels and putti.

Some of the finest monuments erected by lay persons are at Salisbury and Winchester. A pompous monument at Salisbury, gaudy with paint and gilding, houses the remains of Edward Seymour, earl of Hertford (d. 1621), and his wife, Lady Catherine Grey. Their reclining effigies are flanked by figures of their sons, Edward Lord Beauchamp and Lord Thomas Seymour. The towering composition, which includes some twenty coats of arms, reminded a former canon of an Indian pagoda. Similar in style but smaller in size is the tomb of Sir Richard Mompesson and his wife Catherine. The Jacobean taste reflected in these monuments can be seen in many of the cathedrals; what is unique at Salisbury is the tomb of Sir Thomas Gorges and his wife Helena Snachenberg, who came to England from Sweden at the age of fifteen and served as a maid of honour to Elizabeth I. This enormous monument, erected in 1635, is all white marble, chaste in comparison to its neighbours put up only a few years earlier. The workmanship is superb – the effigies are simply but elegantly carved – and the symbolism used throughout the monument is exceptional as well: relief panels in the vaulting of the canopy show scenes embodying the seven gifts of the Holy Spirit; female figures representing the four cardinal virtues stand above the canopy; the whole monument is capped by a globe and astrolabe, signs of Gorges's interest in exploration.

Salisbury also has striking memorials to Sir Henry Hyde, who was executed in 1650 for his loyalty to Charles I, and his brother Sir Robert Hyde, the recorder of Salisbury who helped save the cathedral 'from the sacrilegious malice of the Roundheads'. Sir Robert was lord chief justice when he died of the plague in 1665, and his portrait bust shows him wearing his collar of SS (a gold chain, symbolic of his office) with the Tudor rose and portcullis. There are also smaller monuments honouring gentlemen who died young – Milo Sandys, d. 1632 aged twenty-two, and Charles Langford, d. 1635 aged twenty-nine – and women, Elihonor Sadler (d. 1622) and Mary Cooke (d. 1642). A final monument here is worth mentioning because it is one of only two or three in the country commemorating a medical doctor. D'Aubigny Turberville, who died in 1696 aged eighty-five, was an oculist who practised briefly in London and then moved to Salisbury, where he worked for thirty years. His patients included Samuel Pepys. The conclusion of his Latin epitaph has been translated 'Beneath this stone extinct he lies, the only doctor for the eyes'.

At Winchester the best monuments of this period depict Sir Richard Weston, earl of Portland (d. 1635), who as lord treasurer helped Charles I find non-parliamentary sources of revenue during the Personal Rule, and Sir John Cloberry (d. 1687), who as an officer under General Monk helped restore Charles II. Portland was a patron of the French sculptor Hubert Le Sueur, whose bronze statues of James I and Charles I were originally part of Inigo Jones's screen, and his reclining effigy (holding the lord treasurer's

wand) is also Le Sueur's work. Cloberrry is of interest because he is virtually the only former member of a parliamentary army to be memorialized
in a cathedral; his marble statue was originally surrounded by carved pikes,
guns and flags, but these were removed during the nineteenth century. No
doubt the fact that he entered the army only after the execution of Charles
I and later supported the Restoration helped earn him his niche. He too
bears a staff of office; during the reign of Charles II he was a member of the
city corporation and an MP for Winchester. Small mural tablets at Winchester commemorate Mary Young and Elizabeth Dingley; a cartouche
memorializes Catherine Fulham (d. 1699), and ledger stones in the floor
mark the burials of William Symonds, a mayor and alderman (d. 1606), and
George Pemerton, twice mayor (d. 1627).

As one might expect many of the monuments at Christ Church Cathedral
in Oxford commemorate members of the college and university. An affecting memorial (originally a carved brass) laments the death of Henry Dow,
son of a merchant tailor of London, who died in 1578 at the age of twenty-
one after having studied at Christ Church for two and a half years. The first
bishop of Oxford, Robert King (d. 1557), is buried in the south transept of
his cathedral, in a tomb boasting an elaborately carved canopy but without
an effigy. The memorial to Bishop John Fell (the unfortunate subject of Tom
Brown's epigram 'I do not like you, Dr Fell', d. 1686) is simple but elegant.
There are also a number of monuments commemorating royalists, including Sir William Brouncker, who shared Charles I's residence in Oxford
during the years of the Civil War.

One of the most striking monuments to a woman of the early Stuart
period is that depicting Lady Dodderidge (d. 1614) at Exeter. Lady Dodderidge regularly attended services in the cathedral, and in 1609 it was
ordered that she have 'a fit seat in a convenient place before the pulpit to sit
in at sermon time'. The chapter acts specifically record consent to the erection of her tomb, which includes a skull as a *memento mori*. The companion
monument to Sir John Dodderidge (d. 1628), who had been solicitor general and a member of the Commons, is more conventional. Aside from
these, the most important monuments at Exeter memorialize clergy. There
are the large alabaster tombs of bishops William Cotton (d. 1621) and Valen-
tine Carey (d. 1626) – Carey, a former dean of St Paul's, is actually buried
in London – and a fine portrait bust and Latin inscription honouring
Edward Cotton (d. 1675), grandson of the bishop, son of the precentor, himself treasurer of the cathedral and a residentiary canon. Bishop John Still
(d. 1608) has a typical Jacobean tomb at Wells, so similar to Bishop Cotton's
at Exeter that one wonders if the effigies are from the same hand, but
Richard Kidder (bishop 1691–1703) lies beneath a voluptuous female

mourner surmounted by urns and putti, very much in the Baroque style of
the eighteenth century. Ordinary lay people were likely to be buried under
simple floor slabs, as were three members of the Prickman family.[4]

Cathedrals collected fees from lay persons wishing to erect monuments.
In 1685, for instance, Worcester determined that the charge would be £5,
which was to be used for maintaining the library. The size of monuments
was restricted as well; they could not exceed 2 feet 9 inches in width or 5 feet
6 inches in height. Perhaps because Durham never needed the money which
other cathedrals collected, it has few monuments. Here a simple wooden
panel, not a flamboyant tomb, was thought sufficient to honour Richard
Hunt, dean from 1620 to 1638. The Latin inscription is nevertheless moving.
It concludes, in translation,

> May every stranger pray, with us that love him,
> Soft lie his bones, light rest the earth above him ...
> He taught the lame to walk, the blind to see,
> The stranger's host, the poor man's fortress he.

Fees were also charged for burials, even if monuments were not erected.
In 1608 burial in the nave at Wells cost 20s., 30s. being charged for interment in the choir or a chancel aisle; special permission had to be granted by
the dean and chapter for burial in the chancel itself. At Worcester the charge
was set at 20s. in 1609. In 1670 this was raised to 20 nobles (£8 6s. 8d.). The
following year, 'to preserve the Quire from the Incumbraunce of Buryalls, it
[was] ordered that for the future there shall be no more interment there',
although burial in the nave was still allowed. At the end of the century it was
possible to be buried in the 'new ground on the north side of the church'
for 5s. After 1637 no one but bishops and noblemen could be buried in the
choir of Winchester Cathedral; the lay aristocrats were charged £10. The
charge for the nave and aisles was £3, or 30s. for children under the age of
twelve; as usual members of the chapter and their families were buried free.

At Canterbury the fee for burial in the north aisle was £5 in 1675. During
the same period there were varying rates at Carlisle: £1 for burial in the
choir; 10s. in the aisles; 6s. 8d. 'within the Low Church now standing', that
is, the truncated nave; 3s. 4d. 'within the demolished Low Church' or
churchyard. During the reign of Charles I Salisbury received 20s. for the
burial of Mistress Mompesson and £13 6s. 8d. for the burial of the earl of
Pembroke, but it is not certain whether these were gifts or charges. At
Chester Lady Jane Montgomery, sister to the earl of Mount Alexander in
Ireland, 'being a great lover of the Ceremonyes of our Church while shee
lived, desired to be buried in our Quire' when she died in 1637. The bishop
approved but did not know the correct fee; he was informed that it was

£10 for interment within the choir itself, or £5 in the choir aisles. Exeter Cathedral allowed Alice Hale, who had given £100 for adorning the choir in 1636, to be buried beside her husband at no charge. In addition to these fees there were charges for ringing the bells or having the choir sing at the funeral service.

If conclusions based on such miscellaneous evidence are justified, they are that the cathedrals were sought out as burial sites less frequently following the Restoration than they had been earlier and that a larger proportion of the later monuments were erected to honour bishops and other clergymen. This may be a sign that the cathedral communities were becoming increasingly inbred. Monuments also confirm the view that the cathedrals had closer ties with noblemen, gentry and members of the civic aristocracy than with the lower orders in society. The number of women buried and memorialized, however, may appear surprisingly large, especially considering that they were excluded from the ranks of the clergy.

All of the cathedrals gave alms to the poor. Their charitable contributions were of several sorts. The statutes of cathedrals of the new foundation required them to maintain specified numbers of almsmen or bedesmen. The numbers varied in rough proportion to the wealth of the cathedral: Oxford had twenty-four, Canterbury and Winchester twelve, Bristol and Gloucester only four. In other places the number was six or eight. Almshouses, often dating back to the period before the Reformation, were associated with many of the cathedrals of the old foundation, for instance Lincoln and Exeter. New almshouses were erected at several places during the era of the Restoration. Bishop Cosin was responsible for the construction of an attractive building near the cathedral at Durham, while at Exeter the dean and chapter converted a portion of the cloisters used as a market during the Interregnum into a hospital for six families who had fallen into distress 'chiefly for their loyaltie to his Majestie'. They lived in 'handsome houses' which were built between the buttresses of the nave and can be seen in a contemporary engraving.

Bedesmen received modest stipends, usually £6 13s. 4d. a year, and sometimes housing and food as well. They were generally expected to attend services and they might be assigned other minor duties. At Canterbury two of them served as organ blowers and received an additional payment of 6s. a quarter. They were usually named by the king; since the monarch could not be expected to keep track of vacancies in the several cathedrals, he often nominated persons for the next opening, and he sometimes became confused and named several persons for the same position. Especially during the later years of the seventeenth century, almsmen were generally persons who had suffered injuries in military service. Charles II attempted to reward a number of decayed royalists with these positions. In a few instances royal nominees proved unsuitable; at Chester an almsman named by the king in 1670 was contumacious and refused to take the oath, so he was suspended and Charles was told to nominate someone else. It is interesting to note that Oliver Cromwell nominated an almsman for Oxford in 1652. Oxford was the only cathedral to maintain some semblance of continuity during the Interregnum.

Occasional references suggest that members of the chapter did care about their almsmen: at Canterbury they gave an old ill bedesman an additional 10s., and they agreed to pay another while he was in a London hospital seeking treatment for deafness 'gotten by greate colds taken at sea in his Majesties service'. More often, however, one finds complaints about the almsmen's failure to attend services and their generally irreverent life. A unique complaint was lodged against an almsman of Worcester: he was found making shoes in his room over the north porch, to the 'great profanation of the place', and was ordered to withdraw.

Small gifts to persons in special need were common. The recipients include poor ministers, shipwrecked seamen, prisoners, widows and victims of fires. At Chester we read of 'a poor scholar', 'a musician that came out of Ireland', 'a poor man that had his goods burned', 'a poor boy to buy him a hat', 'a converted friar', 'a poor woman whose son is distracted', 'a gentleman beggar', 'half a dozen soldiers that lately came out of Germany and the Low Countries', and 'a minister yt came to looke for a place and told me yt yf he were furnisht with clothes he should be received at Tarporley'. Funds were also provided for 'setting a poor boy prentice'. In 1682 Wells relieved 'eighteen seamen rescued from the Turks', 'a poor man having no arms', 'a distressed Old Cavalier', 'a ministers orphan', and 'a poor Yorkshire woman'. Rather than money Exeter gave a Bible to William Jones of St Sidwell's parish, 'a poor man desiring the same'.

Sometimes contributions were made to groups. Worcester, Norwich and Canterbury sent aid to the poor who had suffered from a fire at Northampton in 1675, while Winchester and Exeter provided relief for plague victims in 1670. Many of the cathedrals sent aid to the victims of the Great Fire of London and most of them subscribed funds for the rebuilding of St Paul's. In January 1697 the dean and chapter of Exeter ordered that £5 be given to the poor on account of 'the present Difficultys of ye times and Severity of ye Season'. On several occasions Canterbury gave £40 or £50 to poor Irish Protestants, and in 1662 it sent £10 in relief to the reformed church in Strasbourg. In 1699 Norwich dispatched £10 to the 'poor French Protestants (3500 souls)' who had been banished from their native country by 'popish cruelty' and survived only because of the charity of the Protestant cantons of Switzerland. Following the Restoration a concerted effort was made to raise £30,000 for the release of captives of the Turkish pirates in Algiers; we know that Chichester, Durham, Lincoln, Peterborough, Wells and Worcester sent contributions. Funds were also allocated for the repair of roads and bridges (the statutes sometimes ordered this) and for maintenance of parish churches at which the chapter held the right of presentation.

Although a number of municipalities and individual philanthropists conceived schemes for setting the poor to work, Durham was the only cathedral to experiment with an enterprise of this sort. In 1695 the dean and chapter agreed to purchase spinning wheels for twelve poor children and allow them £6 a week for one quarter. We do not know whether this effort met with success.

In several places foundling children were cared for at the expense of cathedrals. In 1692 Chester paid £4 7s. 0d. for 'an upper and an under coat for the bastard child', and two years later it spent 11s. 3d. to care for an 'exposed child' for a quarter. Worcester paid 'Nurse Hill for looking to a young Childe found at Mr Thornborough's Doore February 25, [1674]'. The child was looked after for more than a year at a charge of 2s. a week, but the pathetic tale had a sad ending. In the accounts for 1676 we read:

To ye Nurse in ye Child's sickness, 2s.

To Mr Bullard for Powder and syrup, 9d.

For a shroud to bury it, 1s.

For Diet Cakes and Beere at ye Buryall, 7s.

For a Coffin, £1 10d.

For Grave, and Ringing and Buriall, 2s. 6d.

Lichfield Cathedral, on the other hand, insisted that the cost of caring for a 'female bastard' in one of the cathedral parishes be borne by the 'reputed father', not the dean and chapter. When a poor woman was found in labour within the precincts of Rochester Cathedral, the dean and chapter thought themselves 'therein nothing concerned'.

Despite many acts of kindness and charity, one frequently has the feeling that the cathedral chapters regarded the poor as a nuisance, who might be given alms so long as they did not trouble the clergy. In 1618 the dean and chapter of Winchester proposed to give the poor of the city £40 a year instead of doling out 13s. 4d. a week, 'so that we may be freed from them'. In 1661 alms were still being distributed to sixty poor people after the service on Sunday mornings, but it was decided to have the churchwardens or over-seers of the poor compile lists of suitable recipients so that beggars could be excluded. In the future twenty loaves of bread were to be distributed daily, one-third to those who lived within the city walls and two-thirds to those outside. The names of those to whom the baker gave bread were to be checked quarterly in 1690, 'that it may appear how the number of the said Poor doe diminish and cease'. A forlorn hope! In 1630 Exeter agreed to give the poor £18 a year on condition that they did not resort to the homes of the dean and canons. Ely also provided bread for the poor, at a cost of 10s. a week, but did not permit them to come into the cathedral grounds. A bea-dle was hired at Durham in 1625 to keep disorderly wandering beggars out of the college. In 1692 Durham gave a local bookbinder 40s. 'in his great need' but added, rather irritably, 'on condition that he never ask more'. A greater sense of compassion appeared at Exeter in November 1642: the mayor had pressed the chapter on several occasions to help pay for the for-tification of the city, but the clergy decided to make a contribution to poor tradesmen instead, 'because of the great decay of trading' caused by the war.

Alms never constituted one of the major charges in the cathedral accounts and it would be a mistake to exaggerate the involvement of cathedral chap-ters in meeting the needs of the poor in the sixteenth and seventeenth centuries. Since the annual income of Durham was about £1800 the annual allocation for charity was less than 4 per cent. Canterbury, refounded with an endowment of £2542, also spent less than 4 per cent on alms. This evi-dence can perhaps be read as suggesting a less compassionate attitude than that which had prevailed in the middle ages. Nevertheless, substantial gifts continued to be made to groups of sufferers, and a number of needy individuals received help.

The educational institutions associated with the cathedrals made a much greater impact on society than their charitable activities. The situation had been altered dramatically by the Reformation, but the role of the cathedrals remained undiminished and was if anything greater than it had been in earlier centuries.

In all of the medieval cathedral cities, except perhaps Rochester, ancient schools flourished in the fifteenth century. Song schools were of course needed for the choristers. The monastic cathedrals had almonry schools that provided education for poor boys, often relatives of the monks. Grammar schools were affiliated with the secular cathedrals. St Peter's School at York Minster was the largest and most distinguished of these; it probably had more than one hundred students, both poor boys and fee-paying sons of local merchants or wealthy country families. Lincoln, Exeter, Salisbury and

Wells also possessed grammar schools that were quite separate from the choristers' school. In some places new endowments were provided during the reign of Henry VII: at Lichfield, Bishop William Smith turned a decayed hospital into a grammar school in 1495; at Chichester, Bishop Edward Story converted one of the prebends into an endowment for the cathedral school.

The impact of the New Learning was first evident in London, when John Colet established the new St Paul's School in 1509 to provide education in classical Latin and Greek. Dean Colet gave most of his own estate to the school as an endowment, so that free education could be provided to all the students. (He was a rich man, since his father had been lord mayor of London and he was the sole surviving heir out of a family of twenty-two children.) His stated desire was to provide education for young men who sought careers in the world, not in the church; for this reason, and probably because he distrusted the conservative canons of the cathedral, he left the government of the school in the hands of the Mercers' Company rather than the dean and chapter. This arrangement was not emulated elsewhere, but the classical curriculum and to some extent the secular emphasis became increasingly common.

Schools were provided for in virtually all the cathedrals of the New Foundation. Expansive original proposals that would have established centres of higher learning at Canterbury, Westminster and Durham as well as grammar schools in all the cathedrals were scaled down, but the provisions written into charters and statutes were still substantial. The new institutions regarded Henry VIII as their founder and are generally still called the King's Schools. Their size varied according to the wealth and prestige of the cathedral in question: Canterbury was to provide free instruction for fifty boys, Worcester for forty, Chester and Ely for twenty-four, Peterborough and Rochester for twenty. Durham, probably because its statutes were not issued until Mary's reign, was ordered to maintain only eighteen scholars. No new foundation was thought necessary at Winchester, where William of Wykeham's college remained intact and began to admit more local boys as commoners. The school at Oxford did not survive the transfer of the cathedral to Christ Church and its amalgamation with the college. Henry VIII's original letters patent for Norwich ordered that twenty poor children be educated, but statutes were never provided during the Tudor period and, probably for that reason, the cathedral does not actually seem to have had a school at all.

Edward VI's royal injunctions for cathedrals, issued in 1547, required the old secular cathedrals as well as the new foundations to maintain free grammar schools. No details were set out, and no new endowments were given to the cathedrals, which were told to pay the headmaster 20 marks a years and the usher or junior master half that sum out of normal cathedral revenues. Under Mary an attempt was made to turn some of the schools into seminaries for Catholic priests, but, except perhaps at Lincoln and York, it had little effect.

Students accepted into the cathedral schools were to know how to read and write and to possess an elementary knowledge of grammar. Ordinarily they were to be fifteen or younger when admitted and were to remain for four years, or five if the dean judged that appropriate; former choristers might be allowed to enter even if older than fifteen, and were to have preference over other boys. Those who proved to be slow or dull were to be expelled by the dean, 'lest', say the statutes, 'like mildew, [they] consume the honey of the bees'. The masters were to be named by the dean and chapter; an undermaster was to instruct the younger boys, with the headmaster handling the upper forms.

It was originally planned that cathedrals would provide exhibitions (scholarships) for the brightest young men graduating from the grammar schools, so that they could attend Oxford or Cambridge. The number of such awards was to vary from twenty-six at Canterbury to four at Rochester. Financial records at Chester, Hereford, Winchester and Worcester, as well as Canterbury, show that university students were indeed supported for a few years in the 1540s, but the system did not survive the financial crisis of Henry VIII's last years; the cathedrals were forced to restore the endowments devoted to higher education to the crown, and the exhibitions vanished. In a few places private philanthropy helped fill the gap. Archbishop Parker endowed four exhibitions at Corpus Christi College, Cambridge, where he had been master, for boys from the King's School, Canterbury; these were to run for three years, or six if the scholars were candidates for ordination. While dean of Exeter, Simon Heynes had proposed the establishment of scholarships for twelve students at Oxford and twelve at Cambridge, but his scheme was never put into effect.

The largest and finest of the new establishments, both still flourishing, were the King's Schools established at Canterbury and Worcester. The first headmaster at Canterbury, John Twyne, was an active, picturesque character, a Member of Parliament, alderman and sheriff as well as a scholar. Suspected of conjuring and popery, and dismissed for drunkenness in 1560, he lived on until 1581, spending his last years studying early British history. Less is known about John Pether, the first headmaster at Worcester, but he was described as a fit man for the position and held a M.A. from Oxford. His successor, Thomas Bradshaw, was able to take over the former monastic refectory in the cathedral cloister as College Hall; in the early seventeenth century as many as two hundred boys were educated there.

Alexander Nowell was headmaster of Westminster School. When he became dean of St Paul's, Nicholas Udall followed him at Westminster. Famous as the author of *Ralph Roister Doister* and as a grammarian, Udall was thought guilty of sexual relations with his students and would probably have been removed had he not conveniently died. When Westminster Abbey ceased to be a cathedral the school was refounded a second time (it thus regards Elizabeth as *fundatrix*), and provision was made for as many as 120 students. Scholarships were also created so that five or six graduates a year could go on to Christ Church, Oxford, and Trinity College, Cambridge. The first two headmasters at Durham were not university graduates, and Dean Whittingham wrote to Cecil that he had to teach the boys himself three or four hours a day. But Robert Cooke, Francis Key, James Calfhall and Peter Smart, successive masters between 1570 and 1600, all held M.A.s from Oxford or Cambridge. The founding headmaster of College School, Gloucester, was Robert Alfield, who had studied at Eton and King's College, Cambridge, and had taught at Eton before moving to Gloucester. Described as 'eminent for his learning and piety' and notable for the ease with which he shifted his religious views under Edward and Mary, he remained at the school until 1575, when he left to become rector of Bourton-on-the-Water.

During the seventeenth century there were some signs of disciplinary problems among both students and masters. In 1685 Hereford resolved to introduce the discipline of Westminster School and ruled that there be no 'play days' except Tuesday and Thursday afternoons, unless ordered by the bishop, dean, or chapter. A few years later the chapter of Worcester decreed that 'the schoolmaster shall never grant any whole day for Play [and] he shall never grant any time for play upon a Friday, [or] in a week wherein there shall be a Holy-day'. The scholars of Wells were told not to play in the cloisters. Members of the grammar school at Salisbury were warned to avoid fights, fortune tellers and jugglers, and the schoolmaster at Lincoln was reprimanded for not teaching at the prescribed hours.

The most notable problems with schoolmasters occurred at Carlisle. Here it was the mayor and aldermen who initiated a complaint in 1632: since they paid part of the schoolmaster's salary they had a right to be concerned about his performance. In former times, they wrote, 'by reason of painfull schoole-masters', boys from both the city and the country were 'partakers of the inestimable benefitt that came thereby (for this Seminarye was like another Athens to us.)' But 'now it is far otherwise' and townspeople have begun to send their children away to school. The dean and chapter were asked to appoint a new master who 'has the right way of teaching [as well as] good life and manners'. After due examination of those complaints and 'some other abuses (which we forebeare to sett downe herein)', the chapter gave three successive admonitions to the schoolmaster, John Wood. Evidently these were not efficacious. The mayor wrote again to charge Wood with 'unaptnes and want of methode in teaching Grammar [and] alsoe great neglect and want of ordinary paines in instructing his schoolers either in learning or good manners'. He hoped that the 'church and cyttie of Carlisle' might once again be made 'famous and honoured by the painefull labors of a profitable Schoolemaster'. Wood was finally expelled in 1634.

Affairs were no better after the Restoration. In 1689 the schoolmaster, Robert Harrison, was said to be 'negligent and careless, of a very vicious Deportment, and Scandalous Example, by being frequently drunk, and uttering and maintaining very ill Principles'. After two admonitions he was found to 'continue in his former immoralities', but by 1692 the city council thought he could be continued rather than discharged; he had said that he was 'heartily sorry' for his immorality and would live as a good Christian.

All the cathedrals had libraries, sometimes very large ones. These held the most important collections of books outside London and the universities; indeed, in the era before the institution of public libraries, they were almost the only places outside of private homes where books were gathered together.

At several cathedrals library buildings were erected or improved during the seventeenth century. The mayor and aldermen of Gloucester, not the dean and chapter of the cathedral, were responsible for the new library established there in 1648. Since the cathedral was no longer functioning, the chapter house was available for a new use; Thomas Purdy, a local gentleman, was responsible for having it fitted out as a library and for acquiring books, partly at his own expense. Following the Restoration the library was taken over by the dean and chapter, who surprisingly allowed it to remain in the chapter house: since it held only 150 volumes at the end of the Interregnum, it might have been transferred elsewhere. John Evelyn, visiting Gloucester in 1654, commented that this 'new Library' was 'very noble though a private designe'.

The finest new building was the Wren Library at Lincoln. Another major project of the Restoration era was the rebuilding of the former prior's chapel at Canterbury, a thirteenth-century building near the water tower, for use as a library. Earlier in the century the library at Durham, which housed the largest collection of books at any of the cathedrals, was improved with the addition of a new chimney in 1622, shelves and stalls in 1628, and a convenient passage to the cloister in 1636. A former schoolroom was converted into a library at Worcester in 1636, but this did not prove adequate and the chapter house was fitted out as a library in 1671. Considerable sums were spent to repair and beautify the library at Wells in 1670 and 1685. During the 1670s a former vesting room was made into a library at Ely and part of the organist's house at Norwich was reserved for use as a library. At Hereford the vicars choral had their own library, separate from the library of the dean and chapter, and in 1678 they added two new desks, 'uniform with those already set up'.

The appointment of library keepers was often recorded in chapter act books. Thomas Roper, named keeper of the library at St Paul's in 1626, was allowed to serve in person or by deputy but was directed to keep an inventory of the volumes in his care. A minor canon was appointed library keeper at Worcester in 1676, at a salary of £4 a year. This sort of arrangement was common elsewhere, and it provided a convenient way in which members of the choir might supplement their stipends. But greater supervision was perhaps needed: thus the subdean of Worcester assumed the office of library keeper in 1682, with permission to have a deputy (perhaps still a minor canon) who would receive the same £4. Thomas Hitch, a minor canon and sacrist of Ely – the man who had confronted Oliver Cromwell in 1644 – was named library keeper there in 1678. Two library keepers, at salaries of £5 and £2, were appointed at Canterbury in 1672; their duties, including compiling a catalogue, were set out, and in 1674 it was ordered that they not be paid until they fulfilled them. In 1679 the librarian of Wells was also ordered to make an alphabetical catalogue. The books belonging to Winchester, which had been sold in London during the Interregnum but recovered thereafter, were to be 'disposed in some order' and catalogued in 1677; this work was evidently not completed until 1685, when the keepers were given £5 as a reward for their pains. The 'ancient writings' of the church, stored in two barrels, who also sorted and indexed. William Fane, a canon of Wells, arranged and catalogued the books there in 1670. In 1679 it was decided that the care of the library should be committed to someone 'skilled in letters' and a university graduate, Richard Healey, M. A., was appointed. Once again it was said that an alphabetical catalogue was needed.

Libraries were funded in various ways. Gifts and bequests were common. In 1670 a legacy of £500 given to Canterbury by John Warner, the late bishop of Rochester, was used to buy books, and in 1685 part of a bequest from a former canon was designated for beautification of the library at Wells. More than one hundred people contributed funds for the library of the vicars choral at Hereford; the donors included Thomas and John Tomkins, organists of the Chapel Royal, and 'the Right Honourable John Lord Viscount Scudamore, an honourable Friend to this Place, [who] amongst other Testimonies of his Love, gave to this College seven Pounds; with which Sum was bought Ortelii Geographic'. In 1661 Edmund Prideaux gave £100 to the library at Exeter and Thomas Isack left it all his books. Neither of these donors appears to have been a member of the chapter, but at Salisbury one of the prebendaries, Richard Watson, did bequeath all his printed books to the cathedral library on condition he might keep them during his lifetime. Sixty-five books, valued at £50, were given to Worcester Cathedral library by Bishop Walter Blandford; following his death in 1675 they were selected from his personal library by several of the prebendaries. Alexander Hyde, a prebendary of Winchester, bequeathed his five-volume Polyglot Bible to the cathedral. What was probably the largest single gift was a collection of 240 volumes donated to Carlisle Cathedral by the vice-dean, Arthur Savage, shortly before his death in 1700. These included 139 folios, books published on the Continent as well as in England, writers ranging from the church fathers to Erasmus, Luther and Meric Casaubon.

Sometimes ordinary cathedral revenues were used for library purposes. At Durham a special sum of £33 6s. 8d. was allocated to the library in 1679. The accounts at Worcester record a payment of £9 3s. in 1677 for 'Bookes bought for ye Library in London', with further purchases of more than £20 in 1683 and £12 in 1685. The volumes acquired included the Bibliotheca Patrum and the works of Origen. Canterbury paid £5 for 'Dr Morrison's Botanicke Booke' in 1673. We know that Dean Honywood of Lincoln frequently purchased books from a London bookseller, Christopher Wilkinson. Richard Chiswell, a prominent London publisher and bookseller, sent twenty books costing £33 14s. to Durham in 1680. On rare occasions duplicate volumes might be given away; thus in 1623 Worcester Cathedral sent twenty duplicate manuscripts, including the works of Anselm and Augustine, decretals, digests, glosses and dictionaries, to the lord keeper 'towards the furnishing of his library in the Church of Westminster newly erected'.

Some of the cathedral libraries were open to be public. This was stated to be the case at Ely in 1674 and Carlisle in 1691. Strangers wishing to use the library at Wells were required to apply to the dean and pay a fee of 2s. 6d. At Gloucester men who were 'qualified by their birth, their learning, or their devotion to liberal studies, and by their character' might be admitted. At Exeter only the dean and canons were permitted to borrow books, but other persons were probably allowed to use them. A similar rule applied at Worcester. No one was supposed to take books out of the library at Durham without the consent of the dean or a prebendary. In general the implication is that serious students were allowed access to the cathedral libraries but that borrowing privileges were extended only to the cathedral clergy themselves.

Not all comments on the cathedrals and their clergy were critical. In 1675 Thomas Barlow, the newly appointed bishop of Lincoln, wrote to Dean

Honywood of his desire to live at Lincoln as soon as proper accommodation could be provided: 'I have seene, and love ye place, and like it as ye
fittest place of my abode; as for other reasons, soe principally for ye hap-
pines I should injoy in the society of your selfe, and your and my brethren'.

A valedictory comes from the will of Ralph Bathurst, the dean of Wells,
who died in 1704.

> And here I cannot but with a thankfull heart acknowledge and celebrate that good
> providence, by which I first obtained, and have through Gods goodness, these
> many years enjoy'd a serene and well established mind, and that mine own stud-
> ies, and the conversation of many learned and engenuous friends (wherein I have
> long been exceedingly happy) have carried me far above those anxieties, to which
> my self in times past, have not been a stranger and under which the greatest part
> of mankind do labor ... My cup is not only filled, but something there is that
> probably may run over.

It is a moving expression of a cleric's love for the environment provided by
the cathedral close.

16

The Eighteenth
and Nineteenth Centuries

The eighteenth century is often regarded as being a low point in the history of the cathedrals and, indeed, of the Church of England generally. The cathedrals are frequently characterized as being pockets of privilege, lethargy and decadence, inbred and self-centred, staffed by lazy and pompous clerics, little concerned with ordinary people or the hardships of their lives. Many deans and canons were drawn from genteel families and served for long periods of time with minimal duties, sometimes neglecting those obligations they did have. Daniel Defoe, for instance, commented that the clergy at Wells lived very handsomely with 'no want of good company', while a prebendary of Winchester, Edmund Pyle, wrote that 'the life of a prebendary is a pretty easy way of dawdling away one's time; praying, walking, visiting; and as little study as your heart would wish'. The cathedral clergy have been described as 'blameless but idle'. Following the upheavals of the Civil War and Glorious Revolution there was a great desire for stability, and cathedrals sought to support the established order rather than welcoming change. They upheld a faith based on reason and morality; they paid little attention to the Methodists, whose zeal and enthusiasm they despised.[1]

Although there is truth in such judgments, they are probably too harsh. Many members of cathedral chapters were outstanding scholars, and their cathedral appointments gave them the leisure they needed for study. A number held positions at Oxford or Cambridge concurrently with their cathedral appointments. An examination of the writings of the eighteenth-century clergy of Canterbury, in this case including the archbishops as well as members of the cathedral chapter, shows that more than half of the ninety-six clerics published one or more books.[2] These included 268 volumes of sermons, sixty-three theological studies, thirty-eight political or controversial works, thirty-four devotional or popular tracts, twenty-one sets of visitation articles, and fourteen histories, together with a few works of literature and scientific studies. Several of the deans were notable preachers, occupying pulpits at court and in London as well as at Canterbury. George Stanhope, dean from 1704 until his death in 1728, published fifteen sermons in 1700 and twelve more in 1726, as well as translations and pieces of devotional literature. Some of his sermons which were issued separately reveal both the subjects that interested him and the groups before which he was asked to preach. They include *Of Preparation for Death and Judgment*, for the ladies of the late Queen Mary's bedchamber; *The Perfection of Scripture Stated, and its Sufficiency Argued*, a Cambridge University commencement sermon; *The Sea-Man's Obligations to Gratitude and a Good Life*, preached at Dartford for the Corporation of Trinity House; *The Case of Mistaken Zeal*, for the mayor and aldermen of London; *The Duty of Juries*, for the Lent Assizes at Maidstone; *The Danger of Hard-Heartedness to the Poor*, for the charity schools in London and Westminster; *Christianity the Only True Comfort of Troubled Minds*, for Queen Anne; *The Early Conversion of Islanders a Wise Expedient for Propagating Christianity*, for the Society for Propagating the Gospel, and *Death Just a Matter of Joy to Good Men*, at the funeral of a London bookseller. A later dean, George Horne (1781–92), divided his time between Canterbury and Oxford, where he was President of Magdalen College; his published sermons bear such titles as *The Influence of Christianity on Civil Society, Works Wrought through Faith a Condition of our Justification, The Character of True Wisdom*, and *The Providence of God Manifested in the Rise and Fall of Empires*.

Winchester also provided a home for eighteenth-century scholars, who were (as the chapter later maintained) 'free from the anxieties attendant upon a narrow income, and from the incessant cares which belong to the cure of souls'. These men included deans Zachary Pearce, a classicist who produced new editions of Cicero and Longinus as well as commentaries on the books of the New Testament, and Jonathan Shipley, who published two volumes of sermons and delivered notable speeches in the House of Lords praising the settlers in the American colonies. Among the prebendaries one finds William Louth, author of a popular treatise called *Directions for the Profitable Study of Holy Scripture* in addition to commentaries on the Old Testament prophets. His son Robert was even more distinguished. After serving as professor of poetry at Oxford he became archdeacon of Winchester and published a series of lectures in Latin on the sacred poetry of the Hebrews (*De sacra poesi Hebraeorum*). Another archdeacon, Edmund Gibson, later Bishop of London, studied canon law and wrote a standard work, *Codex Iuris Ecclesiastici Anglicani*. The century was also notable for the publication of the earliest books about the cathedral itself, beginning with Samuel Gale's *History and Antiquities of the Cathedral Church of Winchester* (1715). It was not until 1774 that William Gostling produced his famous guide, *A Walk in and about the City of Canterbury*. Gloucester also supported some scholars. Josiah Tucker, who served as dean for most of the second half of the century, was a prolific writer on economic matters. His *Principles of Commerce*, published in 1755, was originally written for the young Prince George, later King George III. In it he attacked slavery and predicted the rise of American prosperity and power. Exeter (to take one more example) had two notable antiquarians, Charles Lyttelton (dean and then bishop, 1747–68) and Jeremiah Milles (dean from 1762 to 1784). Both were fellows of the Royal Society and Lyttelton served as president of the Society of Antiquaries.

Throughout the eighteenth century the financial arrangements for the cathedrals remained essentially the same as those put in place at the time of the Reformation. There were still two sorts of cathedrals. In cathedrals of the old foundation – those that had been secular cathedrals – the dean and individual cathedral clergy held their own landed endowments, known as prebends. The income of the prebendaries was regarded as being personal and was not included in the general funds or accounting of the cathedral. The cathedral itself also held landed estates. Cathedrals of the new foundation, those which had been monastic prior to the Reformation, had more unified procedures. They had been given specific properties that formerly belonged to the monastery. The revenue from these was paid into the cathedral's general fund, which then provided stipends for the clergy. Revenues had changed very little since the sixteenth century. Canterbury, for instance, had been allocated properties that brought in £2542 at the time of the Reformation, and in 1700 they yielded £2628. The wealth of the cathedrals varied enormously. Durham and Winchester were nearly as well endowed as Canterbury. Lincoln was another prosperous cathedral. The lowest revenues continued to be received at Carlisle, which always remained remote and poor. Everywhere the dean was paid substantially more than prebendaries or canons. The stipend of the dean of Canterbury was fixed at £300 while canons received £40. The total income, however, might be substantially higher: the receipts of the dean of Durham usually exceeded £1000 and a residentiary canon there might have as much as £800. Thus the deans were able to live as well as members of the aristocracy and the canons as country gentlemen. Singing men and schoolmasters might be more comfortable than ordinary working people but were little better paid.

Cathedral revenues continued to be derived mainly from endowments in the form of landed estates. Until the 1850s these were usually let on long leases at low and static annual rents. Substantial fines were collected when the leases were renewed. Most leases ran for twenty-one years, but it was common to renew them after the first seven years had expired. Annual rents were substantially below the annual income for each piece of property: an estate worth £50 a year, for instance, normally paid a rent of £10. When the lease was renewed the lessee theoretically paid a fine equal to one year's difference between the income and the rent. Fines were often expressed in some such words as 'one year's rent'; published tables helped the cathedral officials calculate what they should be. Although rents went into the cathedral's general fund, fines were usually divided between the dean and members of the chapter, so that a system which involved low rents and high fines was detrimental to the finance of the cathedral itself.[3]

Although most cathedral estates were agricultural land, there were also properties within the cathedral city. These might be houses, generally located within the cathedral close, shops, taverns and inns, all of which might produce annual rents. They were often leased for forty years, not twenty-one. In some places properties were let for industrial purposes, like the distillery and water mill which operated on land owned by Rochester cathedral. Rochester also profited from chalk mining; in 1758–59 it received £84 for chalk mined on cathedral estates, calculated at the rate of a penny per ton.

It was common for cathedral officials to renew leases without much knowledge of the estates involved. During the earlier part of the eighteenth century rates were rarely raised. The customary leases were adequate to support the clergy and were not inquired into. Rochester, for instance, had a corporate income of about £1300 in 1750 in addition to about £870 from fines. Expenditures also totalled about £1300, of which about £500 went to the dean and prebendaries as stipends, £400 to minor clergy, singers, choristers, scholars in the grammar school and bedesmen, and £273 to running expenses, alms and university exhibitions. Repairs to the fabric were minimal, ranging from nothing to £480 and averaging £113 a year. During the middle years of the century revenues increased because of splendidly successful investments in the South Sea Company. At Norwich the profits shared by the dean and prebendaries rose by a factor of six during the century after 1720; the dean's income increased from £191 to £1254, while the revenues received by each prebendary climbed from £95 to £627. The expenses of running the church in the 1750s were just under £200 a year; they grew by a factor of eight and a half between 1720 and 1820. Financial administration was left in the hands of legal professionals, the chapter clerk, understeward and auditor. At Norwich, and probably elsewhere, such officers served long terms; one auditor, Richard Moss, held office for sixty-one years.

Cathedrals also generally owned the right of presentation to various livings and thus could name the vicars of a number of parish churches within the cathedral city or in neighbouring towns. A modest cathedral like Rochester was patron of twenty-five churches which brought in an annual income of just under £200; rich cathedrals like Durham and York controlled a much larger number of parishes. Such churches had been part of the cathedral estates since the Middle Ages; the cathedral in theory held the rectory, including the right to collect rectorial tithes, while the church was served by a vicar who could collect only the small tithes. In rural areas the great tithes were supposed to equal a tenth of the principal crop and the small tithes a tenth of income from other sources. In towns and cities complex calculations were needed. After the Reformation traditional rates were rarely raised, so the income from such positions was not large, but a parish living could serve as a valuable supplement to the stipend of a minor canon or schoolmaster.

The cathedral services consisted mainly of morning and evening prayer. These were reserved in style and generally conducted with dignity, although one meets a number of references to singers who came late, left early and talked during the prayers. A notorious organist, Stephen Jefferies, astonished the congregation at Gloucester by playing a common ballad following the sermon at a service of thanksgiving in 1688, 'in the hearing of fiftene hundred or two thousand people, to the great scandall of Religion, prophanation of the Church and greivous offence to all good Christians'. When reprimanded he terminated an evensong with another such ballad, so that 'the young gentlewomen invited one another to dance and the strangers cryed it were better that the organs should be pulled down'. Jefferies was also admonished for frequent absences and for failing to educate the choristers, but he remained in office until his death in 1712. Sermons played an important part in the Sunday services; eucharists were rare. At Canterbury weekly communions were introduced in the 1680s through the efforts of Archbishop Sancroft and Dean Tillotson, but it was hard to persuade lay people to attend. At York early morning prayers were said by one of the vicars choral at six o'clock in the summer and seven in the winter. Daily matins were sung at nine and evensong at five; the cathedral was shut at six. By the beginning of the eighteenth century there was a weekly celebration of the eucharist, conducted by three priests. Fast-day sermons were preached in times of national crisis, and there were services of thanksgiving for military victories. Such services were often attended by civic authorities and other persons 'of the better sort'. Weekday congregations were small – Laurence Sterne recorded that on All Saints' Day 1756 he preached to 'one bellows blower, three singing men, one vicar and one residentiary', while another cleric commented that the regular attenders were 'ancient maiden gentlewomen and decayed tradesmen of this town'. During Sunday services, which attracted more people, there were often disruptions; the vicars choral complained that there was such walking, talking and 'shouting with boyes' that their prayers could not be heard, 'though they streine their voices to the

uttermost'. As late as the early nineteenth century attendance at daily services in Norwich averaged only a dozen or so; once there was a single old
woman, in addition to the officials. Yet three hundred or more attended
Sunday services.

In most places the quality of the music was indifferent. Choirs were small
and poorly rehearsed, and singers often remained in office after their voices
decayed. Canterbury did better. During the earlier eighteenth century it was
served by the distinguished organist Daniel Henstridge and the repertory
included services and anthems by Tallis and Tomkins. In most places the
quality of the music appears to have improved after 1760. Musical activity
was stimulated by the beginning of the Three Choirs Festival, held in rotation at Gloucester, Worcester and Hereford. The first advertised meeting was
that at Gloucester in 1723, though in all probability the three choirs had been
joining forces annually several years earlier. William Hine was the Gloucester organist responsible for concerts there. These often included works by
Handel; *Messiah* was first performed in 1742 and *Judas Maccabaeus* thirty
years later. It was not until the nineteenth century, however, that diocesan
choral festivals became common, and the Southern Cathedrals' Festival,
linking Winchester, Salisbury and Chichester, did not begin until 1905.

Cathedral buildings were little altered during the century. A great storm
in November 1703 caused damage at many cathedrals and killed Richard
Kidder and his wife when the chimney stacks of the bishop's palace at Wells
fell and debris suffocated them in their beds. Restoration followed in several
places, including Canterbury. In 1704 the great woodcarver Grinling Gibbons provided a new archbishop's throne at Canterbury. The choir of
Gloucester was refurbished in 1701. A new reredos was installed in 1716 and
a new choir screen was designed by William Kent in 1741. Towers were
repaired at York, Norwich, Rochester and Peterborough. A fire at York in
1753 necessitated reconstruction of part of the roof. Earlier the Minster had
been repaved to an elegant design by Kent and Lord Burlington. The
stained-glass windows also received constant attention throughout the century. At Exeter the great west window was reglazed, utilizing medieval glass
taken from other windows. The architect James Essex saved the west front
at Ely, which was leaning out of the perpendicular, and also worked at Lincoln. At Hereford the west tower fell on Easter Monday 1786; despite earlier
warnings it had not been shored up. Here the reconstruction was done by
James Wyatt, who demolished one bay of the nave and rebuilt the entire
west end. As he did elsewhere, Wyatt succeeded in tidying things up neatly,
but Victorian critics scorned his work and often attacked him as 'the
Destroyer'. A. W. N. Pugin, who had different ideas of Gothic, denounced
him bitterly. 'I rush to the cathedral [at Hereford]', he wrote; 'but horror;

dismay! The villain Wyatt had been there, the West Front was his! Need I say more? No! All that is vile, cunning and rascally is included in the term Wyatt'. In the end the chapter at Hereford came to agree; in 1908 the west front was redesigned by Oldrid Scott. It is fortunate that Wyatt's proposal to knock down the Galilee at Durham and replace it with a roadway was not followed, nor was his design to enlarge the choir at Westminster Abbey by demolishing the shrine of Edward the Confessor. The Gothic Revival began about 1770, but its principal achievements did not come until the nineteenth century.

The cathedral close served as a link between the cathedral and the community. Houses in the precincts provided homes for members of the cathedral staff, but a number were let to outsiders. The precincts might also include alehouses, shops and offices. The wives of prebendaries helped develop a good social and intellectual atmosphere, and cathedral greens provided a place which the children of clergy and their servants could play. But there could be problems. At Canterbury the dean and chapter had to demand the removal of cattle, horses and geese which were grazing in the cloisters, and in the early nineteenth century they objected to the havoc caused by the annual fair – they resolved to allow no swings, puppet shows, gin stalls or wild beasts within the precincts. At Lincoln a constable was appointed to prevent poor dole boys from frequenting the close or the cathedral itself, and in 1733 it was decided that the cathedral doors should be locked except at times of worship 'by reason of the many indecencys and disorders dayly committed in the Minster'. As late as 1858 it was discovered that the statues on the west front of Wells were being damaged by stones thrown at them by boys playing on the green, and in the 1870s the east window at Chichester was broken by a marble fired from a catapault. There were also complaints about women beating carpets or drying clothes within the cathedral precincts. Eventually most of these disorders died out and a more welcoming atmosphere came to prevail. At Hereford, for instance, it was decided in 1876 that the cathedral would be open from 9 a.m. to 6 p.m. daily. Here the city council had passed a resolution in 1851 thanking the dean and chapter for 'the great improvements they had carried out in the close, improvements which the commissioners feel are as much a credit to the city as they are satisfactory to the inhabitants'. In many places city officials were allowed to assume greater control of the grounds adjacent to the cathedrals by the end of the century.[4]

The eighteenth century witnessed an increased vogue for tourism at the cathedrals. This was perhaps most pronounced at Canterbury, not only because of importance of the cathedral's history and architecture but because the city was strategically placed on the main road from London to

Dover and thus on the route of tourists travelling to and from the Continent. The dean and chapter responded by publishing histories and guide books, some of which are notable for the way in which they expounded a Protestant view of the church's development. Norwich, then England's second-largest city, also drew numbers of tourists, although some of them were disappointed in the cathedral and its setting. One visitor commented, 'the cathedral itself is large but I think not fine, though there has been a great deal done towards cleaning and sprucing it up'.

Eighteenth-century attitudes generally continued to dominate the English church until the 1830s. When he attended matins at Winchester on the last Sunday in October 1825, William Cobbett found 'a dean and God knows how many prebends belonging to this immensely rich bishopric and chapter; and there were at this "service" two or three men and five or six boys in white surplices, with a congregation of fifteen women and four men! Gracious God!' Three elements can be seen in such criticisms. There was anger at the wealth of the cathedrals, regret at finding such small congregations, and a worldly approach that acknowledged the artistic beauty of the architecture but found little beyond a curiosity value in the present-day life and work of the institutions.

The demand for ecclesiastical reform ran parallel to the political movement that led to the Parliamentary Reform Act of 1832. It had begun in the late eighteenth century, when such leaders as Bishop Richard Watson of Llandaff acknowledged that a fairer distribution of church revenues was needed. Animosity against the church increased after most of the bishops in the House of Lords voted against the Reform Act proposed in 1831. In June 1832, after the Act finally passed, the Prime Minister (Earl Grey) appointed an Ecclesiastical Commission and charged it with investigating church finances. Two years later his successor, Sir Robert Peel, argued that the influence of the Established Church could be extended and its true interests promoted by an improved distribution of its revenues. A commission report published in 1835 proposed the abolition of all non-residentiary canonries in the cathedrals, a reduction to four in the number of residentiaries, and the appropriation of separate estates of the deans and prebendaries in cathedrals of the old foundation. There was also to be a reduction in the number of vicars choral or minor canons. It was believed that these measures would produce something like £130,000 a year which could be spent to augment poor livings and build new churches in populous urban areas.[5]

Naturally the cathedrals resisted such change and attempted to defend their position. The dean and chapter of Canterbury argued that a reduction in the number of residentiary canons would be disastrous, for the presence of at least two was essential while age and illness often prevented canons from constant attendance. The clergy of Bristol were distressed that no notice was taken of the ancient constitution of cathedral bodies. The dean and chapter of Durham, among the wealthiest in the realm, said that the proposed changes would 'go far to destroy the influence and usefulness of cathedral establishments, and to render them unfit to accomplish the objects for which they are to be preserved'. Lincoln, which had an unusually large number of prebendaries, held that 'fifty-two dignities, or nearly so, abstracted at once from our magnificent foundation we cannot but contemplate as an act nearly allied to sacrilege'.

One of the leading opponents of change was Bishop Van Mildert of Durham, the founder of Durham University. After his death in 1836 the archbishop of Canterbury, William Howley, came to support the calls of Peel and Melbourne for reform. A more powerful advocate was Charles James Blomfield, bishop of London, who made a telling speech in the House of Lords in 1840. As he passed St Paul's Cathedral he saw 'a dean, and three residentiaries, with incomes amounting in the aggregate to between £10,000 and £12,000 a year' as well as twenty-nine clergymen 'whose offices are all but sinecures', yet a mile or two to the east he was 'in the midst of an immense population in the most wretched state of destitution and neglect', with only 'one church and one clergyman for every 8,000 or 10,000 souls'.

So the Cathedrals Act (technically the Ecclesiastical Commissioners Act) finally passed; it came into effect in August 1840. The statute fixed the number of canons in each cathedral at four, except for Canterbury, Durham and Ely, which were allowed six, and Winchester and Exeter, which were given five. Superfluous canonries were to be abolished as they became vacant. The number of minor canons was limited to six, with a minimum of two. The profits of suspended canonries were to be paid to the Ecclesiastical Commissioners, who would also take over the separate estates of the cathedral dignitaries. The stipends of deans were fixed at £1000 except for the deans of Durham (allowed £3000) and St Paul's, Westminster and Manchester (£2000 each). Most canons were to be paid £500.

Some clergy came to appreciate the value of such reforms. Perhaps the most important of these was E. B. Pusey, Professor of Hebrew at Oxford, canon of Christ Church, and a leader of the Oxford Movement. 'The body of cathedral clergy', he wrote, 'have been called to re-examine the nature of their institutions, their duties and responsibilities, and the means of fulfilling them. While impressing upon others the importance of their office in the Church, they have probably deepened their own consciousness of it'.

The revenues taken from cathedrals and transferred to the augmentation of poorer livings amounted to about £300,000 a year. Since the change occurred gradually, as canonries became vacant, most cathedrals did not suffer significant loses immediately. But the agricultural depression of the late nineteenth century led to financial crises as the value of landed estates declined. At Canterbury, for instance, the dean and canons received only half their stipends in 1892 and took only £400 and £200 respectively in 1894. Most cathedrals found themselves in a similar situation. Despite continuing discussion of reform, no further statutes affecting the cathedrals were passed, but in most places landed endowments were transferred to the Ecclesiastical Commissioners during the 1860s.

Financial troubles were compounded by the fact that many of the cathedrals were in poor physical condition at the beginning of the nineteenth century. It is almost unbelievable that the great Galilee at Durham lay in near ruin, but a letter printed in the *Gentleman's Magazine* in 1802 said that its condition 'was the most reprehensible, in regard to the roof being in many parts without covering, the pavement strewed with heaps of coal and all kinds of building materials, the north aisle partitioned off into offices'. In 1806 rain poured through the roof of the nave at Winchester. There was doubt that the Three Choirs Festival should be held at Worcester in 1833 because of fear that the groined vaults might fall. Even Canterbury had broken windows, weed-covered sills, and walls streaked with damp. In addition there were special problems, the most disastrous being two great fires at York. The earlier, on 1 February 1829, was the result of arson planned by a deranged Methodist fanatic who had hid in the north transept following the close of evensong. The minster lost most of its choir, including the fourteenth-century wooden roof, sixty-six carved stalls, the archbishop's throne, the pulpit, the entire organ and a valuable collection of music manuscripts. The great east window barely survived; the nave remained intact, only to be gutted by a second fire in 1840. The architect Sir Robert Smirke was placed in charge of the earlier restoration at York, which he estimated would cost not less than £60,000, not including the organ. To meet these charges the dean and chapter had to sell their most valuable asset, Serjeants' Inn in London, and to undertake one of the earliest campaigns for public support. The other great loss was the collapse of the central tower and spire of Chichester in 1861.

The greatest of the nineteenth-century ecclesiastical architects was a pupil of Smirke, George Gilbert Scott. Named architect of Ely in 1847, he was shortly put in charge at Hereford, Lichfield, Salisbury and Westminster Abbey. In the end all the old cathedrals except St Paul's, Carlisle and Llandaff saw his work. His enormous practice required the assistance of a number of gifted pupils, who included G. E. Street and G. F. Bodley as well as his own sons John Oldrid and George Gilbert Scott, Jr. His knowledge of medieval Gothic work was immense and his taste broad: he refused to follow the Cambridge Ecclesiologists in their single-minded admiration of the Decorated style or, later, the 'first pointed' Early English. Attacked by William Morris, founder of the Society for the Preservation of Ancient Buildings in 1877, he defended himself in his *Personal and Professional Recollections*, saying that he too deplored unnecessary destruction but recognized the desirability of modifying historic buildings to meet present needs. At Hereford and Ely he replaced solid choir pulpitums with lighter choir screens which permitted a view through to the east end. At Ely he also moved the choir stalls to the west and restored the lantern, which had been altered by Essex, to its original form. Scott's plan for refitting the choir of Canterbury, submitted in 1876, proved controversial, primarily because Scott wished to remove the stalls and panelling at the west end of the choir: the 'Gothicists' believed that the existing panelling was carved by Grinling Gibbons and thus inviolable, but Scott was able to show that this was untrue and that its removal would reveal an early fourteenth-century screen which was the work of William of Eastry. Here the main phase of Victorian restoration ended in the late 1870s, and in 1893 the fabric was said to be in good repair, though the cloisters needed attention. Scott was knighted in 1872 and is buried in Westminster Abbey.

At Wells a comprehensive restoration was completed in the 1850s. First the Lady chapel and nave were stripped of whitewash, revealing the beautiful natural stone and carved capitals. Then the choir was cleaned of the offending wash and artificial green marble paint was removed from the bishop's throne. The architect, Anthony Salvin, also introduced new choir stalls. The total cost of work on the choir was nearly £5000, of which the dean, Richard Jenkyns, subscribed £1000. Scott supervised work at Hereford, completed in 1863. Here he restored the Norman choir, moving the stalls to their original position, and rebuilt the north transept, replacing several round windows which had been removed by earlier builders. In addition he stabilized the foundations of the choir aisles and transepts. He was responsible for restoration at Gloucester, where he worked with the local architect F. S. Waller. Scott introduced a new screen, font and reredos, and supervised the laying of a new tile floor in the choir. New choir stalls were carved, but care was taken to include misericords and other medieval work that remained in good condition. Whitewash was also removed from the from the Lady chapel. After Scott's death in 1878 Waller remained in charge, assisted by the London architect John Loughborough Pearson.

Anthony Salvin and Edward Blore were the principal Victorian architects at Norwich. Here they had to rebuild the west front (none too successfully). In 1867 Scott proposed changes to the choir, for he found the arrangement of the organ and galleries 'exceedingly objectionable', but shortage of funds caused the work to be postponed. It was completed later by Pearson, who moved medieval stalls into the transepts and added substalls of his own design. Scott was responsible for restoration and modification of the west front at Bath, about 1860. At Salisbury he removed Wyatt's furniture and fittings from the choir and Lady chapel, introducing new work which in its turn was taken out in the 1950s. Scott also undid much of Wyatt's work at Lichfield, where he was succeeded as architect by his son Oldrid. Both Scott and Pearson modified the fine fifteenth-century choir at Bristol, but it remained for G. E. Street to build a new nave (generally following the style of the choir) and a new west end (generally thought to be undistinguished). Scott also worked in Wales: at St David's he reconstructed the west front, removing an ill-advised scheme by John Nash, and he introduced a much-needed drainage system.

The nineteenth century saw the establishment of a number of new dioceses, created in areas where the old bishoprics were too large for effective administration. Earlier there had been a legal view that the church could not have more than twenty-six bishops, and when the new sees of Manchester and Ripon were established attempts were made to keep the number right by uniting Bristol with Gloucester and attempting to join St Asaph with Bangor. Fortunately this view did not prevail long, and the old arrangements were reinstated. With new dioceses it became necessary to create a number of new cathedrals. This was easiest in places like Manchester and Ripon, where a collegiate establishment had survived from the middle ages. At Manchester Charles I had re-established a foundation with a warden, four fellows and a choir. This was easily converted into a cathedral in 1847; the great Perpendicular building needed little modification.

The earliest scheme for an entirely new cathedral was conceived at Truro in Cornwall by the first bishop, E. W. Benson, about 1877. Although there had been an Anglo-Saxon diocese of Cornwall, it was merged with the diocese of Exeter in 1050 and had Exeter Cathedral as its mother church until 1876. At Truro a small existing parish church was incorporated into a cathedral designed by J. L. Pearson and completed early in the twentieth century by his son Frank. Often considered to be Pearson's finest work, Truro is mainly Early English in style but displays a number of French elements. At Liverpool a new cathedral was built following the creation of the diocese in 1880. A competition was held and was won by Scott's brilliant but Catholic grandson Giles, then only twenty-two years old; building did not begin until 1904 and the nave remained incomplete when Giles died in 1960. The sheer scale of Liverpool cathedral is what amazes the viewer, reminding us of the importance of the great port city in the nineteenth century. The central tower can be seen for miles. The fine detailed craftsmanship is also remarkable.

At St Albans in Hertfordshire, near the northern fringes of London, a great medieval monastery which had become a parish church at the time of the Reformation was raised to cathedral status in 1877. Scott had begun restoration some twenty years earlier, but it is the name of Lord Grimthorpe that is always associated with the building. A successful lawyer and amateur architect, Grimthorpe designed a west front that has been condemned by critics from that day to this. Wherever he found Perpendicular work Grimthorpe eliminated it in favour of the Early English which he preferred. He did allow the great Norman central tower, built mainly of bricks taken from the adjoining Roman city of Verulamium, to remain; it had once had a spire, but this was removed in the 1830s. It may be that criticism of Grimthorpe has been excessive: whatever his failings as an architect, it should be acknowledged that he spent vast amounts of his own money on stabilizing and restoring the cathedral.

The remaining new dioceses of the Victorian era were established in northern England. These included Ripon and Wakefield in Yorkshire (1836 and 1888 respectively), Newcastle (finally carved out of the diocese of Durham, as had been proposed several centuries before, in 1882), and South-well (taken from the diocese of York to serve Nottinghamshire in 1884). In all these places there were fine medieval buildings, the collegiate churches at Ripon and Southwell being the greatest. Additions and restorations were of course necessary; George Gilbert Scott worked at Ripon and Wakefield, and the younger Pearson extended the east end of Wakefield in the early twentieth century. Unlike the old cathedrals, the new establishments also served as parish churches.

The Roman Catholic church was finally allowed to create thirteen English bishoprics in 1850. It was not permitted to adopt territorial titles which were already in use by Anglicans, so Westminster had to be used in place of London and Clifton instead of Bristol. The cathedral in London proved to be such a low priority that construction did not begin until 1895. A scheme for a building in the Early English style was rejected on the grounds that it might compete with Westminster Abbey, which was close to the proposed site in Victoria. The present imposing structure (its interior mosaics still incomplete) was designed by J. F. Bentley in the Byzantine style of the cathedrals at Venice and Ravenna; its grandest features are its tower and its domes.

Changes in cathedral worship during the nineteenth century were as notable as those in the buildings. Eighteenth-century practices remained dominant during the first half of the century: the offices of morning prayer and even-song were said or sung daily, but eucharists were rare. Apparently the only choral eucharist offered in 1802 was at Durham, where it was said to be cel-ebrated with the utmost solemnity, but only on the first Sunday of the month. Non-communicants, probably most of the congregation, retired after the sermon.

Surveys conducted by the Cathedral Commissioners give us a better pic-ture of worship in the 1850s. On Sundays there were two choral services in all the English and Welsh cathedrals except Llandaff. There were sermons at both services in half the cathedrals, only one in the other half. Communion was celebrated monthly in seventeen cathedrals, twice a month in one, and weekly in twelve. Partly because of the growing influence of the Oxford Movement, more frequent celebrations of the eucharist were introduced during the second half of the century. A said weekly communion at 8 a.m. was added at Salisbury in 1851. By 1872 the Sunday services at St Paul's included an 8 o'clock communion in one of the chapels, sung morning prayer and sermon at 10.30, litany, anthem, sermon and hymn at 3.15, and evening prayer with a hymn and sermon at 7 p.m. A weekly sung eucharist was introduced the next year. Choral eucharists on great festivals were first held at Winchester in 1864, and the dean of York had such a service when the Church Congress met there in 1866. Some comments by the precentor of Worcester are interesting. He had no objection to a weekly choral commun-ion but thought it should be offered at 8 a.m.: at later services 'the solemnity of a choral eucharist was disturbed by the withdrawal of a large part of the congregation, first before the sermon and secondly after the Church Militant Prayer, leaving a few old fashioned people behind, to whom the music was not helpful'. But he came to accept a later service, provided that it began no later than 10.30 so that the lay clerks who lived some distance from the cathedral could be home in good time for an early dinner.

It is not easy to get an accurate impression of the size of congregations at these services. In 1839 it was said that St Paul's often had 150 people at week-day evensongs and that on Sundays the choir was 'full to suffocation'. More precise statistics survive for Worcester; in 1847 the number of communicants varied between four and thirty-five on ordinary Sundays with fifty-seven on Christmas Day and sixty-three at Easter. By the end of the century Worces-ter had thirty to forty communicants at the early service and twenty to thirty at 11.30. It was said that services at York in 1847 were 'thinly attended'. In 1848 a Member of Parliament gave the Commons some figures for the aver-age size of congregations at weekday services. For Canterbury he listed twenty-five at matins and fifty-three at evensong. Evensong at Durham attracted a group ranging from twenty-five to thirty-seven. Peterborough had the smallest attendance, only seven. By the end of the century there were improvements in some places. The organist of York Minster, John Camidge, attributed increased attendance to improvements in the quality of the music; he said that the choir, which could accommodate two thousand, was sometimes not large enough to hold all the worshippers. Manchester also had large congregations, allegedly nearly four thousand every Sunday.

It was partly in an attempt to attract larger congregations that many of the cathedrals introduced Sunday evening congregational services, often held in the nave with music by voluntary choirs. Durham took the lead in 1837, followed by Wells in 1841. Experimental nave services were held at St Paul's during the Great Exhibition of 1851 and were revived by Bishop Tait in 1858. In that year a service held on Advent Sunday attracted such an enormous crowd that 2500 chairs were brought in and the floor was covered with matting; it was said that at least ten thousand people were unable to get into the cathedral and that Ludgate Hill was completely blocked. Nave services at Rochester were introduced in 1852 but discontinued in 1865, supposedly because of inadequate heating. Heat was installed in 1866 but the services were not revived until 1880. Such services attracted members of the working class who did not ordinarily frequent the cathedral; their popularity depended in large part on charismatic preaching, such as that by H. P. Liddon, one of the canons of St Paul's. Crowds of up to six thousand flocked to hear him. In 1878 the Manchester *Guardian* noted the success of evening services at Chester, Gloucester, St Paul's, Westminster Abbey, Worcester and York; other sources add Bristol, Ely, Lincoln, Manchester and Norwich to the list. Not all the cathedral clergy were enthusiastic about this form of worship. The dean and chapter of Canterbury, for instance, argued that the nave was too large and cold for use except as a novelty in the summer, and in general they opposed alterations to the traditional pattern of worship. Nor were evening services introduced at Winchester and Chichester. Their popularity seems to have been declining everywhere by the end of the century.

Attendance at traditional sung services, however, increased. In part this was because of improvement in the quality of the music. Throughout the earlier decades of the century many choirs were small and the singers' attendance was irregular. In 1876 the new organist at Gloucester, who had just succeeded S. S. Wesley, found the standard of singing at a very low ebb. On at least one occasion the choir consisted of choristers and a single bass who was also the dean's butler. The training of choristers was left in the hands of one of the lay clerks, and during rehearsals the men merely whispered their parts rather than singing them. Four years later a meeting of cathedral organists said that every choir should have twelve lay clerks and twenty choristers, but this remained a goal which was often not reached. The choir at Lincoln was said to have improved wonderfully between 1850 and 1895; in 1878 the precentor of Worcester also reported 'a great improvement both in the singing and also in the behaviour of the choir during the last few months'. In most places the repertory remained mainly Victorian; few Tudor anthems were sung. Congregational singing became more popular, especially after the publication of *Hymns Ancient and Modern* in the 1860s. In some cathedrals hymns replaced the anthem on one or two days of the week. Diocesan music festivals also became common; among the most successful were those at Winchester and York.

The Victorian age was a high era for cathedrals. New railway lines made them accessible to large numbers of people who travelled in search of history, art or music. Such visitors, however, were not always a blessing. When a trainload of men from Derby came to Lincoln in 1848 the cathedral was filled with 'an immense crowd of the lowest description of mechanics, many, nay most of them, wearing their hats, and all talking aloud, laughing and jesting in the most irreverent way'. At Ripon Cathedral, according to a visiting priest, 'crowds of children were playing at hide-and-seek in all parts of it. A party of youths and girls had made their way to the font and were amusing themselves with splashing the water it contained on each other'. In later years, after travel became less of a novelty, some tourists did respond to notices like that posted at Chichester in 1889 requesting them to abstain from irreverent and unseemly conduct in the house of God. The number of visitors at St Paul's was estimated at 48,000 in 1840 and 71,000 in 1845. At about the same time Manchester had 250 visitors a day.

All the cathedrals of the New Foundation maintained grammar schools, although some of the old ones did not. In several places choristers' schools began taking in other pupils. Here again there were problems during the first half of the century, but the standard rose during its later years. In 1833 Pusey suggested that theological colleges be established at the cathedrals. Five years later such a college was founded at Chichester, with Wells soon following suit. By 1876 there were theological colleges at Ely, Exeter, Gloucester, Lichfield, Lincoln and Salisbury as well. In most places they served to train candidates for the priesthood who had not attended university until the middle of the twentieth century, when most closed their doors. Cathedral libraries remained important, and their condition was notably improved in many places. At the middle of the century Durham had the largest collection of books, 11,000 volumes. There were 8000 at York and St Paul's, with the other libraries holding between 5000 and 2000. Access was generally restricted but in most places serious students as well as members of the cathedral staff were accommodated. Cathedral archives were also put in order. About 1874 a friend of the chancellor of Lincoln wrote that he would never forget the sight of the place – 'deal boxes, shelves, pigeon holes, crammed with bundles of papers black with age, shrivelled parchments, deeds with huge beeswax seals attached, the whole thing incredibly filthy and neglected'. By 1883 most items had been cleaned and catalogued, and a number had been published.

All in all the Victorian era saw vast improvements in cathedrals. Buildings were restored, the standards of liturgy and music were raised, celebrations of the holy communion became more frequent, attendance increased, education was fostered, and crowds of tourists were accommodated. In many places, too, public campaigns to raise funds for the restoration and maintenance of cathedrals were successful and demonstrated a high level of support and affection.

17

The Twentieth Century

The early years of the twentieth century saw the second phase of the movement to create new dioceses and cathedrals, as the church continued to go beyond historic towns into places without any great ecclesiastical tradition but where there were urgent population needs. In all, twelve more bishoprics were established in England and two in Wales. The total number of cathedrals during the later twentieth century was forty-two, and it seemed doubtful that more would be created.[1]

The first of the new twentieth-century cathedrals were Birmingham, where a fine parish church built by Thomas Archer in the classical style in 1708 was raised to cathedral status, and Southwark, south of the Thames in London. In an unfortunate location surrounded by rail lines, surely the least attractive cathedral site in England, this utilized the church of the great dissolved monastery of St Mary Overy. Both became cathedrals in 1905. Southwark was notable because it continued a significant ministry as a parish church, with more communicants than any other cathedral. Sheffield and Bury St Edmunds (also called St Edmundsbury) followed in 1913, Chelmsford in 1914. At Bury an early sixteenth century Perpendicular parish church had already been restored by Sir George Gilbert Scott and had a new tower added at the end of the twentieth century. Sheffield and Chelmsford too had large parish churches, typical of prosperous towns. In both cases the nave had been rebuilt early in the 1800s. An elaborate plan for the extension of Sheffield, prepared by Sir Charles Nicholson in 1936, was abandoned following the Second World War, but Nicholson did extend the building at Chelmsford in the 1920s, adding a chapter house and vestries. The cathedral at Coventry served a diocese founded in 1918. At Bradford in Yorkshire a chapel dating to the thirteenth century became a cathedral in 1919. In 1926 a Victorian Gothic church of about 1820 became the cathedral of Blackburn in Lancashire. Finally, in 1927, new bishoprics were founded at Derby, Leicester, Portsmouth and Guildford. The medieval parish church at Derby had been rebuilt by Gibbs in 1723, while that at Portsmouth received a new nave built by Nicholson in the late 1930s. Although Guildford was originally served by an existing parish church, an entirely new structure was designed by Sir Edward Maufe in 1932. Building was interrupted by the Second World

War but completed in 1961; the cathedral is in a simplified Gothic style but is constructed of brick, not stone. In Wales, the cathedral established at Brecon in 1923 was a twelfth-century priory restored by Scott, while the diocese of Monmouth, created in 1921, remained without a centre until the Norman church at Newport was confirmed as a cathedral in 1949. It was substantially extended eastward in the early 1960s.

Stabilization, restoration and modernization continued at most of the old cathedrals. The earliest important project was at Winchester. Here it was discovered that the great cathedral had been built without proper foundations and that there was water beneath much of it. William Walker, who came to be known as Walker the Diver, worked under the building from 1906 until 1912, handling more than 25,000 bags of concrete and nearly 115,000 concrete blocks. In addition about 900,000 bricks were used. Other workers forced some five hundred tons of grouting into cracked walls and inserted more than sixteen tons of tie rods. The cathedral architect, J. B. Coulson, originally estimated the cost of restoration at £3000 but the final total was £113,000, an enormous sum at the time. In 1908 Oldrid Scott was engaged to rebuild the west front of Hereford, which had been damaged by an earthquake in 1896. Few were sorry to see Wyatt's façade go; Scott's design, if unexciting, is surely superior.

At York it was found that more than half of the 109 medieval windows needed attention. An appeal to raise £50,000 was launched in 1920. At first contributions came in well, but they lagged during the great depression and it was not until the eve of the Second World War that the target was reached. A separate campaign provided funding for the restoration of the Five Sisters windows in memory of the women of the empire who had given their lives in war – in the end more than a thousand names were inscribed on an adjacent oak screen.

In addition to such special appeals, most places saw the foundation of groups of Friends of the Cathedral. The earliest such organization was established at Canterbury in accordance with a suggestion made by Dean G. K. A. Bell in 1926. Membership stood at 750 when the first meeting was held in November 1927. The subscription was fixed at only five shillings, but this proved enough to support urgent work on the medieval water tower. The Friends of York Minster, established in 1928, soon had more than a thousand members. Among the other early groups were the Friends of Norwich, formed in 1929, the Friends of Winchester in 1931 and the Friends of Hereford in 1932. In 1994 the total number of Friends for all the cathedrals stood at 53,713 and their net assets were just under £5 million; 70 per cent of their total income was being distributed in grants and donations. Some groups had American branches.

Most of the cathedrals escaped serious damage during the Second World War. Manchester and Llandaff were hit by bombs, as was Exeter, where the beautiful small chapel dedicated to St James was destroyed. Westminster Abbey was also hit, but only the roof of the lantern at the crossing suffered serious damage. To some extent the city of Canterbury was an innocent target, for German planes which had been unable to drop bombs on their original targets, mainly industrial towns, unloaded them before reaching the coast. But some of the bombing was probably a deliberate 'Baedeker Raid'. The cathedral, almost miraculously, remained intact. Fire watchers spent many nights atop St Paul's during the Battle of Britain and were able to limit the damage from two high explosive bombs which pierced its roof. One of these smashed the high altar. Its great marble reredos, designed in 1888 by G. F. Bodley, remained largely intact, but when restoration was complete it had been replaced by a baldacchino based on Wren's original plans – it had not been constructed in the seventeenth century because it was thought to be reminiscent of St Peter's in Rome and thus popish. In many places stained-glass windows were removed and stored in safe locations, including caves in Wales.

The worst devastation took place in Coventry, a natural target because of its industrial complex. Earlier chapters have hinted at the unusual history of the diocese. From 1121 until 1238 Coventry was a separate bishopric, with St Mary's priory serving as its cathedral. In 1240 a single bishop was consecrated to serve both Lichfield and Coventry. As we have seen, he had two cathedrals until the time of the Reformation, when the Dissolution of the Monasteries brought about the closure of the cathedral priory. In 1918 the bishoprics were again separated, and the parish church of St Michael became the cathedral for Coventry diocese. It was one of the great Perpendicular civic churches and boasted a thirteenth-century south porch. On 14 November 1940 this building was completely gutted by fire bombs. It had not been protected by fire-watchers, as many other cathedrals had been, because the watchers were all employed at the factories and the cathedral was not regarded as being a high priority. As a result, the damage was much worse, and so was the trauma. The walls of the cathedral remained largely intact, and for a time it was suggested that it might be rebuilt. The final decision, however, was to leave it as a ruin memorializing the war's tragedy – there is a poignant inscription, 'Father Forgive' – and to construct a new cathedral, in the style of the mid twentieth century, adjoining it.

A competition was won by Sir Basil Spence. His dramatic entrance porch, supported by tall plain columns, connects the old and new buildings. To its right is a sculpture by Sir Jacob Epstein (one of his last works) depicting St Michael expelling Satan from Paradise. The west wall is almost entirely glass. There is a remarkable baptistery, with a font which is a rough boulder brought from Bethlehem and a vast multi-coloured window designed by John Piper. The east end of the cathedral is dominated by a tapestry made in France to a pattern by Graham Sutherland; seventy-five feet high, it is said to be the world's largest tapestry. A central figure of Christ is surrounded by symbols of the four Evangelists. As one critic wrote, it is 'spiky and thorny like so much of the cathedral's symbolism', a comment that might also be applied to the chapel of Gethsemane which is dominated by a screen representing the Crown of Thorns. At the time of its construction Coventry was much admired; many pilgrims were moved by its conception and those interested in ecclesiastical art praised the works commissioned from leading painters and sculptors. More recent judgments see the cathedral mainly as a work of its era, not timeless like the great churches of the Middle Ages. It remains true that Coventry came out of the blitz experience changed and enlarged, whereas the other cathedrals took the events in stride yet perhaps failed to benefit from them.

In other places restoration continued, generally not associated with war damage. The great spire of Salisbury was worked on twice. The lesser spire at Norwich also needed attention and was stabilized in the 1960s. At Wells a comprehensive scheme of cleaning, involving both walls and sculpture, was undertaken in 1975. Painstakingly done using only a lime poultice and toothbrushes, not sand blasting, this revealed afresh the glories of the west front with its medieval statutes. For a few years the stone glowed a marvellous golden or honey colour; it has now returned to a more normal grey. The unique Vicars' Close with its hall and chapel was also restored. The central tower of York was stabilized in 1967. Scaffolding which had long marred the west front was removed at about the same time. In 1984 a fire broke out in the south transept, destroying the painted wood roof and causing considerable additional damage. Some conservatives said that it was God's judgment on the cathedral, where a supposedly free-thinking new bishop of Durham had just been consecrated, but the true cause was lightning. The ceiling, which was in any case not actually medieval, was superbly restored, but at considerable cost. The foundations of the minster were also underpinned and some of the excavated areas were left open for visitors to see. New heat and lighting were installed at Gloucester in the 1950s and in several other cathedrals at about the same time. Late in the century the façade of Lincoln was cleaned. At Canterbury the library was improved, rectifying war damage, and a programme of replacing decayed stonework in the cloister continued. A new Cathedrals Measure which came into force in 1990 established fabric advisory committees for each cathedral, consisting of experts in architecture, archaeology and art history as well as representatives of local conservation groups. Limited state aid for urgent repairs was made available for the first time in the same year; earlier the cathedrals had stated, accurately, that they received no funding from the government.

The cost of maintaining the cathedral buildings and their staff suggested the necessity of introducing entrance fees for tourists. This was done at Ely, St Paul's, Salisbury, Winchester and a number of other places. Some deans and chapters, however, opposed mandatory charges; instead they sought voluntary contributions from visitors and often posted notices reminding them of the cost of running the establishments. As the century ended only Canterbury, Ely and St Paul's had mandatory admission charges.

In some places the number of tourists created severe problems for the cathedrals. This was particularly true at Canterbury and St Paul's, as well as at Westminster Abbey. The increased number of travellers from the Continent began to strain resources at Canterbury in the 1960s. There were about two and a half million visitors to the cathedral each year in the early 1990s, with 224,000 coming in the single month of May 1994. At peak periods there could be as many as two thousand people an hour. Such throngs made it necessary to employ a director of visits and establish an education office. At Canterbury as elsewhere trained guides, some speaking foreign languages, were made available, and at the end of the century a fine new visitors' centre was built opposite the south porch of the cathedral. In 1994 York had as many tourists as Canterbury; the other most popular cathedrals, all of them receiving more than 500,000 visitors annually, included St Paul's, Chester, Salisbury, Norwich and Winchester. In most places the number of professional staff serving the cathedrals grew. At Hereford, for instance, the payroll increased from twelve in 1984 to fifty-one in 1998. Most cathedrals provided more facilities for the public. These often included restaurants and shops selling cards, recordings and souvenirs as well as books. They could be profitable: again taking Hereford as an example, the revenue increased from £6484 in 1985 to more than £72,000 in 1993. Museums displaying church plate and sometimes needlework or other historic objects were opened in some cathedrals, including York, Ely, Gloucester and Winchester. Perhaps the finest shop and exhibition area were created at Durham in the 1990s. These were in the cloister, in buildings which had been part of the medieval monastery, and did not invade the sanctity of the cathedral itself.

Cathedral services continued to be broadcast and televised. The first live broadcast of choral evensong went out from Westminster Abbey at 3 p.m. on Thursday, 7 October 1926, with Sidney Nicholson's choir singing canticles by Byrd and an anthem by Boyce. Programmes were transmitted first on National Radio, then transferred to the Home Service in the early sixties and to Radio 3 in 1981. The first service broadcast from a northern cathedral came from York in 1938, while Edward Bairstow was director of music; the first stereo broadcast originated at Gloucester in 1971. Among those responsible for the series were the musicians Henry Walford Davies, George Thalben Ball and Barry Rose; the Rev W. D. Kennedy-Bell, a BBC employee, was the producer for many years. Services from some college chapels and parish churches were also broadcast.[2] Services from St Paul's, Westminster Abbey and Canterbury have been televized as well, and have not been limited to coronations and funerals.

Some cathedral musical establishments began to change in the 1970s, when girls' choirs were introduced in several places. The first such experiment was at Salisbury, where the organist, Richard Seal, was a strong advocate of the cause. Another early girls' choir was that at St Edmundsbury. At the end of the century twenty-two of the forty-two cathedrals had girls' choirs, with forty retaining their choirs of men and boys. Initially a number of church musicians feared that girls' choirs might jeopardize the continued tradition of singing by men and boys, but they are now almost universally approved and the opportunity for girls to have experiences formerly denied them is widely appreciated. In some places, too, it has proved difficult to recruit enough suitable boy choristers. Most observers still hold, however, that girls' and boys' choirs should remain separate, as indeed they have nearly everywhere – only two choirs combined boys and girls. Some cathedrals did not fully consider the financial implications of having a girls' choir in addition to their boys' choir and have had a financial struggle to maintain the two, especially since an additional assistant organist or director has often proved necessary. The number of children engaged in cathedral music increased by more than half during the 1990s. In all the cathedrals children continued to sing the 'top' line. Mixed choirs of men and women, long successful at the universities, were introduced at many cathedral churches, though they did not serve as the only or the main choir.

During the year 2000 cathedral chapters invested more than £2,000,000 in scholarships and expenses for children in their choirs. In some places there were successful public appeals for funds to endow choir schools and scholarships. Foundation grants have helped defray the costs of choirs and choir schools. The Ouseley Trust, established in 1989 'to promote and maintain to a high standard the choral services of the Church of England' as well as the churches in Wales and Ireland, has disbursed more than £1,000,000, of which more than half was given to cathedrals which sought endowments for their choir schools and musical establishments. The cathedrals which have benefitted include Birmingham, Carlisle, Chelmsford, Coventry, Ely, Guildford, Hereford, Leicester, Lichfield, Lincoln, Norwich, Peterborough,

Ripon, Rochester, St Alban's, St David's, Salisbury, Southwell, Truro, Wells and Winchester; some of these received several grants during the 1990s. In addition the trust helped provide music scores for choir libraries and pay for restoration of historic organs. The Friends of Cathedral Music have also made significant contributions.

Those who were familiar with cathedral musical establishments at the end of the century generally agreed that they had never been more vigorous or maintained such high standards but argued that they were vulnerable, perhaps as never before, to social change, problems of recruitment and pressures of funding. Some urged collective action, taken by the cathedrals working together, to sponsor a national program to promote cathedral music.

Coventry is not the only cathedral to have been active in commissioning new religious art. Some of the most notable work is at Chichester; it includes a powerful reredos tapestry by John Piper (1966), Graham Sutherland's *Noli Me Tangere* tapestry in the chapel of St Mary Magdalen, and a stained-glass window based on Psalm 150 designed by Marc Chagall (1978). At Llandaff, Epstein's cast-aluminum statue of Christ in Majesty has been made part of the unique installation of the organ in a cylindrical case mounted on top of a great concrete arch straddling the nave. There is also a window designed by Piper depicting the Supper at Emmaus. Chelmsford has a banner made by the noted needleworker Beryl Dean in 1960, while in 2000 Durham commissioned batik banners of St Cuthbert and St Oswald by Thetis Blacker. There are also fine new vestments and altar frontals in many places.

Many cathedrals had notable deans during the twentieth century. At Canterbury these included George Bell and Hewlett Johnson. Bell served only five years, from 1924 until 1929, but he was responsible for a number of changes. He instituted daily prayers for the parishes in the diocese of Canterbury. He directed that the minutes of chapter meetings be typed and that a ladies' cloakroom be provided. He permitted female visitors to enter without covering their heads, though he did expect them to wear hats or scarves when attending services. He allowed nonconformist ministers to preach in the cathedral. A friend of Sir John Reith, the Director General of the BBC, he was responsible for the first broadcast from Canterbury, not an evensong but a commemoration of the tercentenary of the death of the composer Orlando Gibbons held in 1925. He also sponsored religious drama. The first play produced in the cathedral was *The Coming of Christ* by John Masefield, performed in 1928 with music by Gustav Holst. It was Bell who asked T. S. Eliot to write a play about Thomas Becket, though *Murder in the Cathedral* was not performed until after his resignation. Bell's final triumph was the enthronment of Cosmo Gordon Lang as archbishop in December 1928. Ecumenical leaders as well as politicians, professors and union officials attended the service. A special train ran from London to Canterbury. Vaughan Williams provided a new *Te Deum*. A buffet luncheon was served to 240 guests.

Hewlett Johnson's term in office was longer and more controversial. Appointed in 1931, he had a northern industrial background and came to Canterbury from Manchester, where he had also served as dean. He owed his appointment to the Labour Prime Minister Ramsay MacDonald. Always concerned by international issues and inspired by Christian Socialist ideas, Johnson soon involved himself in politics by attending a garden party at the Soviet embassy and inviting the Indian leader Mahatma Gandhi to visit Canterbury. He endorsed a pilgrimage to the cathedral dramatizing the cause of mass unemployment in 1934. Concern about the Spanish Civil War led him to visit Spain in 1937. Long a proponent of Victor Gollancz's Left Book Club, he published *The Socialist Sixth of the World*, in part a eulogy of the Soviet Union, in 1939. Relations with members of the chapter and with the archbishop, Geoffrey Fisher, grew even more strained after Johnson brought the Soviet ambassador and former premier Malenkov to an evensong also attended by the primate in 1956. It was rumoured that Archbishop Michael Ramsey said of Johnson, 'When he was in Canterbury, I wished fervently that he was somewhere else, and when he went somewhere else, I wished even more fervently that he was back in Canterbury'. As the Cold War grew in intensity it was suggested that the 'Red Dean' should retire, but he remained in office until 1963, when he was eighty-eight.

A much happier occasion was the visit of Pope John Paul II to Canterbury in 1982. Carefully planned by Archbishop Robert Runcie and Dean Victor de Waal, it involved the cooperation of Anglican and Catholic Franciscans and demonstrated the ecumenical role played by the cathedrals in the last quarter century.

At York, A. P. Purey-Cust presided over what one historian has called 'a quiet and steady time' from 1880 until his death in 1916, again at the age of eighty-eight. Among his successors the most notable was probably Eric Milner-White, who came from King's College, Cambridge, in 1941 and died in office twenty-two years later. An Anglo-Catholic, Milner-White enriched cathedral services and introduced eucharistic vestments. He had devised the liturgy for Lessons and Carols at King's and soon introduced the service at York. He was an effective fund-raiser; the Friends found his enthusiasm for the minster infectious. His special interest in art attracted a number of gifts: hangings for the high altar in 1942, rare vestments in 1943, nave choir stalls in 1944, a font cover by Ninian Comper in 1946, and a great astronomical clock erected in 1955 as a memorial to airmen from camps in northern England who had died in the Second World War. His successor Alan Richardson provided effective leadership during the restoration of the building between 1967 and 1972, a five-year period which amazingly saw only one day pass without a choral evensong.

A few more deans may be mentioned – their selection may be regarded as arbitrary, and one cannot include all those whose careers were interesting and accomplishments laudable. F. M. Bennett of Chester is often credited with inventing the modern cathedral, open and welcoming to all. At Winchester Gordon Selwyn served from 1931 to 1958. His predecessor William Hutton had brought in eucharistic vestments and the reserved sacrament. Selwyn was responsible for the establishment of a new school for the training of choir boys, known as the Pilgrims' School, the restoration of the roof bosses in the choir and tower, and the organization of a group of embroiderers. Within a year these women, who called themselves broderers, using the medieval term, had made more than one hundred kneelers. Selwyn was in turn followed by a distinguished church historian, Norman Sykes, who had held the Dixie Professorship at Cambridge. Sadly, Sykes became ill soon after going to Winchester and died in 1961; he is buried in the cathedral.

Hedley Burrows was a canon and archdeacon at Winchester before being named dean of Hereford in 1946. During his first week in office he persuaded the chapter to agree to the use of vestments and obtained £10,000 from the Pilgrim Trust for restoration of the cathedral. He was active in encouraging broadcasts, plays, special services and festivals. Joseph Armitage Robinson became dean of Wells in 1911, leaving the more onerous deanery of Westminster Abbey. According to the *Church Times* his sermons were always an intellectual feast and attracted large congregations. Another high churchman, he brought in copes and candles. His most important achievement was the replacement of the figures of Christ, Our Lady and St John which had been removed from the medieval rood screen at the time of the Reformation. Controversial at the time, the restored rood has come to be loved by many. Another long-serving dean was D. H. S. Cranage of Norwich, who held office from 1927 to 1945. A man of great vitality, he presided over a period of change. Medieval history was one of his special interests; he supported educational projects and was a vice-president of the Society of Antiquaries of London. He was also prolocutor of the clergy in the diocese of Canterbury from 1936 until the time of his retirement.

Seriol Evans was dean of Gloucester for twenty years beginning in 1953. He was responsible for major restoration of the cathedral, working with such advisers as Stephen Dykes-Bower and Brian Fedden. Reroofing was one of the most urgent projects, and lightweight concrete was used in some places since it was less likely to decay than wood. New lighting was also provided for the nave. Coming forward to the end of the century we may recognize the fine work of John Arnold, who served a dean of two of the great Romanesque cathedrals, Rochester (1978–89) and then Durham (1989–2002). Surely one of the most thoughtful and spiritual of the deans, his influence has been felt far beyond his cathedral because of his involvement in closer relationships with churches on the Continent and with the University of Durham.

As the century closed no woman had yet been named dean of one of the old cathedrals, but in 2000 Vivienne Faull was installed as provost of the cathedral at Leicester, which also serves as a parish church. A graduate of Oxford and Nottingham universities, Faull had taught in India, been chaplain of Clare College, Cambridge, and served at Gloucester and Coventry cathedrals. Ordained deacon in 1987 and priest in 1994, she became vice-provost of Coventry in 1995. Female priests did serve as canons in some other cathedrals, although they were not eligible to be residentiary canons until they had been in holy orders for six years. The first women residentiaries, appointed in 1993, were Jane Hedges at Portsmouth and Jane Sinclair at Sheffield. At the end of the century there were women residentiary canons at Guildford (the sub-dean), Oxford, St Edmundsbury, Salisbury, Sheffield, Southwark (two, one an archdeacon) and Worcester (also an archdeacon).

A telling episode late in the century involved the famous medieval Mappa Mundi held by the library at Hereford Cathedral. In 1988 the dean and chapter decided that it might be sold in order to help meet the cathedral's expenses. It was sent to Sotheby's for auction, but public outcry was so great that it was withdrawn from sale and returned to the cathedral. In 1990 ownership was transferred to a Mappa Mundi Trust, which was able to raise more than £3,000,000 from the National Memorial Fund with the assistance of Sir Paul Getty. The event had a happy ending when a fine new building to house the map and library was opened by the Queen in 1996.

In 1994 a special Archbishops' Commission on Cathedrals published its report, called *Heritage and Renewal*. Examining the state of cathedrals and suggesting changes in their organization, the study began by noting that 'today, when public observance of religious belief is not as widespread as it once was, the cathedrals are, paradoxically, popular as never before'.

> For some, the majesty of the buildings themselves is an expression of what might otherwise remain inarticulate, a perception of the holy, an anticipation of eternity. For some, there are historical resonances: those cathedrals which were

conceived or adorned as great canopies over the bones of saints, as stone reliquaries on an enormous scale, remain still a witness to sanctity and an insight into fellowship with past believers. Here the least of the world's citizens can experience the dignity of spiritual space; cathedrals are accessible places, where all can see evidence of the effects of Christian truth as living faith. For some others cathedrals are a dimension of heritage, an illustration of historical processes, aesthetically satisfying, the venue of artistic and cultural achievement.

The commissioners were delighted by the high standards of music and preaching and noted improved facilities for visitors. They expressed concern about cathedral finances, which were not always professionally managed. Their surveys, interestingly, showed that the cathedrals spent 46 per cent of their income on the building, 12 per cent on services, music and the choir school, and about 12 per cent on administration. Contributions from tourists and Friends groups helped meet these needs.

In conclusion the commissioners made a number of recommendations for change. They believed that the distinction between the old 'dean and chapter' cathedrals and the newer 'parish church' cathedrals should be ended and a single system of governance introduced; all cathedrals should have deans, not provosts. The time-honoured 'dean and chapter' was replaced by a group simply called the chapter; deans were given reserved powers with regard to the liturgy and the budget. New statutes were to be drafted for each cathedral; the role of the Privy Council in approving these would be terminated. Fabric advisory committees should have primary responsibility for the maintenance of buildings. Lay professionals should be placed in charge of bookshops and other trading facilities, as well as tourism. The most significant change was probably that which added lay canons to cathedral chapters. As the commission acknowledged, the cathedrals were not in a state of crisis and changes could come gradually, following full discussion.

What, then, is the state of the cathedrals in England and Wales fourteen centuries after St Augustine's establishment at Canterbury? Most observers agreed that it was surprisingly good. Almost everywhere buildings had been restored and were in excellent condition, cared for more systematically than in earlier times. Cathedral music had never been better. New works of art had been commissioned and installed in many places. Liturgies remained dignified and sometimes succeeded in combining tradition with newer forms of worship. Groups of Friends remained strong. Some cathedrals had begun attempts to organize social services. Broadcasts, special services and festivals remained popular. Despite the closure of several theological colleges, most schools associated with cathedrals remained strong. Libraries and archives were generally well organized though often underfunded and understaffed. Visitors, many of whom regarded themselves as pilgrims rather than mere tourists, continued to come in large numbers and were welcomed and provided with appropriate facilities. Although financial problems persisted, the cathedrals succeeded in finding support for essential projects. Important help came from English Heritage, which in January 2001 announced major grants to Hereford, Lincoln, Peterborough and Salisbury, with smaller sums for twenty-three other cathedrals. These gifts totaled £2.5 million, bringing the total for the decade to more than £34 million. While the attendance at weekday services was not large – in many places it never had been – Sunday services attracted considerable numbers of worshippers and communicants. In this respect the cathedrals appeared healthier than the parish churches of England, which had suffered a considerable decline in attendance. Indeed 10 per cent of those who attended Sunday services in 2000 worshipped in a cathedral rather than a parish church. A survey reported that 26 per cent of the population visited a cathedral during the year ending in June 2000, as compared with 17 per cent who attended a football match and 14 per cent a rock concert. The cathedrals were better organized and trying harder to work together than was the case in the past.

A fundamental part of the national heritage and indeed of the universal church, the cathedrals of England remained centres of art and architecture, music and liturgy, learning and service. They offered prayer and praise for all people.

Notes

Notes to Chapter 1: The Early Centuries, 597–1066

1. For general histories of this period see Peter Hunter Blair, *Roman Britain and Early England, 55 BC–AD 871* (Edinburgh, 1963); F. M. Stenton, *Anglo-Saxon England* (Oxford, 1943); H. R. Loyn, *Anglo-Saxon England and the Norman Conquest* (2nd edn, London, 1991).
2. Bede, *A History of the English Church and People*, trans. Leo Sherley-Price (Harmondsworth, Middlesex, 1955), book 1, chapters 23–28.
3. Bede, book 2, chapter 3.
4. See Patrick Collinson, Nigel Ramsay and Margaret Sparks, eds, *A History of Canterbury Cathedral* (Oxford, 1995), pp. 1–37; Kevin Blockley, Margaret Sparks and Tim Tatton-Brown, *Canterbury Cathedral Nave: Archaeology, History and Architecture*, i (Canterbury, 1997), pp. 1–14.
5. See G. E. Aylmer and Reginald Cant, eds, *A History of York Minster* (Oxford, 1977), pp. 1–12.

Notes to Chapter 2: Norman, 1066–1170

1. The building and its history are described in Nikolaus Pevsner, *County Durham*, Buildings of England series (London, 1953), pp. 77–116.
2. The rood screen separating the choir from the nave and transepts is a Victorian work by the architect Sir George Gilbert Scott, who was responsible for considerable nineteenth-century restoration. Most of the windows are also Victorian.
3. See J. Philip McAleer, *Rochester Cathedral, 604–1540: An Architectural History* (Toronto, 1999); and Nigel Yates and Paul A. Welsby, eds, *Faith and Fabric: A History of Rochester Cathedral, 604–1994* (Woodbridge, 1996).
4. The standard history is Frederick Bussby, *Winchester Cathedral, 1079–1979* (Southampton, 1979).
5. There is a fine modern history: Ian Atherton, Eric Fernie, Christopher Harper-Bill and Hassell Smith, eds, *Norwich Cathedral: Church, City and Diocese, 1096–1996* (London, 1996).
6. Dorothy Owen, ed., *A History of Lincoln Minster* (Cambridge, 1994).

7. At the time of the Dissolution of the Monasteries Henry VIII said that the church at Peterborough should be spared because it was one of the goodliest in Christendom. He may also have been moved by the fact that his first wife, Catherine of Aragon, was buried there.

8. Quoted in Peter Burman, *St Paul's Cathedral* (London, 1987), p. 8.

Notes to Chapter 3: Early English, 1170–1280

1. Cf. Patrick Collinson, Nigel Ramsay and Margaret Sparks, eds, *A History of Canterbury Cathedral* (Oxford, 1995), pp. 63–66.

2. For more detail see L. S. Colchester, ed, *Wells Cathedral: A History* (Shepton Mallet, 1982) and L. S. Colchester, *Wells Cathedral* (London, 1987).

3. See Jerry Sampson, *Wells Cathedral West Front: Construction, Sculpture and Conservation* (Stroud, 1998); and Pamela Tudor-Craig, *One Half of Our Noblest Art: A Study of the Sculptures of Wells West Front* (Wells, 1976).

4. The best guide is Roy Spring, *Salisbury Cathedral* (London, 1987).

5. Cf. Dorothy Owen, ed., *A History of Lincoln Minster* (Cambridge, 1994), pp. 14–46.

6. The official history of the abbey is Edward Carpenter, ed., *A House of Kings* (London, 1966), but it is now out of date and not always reliable. The best guidebook is Christopher Wilson, Pamela Tudor-Craig, John Physick and Richard Gem, *Westminster Abbey* (London, 1986).

7. As we shall see, Lichfield was damaged more severely than any other cathedral during the fighting of the Civil War. Two spires had to be replaced in the later seventeenth century and much of the façade is Victorian restoration.

Notes to Chapter 4: Decorated, 1280–1350

1. If we were considering parish churches as well as cathedrals we would cite the north door of St Mary Redcliffe in Bristol, which Elizabeth I once called the finest church in her realm.

2. The classic studies are Jean Bony, *The English Decorated Style: Gothic Architecture Transformed, 1250–1350* (Oxford, 1979), and Nicola Coldstream, *The Decorated Style: Architecture and Ornament, 1240–1360* (London, 1994).

3. See L. S. Colchester, *Wells Cathedral* (London, 1987).

4. In the absence of a full history of Exeter Cathedral one should consult Nicholas Orme, *Exeter Cathedral as it Was, 1050–1550* (Exeter, 1986), and Audrey Erskine, Vyvyan Hope and John Lloyd, *Exeter Cathedral: A Short History and Description* (Exeter, 1988).

5. See G. E. Aylmer and Reginald Cant, eds, *A History of York Minster* (Oxford, 1977), pp. 111–92.

6. See John Rogan, ed., *Bristol Cathedral: History and Architecture* (Stroud, 2000), esp. pp. 88–108.

7. One of the great business buildings in Chicago, the Tribune Tower (1925) is also capped by an octagonal tower obviously based on that at Ely.

Notes to Chapter 5: Perpendicular, 1350–1530

1. The most important study of this period is John Harvey, *The Perpendicular Style* (London, 1978). One of Harvey's significant contributions was his identification of individual architects. It is unfortunate that he concluded his work at the year 1500; he regarded later building as Tudor Gothic and as inferior to Perpendicular.

2. See Peter Burman, *St Paul's Cathedral* (London, 1987), pp. 12–17. Hollar's engravings are reproduced on pp. 13–16.

3. David Welander, *The History, Art and Architecture of Gloucester Cathedral* (Stroud, 1991), pp. 164–83; Christopher Wilson, *The Gothic Cathedral* (London, 1990), pp. 204–12.

4. Frederick Bussby, *Winchester Cathedral, 1079–1979* (Southampton, 1979), pp. 37–61.

5. D. Ingram Hill, *Canterbury Cathedral* (London, 1986), pp. 18–20, and Wilson, *The Gothic Cathedral*, pp. 213–15.

6. In John Harvey's view the Perpendicular vault never surpassed Yeveley's work at Canterbury, which he characterized as orthodox, and Wynford's at Winchester, which he called an eccentric fantasy.

7. The chapel is the ceremonial home of the Knights of the Bath, whose banners hang above the stalls and obscure some of the finely ornamented stonework.

Notes to Chapter 6: Stained Glass

1. For more information on this subject see John Baker and Alfred Lammer, *English Stained Glass* (London, 1978); Richard Marks, *Stained Glass in England during the Middle Ages* (London and Toronto, 1993).

2. See Madeline H. Caviness, *The Windows of Christ Church Cathedral, Canterbury*, Corpus Vitrearum Medii Aevi (London, 1981). Caviness believes that the stained-glass artists were probably Frenchmen.

3. Studies of this work are Sarah Brown, *Stained Glass at York Minster* (London, 1999), Thomas French and David O'Connor, *York Minster: The West Windows of the Nave* (London, 1987) and Thomas French, *York Minster: The Great East Window* (London, 1995). The last two volumes are in the series Corpus Vitrearum Medii Aevi.

4. Those interested in stained glass of the modern period, from the eighteenth to the twentieth century, will find a wealth of it in York Minster as well.

5. It is described in David Welander, *The Stained Glass of Gloucester Cathedral* (Gloucester, 1985).

Notes to Chapter 7: Medieval Tombs and Monuments

1. There is some discussion of tombs and monuments in Lawrence Stone, *Sculpture in Britain: The Middle Ages* (Harmondsworth, 1955).

2. Christopher Wilson, Pamela Tudor-Craig, John Physick and Richard Gem, *Westminster Abbey* (London, 1986), pp. 115–40.

3. Cf. Ben Nilson, *Cathedral Shrines of Medieval England* (Woodbridge, 1998).

Notes to Chapter 8: Life in a Medieval Cathedral

1. For fuller information about topics discussed in this chapter, together with detailed references, see Stanford E. Lehmberg, *The Reformation of Cathedrals: Cathedrals in English Society, 1485–1603* (Princeton, 1988), pp. 3–66.

2. See David Knowles, *The Religious Orders in England*, iii (Cambridge, 1959), pp. 108–26.

3. The best edition is that edited by James Raine and J. T . Fowler and issued by the Surtees Society, no. 107 (Durham, 1903).

4. Cf. N. R. Ker, *Medieval Libraries of Great Britain* (2nd edn, London, 1964).

Notes to Chapter 9: The Reformation

1. Detailed references to sources for this chapter may be found in Stanford E. Lehmberg, *The Reformation of Cathedrals: Cathedrals in English Society, 1485–1603* (Princeton, 1988), pp. 67–100.

2. See Stanford E. Lehmberg, *The Reformation Parliament, 1529–1536* (Cambridge, 1970).

3. Lehmberg, *Reformation of Cathedrals*, pp. 84–85.

Notes to Chapter 10: Protestant Ascendancy and Catholic Reaction

1. For references to specific sources, including materials from the cathedral archives, see Stanford E. Lehmberg, *The Reformation of Cathedrals: Cathedrals in English Society, 1485–1603* (Princeton, 1988), pp. 101–38.

2. John Harington, *Nugae Antiquae*, quoted in L. S. Colchester, *Wells Cathedral: A History* (Shepton Malet, 1982), p. 151.

3. Quoted in Lacey Baldwin Smith, *Tudor Prelates and Politics* (Princeton, 1953), pp. 268–69.
4. Cf. Diarmaid MacCulloch, *Thomas Cranmer* (New Haven and London, 1996).
5. See Christina H. Garrett, *The Marian Exiles* (Cambridge, 1938).

Notes to Chapter 11: The Elizabethan Settlement

1. Cf. Stanford E. Lehmberg, *The Reformation of Cathedrals: Cathedrals in English Society, 1485–1603* (Princeton, 1988), pp. 139–63, which includes detailed references to sources.

Notes to Chapter 12: The Early Seventeenth Century

1. Stanford E. Lehmberg, *Cathedrals under Siege: Cathedrals in English Society, 1600–1700* (University Park, Pennsylvania, and Exeter, 1996), pp. 1–24, contains full references to sources and quotations.
2. No place could be found for it at Winchester, but the central portion was removed and incorporated as an architectural feature in the new Museum of Archaeology and Anthropology at Cambridge University.

Notes to Chapter 13: Civil War and Interregnum

1. Cf. Stanford E. Lehmberg, *Cathedrals under Siege: Cathedrals in English Society, 1600–1700* (University Park, Pennsylvania, and Exeter, 1996), pp. 25–56.
2. The records of the treasurers for the sale of dean and chapter lands survive among the declared accounts of the Exchequer Audit Office in the Public Record Office.
3. At the time of the Restoration the materials kept in London, like other ecclesiastical papers from the Interregnum, were transferred to the archbishop of Canterbury's library at Lambeth Palace, where they remain; although Cromwell was not directly responsible for their compilation, they are sometimes called 'Oliver's Surveys'.
4. This is the view of Claire Cross, 'From the Reformation to the Restoration', in Gerald Aylmer and Reginald Cant, eds, *A History of York Minster* (Oxford, 1997), pp. 214–15.
5. While Walker makes no attempt to conceal his own High Church Tory bias, his facts are generally correct, solidly based on documentary sources. In his modern revision A. G. Matthews found it more satisfactory to count positions vacated rather than individuals ejected and produced a total approaching 4000. About 650 of these came from the cathedrals.

Notes to Chapter 14: The Restoration

1. Full references to sources for this chapter may be found in Stanford E. Lehmberg, *Cathedrals under Siege: Cathedrals in English Society, 1600–1700* (University Park, Pennsylvania, and Exeter, 1996), pp. 57–86.
2. In the end the fire did not reach his home, which was east of the City.
3. See Peter Burman, *St Paul's Cathedral* (London, 1987), pp. 34–48, and Jane Lang, *Rebuilding St Paul's after the Great Fire of London* (Oxford, 1956).

Notes to Chapter 15: Houses of Praise and Prayer

1. Full references to materials quoted in this chapter may be found in Stanford E. Lehmberg, *The Reformation of Cathedrals: Cathedrals in English Society, 1485–1603* (Princeton, 1988), pp. 267–306, and Stanford E. Lehmberg, *Cathedrals under Siege: Cathedrals in English Society, 1600–1700* (University Park, Pennsylvania, and Exeter, 1996), pp. 193–257.
2. This is in the collection of the Society of Antiquaries at Burlington House, Piccadilly.
3. This is the painting in the possession of the Society of Antiquaries.
4. See Lehmberg, *Cathedrals under Siege*, pp. 230–43, for an account of the monuments at Bristol, Chester, Chichester, Ely, Gloucester and Hereford.

Notes to Chapter 16: The Eighteenth and Nineteenth Centuries

1. Sources for this chapter may be found in the studies of the several cathedrals listed in the Bibliography below. There is also much interesting information in William Gibson, *The Church of England, 1688–1832: Unity and Accord* (London, 2001), Gerald Cobb, *English Cathedrals: The Forgotten Centuries* (London, 1980), and Philip Barrett, *Barchester: English Cathedral Life in the Nineteenth Century* (London, 1993).
2. This examination is based on the *Eighteenth Century Short-Title Catalogue* issued on CD ROM by the British Library, 1992. See Stanford Lehmberg, 'Writings of Canterbury Cathedral Clergy, 1700–1800,' *Anglican and Episcopal History*, 73 (2004), 53–77.
3. There are good accounts of leases and fines in Nigel Yates, ed., *Faith and Fabric: A History of Rochester Cathedral 604–1994* (Woodbridge, 1996), pp. 78–88, and Dorothy Owen, ed., *A History of Lincoln Minster* (Cambridge, 1994), pp. 205–8.
4. Cf. Philip Barrett, *Barchester*, pp. 26–34; Gerald Aylmer and John Tiller, eds, *Hereford Cathedral: A History* (London, 2000), p. 165.
5. For more detailed information see Philip Barrett, *Barchester*, pp. 12–25.

Notes to Chapter 17: The Twentieth Century

1. Further information may be found in the books on individual cathedrals listed in the bibliography as well as Nikolaus Pevsner's Buildings of England series and Paul A. Welsby, *A History of the Church of England, 1945–1980* (London, 1984).

2. The famous Festival of Nine Lessons and Carols from the chapel of King's College, Cambridge, was brought to its simple perfection by Boris Ord and Sir David Willcocks; it has been heard on Christmas Eve (or in other time zones the following morning) throughout the world for half a century and has been seen by millions on television.

Bibliography

Addleshaw, G. W. O., and Frederick Etchells, *The Architectural Setting of Anglican Worship* (London, 1948).

Anglo, Sydney, *Spectacle, Pageantry and Early Tudor Policy* (Oxford, 1969).

Atherton, Ian, Eric Fernie, Christopher Harper-Bill, and Hassell Smith, eds, *Norwich Cathedral* (London, 1996).

Aylmer, Gerald, and Reginald Cant, eds, *A History of York Minster* (Oxford, 1997).

Aylmer, Gerald, and John Tiller, eds, *Hereford Cathedral: A History* (London, 2000).

Baker, John, and Alfred Lammer, *English Stained Glass* (London, 1978).

Bede, The Venerable, *A History of the English Church and People*, translated by Leo Sherley-Price (Harmondsworth, 1996).

Binski, Paul, *Westminster Abbey and the Plantagenets: Kingship and the Representation of Power, 1200–1400* (New Haven and London, 1995).

Blair, Peter Hunter, *Anglo-Saxon England* (Cambridge, 1956).

Blockley, Kevin, Margaret Sparks and Tim Tatton-Brown, *Canterbury Cathedral Nave: Archaeology, History and Architecture* (Canterbury, 1997).

Bonney, T. G., *Cathedrals and Abbeys of England and Wales* (London, 1891; new edn, 1985).

Bony, Jean, *The English Decorated Style: Gothic Architecture Transformed, 1250–1350* (Oxford, 1979).

Bosher, Robert S., *The Making of the Restoration Settlement* (London, 1951).

Brown, Sarah, *Stained Glass at York Minster* (London, 1999).

Burman, Peter, *St Paul's Cathedral* (London, 1987).

Bussby, Frederick, *Winchester Cathedral, 1079–1979* (Winchester, 1979).

Calamy, Edmund, *Calamy Revised*, ed. A. G. Matthews (Oxford, 1934).

Carlton, Charles, *Archbishop William Laud* (London, 1987).

Carpenter, Edward, ed., *A House of Kings: The Official History of Westminster Abbey* (London, 1966).

Caviness, Madeline H., *The Windows of Christ Church Cathedral, Canterbury*, Corpus Vitrearum Medii Aevi (London, 1981).

Chamberlin, Russell, *The English Cathedral* (London, 1987).

Cobb, Gerald, *English Cathedrals: The Forgotten Centuries* (London, 1980).

Colchester, L. S., *Wells Cathedral* (London, 1987).

Colchester, L. S., ed., *Wells Cathedral: A History* (Shepton Malet, 1982).

Coldstream, Nicola, *The Decorated Style: Architecture and Ornament, 1240–1360* (London, 1994).

Collinson, Patrick, *The Elizabethan Puritan Movement* (London, 1967).

Collinson, Patrick, Nigel Ramsay and Margaret Sparks, eds, *A History of Canterbury Cathedral* (Oxford, 1995).

Cross, Claire, 'From the Reformation to the Restoration', in Aylmer and Cant, eds, *History of York Minster* (Oxford, 1992).

Davies, Julian, *The Caroline Captivity of the Church* (Oxford, 1992).

Dickens, A. G., *The English Reformation* (2nd edn, London, 1989, and University Park, Pennsylvania, 1991).

Dobson, R. B., *Durham Priory, 1400–1450* (Cambridge, 1973).

Dorman, B. E., *Cathedral Shrines of Medieval England* (Woodbridge, 1998).

Duffy, Eamon, *The Stripping of the Altars: Traditional Religion in England, 1400–1580* (New Haven and London, 1992).

Dugdale, Sir William, *The History of St Paul's Cathedral in London* (London, 1658).

Edwards, Kathleen, *The English Secular Cathedrals in the Middle Ages* (Manchester, 1949).

Edwards, Kathleen, *Salisbury Cathedral* (Trowbridge, 1986).

Elton, G. R., *England under the Tudors* (London, 1955).

Erskine, Audrey, Vyvyan Hope and John Lloyd, *Exeter Cathedral: A Short History and Description* (Exeter, 1988).

Evelyn, John, *Diary*, ed. E. S. de Beer (6 vols, Oxford, 1955).

Fegan, Ethel S., ed., *Journal of Prior William More* (Worcester, 1914).

Fernie, Eric, *Architectural History of Norwich Cathedral* (Oxford, 1993).

Fox, John, *Acts and Monuments of the Christian Martyrs*, ed. S. R. Cattley (8 vols, London, 1838).

French, Thomas, *York Minster: The Great East Window*, Corpus Vitrearum Medii Aevi (London, 1995).

French, Thomas, and David O'Connor, *York Minster: The West Windows of the Nave* (London, Corpus Vitrearum Medii Aevi, 1987).

Garrett, Christina H., *The Marian Exiles* (Cambridge, 1938).

Gibson, William, *The Church of England, 1688–1832: Unity and Accord* (London, 2001).

Green, I. M., *The Re-Establishment of the Church of England, 1660–1663* (Oxford, 1978).

Gregory, Jeremy, *Restoration, Reformation and Reform, 1660–1828: Archbishops of Canterbury and their Diocese* (Oxford, 2000).

Gunton, Symon, *The History of the Church of Peterburgh* (London, 1686).

Harrison, Frederick, *Life in a Medieval College: The Story of the Vicars-Choral of York Minster* (London, 1952).

Harvey, John, *Cathedrals of England and Wales* (London, 1972).

Harvey, John, *English Medieval Architects* (London, 1954).

Harvey, John, *The Gothic World* (London, 1950).

Harvey, John, *The Perpendicular Style* (London, 1978).

Heal, Felicity, *Hospitality in Early Modern England* (Oxford, 1990).

Hill, D. Ingram, *Canterbury Cathedral* (London, 1986).

Hudson, Winthrop P., *The Cambridge Connection and the Elizabethan Settlement of 1559* (Durham, North Carolina, 1980).

Hussey, Walter, *Chichester Cathedral* (Chichester, 1970).

Johnson, Paul, *British Cathedrals* (London, 1980).

Jones, Norman L., *Faith by Statute* (London, 1982).

Jordan, W. K., *Edward VI: The Threshold of Power* (Cambridge, Massachusetts, 1970).

Jordan, W. K., *Edward VI: The Young King* (Cambridge, Massachusetts,1968).

Kahn, Deborah, *Canterbury Cathedral and its Romanesque Sculpture* (London, 1991).

Keats, Jonathan, and Angelo Hornak, *Canterbury Cathedral* (London, 1980).

Ker, N. R., *Medieval Libraries of Great Britain* (2nd edn, London, 1964).

Knighton, C. S., and Richard Mortimer, eds, *Westminster Abbey Reformed 1540–1640* (Aldershot, 2003).

Knowles, David, and R. Neville Hadcock, *Medieval Religious Houses: England and Wales* (London, 1953).

Knowles, David, *The Monastic Order in England* (Cambridge, 1940).

Knowles, David, *The Religious Orders in* England (3 vols, Cambridge, 1948, 1955, 1959).

Kreider, Alan, *English Chantries: The Road to Dissolution* (Cambridge, Massachusetts, 1979).

Lang, Jane, *Rebuilding St Paul's after the Great Fire of London* (Oxford, 1956).

Leedy, Walter C., Jr, *Fan Vaulting: Study of Form, Technology and Meaning* (London, 1980).

Lehmberg, Stanford E., *Cathedrals under Siege: Cathedrals in English Society, 1600–1700* (University Park, Pennsylvania, and Exeter, 1996).

Lehmberg, Stanford E., *The Later Parliaments of Henry VIII, 1536–1547* (Cambridge, 1977).

Lehmberg, Stanford E., *The Reformation of Cathedrals: Cathedrals in English Society, 1485–1603* (Princeton, 1988).

Lehmberg, Stanford E., *The Reformation Parliament, 1529–1536* (Cambridge, 1970).

Le Hurray, Peter, *Music and the Reformation in England, 1549–1660* (London, 1967).

Lepine, David, *Brotherhood of Canons Serving God: English Secular Cathedrals in the Later Middle Ages* (Woodbridge, 1995).

Loades, D. M., *The Reign of Mary Tudor* (London, 1979).

Loyn, H. R., *Anglo-Saxon England and the Norman Conquest* (2nd edn, London, 1991).

Macaulay, Thomas Babington, Lord, *The History of England from the Accession of James the Second* (6 vols, London, 1914).

MacCaffrey, Wallace T., *The Shaping of the Elizabethan Regime* (Princeton, 1968).

MacCulloch, Diarmaid, *The Boy King: Edward VI and the Protestant Reformation* (London, 1999).

MacCulloch, Diarmaid, *Thomas Cranmer* (New Haven and London, 1996).

Marks, Richard, *Stained Glass in England during the Middle Ages* (London and Toronto, 1993).

Mayer, Thomas F., *Reginald Pole: Prince and Prophet* (Cambridge, 2000).

McAleer, J. Philip, *Rochester Cathedral, 604–1540: An Architectural History* (Toronto, 1999).

McAleer, J. Philip, *The Romanesque Church Façade in Britain* (New York, 1984).

Morrill, John, *The Nature of the English Revolution* (London, 1993).

Neale, J. E., *Elizabeth I and Her Parliaments, 1559–1581* (London, 1953).

New, Anthony, *A Guide to the Cathedrals of Britain* (London, 1980).

Nichols, John, *The Progresses, Processions, and Magnificent Festivities of King James the First* (4 vols, London, 1828).

Nichols, John, *The Progresses and Public Processions of Queen Elizabeth* (3 vols, London, 1823).

Nichols, J. G., *The Chronicle of the Grey Friars of London* (London, 1852).

Nilson, Ben, *Cathedral Shrines of Medieval England* (Woodbridge, 1998).

Orme, Nicholas, *Education and Society in Medieval and Renaissance England* (London, 1989).

Orme, Nicholas, *Exeter Cathedral as it Was, 1050–1550* (Exeter, 1986).

Orme, Nicholas, *Medieval Children* (New Haven and London, 2001).

Owen, Dorothy, ed., *A History of Lincoln Minster* (Cambridge, 1994).

Pevsner, Nikolaus, *The Buildings of England* (a series of guides arranged by county, 46 vols, Harmondsworth, 1951–74. Some volumes have a co-author).

Pevsner, Nikolaus, *The Englishness of English Art* (London, 1956; based on the Reith Lectures broadcast on the BBC in 1955).

Poole, A. L., *From Domesday Book to Magna Carta* (Oxford, 1955).

Quiney, Anthony, *John Loughborough Pearson* (New Haven and London, 1979).

Rogan, John, ed., *Bristol Cathedral: History and Architecture* (Stroud, 2000).

Royal Commission on Historical Monuments, *Salisbury: The Houses of the Close* (London, 1993).

Russell, Conrad, *The Causes of the English Civil War* (Oxford, 1990).

Russell, Conrad, *The Fall of the British Monarchies, 1637–1642* (Oxford, 1991).

Ryves, Bruno, *Mercurius Rusticus* (London, 1685).

Sampson, Jerry, *Wells Cathedral West Front* (Stroud, 1998).

Scarisbrick, J. J., *Henry VIII* (Berkeley and Los Angeles, 1968).

Scarisbrick, J. J., *The Reformation and the English People* (Oxford, 1984).

Schellinks, William, *The Journal of William Schellinks' Travels in England, 1661–1663*, ed. Maurice Exwood and H. L. Lehmann (London, 1993).

Shaw, William A., *History of the English Church during the Civil War and under the Commonwealth* (2 vols, London, 1900).

Smith, M. Q., *The Stained Glass of Bristol Cathedral* (Bristol, 1983).

Smith, R. A. L., *Canterbury Cathedral Priory* (Cambridge, 1943).

Spence, Basil, *Phoenix at Coventry* (London, 1962).

Spring, Roy, *Salisbury Cathedral* (London, 1987).

Spurr, John, *The Restoration Church of England, 1646–1689* (New Haven, 1991).

Stenton, F. M., *Anglo-Saxon England* (Oxford, 1943).

Stone, Lawrence, *Sculpture in Britain: The Middle Ages* (Harmondsworth, 1955).

Stranks, C. J., *This Sumptuous Church: The Story of Durham Cathedral* (London, 1973).

Sykes, Norman, *Church and State in England in the Eighteenth Century* (Cambridge, 1934).

Sykes, Norman, *William Wake, Archbishop of Canterbury, 1657–1737* (2 vols, Cambridge, 1957).

Tatton-Brown, Tim, and Julian Munby, eds, *The Archaeology of Cathedrals* (Oxford, 1996).

Trevor-Roper, H. R., *Archbishop Laud, 1573–1645* (Oxford, 1940; rev. edn, 1962).

Tudor-Craig, Pamela, *One Half of Our Noblest Art: A Study of the Sculptures of Wells West Front* (Wells, 1976).

Tullie, Isaac, *A Narrative of the Siege of Carlisle* (1840; reprint, Whitehaven, Cumbria, 1988).

Tyacke, Nicholas, *Anti-Calvinists: The Rise of English Arminianism, c. 1590–1640* (Oxford, 1987).

Verey, David, and David Welander, *Gloucester Cathedral* (Gloucester, 1979).

Walker, John, *Walker Revised*, ed. A. G. Matthews (Oxford, 1948).

Webb, Geoffrey, *Architecture in Britain: The Middle Ages* (Harmondsworth, 1956).

Welander, David, *The History, Art and Architecture of Gloucester Cathedral* (Stroud, 1991).

Welander, David, *The Stained Glass of Gloucester Cathedral* (Gloucester, 1985).

Welsby, Paul A., *A History of the Church of England, 1945–1980* (Oxford, 1984).

Wilson, Christopher, *The Gothic Cathedral* (London, 1990).

Wilson, Christopher, Richard Gem, Pamela Tudor-Craig and John Physick, *Westminster Abbey* (London, 1986).

Wood-Legh, K. L., *Perpetual Chantries in Britain* (Cambridge, 1965).

Yates, Nigel, *Buildings, Faith, and Worship: The Liturgical Arrangement of Anglican Churches, 1600–1900* (Oxford, 1991).

Yates, Nigel, and Paul A. Welsby, eds, *Faith and Fabric: A History of Rochester Cathedral, 604–1994* (Woodbridge, 1996).

Index